ASTHMA'S IMPACT ON SOCIETY

LUNG BIOLOGY IN HEALTH AND DISEASE

Executive Editor

Claude Lenfant
Director, National Heart, Lung and Blood Institute
National Institutes of Health
Bethesda, Maryland

The opinions expressed in these volumes do not necessarily represent the views of the National Institutes of Health.

ASTHMA'S IMPACT ON SOCIETY
THE SOCIAL AND ECONOMIC BURDEN

Edited by

Kevin B. Weiss
Rush Medical College
Chicago, Illinois

A. Sonia Buist
Oregon Health Sciences University
Portland, Oregon

Sean D. Sullivan
University of Washington
Seattle, Washington

MARCEL DEKKER, INC.   NEW YORK • BASEL

ISBN: 0-8247-1942-5

This book is printed on acid-free paper.

Headquarters
Marcel Dekker, Inc.
270 Madison Avenue, New York, NY 10016
tel: 212-696-9000; fax: 212-685-4540

Eastern Hemisphere Distribution
Marcel Dekker AG
Hutgasse 4, Postfach 812, CH-4001 Basel, Switzerland
tel: 41-61-261-8482; fax: 41-61-261-8896

World Wide Web
http://www.dekker.com

The publisher offers discounts on this book when ordered in bulk quantities. For more information, write to Special Sales/Professional Marketing at the headquarters address above.

Current printing (last digit):
10 9 8 7 6 5 4 3 2

PRINTED IN THE UNITED STATES OF AMERICA

INTRODUCTION

In the Introduction to the book *Health Care and Its Costs* (1), Carl J. Schramm asks the following question: "Should we, as a people, be dedicated to the notion that health care should be enjoyed equally by all, regardless of personal resources?" The response was: "Health care is an incident of citizenship, and we should seek a consensus on how we develop this right in the future."

Both the question and the answer apply to asthma. Of course, this disease is not new—we know that Pliny the Elder (23–65 A.D.), a Roman historian and encyclopedist, as well as others from ancient history, suffered from it. Nor is asthma a new topic for the Lung Biology in Health and Disease series. All this is to say that today we know a lot about this disease, although not everything. In addition, there is firm belief that death from asthma should be a rare exception and that morbidity should be minimal if all patients receive the full benefit of current treatment options. So, what is the issue? Why is it that not all of our citizens have the benefit of what we know and can do? As we look at the "demography" of asthma throughout the United States, we recognize an uneven distribution of asthma prevalence and morbidity that is largely linked to social and economic variations. Yet, irrespective of these variations, all the people affected are citizens of the same country and should therefore have the same right to reap the full benefit of our knowledge.

This volume is really about good medicine—not about diagnosis, pathogenesis, or treatment, but about the social barriers to applying what we know. As mentioned earlier, this series of monographs has included many volumes on asthma, in fact, more than on any other subject, and still more are planned! However, the topic would not be fully examined in the absence of a discussion of the impact of asthma on society: the social and economic burden. The ultimate objective of each monograph in the series is to inform and to bring about improvements. This particular volume reveals and examines the barriers to better asthma care; by recognizing these barriers we should be able to reach a "consensus on how we develop this right [to better care] in the future."

The editors of this monograph have had years of interest and expertise in the care of asthma, each from a different point of view. Their collaboration in conceptualizing and developing this volume is in itself a remarkable event. But, in addition, they have assembled a roster of contributors whose expertise defines the uniqueness of the volume. As the Executive Editor of this series of monographs, I am proud to present it.

Claude Lenfant, M.D.
Bethesda, Maryland

Reference

1. Schramm, C.J., editor. Health Care and Its Costs: Can the U.S. Afford Adequate Health Care? New York: W.W. Norton, 1987.

PREFACE

Most of our efforts to understand health and disease are aimed at developing comprehensive knowledge of biomedical, physiological, and pathophysiological mechanisms of illness. From this knowledge, new diagnostic and treatment strategies continue to emerge. Although this approach advances science, illnesses—by design—become deconstructed into organ-specific medical interventions. Thus, viewing health care advancement from the perspective of biomedical knowledge alone may improve organ-specific health, but it does not necessarily improve the health of the whole individual—or of society.

Currently, we are seeing a rapid advancement in our understanding of health and disease in the context of quality of life, both as individuals and as part of a larger society. Increasingly, the social sciences are providing us with the necessary tools to view health and disease more comprehensively. Each year, more studies suggest the importance of examining the impact of health and disease from the perspective of the total person with the context of the social environment.

The purpose of this monograph is to provide a state-of-the-art examination of asthma from the perspective of the social sciences. Two important international epidemiological studies have recently demonstrated that asthma is a disease that affects populations throughout most of the world (1,2). The European Community Respiratory Health Survey (ECRHS), which was carried out in 48 centers in 22 countries, found substantial geographic variation in asthma prevalence, ranging from a high of 9–12% at the centers in New Zealand and Australia to 2% or below in parts of East Germany and Spain (2). Similarly, the International Study of Asthma and Allergies in Childhood (ISAAC) found differences in prevalence of more than 20-fold among the 99 centers in 42 countries (1).

What does it mean to a country or even a single community to have this burden of asthma? How can we measure its impact? Perhaps more importantly, how can knowledge of the social impact of asthma be used to improve clinical care? What types of outcomes, in addition to physiological measures or targeted organ function, should be included in our assessment of this important health condition? What is the economic impact of this disease on individuals, the health care system, and society? And finally, how might our understanding of the economic impact help reduce the social burden of asthma?

These are some of the questions that led us, as editors, to develop this monograph in the Lung Biology in Health and Disease series. It is presented in two sections. The first examines our current understanding of the social burden of asthma and reviews newly emerging methods for measuring this burden. In addition, it is well understood that the social burden is increasingly being translated into economic terms. Therefore, the second section examines the economic impact of asthma. Economic evaluations of this type may help us to understand how to characterize and redistribute resources to reduce the burden of asthma. We believe that these two sections, together, provide the reader with a comprehensive summary of what is known about the social impact of asthma and how knowledge in this area may improve care for individuals and society.

This monograph would not have been possible without the administrative and editorial support of Ms. Robin Wagner. We would also like to thank Rhône-Poulenc Rorer for their support by way of an educational grant, which gave the authors an opportunity to come together to present and discuss early versions of their chapters. As editors, we recognize the importance of the academic exchange that took place at that authors' meeting—it substantially added to the overall quality of this monograph. Finally, we would like to thank Dr. Claude Lenfant. This monograph would not have been possible if it had not been for his vision of the importance of social scientific understanding of health and illness. For that we express our sincere appreciation.

Kevin B. Weiss
A. Sonia Buist
Sean D. Sullivan

References

1. The ISAAC Steering Committee (1998). Worldwide variation in prevalence of symptoms of asthma, allergic rhinoconjunctivitis, and atopic eczema. *Lancet* **352**:1225–1232.
2. Chinn, S., Burney, P., Jarvis, D., Luczynska, C., on behalf of the European Community Respiratory Health Survey (1997). Variation in bronchial responsiveness in the European Community Respiratory Health Survey (ECRHS). Eur. Respir. J. **10**:2495–2501.

CONTRIBUTORS

Linda Asmussen, M.S. Senior Research Associate, Department of Research, American Academy of Pediatrics, Elk Grove Village, Illinois

Paul D. Blanc, M.D., M.S.P.H. Associate Professor, Division of Occupational and Environmental Medicine, Department of Medicine, University of California School of Medicine, San Francisco, California

A. Sonia Buist, M.D. Professor and Head, Pulmonary and Critical Care Medicine, School of Medicine, Oregon Health Sciences University, Portland, Oregon

Arlene Manns Butz, R.N., Sc.D. Associate Professor, Department of Pediatrics, Johns Hopkins University School of Medicine, Baltimore, Maryland

Anne Elixhauser, Ph.D. Senior Social Science Analyst, Center for Organization and Delivery Studies, Agency for Health Care Policy and Research, Rockville, Maryland

Jonathan A. Finkelstein, M.D., M.P.H. Instructor, Department of Ambulatory Care and Prevention, Harvard Medical School and Harvard Pilgrim Health Care, Boston, Massachusetts

Neal Halfon, M.D., M.P.H. Professor, Departments of Pediatrics and Community Health Sciences, Schools of Medicine and Public Health, University of California, and UCLA Center for Healthier Children, Families, and Communities, Los Angeles, California

Michael T. Halpern, M.D., Ph.D., M.P.H.   Vice President, Clinical Research, MEDTAP International Inc., Bethesda, Maryland

Paul W. Jones, Ph.D., F.R.C.P.   Professor, Division of Physiological Medicine, Department of Respiratory Medicine, St. George's Hospital Medical School, London, England

Bengt Jönsson, Ph.D.   Professor, Centre for Health Economics, Stockholm School of Economics, Stockholm, Sweden

Elizabeth F. Juniper, M.C.S.P., M.Sc.   Professor, Department of Clinical Epidemiology and Biostatistics, McMaster University Medical Center, Hamilton, Ontario, Canada

Barry Kitch, M.D., M.P.H.   Fellow, Channing Laboratory and Division of Pulmonary and Critical Care Medicine, Harvard Medical School, and Brigham and Women's Hospital, Boston, Massachusetts

Karen M. Kuntz, Sc.D.   Assistant Professor, Department of Health Policy and Management, Harvard School of Public Health, and Brigham and Women's Hospital, Boston, Massachusetts

Nancy Kline Leidy, Ph.D., R.N.   Director and Senior Research Scientist, Center for Health Outcomes Research, MEDTAP International Inc., Bethesda, Maryland

Guy B. Marks, M.B.B.S., Ph.D., F.R.A.C.P., F.A.F.P.H.M.   Senior Lecturer, Institute of Respiratory Medicine, University of Sydney, Sydney, Australia

Peter J. Neumann, Sc.D.   Assistant Professor, Department of Health Policy and Management, Harvard School of Public Health, Boston, Massachusetts

Paul W. Newacheck, Dr.P.H.   Professor, Institute for Health Policy Studies and Department of Pediatrics, University of California School of Medicine, San Francisco, California

Lynn M. Olson, Ph.D.   Director, Division of Child Health Research, American Academy of Pediatrics, Elk Grove Village, Illinois

A. David Paltiel, Ph.D.   Associate Professor, Department of Epidemiology and Public Health, Yale School of Medicine and Yale School of Management, New Haven, Connecticut

Scott D. Ramsey, M.D., Ph.D. Assistant Professor, Departments of Medicine and Health Services, University of Washington, Seattle, Washington

Cynthia S. Rand, Ph.D. Associate Professor, Department of Medicine, Johns Hopkins University School of Medicine, Baltimore, Maryland

Maureen P. M. H. Rutten-van Mölken, Ph.D. Senior Research Fellow, Institute for Medical Technology Assessment, Erasmus University, Rotterdam, The Netherlands

Lauren A. Smith, M.D., M.P.H. Division of General Pediatrics, Boston Medical Center, Boston University School of Medicine, Boston, Massachusetts

Sean D. Sullivan, Ph.D. Associate Professor, Department of Pharmacy and Health Services, and Director, Health Services Research Core, Center for AIDS Research, and Director, Pharmaceutical Outcomes Research and Policy Program, University of Washington, Seattle, Washington

Kevin B. Weiss, M.D. Associate Professor, Department of Medicine, Rush Medical College, Chicago, Illinois

Scott T. Weiss, M.D. Professor, Department of Medicine, and Director of Respiratory and Environmental Epidemiology, Channing Laboratory, Harvard Medical School, and Brigham and Women's Hospital, Boston, Massachusetts

CONTENTS

Part One

SOCIAL IMPACT OF ASTHMA

1

Introduction to Part One
The Social Impact of Asthma

KEVIN B. WEISS

Rush Medical College
Chicago, Illinois

A. SONIA BUIST

School of Medicine
Oregon Health Sciences University
Portland, Oregon

Although much of the medical literature views asthma from the perspective of lung function and cellular immune function, this view is narrow in contrast to the comprehensive impact of the disease on an individual's life as a whole. The day-to-day social functioning of persons with asthma is often altered, either by asthma symptoms or by the medical care required to keep the disease under control. For persons with asthma, fears and anxieties about disease-related morbidity and mortality are likely to influence choices of short-term activities or even long-term life goals. Yet it is not just the individual who is affected; asthma's impact reaches far beyond the individual to include family, friends, coworkers, schools, and the community.

The following chapters explore our current understanding of asthma's impact on individuals, their families, and society. The authors delve beyond simple descriptive analysis of the social impact of this condition to the most recent advances in our understanding of how to measure the social impact of this disease.

This first section of the monograph has three subsections: the first, Chapters 1, 2, and 4, examines the social and environmental dimensions of asthma; the second, Chapters 5–7, explores the tools currently used to measure a key component of social impact—i.e., health-related quality of life; and the third,

Chapters 8 and 9, examines the psychological impact of asthma and how societal factors may affect the expression of this disease.

Mastery of terminology is central to any thoughtful discussion of the social impact of health. To the novice, the terminology in this area can be very confusing. To help with this, Dr. Paul Jones, in Chapter 2, opens the section with an exploration of the terms used to elucidate social impact. Many investigators have sought to define asthma in social terms and, during the past decade, three terms— *quality of life*, *health status*, and *social impact*—have emerged as distinct concepts with obvious overlapping dimensions. This chapter gives the reader a sense of the differences among these three concepts and how each adds to our understanding of the social impact of asthma.

Chapter 3 provides a detailed characterization of the social impact of asthma as it relates to children. In this chapter, Halfon and Newacheck contribute a rather special view of asthma and children. They propose that to understand asthma's influence on children, one must view this condition in light of the ''interaction of the child as a biopsychosocial [entity] within his/her immediate social environment, as well as the role of larger social systems.'' To support this approach, they borrow from Bronfenbrenner's ecological model of child development to account for the influence of family, peer relationships, school settings, and external influences—such as neighborhood—as part of the environment that may affect or be affected by the child with asthma.

For adults, the greatest social impact of asthma probably relates to occupation and work disability. In Chapter 4, Dr. Paul Blanc explores the relationships between asthma and work status and provides a comprehensive review of how asthma affects the working lives of women and men. He further examines the current strengths and limitations of the models used to define and describe the occupational impact of this disease.

Chapters 5 through 7 present a comprehensive examination of issues surrounding asthma-related quality of life. Dr. Elizabeth Juniper presents an overview of the key issues in assessing health-related quality of life, including insights into the two major types of assessments—generic versus condition-specific. She describes the requirements of good instruments, such as measures of face and content validity as well as discriminative and evaluative properties. She also addresses the challenges of the cultural adaptation of such instruments.

Following Dr. Juniper's introduction, Chapters 6 and 7 provide a detailed review of the instruments currently available for measuring quality of life among children and adults. In Chapter 6, Olson and Asmussen review each of the six available asthma-specific instruments constructed for children. In addition, they also examine three generic health status instruments that have been used to study populations of children with asthma. One of the highlights of their chapter is the discussion surrounding the challenges in developing measures for children and how each of the currently available instruments has addressed these issues.

Although there is a limited body of literature examining the use of quality-of-life instruments for children with asthma, there is much more literature defining the use of these instruments for adults. In Chapter 7, Dr. Guy Marks provides a comprehensive review of the six available asthma-specific instruments constructed for adults (a slightly different set than the six instruments for children) as well as two generic instruments. Most notable is the discussion on how each instrument should be examined in terms of its suitability for various types of studies, specifically differences in "between-subject" or cross-sectional studies and "within-subject" or longitudinal studies.

The last two chapters of this section, Chapters 8 and 9, target two additional issues in the study of asthma and its impact on society. Drs. Rand and Butz present a thorough review of the literature surrounding the psychological impact of asthma. They characterize how the social environment can lessen or exacerbate the disease process. Issues such as mental health, behavior problems, coping skills, health belief models, and family social function all appear to play an important role in asthma outcomes.

In Chapter 9, Drs. Smith and Finkelstein examine how society might influence the burden of asthma. There is mounting evidence that asthma is affected by socioeconomic status. This chapter provides a new understanding of the possible interactions between the biomechanical and sociopsychological mechanisms of this disease. On the basis of their review of the literature, the authors construct a useful model of the impact of social risk and its effect on asthma prevalence and related morbidity.

Together, these eight chapters present a comprehensive examination of the social impact of asthma. It is our hope that the reader will gain many new insights in this area. For the novice, there are introductions to key concepts, terms, and reviews of many of the studies that helped to define the concepts related to social impact and disease. For those who are already familiar with this area, this first section provides a state-of-the-art examination of the research issues that are actively being explored.

Beyond the initial value of such a comprehensive review, this first section defines the need for future scholarly work in these areas and begins to delineate the direction for such work. Perhaps one of the notable themes in this section of the monograph is the desire of the various contributors to construct theoretical models that link the pathway of disease mechanisms to that of differing types and intensities of social impact for the affected individual as well as the family and community. Each of the models presents a reasonable characterization of these pathways. However, to date, none of the models have undergone any rigorous investigation; they therefore remain conceptual "best guesses" awaiting further scientific exploration. In reading the various chapters of this section, the reader will discern a lack of clear relationship among the various theoretical models. Again, this lack of agreement on a single model to explain the social impact of asthma represents the current state of the art and thereby provides a venue for future discussions to advance this area of knowledge.

These differing models raise many questions: Are there substantive differences in the social impact of asthma for certain subpopulations, such as gender groups or specific age groups? How much impact do the workplace and school have upon the social expression of this disease? Should the social impact of asthma be viewed from a developmental model, or should its impact be characterized independent of the individual's stage of life? How do we begin to integrate our knowledge of the psychological dimension to this illness with the sociological characterization of its impact?

Regardless of the questions raised, the authors of many of the chapters in this section expressed a clear need to embrace a conceptual model as the cornerstone for building our knowledge of the social impact of asthma. A clear next step is to engage in a debate that will move this issue forward to a more unified and commonly agreed upon model. From this debate, it is likely that an explicit set of research questions will emerge to both test the model and advance our understanding in this area.

Several chapters in this section also made clear the need for better measures of social impact. More than a dozen health status instruments are currently in use or soon to be available, each with a different degree of scientific validity and reliability. Very few of these instruments have been tested on a large population of persons with asthma, and even fewer of them have proved useful in more than one or two clinical trials. It is not clear that any of these instruments, which were principally designed for research settings, would be useful in clinical practice. So what is to be the next step in advancing our ability to better characterize health status and quality of life? Would there be any utility in attempting to seek a single best instrument, or should the direction of scholarly work in this area involve numerous instruments that may or may not have specific applications? While it would be premature to answer such questions, the chapters in this section demonstrate the early nature of this scientific work and our current inexperience in how best to apply these measurement tools in our daily work as researchers, clinicians, and policymakers.

A third major issue that can be gleaned from reading the chapters in this section is the lack of published literature to inform our understanding of the impact of asthma worldwide. Most of the literature on the social impact of asthma relates to countries that would be considered by the World Health Organization to be developed. There is very little information on the impact of asthma in many of the developing countries or countries of lower socioeconomic status, where most of the world's population resides. Many or most of the instruments developed for measuring health status are currently not validated for cross-cultural comparative studies. The few instruments that have been used cross-culturally have done so with very little formal scientific validation.

Furthermore, as one examines the issue of asthma from the perspective of other societies, it becomes important to consider how the impact of asthma relates to the broader health and social needs of a population. Much of the social impact of asthma relates to the morbidity due to acute exacerbations, the need for urgent medical services, and loss of work productivity. The burden of asthma is not commonly measured in terms of mortality because it is a rare event for this condition. This makes the relative impact of asthma difficult to compare to other conditions that more directly contribute to premature mortality.

The last major issue that emerges from this first section of the monograph relates to other audiences that may benefit from further advances in our understanding of the burden of asthma. The authors clearly have composed their chapters with the view of the clinician and clinical research in mind. However, the societal impact of any chronic condition, particularly a condition as prevalent as asthma, is of interest to a number of other professional sectors. Health policymakers require insights into the burden of asthma to inform legislative or regulatory actions to benefit society for purposes of health, education, and public welfare. Health care insurers, whether private or public, need to be informed of the asthma burden in order to stimulate improvements in the delivery of asthma care. The business sector can use this information to understand how this common condition affects productivity in schools and the workplace.

The chapters in this first section on the social impact of asthma provide an extensive overview of the knowledge in this area as well as insights into the areas where further scholarly investigation might improve our understanding of the social burden of asthma. As these chapters serve to emphasize, while much is known, there is much more yet to be learned about how asthma affects individuals, families, and society.

2

Quality of Life, Health Status, and the Social Impact of Asthma

An Overview

PAUL W. JONES

St. George's Hospital Medical School
London, England

I. Introduction

Many other chapters in this monograph address the impact of asthma on patients' quality of life and its broader social impacts. The aim of this chapter is to provide the background to these issues. Three terms will be used to describe the different impacts of asthma: *health-related quality of life*, *health status*, and *social impact*. It will be argued that these theoretical constructs do reflect different effects of the disease and that each construct has a defining characteristic of sufficient utility to justify its separate identity. Areas of overlap between these different effects of asthma are also discussed.

The chapter is developed along two themes. The first concerns the underlying theoretical concepts and the processes by which asthma produces its effect on patients and their lives. The second is concerned with some issues of measurement.

II. Concepts and Definitions

A. Health-Related Quality of Life

Health-related quality of life may be defined as: "the impact of disease on a patient's health and well-being." This definition is clear and simple but lacks precision. In contrast, Patrick and Erickson (1) have provided an exhaustive description that specifies in detail the precise components of health-related quality of life. It is noteworthy that in their description, social function is a core component of health-related quality of life.

In the view of most commentators, the term *quality of life* is strongly linked to the individual. The uniquely personal nature of quality of life is easy to understand, since each of us is different. As a result, the factors that determine the quality of our lives will also differ, whether in health or disease. These factors will depend upon the mind, personality, and experience of the individual and will influence his or her perception of the effects of the illness and their response to it. A patient's health-related quality of life is the result of a generic disturbance to health common to all patients with the disease, modulated by factors that are internal and unique to the individual. For example asthma causes breathlessness on exercise—a generic effect common to many patients. A child for whom sport is important but often not possible may feel heavily stigmatized and frustrated by the physical limitation imposed by their disease. In contrast, another child with no interest in games may not be upset in the same way. One child's quality of life will be considerably disturbed, but the other's may not.

Factors that are external to the patient but lie within his or her social, physical, and economic environment will also have an impact upon health-related quality of life, as implied by the overlap in Figure 1. While recognizing the importance of this overlap, it is still useful to think of health-related quality of life as being that effect of asthma which is determined by the patient's mind and personality.

B. Health Status

The term *health status measurement* is mostly used to described the process of quantifying the impact of disease on a patient's health and well-being in a standardized manner. Such assessments are used to compare the health of different groups of patients or measure health gain following treatment. Elsewhere in this monograph, the term *quality of life* is used in this context. As discussed above, if quality of life is unique to the individual, standardization of such measurements is very difficult to achieve. There is no harm in using the terms *quality of life*, *health-related quality of life*, and *health status* interchangeably in discussing this type of measurement, but it is not correct to assume that quality of life and health status are one and the same thing.

To allow comparisons of the health of different groups of patients or the relative efficacy of different treatments, measurements must be made in a standardized way. This means that each patient should be assessed in exactly the same manner. For this reason, the questionnaire must be appropriate to each individual being studied. The different methods used to develop these instruments are dealt with in Chapters 5, 6, and 7, by Juniper, Olson, and Marks, but the

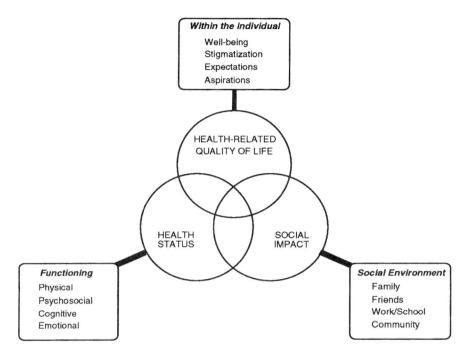

Figure 1   Venn diagram illustrating the overlap between quality of life, health status, and social impact of asthma.

basic principles are enunciated here. In essence, the developer of a health status questionnaire aims to identify and include only those items that are common or potentially applicable to each and every patient who might be studied. To achieve this end, large populations of patients are sampled to ensure that all possible relevant items are identified. Care should then be taken to remove all those items related to age, sex, socioeconomic status, and education level. The end product of this process is a collection of items that form a lowest common denominator of similarity between individuals with the disease for which the questionnaire is designed. These items certainly describe factors that impair quality of life, but since they are potentially common to all patients with asthma, they describe a general effect of the disease on the patient's health. Many other activities disturbed by asthma will be unique to the individual. For example, no health status (or ''quality of life'') questionnaire asks patients specifically whether the activities of scuba diving or pigeon breeding would be affected by their disease. Both of these are important to small numbers of asthmatic individuals but are not common to all patients with the disease. Thus they lie in the domain of quality of life rather than health status.

The process of creating a standardized instrument results in the removal of those items that reflect a patient's individuality. Attempts have been made to produce more individualized questionnaires for asthma, the most notable being the Asthma Quality of Life Questionnaire developed by Juniper and colleagues (2). As described elsewhere, this questionnaire has four components, one of which covers activities that are disturbed by asthma. During the development of this instrument, a large number of different items concerned with disturbance of activity were identified, showing that individuals have a wide range of different activities that might be restricted by asthma. To make a questionnaire that was of manageable size and appropriate to each individual, the developers decided to allow each patient to choose his or her own items for this component. This is the furthest that any of the asthma health status questionnaires go toward allowing the patient to express their individuality. With this partial exception, all of the "quality of life" instruments for asthma described in this book treat each individual as if they were a typical patient with asthma—i.e., they deny their individuality. For this reason these questionnaires would be better termed "health status" measures, to indicate that they quantify generic effects of asthma.

As pointed out in Chapter 7, the content of the various questionnaires developed for asthma does differ, even when robust methodologies have been used in their development. This may be due in part to the background and prejudices of the developers, but it has also been shown that the content of the questionnaire is critically dependent upon small differences in statistical cutoff points chosen by the developers in deciding whether to include or exclude an item (3). That having been said, the similarities in content between the various questionnaires are much greater than the differences (4), despite differences in the theoretical constructs and methodological techniques used.

C. Social Impact

When seen from the perspective of the patient, the social consequences of asthma are to induce handicap and impair quality of life. Handicap has been defined by the World Health Organization (WHO) since 1980 as "disadvantage for a given individual resulting from an impairment or a disability that limits or prevents the fulfilment of a role that is normal (depending on age, sex, social and cultural factors) for that individual." This clearly encompasses issues concerning the individual's role in society and his or her social integration. Asthma also has an impact on the family and the caregivers of patients with asthma, as discussed by Halfon and Newacheck in Chapter 3. Beyond the family, the disease has an effect on the social and work contacts of the patient, including schoolteachers and work colleagues. It also has an impact in terms of reduced productivity due to days lost from school, college, or work that is seen from the perspective of society at large.

The social impact of asthma concerns factors that are external to the patient, but this is not just the effect that an asthmatic patient has upon their environment. It is a two-way process, since external factors will determine the patient's level of handicap. As explained by Blanc in Chapter 4, an asthma trigger may have minimal effect on one patient if he or she is not occupationally exposed to it yet have a major impact on others if it is a frequent or constant feature of their work environment. The nature of this interaction between environment and patient may be multifactorial. The National Health Interview Survey in the United States found that respondents for black children with asthma reported more days of school absence than their white counterparts (mean 6.5 days absent per child per year in blacks vs. 4.0 in whites) (5). Race remained a predictor of absence even after the effect of social deprivation and other confounders was removed (5). This is in contrast to the use of medical services in which race was not a significant covariate after other factors had been taken into account. In the United Kingdom, self-reported school absence was associated with parental separation, poor maternal health, lack of access to a car, and renting of accommodation (6). A more recent study of school attendance records found that absence due to asthma was not related to asthma severity but was related to an index of social deprivation (7). Clearly the social impact of asthma is a complex phenomenon that may in turn be socially determined.

III. Pathways

An alternative way of looking at the impact of asthma is to view it as a sequence or hierarchy of effects (Fig. 2). The primary consequences are symptoms such as wheeze, breathlessness, chest tightness, and cough. These, in turn, have secondary effects upon the patient's daily life and well-being. Many of these will be common to most patients with the disease—for example, disturbance of basic daily activities, social functions, and emotions. As discussed previously, these common secondary effects form the basis of health status as measured by health status questionnaires. Disturbances of quality of life and the social impact of asthma may be seen as tertiary effects.

It is important to note that the tertiary effects of asthma are influenced by factors that may be unrelated to the underlying disease process. Thus, quality of life and social impacts of asthma cannot be predicted with confidence from a knowledge of the disease process in the lungs. The significance of these other inputs may be best understood by analogy with a neurophysiological pathway, as illustrated in Figure 3. In this model, the consequences of asthma progress

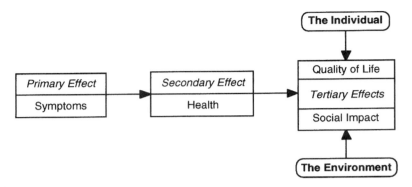

Figure 2 Pathway showing the sequence of effects of asthma.

from symptoms through to handicap. At each stage other signals, unrelated to asthma, feed in and modulate the input such that its size and nature are altered considerably.

The pathways outlined in Figures 2 and 3 are linear models, but this is an oversimplification. Feedback effects operate at both the secondary and tertiary

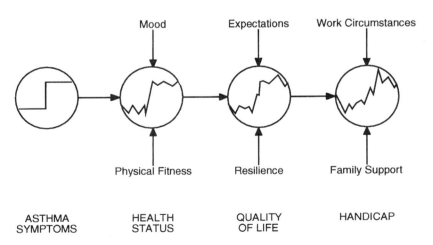

Figure 3 A model based upon an analogy with a neurophysiological model to illustrate the way signals unrelated to the original stimulus may alter the size and morphology of the input as it passes through different stages in the pathway.

levels, and some of the modulating inputs shown in Figure 3 may be derived from feedback arising from further down the signal chain. Two examples are illustrated in Figure 4. Exercise limitation due to breathlessness leads to physical detraining and muscle wasting. Both of these may, in turn, limit exercise performance quite independently of any effect of asthma (Fig. 4A). A behavioral example of feedback is shown in Figure 4B. A number of behaviors would fit this model—for example, leisure pursuits. Asthma symptoms may, from time to time, restrict an individual's ability to play sports or enter smoky environments. After a time, the person may assume that he or she can never carry out these activities and thereby will limit such activities in anticipation of any problems. Thus asthma has shaped these individuals' expectations of life, which, in turn, feeds back to restrict their lives regardless of the level of disease activity. Disturbance to work may follow a similar pattern, and one could easily substitute employment for social restriction in the model in Figure 4B.

From the foregoing, it is clear that the simple model in Figure 2 should be replaced by the more complex nonlinear model shown in Figure 5, in which multiple feedbacks may occur at different stages. If any of these feedbacks are positive (i.e., reinforcing), the disturbance at each step could become autonomous and relatively independent of the events that preceded it. In consequence, lifestyle restriction may persist even though the severity of asthma remits.

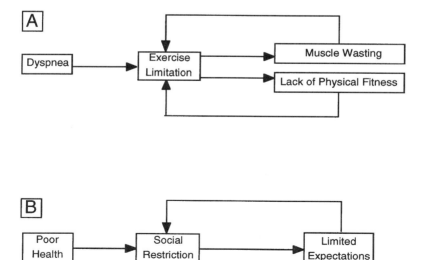

Figure 4   Two examples of feedback in the development of ill health and social impairment due to asthma.

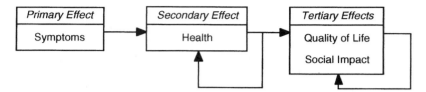

Figure 5   A more accurate reflection of the relationship between the various consequences of asthma, illustrating that feedback may also play an important role in the development of ill health and social impairment.

IV.   Issues of Measurement

A.   Health-Related Quality of Life

The individual and internal nature of quality of life make it difficult to measure in a standardized manner. A tool for the assessment of individual health-related quality of life has been developed (8), but it does not allow comparisons between patients. Interestingly, use of this technique has shown that health factors may not be the most important determinants of quality of life, even in patients with very significant disease (8).

The concept of individual health-related quality of life is very useful in trying to form a coherent view of the various effects of asthma and the factors that form and influence them. It is, however, very difficult to measure. In practical terms, the concept may have greatest value in the context of individual patient management rather than as the basis for a method of measurement.

B.   Health Status

A range of health status instruments are described elsewhere in this book as ''quality of life'' questionnaires. To date, few studies have compared their performance directly. Such comparisons must be carried out using cross-sectional studies to compare the discriminative properties of these instruments (i.e., their ability to distinguish between different levels of health between patients) and in longitudinal studies to examine their evaluative properties (their ability to detect changes within patients). At a minimum, such comparisons should include not only a correlation between the two instruments but also a comparison of the distributions of their scores. The latter will show where the scores lie within the scaling range of each questionnaire, whether the scores are skewed, and whether they exhibit floor or ceiling effects. All of these characteristics may affect an instrument's performance.

Data from a recent study (9) allow a partial comparison of the discriminative properties of two disease-specific health status measures for asthma, the St. George's Respiratory Questionnaire (SGRQ) and the McMaster Asthma Quality of Life Questionnaire (AQLQ(M)). Correlations between the scores and the morning peak expiratory flow (PEFR) were similar: AQLQ(M) vs. PEFR, $r = 0.35$; SGRQ vs. PEFR, $r = 0.48$. There was also a very good correlation between the two questionnaires (Fig. 6). This might suggest that these questionnaires have very similar properties in terms of describing differences between patients, but the frequency distributions of their scores were rather different (Fig. 7). It appears that these two instruments may have different psychometric properties and may behave differently in populations of differing disease severity. Other work suggests that the sensitivity of disease-specific instruments to changes in health may also differ, for example another study compared the responsiveness of the AQLQ(M) and another disease-specific measure, the Living with Asthma Questionnaire (LWAQ). At baseline, there was a good cross-sectional correlation between the LWAQ and the AQLQ(M) scores ($r = 0.73$), but only the AQLQ(M) was able to detect a difference in health gain between the two treatments under examination (10).

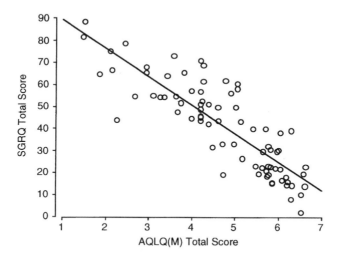

Figure 6 Correlation between two disease-specific health status questionnaires for asthma: the Asthma Quality of Life Questionnaire developed in McMaster (AQLQ(M)) and the St. George's Respiratory Questionnaire (SGRQ). The correlation coefficient was 0.85. The data were derived from a cross-sectional comparison across patients, described in Ref. 9. The mean age of the patients was 46 years and their mean FEV_1 was 73% predicted.

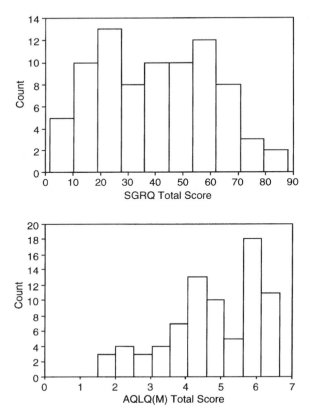

Figure 7 Frequency distribution of scores obtained in asthmatic patients with two disease-specific health status questionnaires for asthma: the Asthma Quality of Life Questionnaire developed in McMaster (AQLQ(M)) and the St. George's Respiratory Questionnaire (SGRQ). Poorer health is indicated by low scores using AQLQ(M) and high scores using the SGRQ. These data are the same as those used in the correlation shown in Figure 6.

In conclusion, there do appear to be differences between health status instruments for asthma, even though their content is quite similar and the methodologies used to develop them appear to be robust. Clearly, any statement about health status should be qualified by adding the identity of the instrument with which it was measured. This should not be a major problem to pulmonary physicians, who have long used two measures of airways obstruction—the FEV_1 and the PEFR—in the knowledge that these measure different aspects of the same functional disturbance.

C. Social Impact

The social impact of asthma may be very wide, depending on how this impact is defined. A number of surveys have listed the frequency of a range of disturbances to leisure and social activities in the families of children with asthma (6,11–13). Often these have been in the form of surveys using techniques derived from market research (14,15). Whilst such studies provide valuable descriptions of the frequency of certain asthma effects, rigorous quantitative estimates of clearly defined asthma impacts may be more useful. By and large such measurements are confined to absence from school or work. In theory, these should be easy to obtain, since the outcomes may be defined quite precisely and form simple dichotomous variables (i.e., absence or no absence).

School absence features prominently in surveys of the social impact of asthma since schooling is important and days of absence are simple to quantify. Most of the data have been obtained using retrospective self-report in study populations recruited in a number of different ways. There is a degree of consistency between such studies (5,14), but this does not necessarily mean these estimates are accurate. The measurements appear to be fairly reliable (i.e., similar estimates were obtained in different settings), but the same sources of recall bias may have been operating in each setting. Another approach to this measurement is to use school attendance registers (7,16). Estimates of absence obtained in this way tend to be a little lower than those obtained through respondent report. In a case-controlled school record study, asthmatic children receiving prophylactic therapy were absent for only 3.5 days per term, compared with 2.8 days per term in controls (7). Furthermore, there was no difference in absentee rate between asthmatic children who were not receiving asthma medication and non-asthmatic controls.

Retrospective self-report may be subject to recall bias. In a study of respondent-reported absence in schoolchildren, the level of absence was stated as being between 1 to 5 days per year, up to a level of 5 days' absence. Above that level, absence was reported uniformly in multiples of five days (P.W. Jones, L. Pearson, J.C. Stinson, and J.B. Klim, unpublished). This suggests that any absence of more than 5 days in a year was recalled as a number of weeks, then converted to the appropriate number of schooldays. Clearly there is a need for a study that compares self-report with recall-independent estimates of school absence.

In adults, time away from work is the corollary of school absence. Reliable data on the amount of time lost from work due to asthma are difficult to obtain.

To date, there have been few studies that have collected such data prospectively, and have controlled for response or recall bias. Sickness certification is a source of data available on a national scale; however, the precision of this estimate will be determined by the criteria used for giving sickness benefit that are current in any particular country at any given time. For example in the United Kingdom, certification occurs only after 5 days consecutive absence—quite a long period for an asthma attack. For the last year for which data are available, asthma accounted for 1% of all days lost by males in employment, as compared with chronic obstructive pulmonary disease (COPD), which accounted for 8%. Other studies have collected data through employers' employment registers, but this may be subject to a different set of biases. In a study in U.S. college students with asthma, self-reported absence from college due to asthma was approximately 3 days per year. In those students who were also in paid employment at the same time, the mean number of missed days of paid employment was little more than a day (17).

When assessing school or work absence, account must be made of seasonal variation. The absence rate in asthmatic children in the United Arab Emirates, obtained from a large study of school records (18), was twice as high in the spring as in the autumn (45 vs. 22% of children). In a U.K. study in which adults were sampled in March and September for 3 consecutive years, a quarter of patients reported 4 or more days away from work over the 6 months up to March of the first year of the study (19). When sampled in September, only 9% of subjects reported 4 or more days' absence over the preceding 6 months. This study also showed that there may be moderate between-year variations in self-reported work absence due to asthma. In the second and third years of the study, the average absence recorded in March was rather lower (16% of subjects reporting 4 or more days absence) than when it was assessed in the first year (19). The higher work absence over the winter season in adults was probably due to the higher frequency of upper respiratory tract and other viral infections at this time of year. These also cause work absence in nonasthmatics, but there are no matched data for absenteeism over the winter in nonasthmatics, so it is not possible to quantify absence specifically due to asthma.

A true estimate of the impact of asthma on work absenteeism requires an accurate and unbiased estimate of absence over a full cycle of seasons in the asthmatic population under study and in matched nonasthmatic controls. Such data do not appear to be available currently for adults, unlike children, where studies of school records have met these requirements.

V. Summary and Conclusions

This chapter has attempted to show that quality of life, health status, and social impact may be viewed as distinct entities, despite their areas of obvious overlap.

It has been argued that health-related quality of life is unique and individual to the patient, since it is dependent upon his or her mind and thoughts. In contrast, health status is a theoretical construct of the impact of asthma on the patient's daily life and well-being that is shorn of all individuality. In this construct, each individual is viewed as if he or she were a typical patient. Finally, the social impact of asthma concerns the two-way interaction between the diseased patient and their social and physical milieu.

The pathways and interactions that result in these effects are complex. At each step, other factors unrelated to asthma may interact to mitigate or intensify the effects of the disease on the patient's life and social functioning. In consequence these effects must be measured directly, not inferred from estimates of airways function. Significant strides have been made in the development of robust and reliable measurements of these effects.

References

1. Patrick, D.L., and Erickson, P. (1993). Assessing health-related quality of life for clinical decision making. In *Quality of Life Measurement: Key Issues for the 1990s.* Edited by S.R. Walker, R.M. Rosser. Dordrecht, Kluwer, pp. 11–64.
2. Juniper, E.J., Guyatt, G.H., Epstein, R.S., Ferrie, P.J., Jaeschke, R., and Hiller, T.K. (1992). Evaluation of impairment of health related quality of life in asthma: development of a questionnaire for use in clinical trials. *Thorax,* **47**:76–83.
3. O'Leary, C.J., and Jones, P.W. (1998). The influence of decisions made by developers on health status questionnaire content. *Qual. Life Res.,* **7**:545–550.
4. Hyland, M. (1992). Quality of life assessment in respiratory disease: an examination of the content and validity of four questionnaires. *Pharmacoeconomics,* **2**:1–11.
5. Taylor, W.R., and Newacheck, P.W. (1992). Impact of childhood asthma on health. *Pediatrics,* **90**:657–662.
6. Anderson, H.R., Bailey, P.A., Cooper, J.S., Palmer, J.C., and West, S. (1983). Morbidity and school absence caused by asthma and wheezing illness. *Arch. Dis. Child.,* **58**:777–784.
7. McCowan, C., Bryce, F.P., Neville, R.G., Crombie, I.K., and Clark, R.A. (1996). School absence—a valid morbidity marker for asthma? *Health Bull.,* **54**:307–313.
8. Hickey, A.M., Bury, G., O'Boyle, C.A., Bradley, F., O'Kelly, F.D., and Shannon, W. (1996). A new short form individual quality of life measure (SEIQoL-DW): application in a cohort of individuals with HIV/AIDS. *Br. Med. J.,* **313**:29–33.
9. Barley, E.A., Quirk, F.H., and Jones, P.W. (1998). Asthma health status measurement in clinical practice: validity of a nes short and simple instrument. *Respir. Med.,* **92**:1207–1214.
10. Rutten van-Mölken, M.P.M.H., Custers, F., Van Doosrlaer, E.K.A., Jansen, C.C.M., Heurman, L., Maesen, F.P.V. Smeets, J.J., Bommer, A.M., and Raaijmakers, J.A.M. (1995). Comparing the performance of four different instruments in evaluating the effects of salmeterol on asthma quality of life. *Eur. Respir. J.,* **8**:888–898.

11. Martin, A.J., Landau, L.I., and Phelan, P.D. (1982). Asthma from childhood at age 21: the patient and his disease. *Br. Med. J.*, **284**:380–382.

12. Donnelly, J.E., Donnelley, W.J., and Thong, Y.H. (1987). Parental perceptions and attitudes toward asthma and its treatment: a controlled study. *Soc. Sci. Med.*, **24**: 431–437.

13. Nocon, A., and Booth, T. (1991). The social impact of asthma. *Fam. Pract.*, **8**:37–41.

14. Lenney, W., Wells, N.E.J., and O'Neill, B.A. (1994). The burden of paediatric asthma. *Eur. Respir. Rev.*, **4**:49–62.

15. The impact of asthma survey (1996). *National Asthma Campaign* (UK).

16. Hill, R.A., Standen, P.J., and Tattersfield, A.E. (1989). Asthma, wheezing, and school absence in primary schools. *Arch. Dis. Child.*, **64**:246–251.

17. Jolicouer, L.M., Boyer, J.G., Reeder, C.E., and Turner, J. (1994). Influence of asthma or allergies on the utilization of health care resources and quality of life of college students. *J. Asthma*, **31**:251–267.

18. Bener, A., Abdulrazzaq, Y.M., Bebuse, P., and Abdin, A.H. (1994). Asthma and wheezing as a cause of school absence. *J. Asthma*, **31**:93–98.

19. White, P.T., Pharoah, C.A., Anderson, A.R., and Freeling, P. (1989). Randomized controlled trial of small group education on the outcome of chronic asthma in general practice. *J. R. Coll. Gen. Pract.*, **39**:182–186.

3

Characterizing the Social Impact of Asthma in Children

NEAL HALFON

Schools of Medicine and Public Health
University of California and
UCLA Center for Healthier Children,
Families, and Communities
Los Angeles, California

PAUL W. NEWACHECK

Institute for Health Policy Studies
University of California School of
Medicine
San Francisco, California

I. Introduction

Asthma is the most common chronic medical condition affecting children. Estimates from the U.S. National Health Interview Survey (NHIS) suggest that 7.2% of children 0–17 years of age had asthma in 1994. Prevalence estimates from other countries range from 2.2–2.7% of 17- to 18-year-olds in Israel to 13–15% in 5- to 17-year-olds in Great Britain (1–3). More disturbing, the worldwide prevalence of asthma in children appears to be increasing; the number of children reported as disabled by their asthma is also increasing, as is the number of children hospitalized and the number of deaths attributed to asthma (2–15).

The effects of asthma on children and adolescent social role function—including children's ability to play, participate in school activities, and construct meaningful social and family relationships—are important to consider in accounting for the overall burden of this disease. Moreover, the dynamic interplay between social, family, and individual psychological factors can influence the onset, course, and severity of the disease as well as the overall burden on the child, family, and society. Thus, in considering the psychosocial impact of asthma, it is important to acknowledge and explore the dynamics of these reciprocal interactions.

In this chapter we review studies on the psychological, social, and family effects of asthma in children. Since children are not just little adults, it is important to consider these effects in the context of the child's changing development. We also use two prominent developmental theories—the ecological model of human development and the transactional model of individual psychological development—to build an ecological/transactional approach for considering how a child's various environments influences the onset, course, and severity of disease.

II. Unique Characteristics of Children with Asthma

Children's health and pathophysiology differ significantly from those of adults in four distinct ways. These differences include children's developmental vulnerability, the dependency of children upon a range of caregivers and institutions, the differential patterns of morbidity and mortality experienced by children, and asthma as a developmental disease. These distinctions have important implications for understanding the context of the psychological, social, and family impacts of childhood asthma (16,17).

A. Developmental Vulnerability

Developmental vulnerability refers to the rapid and cumulative physical and emotional changes that characterize childhood and the potential impact that illness, injury, and adverse social and family circumstances can have on a child's life course trajectory. Physical health conditions such as asthma as well as the child's social environment (e.g., severe poverty, unstable family situations, environmental exposures) can dramatically affect the health development processes. Several conceptual models have been used to specify the dynamic relationship between factors that promote or adversely affect children's capacity to achieve their physical, cognitive and emotional potential (18–20). There is a growing body of evidence suggestive of a substantial and cumulative impact of early exposures to adverse social and biological conditions on health status throughout the life course (18,21–23). In fact, some of the evidence on the life long impact of childhood diseases comes from longitudinal studies of children with asthma (24–30).

B. Dependency

Children also have complex and changing dependency relationships that affect their development and their ability to obtain and utilize appropriate services. Children are dependent on their parents and other caregivers to recognize and respond to their health needs, to organize their care and authorize treatment, and to comply with recommended treatment regimes. The importance of this dependency for children's access to health care is illustrated by studies that find that maternal and child health use of health services are highly correlated irrespective of the level of the child's health status (31). While children are generally dependent upon primary caregivers, other caregivers and caregiving institutions play a vital role in assuring that a child's needs are met in order not to overwhelm the emotional, physical, and financial resources of the primary caregiver. Thus schools, day-care centers, and other neighborhood social institutions play an important role in molding a child's experience and development. These other institutions can also play a significant role in ensuring that a continuum of services are available to the child with asthma.

For the child with asthma, family relationships and response patterns can play a significant role in the presentation and severity of the disease. The family environment can mediate the child's response to disease management approaches, and parents' ideas about educational and self-management programs play a role in the success of such interventions (32–35). Increasingly, comprehensive approaches to asthma therapy involve family level assessment and family level interventions (36–39).

C. Differential Morbidity

Children differ from adults also in the patterns of morbidity and in the basic pathophysiology and pharmacotheraputic responsiveness to treatment. In addition, specific disease expression, drug metabolism and methods of health status assessment differentiate children from adults. Most adults experience serious chronic medical conditions as a consequence of degenerative diseases. In children, such serious chronic conditions are usually related to birth or to congenitally acquired conditions. Patterns of illness in children are also related to unique behavioral comorbidities and social situations that are quite distinct for those that effect adults (40).

D. Asthma as a Developmental Disease

A life course perspective on childhood asthma recognizes that the biological and genetic predisposition toward asthma interacts with behavioral, social, and environmental influences in different ways at different ages. For example, there is some indication that the onset of asthma before age 3 may be more related to exposure to infectious agents, whereas later onset may be more related to other atopic factors (41). Similarly, the factors that influence the onset of acute exacerbation may significantly differ for children as opposed to adults (30).

The relative influence on developmental trajectory of childhood asthma has recently been elucidated by several studies that have clarified key immulogical processes that underlie the development of behavioral hyperresponsiveness to inhaled allergens. These studies have suggested the presence of a causal pathway with several branch points to explain how maternal exposure to inhaled allergens can prime fetal T cells. With subsequent postnatal exposure, different immulogical phenotypes are induced. These are characterized by different patterns and activity of lymphocytes: with the T_H2 lymphocyte predominantly found in asthmatic airways (42–45). While the exact mechanisms and relative magnitude of the lymphocyte response have yet to be worked out, multiple branch points in this pathway show that a range of environmental control mechanisms can differentially impact the progression of this developmental pathway.

This growing body of evidence and emerging developmental model of childhood asthma is a specific case of the general phenomenon of developmental vulnerability. This general model suggests that critical periods are important for the sensitizing response patterns and priming processes to take place. The impact of these priming and sensitizing processes can be manifest in a cumulative way, or as latent characteristics that are only manifest in the presence of specific triggers or combination of triggering and enhancing influences. Platts-Mills et al. (1996) and Holt et al. (1997) have suggested similar models to explain this process (Fig. 1) (44–46).

The developmental immunology of asthma suggests that a response pattern is induced early in life and that it predisposes children to wheeze based on a variety of other interacting features. These differential immulogical developmental trajectories may be related to the development of a different profile of lung function across the life course that has been described by Weiss (47). For example, we know that the exposure to inhaled allergens will have a different effect (prenatally in infancy, than when a child is 3). Similarly, the cumulative impact and interactions between different sensitizers and triggers are different during infancy and as the child ages (48).

We have presented this developmental model of asthma immunology to highlight the dynamic changes that take place early in life and the importance of the timing of exposures and control strategies. This largely biological developmental trajectory is nested in a repertoire of psychosocial processes that have their own developmental trajectory. We turn to a brief explanation of these next.

III. The Ecological/Transactional Approach to Understanding Asthma's Social Impacts

Bronfenbrenner's ecological model of child development suggests that in order to understand the broader influences on a child's developmental trajectory, one needs to understand the interaction of the child as a biopsychosocial organism with his or her immediate social environment as well as the role of larger social systems. The systems approach that Bronfenbrenner puts forth (Fig. 2) accounts

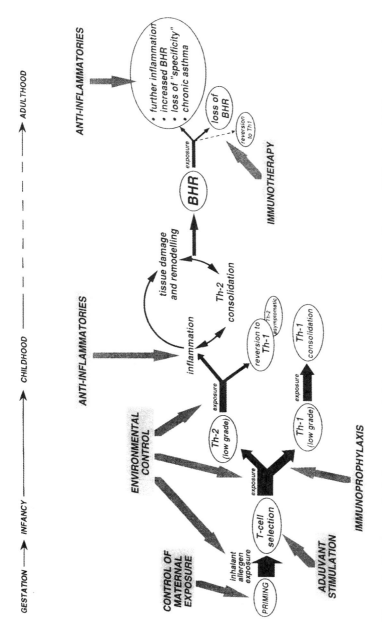

Figure 1 Key immunological processes underlying responsiveness to inhalant allergens. BHR = bronchial hyperresponsiveness. (From Ref. 45.)

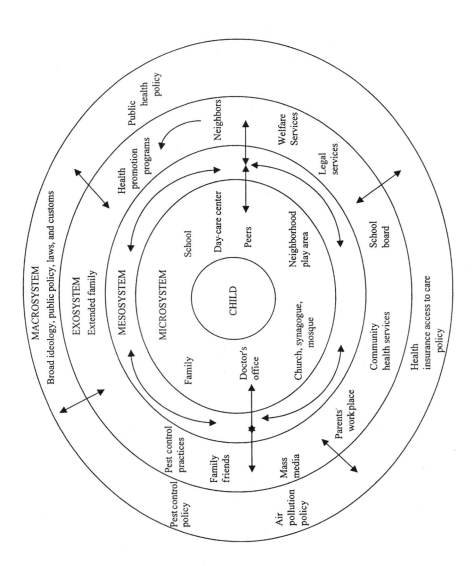

for the influence of family, peer relationships, and schools settings (the microsystem) as well as external influences, such as the neighborhood in which the child grows up and the conditions of the broader social environment in which a child lives (the exosystem). The ecological model also considers how broad ideological, demographic, and institutional influences as well as social policies influence both the exosystem and the microsystem in which a child resides (the macrosystem). This model provides a way of categorizing and accounting for the wide range of environmental factors that influence development. For the child with asthma, this ecological approach can account for the impact that family environment has on children's presentation, symptoms, and exacerbation as well as an understanding of the role that schools, school-based services, and education programs play in providing preventive treatment and rehabilitative services. It can also suggest ways in which community housing and pest-control policies influence children's symptom levels and quality of life.

Sammeroff also proposed a systems approach to understanding human development. His transactional model accounts for how different risk factors influence developmental outcomes (19). The transactional model suggests how biological, psychological, and environmental systems interact through continuous transactions over time. In this approach, developmental outcomes are not the result of individual or experiential context alone, but of transactions between biological, psychological, and environmental systems over time. Gottlieb (1976) and Cicchetti and Lynch (1996) suggest that experience can either induce, maintain, or facilitate the function of different behaviors or biological systems, making the expression of a genetic predisposition dependent on the environmental experience (49,50). Cicchetti and Lynch have combined these transactional and ecological perspectives into an ecological/transactional model of child maltreatment (50).

Figures 3 and 4 suggest how this ecological/transactional approach informs our understanding of childhood asthma. In Figure 3, four domains of child function relevant to asthma are depicted. While it is not exhaustive, interactions are depicted between a child's cognitive skills (knowledge, understanding, and self-management), a child's biological condition (disease severity, airway reactivity, and overall symptom burden) and emotional state (self-esteem, anxiety, and feelings of control). Each of these interacts with peer and family relationships. In Figure 4, a time dimension is added, and we depict how transactions between domains can influence different functional characteristics at the baseline, includ-

---

Figure 2 Ecological model: children's environment as a series of nested systems. (Adapted from Ref. 20.)

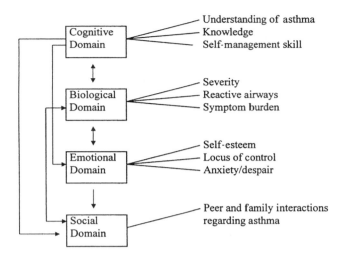

Figure 3 Multiple interacting dimensions of function and impact that can affect manifestations and outcomes of asthma in an individual child.

ing frequent symptoms, high severity, and little knowledge about disease management and concomitant high anxiety. As knowledge and self-management skills improve, medications are more appropriately administered, environments with tobacco smoke are avoided, and disease exacerbations as well as severity decrease, resulting in diminished anxiety and improved self-esteem. Additional behavior therapy continues to address the emotional needs of bolstering psychology functions and further diminishing exacerbations. While the figure does not display all transactions, it is easy to understand how such a developmental trajectory would also result in better peer and family relationships, school attendance, and performance.

It has been suggested that such a model is important in understanding the behavioral influences and consequences of the illness, because the somatic predisposition for the development of asthma interacts with multiple internal and external forces to determine the clinical presentation of asthma and the degree of airway disease and disability (32). The emerging theories about the etiology and predisposition to asthma suggest that, rather than one underlying physiological problem, there are multiple independent vulnerabilities that serve as the basic predisposition to asthma. Several studies have suggested that in addition to the basic biological propensity for reactive airways, social and environmental factors such as maternal smoking, poverty, and viral illness associated with poverty play some role in the onset, course, and severity of the disease (11,52–54). In keeping with the transactional model, the expression of the disease also has an effect on

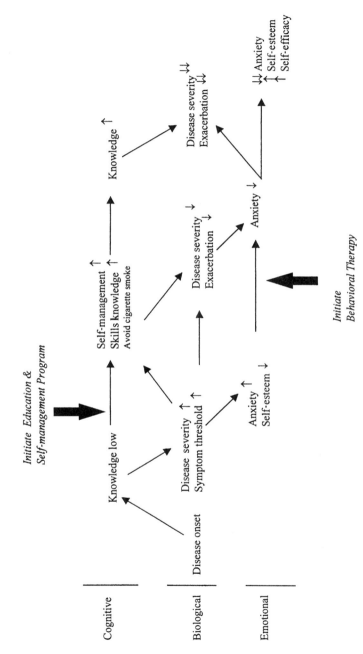

Figure 4 Transactional relationships between functional domains and interventions over time for children with asthma.

the primary caretaking parent, other members of the family unit, peer groups, the local community, and society. The manner in which these groups react to the child's asthma, in turn, affects ongoing exposure to allergens, contact with other inciting factors, and the ability to obtain appropriate care.

An ecological/transactional approach also helps to explain the relationship of potentiating and compensatory factors that influence presentation, course, severity, and long-term consequences of the disease from a developmental perspective. For example, for many children, the onset of asthma occurs between the ages of 1 and 3. This is a period of continued and rapid physical, emotional, and cognitive growth and is a time when the integration of a wide array of behavioral responses occurs. During this developmental period, children learn to regulate their affective responses; they form and develop attachment relationships and develop self-management and self-organizational behaviors that are precursors to the development of an autonomous self. Symbolic development through language, play, and other representational models also helps a child begin to understand and communicate with various environments. Within the microsystem, the family environment—including family dynamics, family interactions, and parenting styles–are all evolving and changing in response to the changing characteristics and potential of the individual child. Longitudinal studies are attempting to unravel the relationship between family response patterns and the onset of asthma in early life (37).

The presentation and course of asthma or any chronic illness are therefore superimposed upon this dynamic set of relationships and developing capacities. The episodic and often unpredictable nature of the asthma attack, the extra work of breathing during an attack, and the demoralization of fatigue and panic that accompany acute exacerbation can profoundly impact and disrupt the developmental pathways to a child's sense of control and their sense of self and well-being. The overlay of asthma symptoms on the transactions that take place between the child and family need to be considered in terms of their mutually interacting impact. From a clinical viewpoint, understanding the behavioral responses of a child with asthma means understanding the way in which a child has learned to respond based not only on physiological experience but also on how others responded in the course of a specific exacerbation. For example, a child who is hypoxic can appear anxious, irritable, and cranky. These behavioral responses to hypoxia can also be reinforced based on the response patterns of parents and other caregivers. Some behavioral responses can serve as buffers and are compensatory, whereas others may have potential long-term adverse consequences.

The proposed ecological/transactional framework allows us to integrate a developmental and life course perspective into our interpretation of the psychological and social impacts of this disease. It allows us to assess different levels of risk factors (child, family, and communities) and understand how different risk factors act independently or in conjunction to influence the presentation on-set, severity, and episodic fluctuations in the disease process. From a clinical and health service planning perspective, the ecological/transactional approach suggests ways in which a child, and family's resilience may be supported, the kinds of protective factors that may be effective, and the services that may be linked to provide more appropriate continuum of care.

IV. Social Basis of Childhood Asthma and Relevance for Assessing Social Impact

The prevalence of childhood asthma in the United States and throughout most of the world seems to be increasing (8,11–13,55). Whether this represents better diagnosis by clinicians, greater recognition by the public, longer-lasting episodes of the disease, or a true increase in incidence has been debated in the literature. The fact that hospitalizations, deaths, and the number of children reported disa-bled by this condition are also increasing suggests that the apparent increase in prevalence is real. Before defining the social impact of asthma, it is important to describe what is understood by the social and psychological factors that con-tribute to the prevalence and severity of asthma.

The prevalence of asthma has been associated with several social demo-graphic characteristics. Social and demographic characteristics, while not neces-sarily directly influencing the onset of disease, may have important associations with known causal factors, such as differential exposure rates to infectious agents, contact with environmental triggers such as house dust mites, or difficulties in access and quality of medical care. In addition, the sociodemographic characteris-tics of the child and family may indirectly influence parental and child perceptions of childhood asthma and related response patterns.

The relationship of sociodemographic characteristics to the prevalence of asthma has been investigated in several large population-based studies over the past 40 years (11,51,56,57). These studies demonstrate strikingly different associ-ations between asthma prevalence and social demographic characteristics. These divergent results may reflect differences in the distribution of social and demo-graphic characteristics among countries or variations in effect size across coun-tries. For example, most studies suggest, that at least in early and middle child-hood, males are more likely to have asthma than females (11,51,56). The role of race, social class, and family structure is less consistent across studies, In an analysis of the U.S. 1981 and 1988 National Health Interview Survey (NHIS) and 1976 and 1980 National Health and Nutrition Examination Sur-vey (NHANES), family income and minority status are associated with higher prevalence rates (11,58–60). A 1992 study of 5472 children 5 to 17 years old in Great Britain also found some association between asthma prevalence and social class (1). In contrast, Christchurch's (New Zealand) child development study of 1056 children in 1984 found that social class as well as most other sociodemographic variables were not significant predictors of asthma prevalence (51).

A recent analysis of the 1993–1994 U.S. NHIS using a multivariate approach that statistically controlled for the impact of multiple factors suggests that the prevalence of asthma increases with age, is more common in males, and is significantly higher in children from one-parent families as compared with two-parent families. Other social demographics such as poverty, family size, regional geographic difference, and place of residence were not significant predictors of asthma prevalence in this multivariate analysis (61). Interestingly, when a similar analysis was conducted for disabling asthma, poverty was found to have a substantial association with prevalence (62).

The potential role of family structure on the prevalence and severity of asthma bears further investigation. Since the trend in single parenthood in the United States parallels the trend of increasing asthma prevalence and severity, this association is important to explore. Single parenting can indicate a parent's individual choice, or it may reflect a divorce or other family disruption. Single parenting is often associated with poverty, which is, in turn, associated with a range of adverse child outcomes (63). It has yet to be determined however, whether single parenting is associated with fewer parental resources and/or more family disruption and stress and how it might be related to asthma. Almost all large population-based studies have shown an association between asthma severity and family structure (30,55,64–67).

The association between social class and asthma severity may be further explained by other factors that follow the same social distribution. For example, exposure to cigarette smoking has been linked to increased severity of asthma symptoms in childhood, and, as in a U.S. study using the 1981 NHIS, smoking accounted for some of the poverty-related disparities in prevalence (11).

V. Impact on Children's Functioning

In order to describe the impact of asthma on children's functioning, several different measures can be used. Traditionally, the impact of a health condition can been measured using a range of constructs, including opportunity, symptoms and health perceptions, functional status, impairment, and duration of life (68,69). These domains can be measured using indicators of resilience and ability to withstand stress, general health perceptions, and functional status defined in terms of health, social, psychological, and physical domains. More recently, integrative measures of health related quality of life have been used to measure the impact of disease and impaired function. These measures can integrate the impact of health across a variety of domains into a single measure, index, or summary score (68–70). While there are clear advantages to measure health-related quality of life, there have been very few quality-of-life measures used for pediatric illnesses and only a few using such measures for children with asthma (70; Chap. 6).

For asthma, several different outcome measures have also been used. These include classical signs and symptoms, measures of lung function, functional stress and health-related quality of life, and family function and impairment. In several recent economic evaluations of adult asthma interventions, *symptom-free days* were used as a multidimensional index that accounts for the frequency, duration, and intensity of wheezing, sputum production, nighttime wakings, and other symptoms (69,71). This measure, as well as other asthma-specific quality-of-life measures, have not been widely used in pediatric practice according to the literature to date.

For the purposes of this chapter, we have analyzed the social and emotional impact of childhood asthma in terms of the child's ability to function in society. We have operationalized the concept of function to include the number of disability days as well as general perception of health status; impact on schooling, including school attendance and academic performance; impact on social interaction with peers, family, and other social and leisure pursuits; and the emotional impact of asthma.

A. Limitations of Current Data

Before critically evaluating the literature on the impact of asthma on various aspects of children's lives, careful consideration must be given to several methodological limitations that may limit the conclusions drawn. First there are few longitudinal studies that use population-based samples to examine impacts. That is, most studies examining the impact of asthma on children are based on clinic populations that often include disproportionate numbers of children with severe asthma and may also differ from the general population in terms of their social, demographic, and service-utilization characteristics. Thus, we have attempted to place more weight on the few longitudinal and cross-sectional studies that use population-based samples because of the potential generalization of the results.

Another persistent methodological problem in comparing studies is the fact that the definition of asthma and the diagnostic distinction between asthma and wheezing is not clearly articulated. For example, Anderson (1983) and William and McNichol (1969) used a screening questionnaire based on symptoms rather than "disease label criteria" (56,66). Several studies report on any wheezy condition, whereas others make clear distinctions between those children with wheezing, those children that are wheeze-free, and those children that have the diagnosis of asthma (72). Another major problem in comparing the results of different studies is that there are no standardized tools to measure impact in childhood, as indicated by disability or quality of life. The absence of standardized measures across studies makes a comparison of impacts for children with asthma difficult. Moreover, few studies account for the effects of confounding variables such as social class when examining impacts of asthma.

Last, there are very few population-based intervention studies that examine the role of specific medical, behavioral, or community-based interventions on ameliorating the impact of asthma on children's lives. There is some evidence that comprehensive intervention programs do lead to better outcomes as measured by educational attainment and school days lost (73,74). However, with most studies, it is difficult to know what level of baseline intervention children are routinely receiving and what impact this has on outcomes.

B. Global Measures of Asthma Impact

The impact of asthma on children's function is dependent on the severity of the underlying disease processes as well as the social and emotional factors that exacerbate the disease process. Several authors have attempted to measure the severity of asthma in children. Mortality is one obvious measure of asthma severity, but its fortunate rarity does not lead it to be a useful measure of severity for clinical purposes. Severity measures have often been based on a combination of physiological measures such as forced expiratory volume, (FEV_1); social role limitations, such as the inability to conduct age-specific activities; and health care utilization characteristics, such as hospitalizations or emergency room visits for severe attacks. As Mitchell and colleagues have suggested, many routinely used indicators serve to distinguish only the most severe cases, so that a large majority of children with no hospitalizations or mild disability are indistinguishable from each other (4). Understanding how such classifications are applied is important for interpreting results concerning the impacts of asthma, since several of the longitudinal studies intentionally oversample more severely afflicted children. For example, in the Melbourne longitudinal studies of children with asthma, an additional 75 children with severe asthma were added to the 400 children randomly selected from the sample population of asthmatic children.

Using large population-based databases, other authors have attempted to classify the severity of asthma based on social role function as well as degree and amount of bother-caused care by the disease. Taylor and Newacheck (1992), in an analysis of the U.S. NHIS, used limitation in usual activity and the amount and type of bother to classify children as (58%) mild, (32%) moderate, and (10%) severe (58). Several authors have used similar methodology. More recently, Mitchell et al. have suggested an array of measures that could be used in a clinical setting to develop a more refined notion of morbidity due to asthma (4). In general, reviewing the literature on the classification of severity, it appears that 50–60% of children with asthma can be classified as having mild asthma, 30–40% as having moderate asthma, and 10–20% as having severe asthma.

Several studies have measured the level of childhood disability associated with asthma. These include studies that use general measures of disability, such as a child's limitation in the ability to conduct normal age-appropriate activities or the number of disability and sick days a child experiences over some specified period of time. The U.S. NHIS uses the notion of the limitation of activity as a way of classifying disability in the U.S. population.

In an analysis of the 1992–1994 NHIS, 1.5% of U.S. children (approximately 1.59 million children) were reported to be limited in their activities due to asthma. This represented approximately 33% of all children with asthma. Prevalence of limitation of activity due to asthma was reported to be higher for older children, males, and children from low-income and single-parent families. Disabling asthma was reported to result in 21 million restricted activity days annually, including 9 million days lost from school. Furthermore, asthma disability in childhood resulted in an added 7 million physician contacts and 750,000 million hospital days annually during 1992–1994 (61).

Taken together, these results suggest that asthma is associated with significant impact on normal social role function as measured by global indicators of function. In the next section, we examine the impact of asthma on children and their families in three categories; schools; emotional effects; and family, social, and peer interactions.

C. Schools

Regular school attendance is a common activity for children and is assumed to be necessary for normal social and educational development. School absence is a useful indicator of impact, since both prolonged and multiple brief absences interfere with children's academic performance and peer relationships in the school setting. School absences can also be expressed quantitatively, making it relatively easy to measure via school records (66). When children are frequently absent from school, they not only tend to perform poorly but also are more likely to drop out before graduation from high school (75–77) and to have problems with reading skills (78).

Asthma is one of the most common reasons for children's absence from school and accounts for a substantial number of total days lost from school (78–80). Several studies have highlighted the impact of asthma on school absences (77,81).

Data that report mean rates of school absences do not capture the variation in attendance across the population of children with asthma. In fact, some children are reported to experience very long school absences or multiple, frequent absences in the school year. In the Croydon studies reported by Anderson, 35% of wheezing children had over three times the normal rates of absences (66). There is some indication that the pattern of school absence differs by age, with younger children more likely to be absent due to increased proneness to chest infections, leading to exacerbation (82,83). While most studies have not controlled other factors that may be associated with lost school days, Anderson found that school absence for asthmatic children was also associated with social circumstances and psychological factors, such as parental marital status, poor maternal mental health, maternal occupation, number of children in the household, and lack of access to health care.

Decreased school performance has been attributed to increased absences but has also been attributed to the effect of asthma medications, the perception of teachers or parents that the child is vulnerable, acute exacerbation, and stress associated with this chronic illness (79). Teasing out the relationships of absences to school performance in children with asthma is not straightforward. First, several studies from the United Kingdom and one from Israel have suggested that children with asthma have higher-than-normal IQs (2,64,65,84), implying that these children might be expected to perform better in school than other children. Above-average levels of intelligence may allow students to compensate for missed time from school and maintain their expected academic performance (85). However at least two studies examining school performance did not find a direct relationship between asthma and school performance. Gutstadt et al. (1989) found a negative correlation between school absence and performance after examining school performance in 99 previously hospitalized children with asthma (85). This investigation found that socioeconomic status, history of oral steroid use, and abnormalities on the Child Behavior Checklist (CBCL) predicted most of the variance on the reading scores. Fowler et al. (1992), using the 1988 U.S. NHIS on Child Health, found that children with asthma had similar rates of grade failure and suspension as other children (86).

Current research has yet to clearly define whether poor school performance is related to absence or associated with other related neuropsychiatric factors. A series of studies conducted by different investigators using different methods have produced inconsistent findings concerning whether children with asthma suffer from neurocognitive problems (87–89). Some of the methodological problems with these studies include different sample definitions, lack of control for severity, inability to account for different medications, and other emotional factors that could influence neurocognitive functioning.

Data from the 1994 U.S. NHIS indicates that parents of children with asthma are twice as likely to report the presence of behavioral problems in school, including problems communicating, paying attention in school, behaving in school, and understanding their lessons in school. It should be noted that school behavioral problems are infrequent in absolute terms irrespective of the relative magnitude of difference between the asthmatic and nonasthmatic child (64).

Thus, we can clearly state that children with asthma have higher rates of school absences; however, it is unclear from the current research literature whether these absences result in poor school performance or whether other neuro-cognitive or emotional problems associated with asthma are responsible for differences in school performance for some children. In addition to possible impact on academic performance, school absenteeism can lead to psychological symptoms of feeling ostracized, different, and inferior, and these problems can, in turn, interfere with school performance, potentially further exacerbating the symptoms of asthma (90).

Related to children's attendance and performance in schools is the ability of schools to respond to the needs of children with asthma. Many clinicians have anecdotally observed that schools do not take appropriate precautions with asthmatic children and that children are often pushed beyond their ability to participate in athletic and other events. In addition, several studies have found that neither teachers nor schools are adequately prepared to understand the needs of asthmatic children or to participate in comprehensive care plans that must necessarily include school participation. In a study of 98 schoolteachers in London, it was found that most teachers did not have a basic understanding of asthma and felt inadequate coping with the management of their asthmatic students (91). In another study of 87 teachers at 11 different schools in South Hampton, teachers' knowledge about asthma was rated as very low and delivery of care in the schools described as disorganized (92). In an attempt to improve the ability of schools to identify and attend to the needs of children with asthma, a study was conducted in Nottingham, England, where 102 primary schools were randomized to receive a school-based asthma identification and treatment service. The result of this school-based intervention showed a significant increase in visits to physicians for the care of asthma, diagnosis of asthma and changes in their treatment regimen and increased knowledge on the part of teachers. There was a decrease in school absences due to wheezing in both intervention and control schools. At the end of the study, schools were more likely to have improved aspects of asthma management and teachers were more knowledgeable (93). Several other school-based health and educational programs have demonstrated improved efficiency of self-and parent management, fewer episodes of asthma, and better school performance (81,94).

VI. The Impact of Asthma on Social, Leisure, and Peer Relationships and Family Life

Asthma also impinges on children's recreational and leisure activities as well as peer and family relationships. Several studies have documented that children with asthma report adverse effects of asthma on their ability to participate in sports programs (34,95). The inability of children to participate in normal school and athletic activities can have a profound effect on their relationships with peers and friends. Donnelley also reported that parents perceive their children as having poor relationships with peers. Communities as a whole may have a generally negative perception of the disease. This critical attitude can lead to disturbances in normal development. One study conducted by a general practitioner in Bristol, England, explored how children feel asthma affects their life at school. Children in this study reported feeling that their inability to participate in school-related sports and activities was one of the most profound effects that asthma had and they also reported that it disrupted their relationships with peers. Parents and siblings can also become overly protective and prevent children from participating in activities necessary for normal development for fear that it might trigger episodes. This encourages increased dependency, which the child may not require (96).

Asthma has other effects on a range of family-related activities. Families report that having a child with asthma influences decisions concerning holidays, pets, furnishings, carpets, and soft toys—all of which have important financial, lifestyle, and esthetic implications for the families (34,97). Moreover, families are frequently confronted with extra housework related to dusting and cleaning. Parents also report taking time off from work to care for children with asthma (98–100). In addition to these instrumental and financial changes in family life, parents often report that they are afraid to leave their children (101). Families also experience clear financial burdens because of asthma. These include uncompensated medical care expenses as well as expenses for special equipment like humidifiers, special bedding, and other costs associated with asthma (98). A study by Reddihough et al. (1977) found a lack of communication between doctors, patients, and families leading to coping difficulties and a negative impact on family life (100).

VII.   Impact on Emotional and Psychological Functioning

Asthma, like many other chronic illnesses, is associated with a certain degree of stigma, loss of self-esteem, and a variety of stresses that can influence how children perceive themselves and how they function in the world (102–104). Understanding the psychological and emotional impact of asthma on children is complicated given the transactions that take place between psychological causes and consequences of the disease as well as with underlying developmental changes. For many years, asthma was viewed as a ''psychosomatic disease'' in which psychological variables were seen as principal causes of asthma. While this viewpoint has not been supported by the research literature, the effect of psychological factors on severity is well documented (105). Moreover, several studies have demonstrated that behavioral and family-focused psychotherapy can play an important role in diminishing symptoms, diminishing exacerbation, and promoting rehabilitation (37,103,106,107).

Few population-based studies have attempted to examine the emotional and behavioral problems associated with asthma (40,57). Psychological variables clearly influence the medical management of asthma. Several studies have shown that psychological variables are associated with medication noncompliance. Children with poor psychological adjustment in dysfunctional families are more likely to have reduced compliance with medical regimens and worse outcomes (108). Moreover, children with poor psychological adjustment experience asthma that is more difficult to control. This has been demonstrated in children through greater use of steroids (104), emergency room visits (109), hospitalizations (104,110), reduced compliance with medication, and higher rates of mortality (111,112).

Children suffering with asthma clearly feel differently about themselves (112,113). In a study of a clinical cohort of Australian children, those with asthma expressed more self-pity (41%), and lower self-esteem (21%) than controls (39). Other studies have suggested that a large percentage of children with asthma have had anxiety disorders. Anxiety and panic attacks can in turn lead to hyperventilation and the initiation of an asthmatic attack (114). Mrazek has suggested that because respiratory symptoms can be precipitated by emotional stressors, a vicious cycle can be generated by the conditioned response that links the two. This and other illness-specific stressors create the preconditions for developing psychopathology (98).

Several studies have been conducted to formally evaluate the psychological function of children with asthma. These studies have yielded decidedly mixed results. Part of the difficulty in interpreting results is the lack of control for medication, severity, and other possible comorbid conditions as well as the absence of adequate comparison groups. Some of these studies have shown that children with asthma have emotional difficulties, as indicated by greater facial emotional expression, higher levels of hostility and helplessness, and more aggressiveness (115).

Several recent studies using standardized psychological assessment suggest that children with asthma have higher rates of behavioral abnormalities, as measured by the widely used Child Behavioral Checklist (CBCL). In a clinic-based study, conducted by Maclean and Perrin, of 81 asthmatics, 11.5% of children had CBCL scores above 98%. Abnormal scores in children with asthma were also associated with negative life events, more severe illness, and lower socioeconomic status. In a study of children with different types of chronic illness, children with asthma scored significantly higher on measures of depression and internalizing behaviors, significantly lower on self-esteem, and evidenced significantly greater functional impairment than children with diabetes or cancer (116). In a longitudinal population-based study of children in Ontario, Canada,

children with asthma were at risk for decreased psychological adjustment as well
(117).

Using the 1988 U.S. NHIS, Bussing and colleagues documented that children with severe asthma, those with comorbid conditions, had higher rates of emotional and behavioral problems as measured by a modified version of the CBCL called the Behavioral Problems Index. They also demonstrated that children with mild to moderate asthma did not report emotional and behavioral problems at rates that were higher than those among the general population of children. Interestingly, these data did not reveal a unique behavioral profile on the pattern of behavioral problems for children with asthma as compared with that of children with other chronic disabling conditions (40).

Review of the psychological and emotional impact of asthma in children again presents a confusing picture of whether the negative emotion manifested by asthmatics is a cause or consequence of the disease. While is it clear from the literature that children with poor psychological adjustment experience problems in the treatment and control of their asthma, there remain real problems in our understanding of the causal connections.

There is also the potential for emotional impacts on families. These include adverse affects on the parents' relationship as well as an inability for parents to provide appropriate support, discipline, and other family resources (107,117). For example, in one study, parents reported constant worries and sleepless nights (97). Again, the difficulty with these few studies is that they have been conducted on a small group for families with children with asthma and without accounting for other confounding factors.

VIII. Long-Term Impacts

Several studies have attempted to define the long-term prognosis of childhood asthma, both in terms of disease process and social and emotional activities. There is an ongoing controversy in the research literature about the proportion of children whose asthma persists into adulthood and the proportion of children who "outgrow" their asthma. Community-based studies from Britain, Melbourne, and Tasmania show that about 25% of children diagnosed with asthma at age 7 will have persistent disease at age 33 (27–29). In both the Melbourne and British studies, there was a tendency for symptoms to decrease in adolescence and early adulthood, only to recur later (30). Attempts to define factors associated with persistence suggest that disease severity, degree of atopy, and exposure to cigarette smoke in utero and over time play some role in persistent or recurring disease. Longitudinal studies of clinical populations in Great Britain and Sweden have shown even higher rates of persistence of childhood asthma into adulthood (25,118).

With regard to long-term social impacts, data from the British National Child Development Survey, which followed children until the age of 23, found a small increase in unemployment for those with current or past asthma and conclude that there was only a small adverse effect of childhood asthma on adult employment at age 23 (113). A follow-up study of a sample of the Aberdeen cohort showed no difference in educational attainment, unemployment, housing, or social class among participants with diagnosed asthma, wheezing, or no wheezing in childhood (72). Both of these studies of large population-based samples would indicate that in general the cumulative impact of asthma is not significant in adulthood as measured by these indicators.

IX. Summing Up the Impact

In piecing together various fragments of this broad and diverse literature, we are able to develop some sense of the range and magnitude of the health and social impacts of asthma on children. This literature suggests that asthma impacts many functional domains including personal function, psychological distress and well-being, and general health status and social role function. We also know that the personal, social, economic, cultural, and physical environments in which children live influence prognosis as well as the full range of psychosocial impacts.

To date, there are no longitudinal studies of children with asthma that have used integrative measures of health-related quality of life, but several independent studies have demonstrated that asthma impacts all of the core dimensions of health-related quality of life as suggested by Patrick and Erickson (68). Asthma can reduce the opportunities for children due to the stigma associated with the disease and inappropriate responses by their parents, teachers, schools, and peers. The disease can influence a child's resilience, compromising physiological reserves, and affect the ability to withstand other stressors. It can diminish their social role functioning, including their ability to play and ability to attend and participate fully in school. It can also limit a child's integration into social, peer and community groups, which have been increasingly shown to be important for appropriate social and emotional development.

In terms of psychological function, asthma can affect a child's attitudes, behaviors, sense of self-esteem, and level of despair. In the cognitive domain, asthma can affect alertness, reasoning abilities, and capacity to understand directions and other complex forms of communication. The physical impact of asthma includes limitations in physical activity and communication as well as overall fitness and ability to approach normal physical challenges without excessive fatigue. Asthmatic children typically experience a range of comorbidities, including a range of allergic, emotional, and behavioral conditions that frequently potentiate their asthma symptom burden. Thus from a health-related quality-of-life perspective, the impact of asthma on children and their families is far-reaching.

While the potential effect on children is manifold from an epidemiological standpoint, it is also clear that for most children, asthma is a mild to moderate disease whose impacts can be minimized by providing access to an appropriate range of services. Unfortunately, the research to date does not provide enough information about the impacts of asthma at different levels of severity. More work is needed here to develop better and more enhanced measures.

We have learned from this review that asthma can affect a variety of functional domains. We were not able to determine from the literature whether the prevalence and magnitude of impacts is increasing. Developing a better understanding of the patterns of impact, the prevalence, and cumulative effects is very important for the development of population and community-based interventions that could ultimately lead to a more comprehensive, effective, and efficient continuum of prevention, treatment, and rehabilitation services.

We were also unable to determine the availability of different types of asthma-specific services and how these services affect asthma outcomes at the population level. There are numerous studies showing that asthma self-management and education programs can provide individual children and families with the tools to more appropriately care for their disease. These studies show decreased symptom burden and improved functional and educational status (75,94,119,120). Other studies have shown that providing asthmatic children with comprehensive medical services—including additional education and intervention, access to an "on-call nurse," availability of appropriate medications, and contingency plans for acute exacerbation—can also diminish symptom burden, improve functional status, decrease the number of physician visits, hospitalizations and days lost from school (74) Similarly, studies examining behavioral and family therapy have also been shown to impact individual and family coping mechanisms and to modify maladaptive behavioral patterns that also result in decreased symptom burden and improved functional status (104,105,107). There is also a growing literature on these type of community-based approaches to asthma prevention and management (121–123). These interventions vary from health educational–focused efforts to full-scale community engagement and health improvement campaigns. In most cases, these represent efficacy studies and do not provide the necessary effectiveness data on how such programs work in "real world" settings. We also do not know whether such programs are widely available and whether they are being applied to populations of children in a systematic way.

A. Implication for Service Delivery

Our review of the empirical literature identified a number of interventions that have been shown to improve functional status and minimize adverse outcomes.

This literature, largely based on efficacy studies, would suggest that a rational approach to the provision of services to asthmatic children and their families would include a full continuum of educational, medical, and behavioral services as well as environmental modifications where needed. Considering what such a continuum of prevention, treatment, and rehabilitation services for children and families with asthma would look like is an important exercise not only for public health officials interested in primary, secondary, and tertiary prevention but also for private and public health care delivery organizations that are attempting to develop population-focused intervention strategies.

One approach that informs how services can be organized for chronically ill and other vulnerable populations has been presented by Luann Aday (124). Adapting the Aday model of a service continuum by including more ecological considerations regarding the different environments in which children live, we can suggest a range of appropriate services for children that may begin to address the broad health and social impact that we have reviewed above.

Table 1 portrays the principal programs and services for children with asthma. The continuum ranges from prevention to treatment-oriented care and finally to long-term rehabilitative care. Services are provided by population/community-providers, the medical care system, and through other community resources. In order to portray some of the ecological considerations, we have suggested that the focus of services can also be specified at the child, family, and community levels. Such a comprehensive, multidimensional approach should guarantee the greatest likelihood of interrupting negative transactions and promoting positive impacts. A comprehensive continuum of asthma care can also be used as a normative guide by a community to evaluate the comprehensiveness and availability of appropriate components of the service delivery system that a community has in place. In addition, it can serve as a planning aid for determining how to develop services to meet the range of needs in a particular population.

We would also have to caution communities to recognize that while the literature on childhood asthma suggests a range of important and costly impacts, this subject is beyond the scope of this chapter's primary focus. More fundamentally, there are no community-based efficacy studies in which a continuum of asthma-care services has been instituted and the impacts evaluated. However, since various components of the service continuum have been evaluated favorably, we might predict that the additional synergy realized from a comprehensive approach would also produce added efficiencies not present in the current piecemeal approach.

With the advent and expansion of managed health care systems, and a greater focus on population approaches, the potential to institute a developmentally appropriate continuum of care for childhood asthma is even greater. Moreover, organized health systems also have the potential to use other quality-im-

Table 1 Principal Programs and Services for Children with Asthma

Level of intervention	Prevention-oriented care		Treatment-oriented care		Long-term care
	Public health/community	Prevention-oriented (Ambulatory)	Treatment-oriented (Ambulatory)	Acute care (Institutional)	Home- and community-based care
Child Focus	School-based asthma education Prenatal care focus on smoking prevention	Case identification Self-management education programs Well-child care Psychological evaluation Anticipatory guidance Child counseling	Chronic disorder management Self-management programs Medications management Respiratory treatments Emergency medical services Psychological counseling	Acute hospital intensive care	Home visiting for environmental education Case management School-based clinics/services Peer support groups
Family Focus	Smoking prevention programs Stress reduction programs Parenting skills and chronic disease Media education	Parental/family education Anticipatory guidance Family counseling	Smoking cessation programs Treatment for family conditions		Family therapy Psychiatric rehabilitation
Community Focus	Environmental abatement programs: Roach, dust-mite, pest elimination Air pollution policy	Practice guidance and quality measurement for providers	Office-based quality improvement system	Hospital-based guidelines, quality measurement, and improvement	School-based policy Disease management programs

provement techniques that can be useful in building service connections at different levels: child, family, and community.

Improving the effectiveness and efficiency of asthma services through development of appropriate continuums of care will also depend on outcomes and effectiveness research targeted at the community level. An asthma service continuum has the potential to provide the most appropriate services based on need as well as increasing the synergy that comes from appropriate linking of service types, and modalities. However, it is also a well-established principle that for efficiency to be maximized, targeting of services is necessary. All children with asthma do not need all possible services. In the childhood asthma services continuum, many of the proposed preventive services would be targeted at the full population of asthmatic children, while the rehabilitative services would be targeted at those with the greatest need (i.e., highest severity). Future research will be necessary to determine not only what constitutes an appropriate and effective continuum but how to maximize cost-effectiveness in the delivery of services across the continuum to minimize the social impact of asthma.

References

1. Strachan, D.P., Anderson, H.R., Limb, E.S., O'Neill, A., and Wells, N. (1994). A national survey of asthma prevalence, severity, and treatment in Great Britain. *Arch. Dis. Child.*, **70**:174–178.
2. Sacher, Y. Laor, A., and Danon, Y.L. (1994). Longitudinal study on the prevalence of asthma among Israeli young adults. *Isr. J. Med. Sci.*, **30**:564–572.
3. Ulrik, C.S., Backer, V., Hesse, B., and Dirksen, A. (1996). Risk factors for development of asthma in children and adolescents: findings from a longitudinal population study. *Respir. Med.*, **90**:623–630.
4. Mitchell, E.A., Stewart, A.W., Rea, H.H., McNaughton, S., Taylor, G., Smith, L.T., Asher, M.I., Mulder, J., and Seelye, E.R. (1997). Measuring morbidity from asthma in children. *N.Z. Med. J.*, **110**:3–6.
5. Halfon, N., and Newacheck, P. (1986). Trends in the hospitalization for acute childhood asthma, 1970–84. *Am. J. Public Health*, **76**:1308–1311.
6. Weiss, K.B., and Wagener, D.K. (1990). Changing patterns of asthma mortality: identifying target populations at high risk. *J.A.M.A.*, **264**:1683–1687.
7. Robertson, C.F., Heycock, E., Bishop, J., Nolan, T., Olinsky, A., and Phelan, P.D. (1991). Prevalence of asthma in Melbourne schoolchildren: changes over 26 years. *Br. Med. J.*, **302**:116–118.
8. Anderson, H.R., Butland, B.K., and Strachan, D.P. (1994). Trends in prevalence and severity of childhood asthma. *Br. Med. J.*, **308**:1600–1604.
9. Peat, J.K., Salome, C.M., Sedgwick, C.S., and Kerrebijin, J., et al. A prospective study of bronchial hyperresponsivenes and respiratory symptoms in a population of Australian schoolchildren. *Clin. Exp. Allergy*, **19**:299–306.
10. Peat, J.K., vandenBerg, R.H., Green, W.F., Mellis, C.M., Leeder, S.R., and Wool-

cock, A.J. (1994). Changing prevalence of asthma in Australian children. *Br. Med. J.*, **308**:1591–1596.

11. Weitzman, M., Gortmaker, S.L., Sobol, A.M., and Perrin, J.M. (1992). Recent trends in the prevalence and severity of childhood asthma. *J.A.M.A.*, **268**:2673–2677.

12. Burr, M.L., Butland, B.K., King, S., and Vaughan-Williams, E. (1989). Changes in asthma prevalence: two surveys 15 years apart. *Arch. Dis. Child.*, **64**:1452–1456.

13. Burney, P.G., Chinn, S., and Rona, R.J. (1990). Has the prevalence of asthma increased in children? Evidence from the national study of health and growth 1973–86. *Br. Med. J.*, **300**:1306–1310.

14. Ninan, T.K., and Russell, G. (1992). Respiratory symptoms and atopy in Aberdeen schoolchildren: evidence from two surveys 25 years apart. *Br. Med. J.*, **304**:873–875.

15. Hyndman, S.J., Williams, D.R.R., Merrill, S.L., Lipscombe, J.M., and Palmer, C.R. (1994). Rates of admission to hospital for asthma. *Br. Med. J.*, **308**:1596–1600.

16. Jamison, E.J., and Wehr, E. (1993). Drafting national health care reform legislation to protect the health interests of children. *Stanford Law Pol. Rev.*, **5**:152–176.

17. Halfon, N., Inkelas, M., and Wood, D. (1995). Nonfinancial barriers to care for children and youth. *Annu. Rev. Public Health*, **16**:447–472.

18. Hertzman, C. (1994). The lifelong impact of childhood experiences: a population health perspective. *Daedelus*, **123**(4):167–180.

19. Sameroff, A., and Chandler, M. (1975). Reproductive risk and the continuum of caretaking casualty. In Horowitz F., ed. (1975). *Review of Child Development Research*. Chicago, University of Chicago Press.

20. Bronfenbrenner, U., Moen, P., and Garbarino, J. (1984). Families and communities. In *Review of Child Development Research*. Edited by H.R. Parke. Chicago: University of Chicago Press.

21. Barker, D.J.P. (1990). *Fetal and Infant Origins of Adult Disease*. Great Britain, *Br. Med. J.*, **301**(6761):1111.

22. Werner, E.E. (1989). High risk children in young adulthood: A longitudinal study from birth to 32 years. *Am. J. Orthop.*, **59**:72–81.

23. Schwartz, J.E., Friedman, H.S., Tucker, J.S., Tomlinson-Keasey C., Wingard D.L., and Cariqui, M.H. (1995). Sociodemographic and psychosocial factors in childhood as predictors of adult mortality. *Am. J. Public Health*, **85**:1237–1245.

24. Rackemann, F.M., and Edwards, M.C. (1952). Asthma in children. *N. Engl. J. Med.*, **246**:815–858.

25. Blaire, H. (1977). Natural history of childhood asthma. *Arch. Dis. Child.*, **52**:613–619.

26. Holland, W.W., Bailey, P., and Bland, J.M. (1978). Long-term consequences of respiratory disease in infancy. *J. Epidemiol. Community Health*, **32**:256–259.

27. Martin, A.J., McLennan, L.A., Landau, L.I., and Phelan, P.D. (1980). The natural history of childhood asthma to adulthood. *Br. Med. J.*, **280**:1397–1400.

28. Oswald, H., Phelan, P.D., Lanigan, A., Hibbert, M., Bowes, G., and Olinsky, A. (1994). Outcome of childhood asthma in mid-adult life. *Br. Med. J.*, **309**:95–96.

29. Jenkins, M.A., Hopper, J.L., Bowes, G., Carlin, J.B., Flander, L.B., and Giles, G.G.

(1994). Factors in childhood as predictors of asthma in adult life. *Br. Med. J.*, **309**: 90–93.

30. Strachan, D.P., Butland, B.K., and Anderson, H.R. (1996). Incidence and prognosis of asthma and wheezing illness from early childhood to age 33 in a national British cohort. *Br. Med. J.*, **312**:1195–1199.

31. Newacheck, P., and Halfon, N. (1986). The association between mother's and children's use of physician services. *Med. Care*, **24**:30–38.

32. Creer, T.L., Stein, R.E.K., and Rappaport, L., et al. (1992). Behavioral consequences of illness: childhood asthma as a model. *Pediatrics*, **90**:808–815.

33. Brook, U., and Tepper, I. (1997). Self-image, coping and familial interaction among asthmatic children and adolescents in Israel. *Patient Educ. Couns.*, **30**:187–192.

34. Donnelly, J.E., Donnelly, W.J., and Thong, Y.H. (1987). Parental perceptions and attitudes toward asthma and its treatment: a controlled study. *Soc. Sci. Med.*, **24**: 431–437.

35. Brook, U., Mendelberg, A., and Hei, M. (1993). Increasing parental knowledge of asthma decreases the hospitalization of the child: a pilot study. *J. Asthma*, **30**:45–49.

36. Klinnert, M.D., McQuaid, E.L., and Gavin, L.A. (1997). Assessing the family management system. *J. Asthma*, **34**:77–88.

37. Gustafsson, P.A., Kjellman, N.I.M., and Cederblad, M. (1986). Family therapy in the treatment of severe childhood asthma. *J. Psychosom. Res.*, **30**:369–374.

38. Liebman, R., Minuchin, S., and Baker, L. (1974). The use of structural family therapy in the treatment of intractable asthma. *Am. J. Psychiatry*, **131**:535–540.

39. Donnelly, E. (1994). Parents of children with asthma: An examination of family hardiness, family stressors, and family functioning. *J. Pediatr. Nurs.*, **9**:398–408.

40. Bussing, R., Halfon, N., Benjamin, B., and Wells, K.B. (1995). Prevalence of behavior problems in US children with asthma. *Arch. Pediatr. Adolesc. Med.*, **149**: 565–572.

41. Gauthier, Y., Fortin, C., Drapeau, P., Breton, J.J., Gosselin, J., Quintal, L., Weisnagel, J., Tetreault, L., and Pinard, G. (1978). Follow-up study of 35 asthmatic preschool children. *J. Am. Acad. Child. Psychiatry*, **17**:679–694.

42. Robinson, D.S., Hamid, Q., Ying, S., et al. (1992). Predominant TH2-like bronchoalveolar T-lymphocyte population in atopic asthma. *N. Engl. J. Med.*, **326**:298–304.

43. Robinson, D., Hamid, Q., Bentley, A., Ying, S., Kay, A.B., and Durham, S.R. (1993). Activation of CD4+T cells, increased TH2-type cytokine mRNA expression, and eosinophil recruitment in bronchoalveolar lavage after allergen inhalation challenge in patients with atopic asthma. *J. Allergy Clin. Immunol.*, **92**:313–324.

44. Holt, P.G., Sly, P.D., and Bjorksten, B. (1997). Atopic versus infectious diseases in childhood a question of balance? *Pediatr. Allergy Immunol.*, **8**:53–58.

45. Holt, P.G., and Sly, P.D. (1997). Allergic respiratory disease: strategic targets for primary prevention during childhood. *Thorax*, **52**:1–4.

46. Platts-Mills, T.A.E., Woodfolk, J.A., Chapman, M.D., and Heymann, P.W. (1996). Changing concepts of allergic disease: the attempt to keep up with changes in lifestyles. *J. Allergy Clin. Immunol.*, **98**:S297–S306.

47. Weiss, S.T. (1995). Early life predictions of adult chronic obstructive lung disease. *Eur. Respir. Rev.*, **5**:303–309.
48. Duff, A.L., Pomeranz, E.S., Gelber, L.E., Price, G.W., Farris, H., and Hayden, F.G., et al. (1993). Risk factors for acute wheezing in infants and children: viruses, passive smoke, and IgE antibodies to inhalant allergens. *Pediatrics*, **92**:535–540.
49. Gottlieb, G. (1976). Conceptions of prenatal development: Behavioral embryology. *Psychol. Rev.*, **83**:215–234.
50. Cicchetti, D., and Lynch, M. (1993). Toward an ecological/transactional model of community violence and child maltreatment. *Psychiatry*, **56**:96–118.
51. Horwood, L.J., Fergusson, D.M., Hons, B.A., and Shannon, F.T. (1985). Social and familial factors in the development of early childhood asthma. *Pediatrics*, **75**:859–868.
52. Wood, P.R., Hidalgo, H.A., Prihoda, T.J., and Kromer, M.E. (1993). Hispanic children with asthma: Morbidity. *Pediatrics*, **91**:62–68.
53. Schwartz, J., Gold, D., Dockery, D.W., Weiss, S.T., and Speizer, F.E. (1990). Predictors of asthma and persistent wheeze in a national sample of children in the United States: association with social class, perinatal events, and race. *Am. Rev. Respir. Dis.*, **142**:555–562.
54. Ernst, P., Demissie, K., Joseph, L., Locher, U., and Becklake, M.R. (1995). Socioeconomic status and indicators of asthma in children. *Am. J. Respir. Crit. Care. Med.*, **152**:570–575.
55. Newacheck, P., and Halfon, N. (1998). Prevalence and impact of disabling chronic conditions in childhood. *Am. J. Public Health*, **88**:610–617.
56. Williams, H.E., and McNichol, K.N. (1969). Prevalence, natural history and relationship of wheezy bronchitis and asthma in children: an epidemiological study. *Br. Med. J.*, **4**:321–325.
57. McNichol, K.N., and Williams, H.E. (1973). Spectrum of asthma in childhood: 1. Clinical and physiological components. *Br. Med. J.*, **4**:7–11.
58. Taylor, W.R., and Newacheck, P.W. (1992). Impact of childhood asthma on health. *Pediatrics*, **90**:657–662.
59. Halfon, N., and Newacheck, P. (1993). Childhood asthma and poverty: Differential impacts and utilization of health services. *Pediatrics*, **91**:56–61.
60. Gergen, P.J., Mullaly, D.I., and Evans, R. III. (1988). National survey of prevalence of asthma among children in the United States 1976–1980. *Pediatrics*, **81**:1–7.
61. Halfon, N., Newacheck, P., Ahn, P., and Bastian, A. (1998). Prevalence and impact of childhood asthma in US Children (abstr). APA-SPR meeting.
62. Newacheck, P., and Halfon, N. (1998). Prevalence, impact and trends in childhood disability due to asthma. submitted to *Pediatrics*.
63. Brooks-Gunn, J., and Duncan, C.J. (1997). The Effects of Poverty on Children. *The Future of Children*, **7**:55–71.
64. Peckham, C., and Butler, N. (1978). A national study of asthma in childhood. *J. Epidemiol. Community Health*, **21**:79–85.
65. Dawson, B., Hoborin, G., Illsley, R., and Mitchell, R. (1969). A survey of childhood asthma in Aberdeen. *Lancet*, **1**:827–830.
66. Anderson, H.R., Bailey, P.A., Cooper, J.S., Palmer, J.C., and West, S. (1983). Morbidity and school absence caused by asthma and wheezing illness. *Arch. Dis. Child.*, **58**:777–784.

67. Littlejohns, P., and Macdonald, L.D. (1993). The relationship between severe asthma and social class. *Respir. Med.*, **87**:139–143.
68. Patrick, D.L., and Erickson, P. (1993). *Health Status and Health Policy: Allocating Resources to Health Care*. New York, Oxford University Press.
69. Sulllivan, S., Elixhauser, A., Buist, A.S., Luce, B.R., Eisenberg, J., and Weiss, K.B. (1996). National asthma education and prevention program working group report on the cost effectiveness of asthma care. *Am. J. Respir. Crit. Care Med.*, **154**:S84–S95.
70. Ware, J.E. (1984). Conceptualizing disease impact and treatment outcomes. *Cancer*, **53**:2316–2323.
71. Schulper, M.J., and Buxton, M.J. (1993). The episode-free day as a composite measure of effectiveness. *Pharmacoeconomics*, **4**:345–352.
72. Usherwood, T.P., Scrimgeour, A., and Barber, J.H. (1990). Questionnaire to measure perceived symptoms and disability in asthma. *Arch. Dis. Child.*, **65**:779–781.
73. Mitchell, R.G., and Dawson, B. (1973). Educational and social characteristics of children with asthma. *Arch. Dis. Child.*, **48**:467–471.
74. Ross, S., Godden, D., McMurray, D., Douglas, A., Oldman, D., Friend, J., Legge, J., and Douglas, G. (1992). Social effects of wheeze in childhood: a 25 year follow up. *Br. Med. J.*, **305**:545–548.
75. Clark, N.M., Feldman, C.H., Evans, D., Wasilewski, Y., and Levison, M.J. (1984). Changes in children's school performance as a result of education for family management of asthma. *J. School Health*, **54**:143–145.
76. Hughes, D.M., McLeod, M., Garner, B., and Goldbloom, R.B. (1991). Controlled trial of a home and ambulatory program for asthmatic children. *Pediatrics*, **87**(1): 54–61.
77. Lloyd, D.N. (1976). Concurrent prediction of dropout and grade of withdrawal. *Educ. Psychol. Meas.*, **36**:983.
78. Rozelle, R.M. (1968). The relationship between absenteeism and grades. *Educ. Psychol. Meas.*, **28**:1151.
79. Weitzman, M. (1986). School absence rates as outcome measures in studies of children with chronic illness. *J. Chronic Dis.*, **39**:799–808.
80. Freudenberg, N., Feldman, C.H., Clark, N.M., Millman, E.J., Valle, I., and Wasilewski, Y. (1980). The impact of bronchial asthma on school attendance and performance. *J. School Health*, **Nov**:522–526.
81. Celano, M.P., and Geller, R.J. (1993). Learning, school performance, and children with asthma: how much at risk? *J. Learning Disabil.*, **26**:23–32.
82. Fowler, M.G., Johnson, M.P., and Atkinson, S.S. (1985). School achievement and absence in children with chronic health conditions. *J. Pediatr.*, **106**:683–687.
83. Parcel, G.S., Nader, P.R., and Tiernan, K. (1980). A health education program for children with asthma. *J. Dev. Behav. Pediatr.*, **1**:128–132.
84. Sutherland, S. (1987). *Help Me Mummy: I Can't Breathe*. London, Souvenir Press.
85. Gutstadt, L.B., Gillette, J.W., Mrazek, D.A., Fukuhara, J.T., LaBrecque, J.F., and Strunk, R.C. (1989). Determinants of school performance in children with chronic asthma. *Am. J. Dis. Child.*, **143**:471–475.
86. Fowler, M.G., Davenport, M.G., and Garg, R. (1992). School functioning of U.S. children with asthma. *Pediatrics*, **90**:939–944.

87. Dunleavy, R.A., and Baade, L.F. (1981). Neuropsychological correlates of asthma: effect of hypoxia or drugs? *J. Consult. Clin. Psychol.*, **49**:137.

88. Seuss, W.M., and Chai, H. (1981). Neuropsychological correlates of asthma: brain damage or drug effects? *J. Consult. Clin. Psychol.*, **49**(1):135–136.

89. Bender, B.A.G. (1996). Measurement of quality of life in pediatric asthma clinical trials. *Ann. Allergy Asthma Immunol.*, **77**:438–447.

90. Richards, W. (1990). Allergy, asthma and school problems. *J. School Health*, **56**(4): 151–152.

91. Bevis, M., and Taylor, B. (1990). What do school teachers know about asthma? *Arch. Dis. Child.*, **65**:622–625.

92. Brookes, J., and Hones, K. (1992). Schoolteachers' perceptions and knowledge of asthma in primary schoolchildren. *Br. J. Gen. Pract.*, **42**:504–507.

93. Hill, R., Williams, J., Britton, J., and Tettersfield A. (1991). Can morbidity associated with untreated asthma in primary school children be reduced? A controlled intervention study. *Br. Med. J.*, **303**:1169–1174.

94. Evans, D., Clark, N.M., Feldman, C.H., Rips, J., Kaplan, D., Levison, M.J., Wasilewski, Y., Levin, B., and Mellins, R.B. (1987). A school health education program for children with asthma aged 8–11 years. *Health Educ. Q.*, **14**:267–279.

95. Coughlin, S.P. (1988). Sports and the asthmatic child: a study of exercise-induced asthma and the resultant handicap. *J. R. Coll. Gen. Pract.*, **38**:253–255.

96. Meijer, A. (1980). Maternal feelings towards asthmatic children. *Child. Psychiatry Human Dev.*, **11**:33–40.

97. Wasilewski, Y., Clark, N., Evans, D., Feldman, C.H., Kaplan, D., Rips, J., and Mellins, R.B. (1988). The effect of paternal social support on maternal disruption caused by childhood asthma. *J. Community Health*, **13**(1):33–42.

98. Marion, R.J., Creer, T.L., and Reynolds, R.V.C. (1985). Direct and indirect costs associated with the management of childhood asthma. *Ann. Allergy*, **54**:31–34.

99. Quinn, C.M. Children's asthma: new approaches, new understandings. *Ann. Allergy*, **60**:283–292.

100. Hookham, V. (1985). Family constellations in relation to asthma. *J. Asthma*, **22**(2): 99–114.

101. Reddihough, D.S., Landau, L., Jones, H.J., and Richards, W.S. (1977). Family anxieties in childhood asthma. *Aust. Paediatr. J.*, **13**:295–298.

102. Mrazek, D.A. (1992). Psychiatric complications of pediatric asthma. *Ann. Allergy*, **69**:285–294.

103. MacLean, W.E., Perrin, J.M., Gortmaker, S., and Pierre, C.B. (1992). Psychological adjustment of children with asthma: effects of illness severity and recent stressful life events. *J. Pediatr. Psychol.*, **17**(2):159–171.

104. Fritz, G.K., Yeung, A., Wamboldt, M.Z., Spirito, A., McQuaid, E.L., Klein, R., and Seifer, R. (1996). Conceptual and methodologic issues in quantifying perceptual accuracy in childhood asthma. *J. Pediatr. Psychol.*, **21**:153–173.

105. Colland, V.T. (1993). Learning to cope with asthma: a behavioural self-management program for children. *Pat. Educ. Couns.*, **22**:141–152.

106. Park, S.D.I., Sawyer, S.M., and Glean, D.E. (1996). Childhood asthma complicated by anxiety: an application of cognitive behavioral therapy. *J. Paediatr. Child. Health*, **32**:183–187.

107. Lask, B. (1992). Psychological treatments for childhood asthma. *Arch. Dis. Child.*, **67**:891.

108. Christiaanse, M.E., Lavigne, J.V., and Lerner, C.V. (1989). Psychosocial aspects of compliance in children and adolescents with asthma. *Dev. Behav. Pediatr.*, **10**(2): 75–80.

109. Dirks, J.F. (1977). Panic-fear, a personality dimension related to length of hospitalization in respiratory illness. *J. Asthma Res.*, **14**:61–71.

110. Baron, C., Veilleux, P., and Lamarre, A. (1992). The family of the asthmatic child. *Can. J. Psychiatry*, **37**:12–16.

111. Kravis, L.P. (1987). An analysis of 15 childhood asthma fatalities. *J. Allergy Clin. Immunol.*, **80**:467–472.

112. Sears, M.R. (1987). Asthma mortality: a review of recent experience in New Zealand. *J. Allergy Clin. Immunol.*, **80**:319–325.

113. Sibbald, B., Anderson, H.R., and McGuigan, S. (1992). Asthma and employment in young adults. *Thorax*, **47**(1): 19–24.

114. Padur, J.S., Rapoff, M.A., Houston, B.K., Barnard, M., Danovsky, M., Olson, N.Y., Moore, W.V., Vats, T.S., and Lieberman, B. (1995). Psychosocial adjustment and the role of functional status for children with asthma. *J. Asthma*, **32**:345–353.

115. Lehrer, P.M., Isenberg, S., and Hochron, S.M. (1993). Asthma and emotion: a review. *J. Asthma*, **30**:5–21.

116. Cadman, D., Boyle, M., Szatmari, P., and Offord, D.R. (1987). Chronic illness disability and mental and social well-being: findings of the Ontario child health study. *Pediatrics*, **79**:805–813.

117. Nocon, A., and Booth, T. (1989–1990). The social impact of asthma: a review of the literature. *Soc. Work. Soc. Sci. Rev.*, **1**:177–200.

118. Kjellman, B., and Hesselmar B. (1994). Prognosis of asthma in children: a cohort study into adulthood. *Acta Paediatr.*, **83**:854–861.

119. Lewis, C.E., Rachelefsky, G., and Lewis, M.A., et al. (1984). A randomized trial of ACT (Asthma Care Training) for kids. *Pediatrics*, **74**:478–486.

120. Wilson, S.R., Austin, D.M., Starr-Schneidkraut, N., Fish, L., Loes, L., Page, A., and Kubic, P. (1993). Early intervention with parents of very young children with asthma: a developmental evaluation of the Wee Wheezers program. *J. Asthma*, **33**: 239–254.

121. Fisher, E., Strunk, R., and Sussman, L., et al. (1996). Acceptability and feasibility of a common approach to asthma management: the neighborhood coalition. *J. Asthma*, **33**:367–383.

122. Toelle, B.G., Peat, J.K., Salome, C.M., Mellis, C.M., Bauman, A.E., and Woolcook, A.J. (1993). Evaluation of a community based asthma management program in a population sample of schoolchildren. *Med. J. Aust.*, **158**:742–746.

123. Wilson, S.R., Scamagas, P., Grado, J., Norgaard, L., Starr, N.J., Eaton, S., and Pomaville, K. (1998). The Fresno asthma project: A model intervention to control asthma in multiethnic, low-income inner-city communities. *Health Educ. Behav.*, **25**:79–98.

124. Aday, L. (1993). *At Risk in America: The Health and Health Care Needs of Vulnerable Populations in the United States*. San Francisco, Jossey-Bass.

4

Characterizing the Occupational Impact of Asthma

PAUL D. BLANC

University of California School of Medicine
San Francisco, California

I. Introduction

Asthma has multiple attributes that make it one of the most important chronic medical conditions in relation to occupation and work disability. First, asthma is an extremely common condition among adults in the age range with greatest labor-force participation. Second, asthma is a chronic health condition marked by potentially severe exacerbations during which functional impairment leading to disability can be anticipated. For this reason, decreased productivity and work loss are major contributors to the overall costs of asthma. Finally, asthma has specific characteristics, in particular its responsiveness to a variety of chemical and physical stimuli, making persons with this condition especially vulnerable to work-related worsening of health status.

Although the general impact of asthma on work is vitally important, it has received relatively little research attention. Imprecise distinctions between disability and impairment and overlapping concepts such as handicap and quality of life have led to potential confusion in the definition of study questions and in the interpretation of research findings addressing asthma-related work loss. The inherent multifactorial nature of work disability further complicates the identification of risk factors for this potentially preventable adverse outcome. Among the subset of those with occupationally related asthma, the risk of work and wage loss appears to be especially great. Yet estimating the proportion of asthma attributable to workplace exposures (the work-related etiological fraction) has proved an elusive research goal. Even less research attention has been given to the impact of asthma on work in the home or other unsalaried vocational activities.

The purpose of this chapter is to explore the interrelationships between asthma and work status. Summarizing existing epidemiological data underscores the scope of this problem. Better delineating the risks and defining outcomes can help set priorities for an appropriate research and public policy agenda.

II. Asthma Prevalence Among Those of Working Age

Asthma clearly affects those of working age. Based on the 1994 U.S. National Health Interview Survey (NHIS), the estimated prevalence rate of asthma among those 18 to 44 years of age in the United States was 51.7 per 1000 (5.2%), totaling 5.6 million adults. Although this is lower than the 6.9% (69 per 1000) prevalence estimate for the age stratum under 18 years, it is slightly higher than the estimated prevalence of 5.1% for those aged 45 to 64 years (1). Earlier U.S. NHIS data (1990–1992), for which gender-stratified estimates are available, reveal significant female:male differences within the 18- to 44-year-old stratum. The overall asthma prevalence was estimated at 41.2 per 1000 (4.1%), but the rate was considerably higher among women (48.0 per 1000) than men (34.2 per 1000), representing a 40% difference in prevalence rates by gender (2).

As with other age groups, the prevalence of asthma among working-age adults appears to be on the rise. The overall increase in the prevalence rate of asthma among 18- to 44-year-olds between 1987 and 1994 went from 36.5 to 51.7 per 1000, representing a 42% increase (1,3). Temporal trends also display a disproportionate gender effect. Based on 1986–1988 U.S. NHIS data, the estimated prevalence of asthma among females 18 to 44 years old was 39.8 per 1000, while that for males was 33.2 per 1000 (3). The overall increase over 4 years from 1986–1988 until 1990–1992 was 12.9%. Almost all of this increase can be accounted for by a 20.6% increase among working-age females, in contradistinction to a male-specific increase of only 3% (2,3). The etiology of these gender differences and their temporal trends has not been identified and any explanation of their root causes remains highly speculative.

International data for this age stratum are consistent with U.S. estimates. Based on the European Community Respiratory Health Survey (ECRHS), reflecting data collected between 1988 and 1994 for those 20–44 years of age residing in 22 countries, the median prevalence of asthma was 4.5% (4). This is remarkably similar to the 1990–1992 U.S. NHIS estimate of 4.1%, despite a somewhat narrower age range (excluding 18–19 year olds) and somewhat differing criteria for the case definition of "asthma" for epidemiologic purposes.

Published follow-up data from the ECRHS are not available in order to assess temporal trends. One of its cooperating centers in Australia, however, employed similar prevalence measures in an earlier 1990 survey and in its ECRHS study in 1992, allowing an estimation of temporal trends. Over the two year interval, that group observed a statistically significant increase in the proportion of subjects who reported use of asthma medications ($p < 0.001$) and a statistically borderline increase ($p = 0.08$) in the proportion of those reporting asthma attacks (the ECRHS definition of asthma is based on these two questionnaire items) (5).

III. Asthma-Related Work Limitations

Not only is asthma a common and increasingly prevalent chronic condition among those of peak working age, it also is a condition characterized by variable symptoms and functional impairment over time. Even in persons with otherwise mild to moderate asthma, exacerbations may result in limitation of routine activities. Over all age groups including children (18- to 44-year-old age-specific data not available), 21% of those with asthma report some limitation of activity (including activities inside and outside the home) (2). A similar proportion (22%) report one or more hospitalizations annually due to this condition (2). For comparison with two other common chronic medical conditions, the relative proportion of reported activity limitation among all persons with hypertension is 11% and for diabetes mellitus among all ages, 35%. For hospitalization in hypertension, the proportion is 8%, and for diabetes 27% (2).

The prevalence of asthma-specific work limitation is shown in Table 1. These data are derived from the 1992 U.S. NHIS (6). In the NHIS, occupation and industry of employment are based on subject self-report. NHIS data may underestimate current rates if one assumes a continuing rise in asthma prevalence and associated work limitations. These 1992 data underscore the powerful impact of asthma on work productivity and labor-force participation. Given a 1990–1992 NHIS estimate of 4.35 million persons in the 18- to 44-year-old stratum with asthma, an estimated 7.1% report some work limitation (2,6). The economic ramifications of these widespread limitations are addressed in a later section.

As can be seen from Table 1, exclusive of specific musculoskeletal impairments and mental retardation, asthma is the most common medical condition associated with working-age work disability in the United States (6). For example, it surpasses the combined occupational disability impact of hypertension and diabetes in the 18- to 44-year-old age group. Moreover, there are marked gender differences in the relative contribution of asthma to work disability. Among females, asthma ranks third among specific conditions as the primary cause of work

Table 1 Reported Health Conditions as the Primary Cause of Any Work Limitation Based on 1992 National Health Interview Survey Data

Condition	All Number (%)	Males Number (%)	Females Number (%)
All	7,628,000 (100.0)	3,944,000 (100.0)	3,683,000 (100.0)
Leading causes			
Back impairment	1,051,000 (13.8)	531,000 (13.5)	521,000 (14.1)
Disk disease	752,000 (9.9)	456,000 (11.6)	295,000 (8.0)
Lower extremity impairment	420,000 (5.5)	283,000 (7.2)	137,000 (3.7)
Mental retardation	369,000 (4.8)	231,000 (5.9)	138,000 (3.7)
Asthma	308,000 (4.0)	115,000 (2.9)	193,000 (5.2)
Upper extremity impairment	299,000 (3.9)	163,000 (4.1)	135,000 (3.7)
Comparison conditions			
Hypertension	60,000 (0.8)	25,000 (0.6)	35,000 (1.0)
Diabetes mellitus	147,000 (1.9)	68,000 (1.7)	79,000 (2.1)

Source: Derived from Ref. 6.

disability; among males, its rank order falls to sixth. Moreover, these data apply only to employment disability as defined in the analysis cited, which includes NHIS respondents who were either salaried employees or students but excludes from the work-disabled those limited to "keeping house" as their major vocational activity (6).

As with the overall prevalence of asthma among 18- to 44-year-olds, asthma-attributable work disability also appears to be on the rise. Compared to 1983–1985 U.S. NHIS data analyzed by the same investigator, by 1992 there was an overall 14% increase in the prevalence of asthma-caused disability in this age stratum, from 270,00 to 308,000 (6,7). Paralleling general asthma prevalence trends, the increase in asthma-caused work disability was greater among females (24%) than males (6%). Once again, the factors underlying this gender disparity are unknown.

Published data estimating the international impact of asthma in terms of employment and work incapacity are limited but support the view that occupational disability is a major adverse outcome among adults with this condition. A study of young adults in the United Kingdom found that those with a current ($n = 192$) or past history of asthma ($n = 1522$) were more likely to have been unemployed, had more job changes, and experienced less recent full-time employment than respondents with no asthma history ($n = 2505$). However, a statistically significant increased risk was observed only for the outcome measure of unemployment (8).

In a study from New Zealand, 14% of adult subjects with asthma and a history of labor-force participation ($n = 93$) stated that their condition contributed to job dismissal, lack of advancement, or poorer working standards. In total, nearly half (46%) reported that asthma affected their occupational activities (9). A Spanish study of asthma self-management reported a mean of over 20 lost workdays per person due to asthma over a 6-month baseline run-in period prior to intervention ($n = 94$ subjects) (10). A study of 802 adults with asthma aged 21 to 58 years recruited from government clinics in Singapore found that 62% experienced at least one day of work or school absence in the previous year due to asthma and 21% had missed a week or more (the precise breakdown of work as opposed to school absence was not provided) (11). A population-based analysis of data from the Israeli armed forces found that new-onset asthma was commonly associated with change in duties, with moderate asthma having a greater impact on technical (noncombat) jobs than mild asthma (71% versus 52% changing duties) (12). These data underscore the limited nature of our current international understanding even of the descriptive epidemiology of work disability in asthma. Internationally, as in the United States, the issue of vocational disability in keeping house has not been the focus of detailed epidemiological study.

IV. Costs of Asthma-Related Work Limitations

The estimated costs of work disability due to asthma are substantial. In the United States, asthma-related costs of lost workdays were calculated at $284.7 million per annum in 1990 (13). This estimate, which did not include work disability among those who had stopped working completely (indirect work loss for asthma child care was included), was equivalent to the total cost of outpatient health care services for asthma. In that study, the cost of lost workdays was found to be on the upswing, growing by 18% among men and 24% among women from 1985 to 1990 (13). The estimated economic value of lost housework activity, an important measure of uncompensated work, amounted to over $500 million annually, a sum equivalent to hospital-based charges for outpatient and emergency department asthma care combined.

Following the estimate by Weiss and coworkers, Smith and coinvestigators also estimated the U.S. economic impact of asthma (14). It differed from the previous study by being expenditure-based for the direct health care costs, utilizing the 1987 National Medical Expenditure Survey rather than Weiss's charge-based estimate derived from 1990 sources. The Smith study estimated that the total indirect costs of asthma due to lost labor productivity were $532 million

(1987 dollars). This accounted for only 15% of total asthma costs and was considerably lower than Weiss's estimate both in absolute and relative terms, driven largely by lower estimates of the indirect costs of lost housekeeping labor productivity. The breakdown by source of estimated lost labor productivity costs was as follows: lost salaried workdays, 33% of total indirect costs; lost housekeeping days, 3%, adult restricted activity days impacting work capacity, 32%; and adult lost productivity due to care of children with asthma, 31% (the latter two categories were calculated as the loss of either salaried work or nonsalaried housekeeping) (14). As with Weiss's estimate, the costs of work loss for those completely disabled (e.g., no longer in the labor force) would not be valued in these calculations, leading to a potentially important source of underestimated costs.

There are few other North American data estimates of general asthma disability costs. A recent small U.S. cohort study found that lost employment income due to asthma accounted for 50% of all indirect asthma costs, 17% as much as the direct medical costs, and 13% of the total cost of asthma (15). In Canada, a national estimate for asthma costs in 1990 ranged from $76 to $98 million for lost work outside and inside the home, with an additional $20.6 million in disability insurance payments of varying kinds (16). As a proportion of total costs, the aggregate work-disability costs amounted to no more than 19% of all direct and indirect health costs for asthma in Canada. This represents a proportionately lower impact than the U.S. national estimate by Weiss (13) but more than that of Smith (14).

Cost estimates for asthma-related work loss outside North America were addressed in detail in a recent analysis by Barnes and colleagues (17). Although a secondary review, it serves as a useful metanalysis of nine primary reports, of which six were consultative or governmental documents. The cost estimates cited were huge but varied widely both in absolute terms and relative to direct health care costs. The highest proportion of indirect costs, largely reflecting the value of work loss, was estimated for the United Kingdom and Sweden, while the lowest relative proportion was for Canada and Australia. The United States and France fell in the middle. For the United Kingdom, two cited estimates for asthma work-loss costs, both from 1990, differed from each other by 23%, underscoring the extent to which estimates of the indirect costs of illness are driven by the assumptions underlying them. A population-based study from New South Wales, Australia, also cited by Barnes, estimated that the annual cost of asthma due to lost work productivity was $48 million, 33% of the total asthma direct medical costs for adult and childhood asthma combined (18).

V. Asthma and the Working Environment

The working environment can interact with asthma in a complex manner, potentially impacting the employed person with asthma in a variety of different ways.

This critical characteristic of adult asthma makes occupational disability such a vitally important issue. The potential interactions between work and asthma are illustrated graphically in Figure 1. Job attributes and occupational factors can initiate asthma de novo or worsen preexisting asthma. "Occupational asthma," in its classic meaning, describes disease initiation through work-related exposures. A myriad of specific agents that can cause occupational asthma have been identified (19,20). These agents include low- and high-molecular-weight naturally occurring and synthetic sensitizing chemicals and nonsensitizing irritant work exposures.

In contrast to substances that *initiate* occupational asthma, other work exposures may worsen the physiological impairment of preexisting asthma. The term *work-related asthma* is sometimes used to describe such work-related exacerbations of preexisting asthma. For example, certain chemical exposures can clearly precipitate bronchospasm among persons with underlying airway hyperresponsiveness. The best-studied of these is sulfur dioxide, but chlorine gas also seems capable of inducing an exaggerated response in persons with asthma (21,22). Ozone, in contrast, is less predictable in its effects (23). Similarly, exposure to certain nonchemical environmental conditions on the job, such as aeroallergens (e.g., molds or even a workplace cat) or abrupt temperature changes, can worsen airflow obstruction and increase asthma symptoms. These exposure scenarios would fall under the rubric of *work-aggravated asthma*.

Beyond occupational asthma and work-related asthma, the nature of work itself may modify outcomes without affecting asthma's underlying physiological impairment. The physical demands of the job may exceed the respiratory capacity of the individual with asthma. This factor would be most relevant to jobs with ongoing, heavy physical demands, although symptoms due to exercise-induced asthma could be aggravated by intermittent vigorous effort.

More broadly, other job attributes unrelated to the physical demands of work may affect the individual's ability to maintain employment. One such set of attributes is termed the *social characteristics of work*, which concern the individual's discretion over the pace and scheduling of work activities (24). During exacerbations of illness, for instance, persons with chronic disease may need to limit work activities to garner rest and secure medical care. Inability to do so may lead to work disability. In cross-sectional and longitudinal studies of muscu-

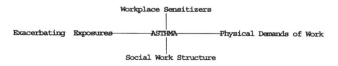

Figure 1 Potential interactions between workplace actors and asthma.

loskeletal disease (24), cancer (25), and other chronic diseases (26,27), persons with greater autonomy and flexibility at the workplace were much less likely to stop working. The impact of the social characteristics of work appears to be independent of the severity of the medical condition or other covariables that had been previously found to predict work disability status. The social characteristics of work may also impact asthma caregivers. As discussed previously, work and productivity loss for asthma caregivers is a major contributor to the estimated indirect costs of asthma (13,14). Decreased job autonomy and flexibility may result in greater work loss for caregivers.

The multifactorial nature of workplace-asthma interactions raises critical methodological challenges in interpreting other important covariates of asthma status and outcome. Socioeconomic status and educational level are two examples of covariates that can, in part, be unintended surrogates for work-related exposures. Specifically, low socioeconomic status or educational level can be associated with jobs whose workplace conditions are more likely to initiate asthma, aggravate preexisting asthma, or allow for reduced job autonomy and flexibility. To the extent that socioeconomic status or education acts as a surrogate measure for these risk factors, it becomes more difficult to analyze the impact of these variables on asthma independent of their potential occupational ramifications.

Workplace factors initiating asthma, exposures aggravating asthma, physical demands outstripping functional capacity, and a social work structure poorly adaptive to chronic illness represent the broad pathways through which occupation can intersect with adult asthma. These factors, singly or in concert, may act to amplify the risk of work disability among adults with asthma. As such, they can be critical to the socioeconomic impact of this condition.

VI. Work in the Home

Although largely unsalaried, work in the household environment embodies many of the same potential interactions delineated in Figure 1. Asthma caused by sensitization to natural or synthetic chemical antigens can occur through household activities. Perhaps as common, acute irritant-induced asthma can result from cleaning product misadventure, especially exposures involving chlorine or chloramine gas release (28). Worsening of preexisting asthma has been linked to the use of home gas stoves, likely to be a common exposure in household work. This risk factor was associated with more than doubling of the odds of restricted activity [occupational risk (OR) 2.9; 95% CI 2.3–3.6] and of physician or emergency department visits for asthma (OR 2.5; 95% CI 1.5–4.4) in a longitudinal panel study of 164 adults with asthma (29). The same study also identified use of wood-burning fireplaces and heating stoves as a risk factor for worsening asthma, especially for nocturnal symptoms (OR 1.6; 95% CI 1.3–2.0). This may be particularly relevant to household work in environments where biomass fuel is used for primary home heating and cooking. Such fuels have been epidemiologically associated with chronic obstructive lung disease (30). Among those sensitized to house dust-mite antigen, routine household dusting and cleaning activities may aggravate asthma. For example, standard vacuuming can entrain allergen (31). Finally, the social characteristics of household work may be disadvantageous to persons with asthma, since such individuals may be unable to modify job duties or the work environment to significantly reduce aggravating exposures.

VII. Defining Work Disability in Asthma

In asthma, it is easy to blur the concepts of impairment and disability. *Impairment*, which refers to a functional decrement, can be directly quantified in asthma by pulmonary function testing. *Disability*, which refers to compromised performance of activities, is not readily quantifiable. To define work disability in asthma, it is critical to delineate the differences between impairment and disability.

Conceptually, the quantification of an asthma-associated physiological impairment is straightforward. It assumes an expected level of normal function, adjusting for established determinants (demographic and anthropomorphic). Any deviation from the projected normal level of function yields the quantified measurement of functional impairment. Quantification of impairment, consistent with the common practice of reporting pulmonary function data as a percentage of age-, height-, and gender-adjusted normal values, has been widely used in rating schemes that assess functional status. This is most evident in the widely used American Medical Association (AMA) Guidelines for Evaluation of Permanent Impairment (32), which, in turn, echo American Thoracic Society recommendations (33). Internationally, the assessment of asthma impairment in a variety of social insurance systems is also predicted on pulmonary function testing (34).

By inappropriate analogy, this often leads to the misconception that disability equates with impairment and that it can be quantified in the same manner. Disability, however, is relative and qualitative, not a fixed and measurable absolute. It reflects a compromised ability to perform activities or to fulfill duties over a wide spectrum of human endeavors. This can include work, the activities of daily living, or leisure pursuits (35–37).

The concept of work disability in asthma attempts to define the attributes of this specific condition that lead to a compromised capacity for work. The compromised work capacity is, nonetheless, relative to each job environment. Consider the example of a butcher whose asthma is aggravated by cold air exposure from entering a refrigerated meat locker multiple times each day. The butcher may come to a point where these job duties cannot be performed and would, therefore, experience asthma-related work disability as defined. This hypothetical butcher may have precisely the same degree of physiological impairment as a twin sibling who, being employed as a computer programmer in a temperature- and humidity-controlled office building, experiences no work disability.

Not only is work disability relative, it can also be defined by varying criteria. Defining asthma-related work disability narrowly as complete work cessation provides a well-demarcated but excessively narrow criterion. This definition excludes less severe but more frequent outcomes such as restriction in work duties, change in job, increased days of work loss, or even limitation in work hours at the same job. For example, in a study of adults with asthma recruited from a university-based pulmonary subspecialty practice, subjects ($n = 53$) were contacted for a brief structured telephone interview at baseline and follow-up. The estimated 5-year cumulative incidence of work disability by various measures was as follows: change in work duties attributed to asthma, 19%; reduced pay due to asthma, 17%; change in job status (new job or left work), 20%; and any of these, 36% (95% CI 23–40%) (38). Even such an expanded approach to defining work disability is still not all-inclusive, however. None of these definitions subsumes work disability in non-salaried employment at home or elsewhere, which could be defined by asthma-attributed avoidance of specific duties (e.g., vacuuming or using certain cleaning agents in housework) or cessation of certain activities, such as service as a volunteer fireman.

VIII. Handicap and Quality of Life

Further confusion can arise because disability is related to, but does not equate with, either handicap or quality of life. As a construct, handicap subsumes an individual's adaptation to impairment and disability. There are no widely used survey instruments that quantify gradations or scales of handicap as such. Health-related quality of life (QOL) attempts to capture the ways in which illnesses impact patient-perceived functioning and status. Clearly, QOL is not unrelated to work disability for those with asthma and impaired labor force participation. In contradistinction to handicap, there are a number of generic and disease-specific instruments that are intended to quantify differing domains of QOL (these QOL instruments are covered in detail in later chapters by Juniper and Marks). Two widely used disease-specific QOL instruments do include specific measures of work disability. The asthma questionnaire battery of Juniper and coworkers (39) allows respondents to identify work as one of the selected activities for which limitations are assessed. The St. George's Respiratory Questionnaire of Jones and coworkers (40) specifically includes work impairment, as does a shorter, asthma-specific battery (the "AQ2O") derived from it. The widely used generic health status instrument, the Medical Outcomes Study SF-36, which has been employed in the study of asthma, includes work among daily activities assessed in the domains of both physical and emotional functioning (41,42).

Clearly defining work disability and related constructs is critical to the task of assessing the occupational impact of asthma. The differences and overlap among impairment, disability, handicap, and quality of life must be kept in view in the design of studies, the interpretation of data, and the development of public policy relating to this question.

IX. Identifying Predictors of Work Disability in Asthma

There are multiple factors that, on theoretical grounds, would be likely candidates as risk factors for work disability and decreased productivity among adults with asthma. There are no established, widely accepted predictive models of work disability in asthma. Some potential risk factors in one hypothetical schema are illustrated in Figure 2. As shown, illness severity is one predictor of disability but not its sole predictor. A number of other factors may modify asthma-disability risk. Thus, for a given degree of severity, the model predicts that risk factors such as demographic cofactors (for example, educational level), psychosocial characteristics, or working conditions themselves will be associated with poorer or better outcomes. Figure 2, as drawn, reflects a simplified model. Conceptually, however, the model allows for interactions among the risk factors so that, acting together, they may modify any given asthma-specific outcome. Furthermore, the model may differ markedly in the relative contributions of various predictors depending on the work outcome in question, such as asthma-related complete cessation of work, change in job duties, or reduction in work hours.

This theoretical model has been tested, at least in part, in a recent cross-sectional study of adults with asthma recruited from a random sample of internal medicine pulmonary or allergy and immunology subspecialists (43). Subjects underwent lengthy structured interviews assessing asthma severity, general health status and well-being, demographics, and work status. Work disability was com-

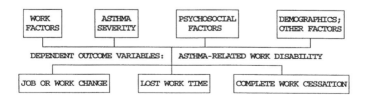

Figure 2 Predictive model of work disability among adults with asthma (independent predictor variables).

mon. Among those interviewed with any history of labor force participation (*n* = 550), the prevalence of complete work cessation attributed to asthma was 7% (95% CI 5–9%). When disability was defined as complete work cessation attributed to asthma, job change, or job limitations, the prevalence climbed to 17% (95% CI 14–20%). In a multiple logistic regression analysis, key risk factors for disability included asthma severity, general health status, cigarette smoking status, educational level, and atopic history. Addition to predictive models of patient characteristics (such as age, gender, race, marital status, and childhood asthma) provided little additional explanatory effect.

Table 2 presents an analysis of work-related factors studied for their potential disability risk, adjusted for severity and the other covariates delineated previously. In essence, this analysis examines in detail predictors that fall within the domain of ''work factors'' illustrated in Figure 2. Occupational conditions— when converted into a single combined measure including chemical exposures, temperature changes, and physical demands together—predicted work disability as powerfully as greater asthma severity, measured as the difference in severity going from the lowest to the highest quartile of severity scores. This further supports the theoretical construct illustrated in Figure 2. Work disability in asthma does indeed appear to be multifactorial in nature. Severity of disease is an important factor but not the sole or even the most potent risk factor for work disability.

This analysis still leaves unexplained much of the variation in asthma-related work disability, particularly within the psychosocial realm. For example, a

Table 2 Occupational Risks (OR) for Work Disability (*n* = 550 with work history)

Occupational variable	Frequency	OR	95% CI
Reported exposure to chemicals or dusts	167 (30%)	1.6	0.97 to 2.7
Job-based exposure matrix (score range)	(1.3–3.8)	1.7	1.2 to 2.5
Reported exposure to temperature changes	64 (12%)	2.2	1.1 to 4.3
Physical exertion on job			
Minimal (referent)	365 (66%)	—	—
Intermittent moderate to heavy	45 (8%)	2.0	0.8 to 4.6
Sustained moderate to heavy	140 (25%)	1.6	0.9 to 2.8
Occupation prior to disability			
Managerial or professional (referent)	153 (28%)	—	—
Technical	38 (7%)	2.9	1.03 to 8.1
Administration, sales, support	184 (34%)	1.2	0.6 to 2.5
Service	81 (15%)	2.3	1.1 to 5.1
Crafts, operatives, laborers, farm	94 (17%)	2.5	1.2 to 5.5

Source: Derived from Ref. 43.

novel scale assessing patient-perceived asthma control, when tested in this cohort, demonstrated a strong association with work disability: those with poorer self-assessed control were more likely to be work-disabled due to asthma, even taking disease severity into account (44).

Another community-based study of work disability among adults with asthma from Sweden reported findings consistent with the previously cited panel study. Investigators identified 332 adults with labor force participation and new-onset asthma over a 4-year period in Goteborg, Sweden, from an adult population of 370,000 (45). Based on self-rated work ability (which correlated with lost workdays), 2% were disabled (greater than 50% impairment); 25% moderately impaired; and 17% minimally impaired (≤10% impairment). In a multiple logistic regression analysis taking asthma severity and methacholine responsiveness into account, the presence of respiratory symptoms at work was a potent risk factor for decreased work ability (odds ratio of 2.6; 95% CI 1.6–4.2). In the same model, physically demanding jobs and workplace exposure to irritants also carried increased risk of disability (odds ratio of 1.5 in both instances), although these associations were of borderline statistical significance.

X. Work-Related Asthma

Work-related asthma, especially occupational asthma arising from sensitization in the workplace, represents a special subset of adult asthma. As stated earlier, there are numerous heterogenous causes of occupational asthma. Whatever the initiating agent, however, a growing number of studies suggest that the outcomes of occupational asthma are particularly poor in terms of work disability.

Although earlier studies had examined the natural history of occupational asthma after cessation of ongoing workplace exposure, the seminal report by Burge and coworkers in 1993 was one of the first to emphasize the socioeconomic impact of the illness (46). They showed that persons with documented occupational asthma from a variety of causes fared poorly at follow-up. Those removed from further exposure ($n = 78$) had fewer symptoms and required less medication than those still exposed ($n = 34$) but also reported a median loss of income of 54%. Remarkably, those remaining exposed at work also reported a 35% median loss of income. The authors state: ''More workers who had changed jobs thought that they had suffered financially compared with those who remained exposed. Those who stayed suffered financially because of sickness, lack of promotion, or reduced opportunity for overtime'' (46).

These findings have been amplified in other studies. A study of 128 Western red cedar workers found a high prevalence of work disability at 5-year follow-up evaluation: 41% were unemployed, another 38% were working but still exposed to the agent, and only 27% were employed but not exposed (47). Monthly income was only 54% of baseline in the unemployed individuals. A smaller study in the United Kingdom, comparing patients with occupational asthma ($n = 26$) with nonoccupational cases ($n = 29$), found that 62% of the occupational cases had changed jobs at some point because of their asthma, compared with 21% of the referents; 50% of the occupational cases were currently unemployed at the time of study, compared with only 3% of the nonoccupational asthma group (48). Another study, also from the United Kingdom, also compared occupational with nonoccupational cases while including a third group of subjects with preexisting asthma aggravated at work. Of those with occupational asthma ($n = 87$) or work-aggravated asthma ($n = 26$), 50% reported that asthma made getting employment more difficult; but only 23% of those ($n = 65$) without a work component to their disease reported such disability (49). Finally, a French cohort study of occupational asthma cases ($n = 209$) found that after a mean of 3 years of follow-up, 28% were unemployed or retired, 16% had found new employment, and 56% were with the same employer (most of these with different duties or some modification). Of those that were no longer with the same employer, 84% reported an income reduction with a 50% mean loss (50).

In every study in which it has been examined, the impact of occupational asthma on work disability appears to be immense, markedly surpassing the general proportion of work disability among persons with non-occupational asthma. This disproportionate risk raises the question: "To what extent is adult asthma generally attributable, etiologically, to work factors?" This issue gains in importance as a matter of social policy because even a modest proportion of occupational asthma could be contributing a major proportion of adult asthma's indirect costs. For example, assume that occupationally related asthma incurs three times as much indirect health costs on average per case as nonoccupational adult asthma. This would be in line with the degree of work loss noted previously. Were this to be compounded by a 7% etiological fraction of occupational causes among all adult asthma, then approximately 18% of the indirect health costs of adult asthma would be attributable to this factor.

Table 3 summarizes data from a variety of studies that have attempted to estimate the etiological fraction or population attributable risk percent (PAR%) for occupationally related asthma among all adults with asthma (51–66). The estimates, based on data from nine different countries, vary widely, from a low of 2% to a high of 33%. Nonetheless, many of the estimates fall within a 6–10% range, which may reflect the best available estimate of the proportion of adult asthma attributable to occupational factors.

Moreover, each of the estimation approaches used has important limitations. The theoretical model cited (61) may be as legitimate as any: it assumes that 9% of the adult working-age population have jobs that can initiate asthma, with an overall relative risk of 2.0 for these occupations. A simple averaging

Table 3 Estimates of the Proportion of Adult Asthma Due to Occupation

Location	*n*	Methods	Estimated PAR%[a]	Ref.
U.S.A.	NA	Consensus statement	2.0%	51
Japan	813	Population-based, males only	3.4 to 14.5%	52
U.S.A.	6063	Weighted disability sample	15.4%	53
Zambia	580	University clinic	5.9%	54
U.S.A.	94	Hospitalized cases	3.0 to 20.2%	55
China	3606	Population sample	5.0 to 15%	56,57
Singapore	787	Community-based clinics	33%	58
Spain	2646	Random population survey	2.6 to 6.7%	59
U.S.A.	601	Community-based sample	6.0 to 17%	60
U.S.A.	NA	Theoretical model	8.3%	61
U.S.A.	42487	Weighted population sample	6.9%	61,62
Finland	4717	National incidence	4.8%	63
New Zealand	1609	Random population survey	1.9 to 3.1%	64
Canada	731	University referral clinic	7.0%	65
U.S.A.	68	Incident cases from large HMO	9.1 to 21.2%	66

[a]PAR% = Population attributable risk percent.

yields a PAR% of 8.3%. Whatever the precise value is, the occupational contribution to asthma prevalence is substantial.

A recent review of the incidence of occupational asthma per se, as opposed to its population attributable risk, also found that those estimates vary widely among different countries, ranging from 10.4 per million employed persons per year (United States—based on four different surveillance programs) to 140 per million per year in Finland, with Quebec (Canada) and the United Kingdom the midrange (23 to 24 per million per year) (67). An incidence study from Sweden, based on data from a similar time period to the others cited above, estimated an annual incidence rate of 80 per million (68). Data from Finland, which are particularly rigorous, suggest an increasing incidence of work-related asthma over time, paralleling the increases in adult asthma generically (63).

Although a variety of differing factors may impact estimates of work-related asthma incidence and prevalence, cigarette smoking status merits specific discussion. Diagnostic bias would likely shift some working persons with a history of cigarette smoking from a categorization of "asthma" to "chronic obstructive pulmonary disease"(COPD), even in the face of known or suspected asthma-causing exposures. This is apt to be particularly true of those older than 45 years of age and could lead to underestimation of the occupationally related PAR%

for adult asthma. Even taking into account diagnostic overlap, cigarette smoking (any history of past or current smoking), is surprisingly prevalent among adults with asthma. In the U.S. NHANES I follow-up study lifetime, ever-smoking rates among those with asthma were similar to those in the general population (e.g., >50%), even after excluding those with emphysema, COPD, or chronic bronchitis from the asthma group (69). In the population-based Tucson, Arizona, study, among 261 persons with asthma, 29% were current and 24% ex-smokers (the mean age was 41 years; those with emphysema were excluded) (70). A study of 238 adults with asthma from a university-based specialty clinic, where diagnostic homogeneity was assured and asthma severity would be expected to be higher than a community-based sample, found that 15% were current smokers and that nearly 50% ever smokers (71). Among certain cohorts there is strong evidence that cigarette smokers are indeed at greater risk of sensitization to specific workplace exposures (72,73). Cigarette smokers also appear to be at greater risk of persistent symptoms after acute irritant inhalation exposures, consistent with diagnostic criteria for irritant-induced work-related asthma (74). The potential impact on the incidence and prevalence of adult asthma from interactions between workplace factors and smoking exposure is a very real consideration that warrants further investigation.

XI. Conclusions

Overall, asthma has a major impact on the working lives of women and men around the world. The condition is common and costly among those of working age. The inherent variability of the condition may be critical to its general morbidity, but well delineated risk models of asthma-caused work disability have yet to be tested prospectively. This is all the more important in an ever-changing work environment, where increasingly flexible hours and "telecommuting" may decrease the risk of asthma disability for one group, just as novel work processes may introduce new and potent hazards for another. It is clear that among the subset of those with occupationally related asthma, poor work outcomes are particularly important and likely to be of huge societal burden and cost. The impact of asthma on work in the home may be as great as in the salaried workplace, yet this issue has gone virtually unstudied.

The role of primary asthma prevention emerges as particularly important among those at risk of occupationally initiated asthma and is addressed in greater detail in a later chapter by Elixhauser. In a broader sense, the workplace, for both salaried and unsalaried employees, must be a priority for environmentally focused asthma prevention activities. This includes not only primary prevention but secondary and tertiary prevention as well. Such activities include both prevention of work-initiated asthma and prevention of adverse outcomes for those with preexisting asthma, whether worsened by work factors or through other pathways (see Fig. 2). The Americans With Disabilities Act sets a framework for reassessing the relationship between workplace accommodation and pre-existing employee health conditions that is especially relevant to asthma (75). Importantly, such legislation also addresses the potential for job discrimination against employees with health conditions often as clearly manifest as asthma. Although legislation that is as far-reaching has not yet been promulgated by members of the European Community and other industrialized countries, international prevention of asthma-related disability will inevitability expand to more fully address the working environment in all its ramifications.

Acknowledgments

Supported by a Research Career Development Award (KO4 HL03225) and additional funding (R01 HL56438) from the National Heart, Lung and Blood Institute and from the National Institute for Occupational Safety and Health (R01 OH03480).

References

1. U.S. Department of Health and Human Services. (1996). *Vital and Health Statistics: Current Estimates from the National Health Interview Survey*. Series 10, Data from the National Health Survey; no. 193. DHHS publication no. PHS 96-1521. Hyattsville, Md.
2. Collins J.G. (1997). *Vital and Health Statistics: Prevalence of Selected Chronic Conditions: United States, 1990–1992*. Series 10, Data from the National Health Survey; no. 194. DHHS publication no. PHS 97-1522. Hyattsville, Md.
3. Collins J.G. (1993). *Vital and Health Statistics: Prevalence of Selected Chronic Conditions: United States, 1986–1988*. Series 10, Data from the National Health Survey; no. 182. DHHS publication no. PHS 93-1510. Hyattsville, Md.
4. European Community Respiratory Health Survey (1996). Variations in the prevalence of respiratory symptoms, self-reported asthma attacks, and use of asthma medication in the European Community Respiratory Health Survey (E.C.R.H.S.). *Eur. Respir. J.*, 9:687–695.
5. Abramson M., Kutin J., Czarny D., and Walters E.H. (1996). The prevalence of asthma and respiratory symptoms among young adults: is it increasing in Australia? *J. Asthma*, 33:189–196.
6. LaPlante, M.P., and Carlson D. (1996). Disability in the United States: prevalence and causes, 1992. Disability Statistics Report no. 7. Washington, D.C., Department of Education, National Institute on Disability and Rehabilitation Research.
7. LaPlante M.P. (1988). *Data on Disability from the National Health Interview Survey, 1983–1985: An InfoUse Report*. Washington, D.C., U.S. National Institute on Disability and Rehabilitation Research.

8. Sibbald, B., Anderson, H.R., and McGuigan, S. (1992). Asthma and employment in young adults. *Thorax*, **47**:19–24.

9. McClellan, V.E., and Garrett, J.E. (1990). Asthma and employment experience. *N.Z. Med. J.* **103**:399–401.

10. Ignacio-Garcia, J.M., and Gonzales-Santos, P. (1995). Asthma self-management education program by home monitoring of peak expiratory flow. *Am. J. Respir. Crit. Care. Med.*, **151**:353–359.

11. Goh, L.G., Ng, T.P., Hong, C.Y., Wong, M.L., Koh, K., and Ling, S.L. (1994). Outpatient adult bronchial asthma in Singapore. *Singapore Med. J.*, **35**:190–194.

12. Kivity, S., Shochat, Z., Bressler, R., Wiener, M., and Lerman, Y. (1995). The characteristics of bronchial asthma among a young adult population. *Chest*, **108**:24–27.

13. Weiss, K.B., Gergen, P.J., and Hodgson, T.A. (1992). An economic evaluation of asthma in the United States. *N. Engl. J. Med.*, **326**:862–866.

14. Smith, D.H., Malone, D.C., Lawson, K.A., Okamoto, L.J., Battista, C., and Saunders, W.B. (1997). A national estimate of the economic costs of asthma. *Am. J. Respir. Crit. Care. Med.*, **156**:787–793.

15. Taitel, M.S., Kotses, H., Bernstein, I.B., Bernstein, D.I., and Creer, T.L. (1995). A self-management program for adult asthma. Part II: Cost benefit analysis. *J. Allergy Clin. Immunol.*, **95**:672–676.

16. Krahn, M.D., Berka, C., Langlois, P., and Detsky, A.S. (1996). Direct and indirect costs of asthma in Canada. *Can. Med. Assoc. J.*, **154**:821–843.

17. Barnes, P.J., Jonsson, B.M., and Klim, J.B. (1996). The costs of asthma. *Eur. Respir. J.*, **9**:636–642.

18. Mellis, C.M., Peat, J.K., Bauman, A.E., and Woolcock, A.J. (1991). The cost of asthma in New South Wales. *Med. J. Aust.*, **155**:522–528.

19. Chan-Yeung, M., and Malo, J.L. (1993). Compendium I: Table of the major inducers of occupational asthma. In *Asthma in the Workplace*. Edited by I.L. Bernstein, M. Chan-Yeung, J.L. Malo, and D.I. Bernstein. New York, Marcel Decker, pp 595–623.

20. Venables, K.M., and Chan-Yeung, M. (1997). Occupational asthma. *Lancet*, **349**:1465–1469.

21. Sheppard, D., Wong, W.S., Uehara, C.F., Nadel, J.A., and Boushey, H.A. (1980). Lower threshold and greater bronchomotor responsiveness of asthmatic subjects to sulfur dioxide. *Am. Rev. Respir. Dis.*, **122**:873–878.

22. D'Alessandro, A., Kuschner, W., Wong, H., Boushey, H.A., and Blanc, P.D. (1996). Exaggerated responses to chlorine inhalation among persons with nonspecific airway hyperreactivity. *Chest*, **109**:331–337.

23. Aris, R.M., Tager, I., Christian, D., Kelly, T., and Balmes, J.R. (1995). Methacholine responsiveness is not associated with O_3-induced decreases in FEV_1. *Chest*, **107**:621–628.

24. Yelin E, Nevitt M, and Epstein W. (1980). Toward an epidemiology of work disability. *Milbank Q.*, **58**:386–415.

25. Greenwald, H.P., Dirks, S.J., Borgatta, E.F., McCorkle, R., Nevitt, M.C., and Yelin E.H. (1989). Work disability among cancer patients. *Soc. Sci. Med.*, **29**:1253–1259.

26. Yelin, E. (1986). The myth of malingering: why individuals withdraw from work in the presence of illness. *Milbank Q.*, **64**:622–649.

27. Yelin, E., and Katz, P. (1994). Making work more central to work disability policy. *Milbank Q.*, **72**:593–620.
28. Das, R., and Blanc, P.D. (1993). Chlorine gas exposure and the lung. *Toxicol. Ind. Health*, **9**:439–455.
29. Ostro, B.D., Lipsett, M.J., Mann, J.K., Wiener, M.B., and Selner, J. (1994). Indoor air pollution and asthma: results from a panel study. *Am. J. Respir. Crit. Care Med.*, **149**:1400–1406.
30. Dennis, R.J., Maldonado, D., Norman, S., Buena, E., Castano, H., Martinez, G., and Velez, R.J. (1996). Wood smoke exposure and risk for obstructive airways disease among women. *Chest*, **109**:55s–56s.
31. Hegarty, J.M., Rouhbaksh, S., Warner, J.A., and Warner, J.O. (1995). A comparison of the effect of conventional and filter vacuum cleaners on airborne house dust mite allergen. *Respir. Med.*, **89**:279–284.
32. Doege, T.C., and Houston, T.P. eds. (1993). *Guides to the Evaluation of Permanent Impairment*, 4th ed. Chicago, American Medical Association, pp. 153–167.
33. American Thoracic Society (1993). Guidelines for the evaluation of impairment/disability in patients with asthma. *Am. Rev. Respir. Dis.*, **147**:1056–1061.
34. Balmes, J.R., and Barnhart, S. Evaluation of respiratory impairment/disability. In *Textbook of Respiratory Medicine*, 2nd ed. Edited by Murray, J.F., and Nadel, J.A. Philadelphia, Saunders, pp. 920–942.
35. Nagi, S. (1976). An Epidemiology of Disability among Adults in the U.S. *Milbank Q.*, **54**:439–468.
36. Haber, L. (1971). Disabling effects of chronic disease and impairments. *J. Chronic Dis.*, **24**:469–487.
37. Institute of Medicine (1991). *Disability in America*. Washington, D.C., National Academy Press.
38. Blanc, P.D., Jones, M., Besson, C., Katz, P., and Yelin, E. (1993). Work disability among adults with asthma. *Chest*, **104**:1371–1377.
39. Juniper, E.F., Guyatt, G.H., Ferrie, P.J., and Griffith, L.E. (1993). Measuring quality of life in asthma. *Am. Rev. Respir. Dis.*, **147**:832–838.
40. Jones, P.W., Quirk, F.H., Baveytock, C.M., and Littlejohn, P. (1992). A self-completed measure for chronic airflow limitation—the St. George's Respiratory Questionnaire. *Am. Rev. Respir. Dis.*, **145**:1321–1327.
41. Bousquet, J., Knani, J., Dhivert, H., Richard, A., Chicoye, A., Ware, J.E. Jr., and Michel, F.-B. (1994). Quality of life in asthma: I. Internal consistency and validity of the SF-36 questionnaire. *Am. J. Respir. Crit. Care Med.*, **149**:371–375.
42. Ware, J.E., and Sherbourne, C.D. (1992). The MOS 36-item short-form health survey (SF-36): I. Conceptual framework and item selection. *Med. Care*, **30**:473–483.
43. Blanc, P.D., Cisternas, M., Smith, S., and Yelin, E. (1996). Asthma, employment status, and disability among adults treated by pulmonary and allergy specialists. *Chest*, **109**:668–696.
44. Katz, P.P., Yelin, E.H., Smith, S., and Blanc, P.D. (1997). Perceived control of asthma: development and validation of a questionnaire; *Am. J. Respir. Crit. Care Med.* **155**:577–582.
45. Balder, B., Lindholm, N.B., Lowhagen, O., Palmqvist, M., Plaschke, P., Tunsater,

A., and Toren, K. (1998). Predictors of self-assessed work ability among subjects with recent onset asthma. *Respir. Med.* **92**:729–734.

46. Gannon, P.F.G., Weir, D.C., Robertson, A.S., and Burge, P.S. (1993). Health, employment, and financial outcomes in workers with occupational asthma. *B.M.J.*, **50**: 491–496.

47. Mrabani, A., Dimich-Ward, H., Kwan, S.Y.L., Kennedy, S.M., Waxler-Morrison, N., and Chan-Yeung M. (1993); Clinical and socioeconomic features of subjects with red cedar asthma: a follow-up study. *Chest*, **104**:821–824.

48. Axon, E.J., Beach, J.R., and Burge, P.S. (1995). A comparison of some of the characteristics of patients with occupational and non-occupational asthma. *Occup. Med.*, **45**:109–111.

49. Cannon, J., Cullinan, P., and Taylor, A.N. (1995). Consequences of occupational asthma. *B.M.J.* **311**:602–603.

50. Ameille, J., Pairon, J.C., Bayeux, M.C., Brochard, P., Choudat, D., Conso, F., Devienne, A., Garnier, R., and Iwatsubo, Y. (1997). Consequences of occupational asthma on employment and financial status: a follow-up study. *Eur. Respir. J.*, **10**: 55–58.

51. Salvaggio, J., ed. (1979). Occupational and environmental respiratory disease in the NIAID task force report: asthma and other allergic disease. NIH publication No. 79–387. Washington, D.C., U.S. Department of Health Education, and Welfare.

52. Kobayashi, S. (1980). Different aspects of occupational asthma in Japan. In *Occupational Asthma*. Edited by Frazier, C.A. New York: Van Nostrand Reinhold, pp. 229–244.

53. Blanc, P. (1987). Occupational asthma in a national disability survey. *Chest*, **92**: 613–617.

54. Syabbalo, N. (1991). Occupational asthma in a developing country (letter). *Chest*, **99**:528.

55. Timmer, S.T., and Rosenman, K. (1993). Occurrence of occupational asthma. *Chest*, **104**:816–820.

56. Xu, X., and Christiani, D.C. (1993). Occupational exposures and physician-diagnosed asthma. *Chest*, **104**:1364–1370.

57. Milton, D., and Christiani, D. (1997). The risk of asthma attributable to occupational exposures: a population-based study in Spain (letter). *Am. J. Respir. Crit. Care Med.*, **155**:382.

58. Ng, T.P., Hong, C.Y., Goh, L.G., Wong, M.L., Koh, K.T.C., and Ling, S.L. (1994). Risks of asthma associated with occupations in a community-based case-control study. *Am. J. Ind. Med.*, **25**:709–718.

59. Kogevinas, M., Anto, J.M., Soriano, J.B., Tobias, A., and Burney, P. (1996). The risk of asthma attributable to occupational exposures: a population-based study in Spain. *Am. J. Respir. Crit. Care. Med.*, **154**:137–143.

60. Blanc, P.D., Cisternas, M., Smith, S., and Yelin, E. (1996). Occupational asthma in a community-based survey of adult asthma. *Chest*, **109**:56s–57s.

61. Blanc, P.D. (1996). Occupation and asthma: through a glass, darkly (editorial). *Chest*, **110**:3–5.

62. National Health Interview Survey, 1988. (1992). Occupational health public use data tape. Bethesda, Md., National Center for Health Statistics.

63. Reijula, K., Haahtela, T., Klaukka, T., and Rantanen, J. (1996). Incidence of occupational asthma and persistent asthma in young adults has increased in Finland. *Chest,* **110**:50–61.

64. Fishwick, D., Pearce, N., D'Souza, W., Lewis, S., Town, I., Armstrong, R., Kogevinas, M., and Crane, J. (1997). Occupational asthma in New Zealanders: a population based survey. *Occup. Environ. Med.,* **54**:301–306.

65. Tarlo, S., Leung, K., Broder, I., Silverman, F., Holmes, D.L. (1997). Prevalence and characterization of asthmatics symptomatically worse at work among a general asthma clinic population (abstr.). *Chest,* **112**:133s.

66. Milton, D.K., Solomon, G., Rosiello, R.A., and Herrick, R.F. (1998). Risk and incidence of asthma attributable to occupational exposure among HMO members. *Am. J. Ind. Med.,* **33**:1–10.

67. Meridith, S., and Nordman, H. (1996). Occupational asthma: measures of frequency from four countries. *Thorax,* **51**:435–440.

68. Toren, K. (1996). Self reported rate of Occupational asthma in Sweden 1990–2. *Occup. Environ. Med.,* **53**:757–761.

69. McWhorter, W.P., Polis, M.A., and Kaslow, R.A. (1989). Occurrence, predictors, and consequences of adult asthma in NHANES 1 and follow-up survey. *Am. Rev. Respir. Dis.,* **139**:721–24

70. Cline, M.G., Dodge, R., Lebowitz, M.D., and Burrows, B. (1994). Determinants of percent predicted FEV_1 in current asthmatic subjects. *Chest,* **106**:1089–1093.

71. Bailey, W.C., Richards, J.M. Jr., Manzella, B.A., Brooks, C.M., Windsor, R.A., and Soong, S.J. (1990). Characteristics and correlates of asthma in a university clinic population. *Chest,* **98**:821–828.

72. Cartier, A., Malo, J.L., Forest, F., Lafrance, M., Pineau, L., St-Aubin, J.J., and Dubois, J.Y. (1984). Occupational asthma in snow crab-processing workers. *J. Allergy Clin. Immunol.,* **74**:261–269.

73. Venables, K.M., Dally, M.B., Nunn, A.J., Stevens, J.F., Stephens, R., Farrer, N., and Hunter, J.V. (1989). Smoking and occupational allergy in workers in a platinum refinery. *Br. Med. J.,* **299**:939–942.

74. Blanc, P.D., Galbo, M., Hiatt, P., and Olson, K.R. (1991). Morbidity following acute irritant inhalation in a population-based study. *J.A.M.A.,* **266**:664–669.

75. Harber, P., and Fedoruk, M.J. (1994). Work placement and worker fitness: implications of the Americans with Disabilities Act for pulmonary medicine. *Chest,* **105**:1564–1571.

5

Measuring Health-Related Quality of Life for Persons with Asthma
An Overview

ELIZABETH F. JUNIPER

McMaster University Medical Center
Hamilton, Ontario, Canada

I. Introduction

Many asthma clinicians now recognize the importance of incorporating an assessment of health-related quality of life into their clinical studies and clinical practice. Conventional measures of asthma severity and asthma control—such as spirometry, medication use, symptom severity, airway hyperresponsiveness, and sputum analysis—provide valuable information about the status of the airways but they tell us very little about the functional impairments (physical, emotional, and social) that are important to asthma patients in their everyday lives. One of the aims of treating patients with asthma should be to ensure that the functional impairments that are important to them are identified and that improvement of patient well-being is included in the treatment plan.

II. Health-Related Quality of Life (HRQL)

The quality of a person's life is usually considered in terms of its richness, completeness, and contentedness, and there are a number of factors that are usually considered important in determining this sense of well-being. These factors include good health, a secure social and occupational environment, financial security, spirituality, self-confidence, and strong, supportive family relationships. Each of these factors on its own may be a determinant of a person's quality of life and is also closely interrelated with all the others. For instance, a patient will often be able to deal with an illness better if she has good family support, a strong faith, and the financial ability to acquire nourishing food, adequate shelter, and good treatment.

In recent years, the term *health-related quality of life* (HRQL) has emerged as an important component of health care. HRQL can be considered as that part of a person's overall quality of life that is determined primarily by his or her health status and that can be influenced by clinical interventions. The definition by Schipper and colleagues is both simple and focused (1): "the functional effects of an illness and its consequent therapy upon a patient, as perceived by the patient." The final phrase is important because it emphasizes that these are the impairments that the patients themselves consider important.

In a number of medical conditions, it is often functional impairments, rather than the actual symptoms, that first cause patients to seek medical help. For instance, a patient with asthma may first seek help because she is having difficulties working in an animal laboratory. Another patient may be limited in her sporting activities. Yet another may be having difficulties with her housework and another may be bothered by the cigarette smoke with which her boss surrounds himself and his colleagues. Although these patients may be bothered by asthma symptoms, they seek help primarily because they are unable to do everyday activities as well or as enjoyably as they would like.

For centuries, clinicians depended almost entirely on a medical history, with some clinical signs, for diagnosis and for the evaluation of treatment effectiveness. The medical history usually included not only an exploration of the patient's symptoms but an assessment of the ways in which the patient was limited in daily activities and how this made him feel. Over the last three decades, modern diagnostic technology has developed at a phenomenal rate and the availability of quantified measurements of organ function has tended reduce the preeminence of the medical history for evaluating the status of the affected organ and thus less attention has tended to be paid to a patient's functional status and well-being.

This growth in technology has certainly occurred in asthma, where, starting with spirometry in the 1960s, we began to make measurements of airway function. By the end of the 1980s, we had well-standardized methods for measuring airway responsiveness to such stimuli as histamine, methacholine, cold and dry air, exercise, hypo- and hypertonic solutions, and allergens (2). Now, in the 1990s, we have methods for measuring sputum cells to tell us about the inflammatory status of the airways (3). There can be no doubt that the development of each of these new technologies has been very important in helping clinicians to estimate the inflammatory status of the airways and the adequacy of clinical asthma control and to evaluate the efficacy of interventions on airway function.

Fortunately, with the advent of HRQL instruments during the last decade, the balance is being redressed and we can now include quantified measures of functional status to ensure that this component of overall health status is also taken into consideration. There has been an enormous advance in psychometric methodology and we are now able to develop questionnaires that are rigorous scientific instruments and have the ability to provide a quantified and accurate assessment of a patient's subjective functional status. These subjective experiences of the patient, which we previously considered rather qualitative and nebulous, can now be used with measures of airway function to provide a more complete picture of the patient's overall health status.

III. The Importance of HRQL in Asthma

It has been proposed that there are three reasons for treating patients: to prevent mortality, to reduce the probability of future morbidity, and to improve patient well-being (4). Most conventional clinical measures of asthma control and severity—such as spirometry, medication requirements, symptoms, airway hyperresponsiveness, and sputum cells—assess the status of the airways and are primarily used to gauge whether the first two goals are being achieved. In the past, it was frequently assumed that these measures also provided insight into patients' well-being. Certainly, patients with very severe asthma tend to have a worse HRQL than patients with milder disease, but there is a growing body of evidence showing that correlations between clinical measures and how patients feel and how they are able to function in daily activities are only weak to moderate (5–8) (Table 1). Therefore, to obtain a complete picture of a patient's health status, HRQL must be measured along with the conventional clinical indices.

Why should the relationship between asthma clinical measures and HRQL be so weak? Let us take as an example two hypothetical patients with identical clinical asthma. Both women are 35 years of age with a moderate degree of bronchoconstriction (FEV$_1$: 65% predicted) and moderate airway hyperresponsiveness to methacholine (PC$_{20}$: 1 mg/mL). The first patient has very poor perception of airway narrowing; she works at home and can regulate her lifestyle according to how she feels. She lives a very sedentary life and is generally a very relaxed person. The second patient is very different. She has very acute perception of airway narrowing, she works in a high-pressure job and has to attend meetings where people smoke. She is an athlete and is very "uptight." In the past, she has had a life-threatening asthma episode. Although both of these patients present with similar degrees of airway narrowing and hyperresponsiveness, the second patient is likely to have much greater impairment of HRQL than the former as

Table 1 Longitudinal Correlations Between Quality of Life and Clinical Outcomes in Adults with Asthma

Change in clinical outcomes	Change in Asthma Quality of Life Questionnaire scores				
	Overall HRQL	Symptoms	Emotions	Activities	Environment
PEF[a]—morning	0.58	0.60	0.56	0.43	0.42
PEF—evening	0.48	0.50	0.43	0.36	0.40
Morning symptoms	0.47	0.49	0.45	0.38	0.28
Disturbance-free nights	0.28	0.30	0.26	0.20	0.17
Daytime symptoms	0.54	0.52	0.54	0.45	0.44
FEV_1	0.38	0.36	0.37	0.33	0.28
Salbutamol use	0.43	0.41	0.46	0.35	0.29

[a]PEF = peak expiratory flow.
Source: From Ref. 5.

a result of her asthma. Similar scenarios can easily be imagined for children with asthma where additional factors, such as family support and desire to keep up with peers, will also affect the child's HRQL.

IV. HRQL Impairments in Asthma

A. Adults

Extensive research has highlighted the functional impairments that are most troublesome to adults with asthma (9–17) (Table 2). They are certainly bothered by the symptoms themselves. The most troublesome are usually shortness of breath, chest tightness, wheeze, and cough. Many patients have problems with physical

Table 2 Functional Impairments Most Important to Adults with Asthma

Symptoms	Emotions	Activities	Environment
Shortness of breath	Afraid of not having medications available	Exercise/sports	Cigarettes
Chest tightness	Afraid of getting out of breath	Hurrying	Dust
Wheeze	Concerned about the need to use medications	Social activities	Air pollution
Cough		Pets	Cold air
Tired	Frustrated	Housework	Pollen

Source: From Ref. 9.

Table 3 Functional Impairments Most Important to Children with Asthma

Symptoms	Activities	Emotions
Shortness of breath	Sports and games	Feel different and left out
Chest tightness	Activities with friends	Frustrated
Cough	Playing with pets	Angry
Wheeze	School activities	Sad
Tired	Sleeping	Frightened/anxious

Source: From Ref. 20.

activities such as sports, hurrying, going up stairs, and shopping. Allergens may cause difficulties with daily activities such as vacuuming and other household chores, gardening, and hobbies. Environmental stimuli—such as cigarette smoke, strong smells, and troublesome weather conditions—may limit family and social activities. Asthma patients are bothered by not being able to get a good night's sleep and often feel tired. In addition, they experience fears and concerns about having asthma and the need for medications, and they become frustrated by their limitations. Several studies have now shown that women tend to experience greater impairment of HRQL than men with similar clinical asthma severity (8,9,14,18). Occupational asthma causes its own special problems, with HRQL being poorer in these patients than in clinically matched patients whose asthma is not of occupational origin (19).

B. Children

The burden of illness and functional impairments experienced by children with asthma are similar to those experienced by adults (Table 3). In addition, children are troubled because they cannot integrate fully with their peers; they feel isolated and left out, and this often causes them to feel frustrated, irritable, and angry (20–26). There is growing evidence that parents often have a poor perception of the problems and emotions that are troubling the child, so it is essential to obtain HRQL information directly from the child (27–30). Few studies suggest children as young as 6 years of age have little difficulty understanding HRQL questionnaires, and they are able to provide reliable and valid responses (31,32) (Table 4).

V. Selecting a HRQL Instrument

We now have a range of instruments for measuring HRQL in both adults and children with asthma. There is no best instrument. Each one has been developed for a different purpose and has different measurement properties.

Table 4 Reliability of the Pediatric Asthma Quality of Life Questionnaire in Children with Stable Asthma

	Reliability (intraclass correlation coefficient)			
Age groups	Overall HRQL	Symptoms	Activities	Emotions
All subjects	0.95	0.93	0.84	0.89
7–10 years	0.89	0.87	0.83	0.68
11–14 years	0.96	0.95	0.86	0.92
15–17 years	0.87	0.89	0.67	0.80

Source: From Ref. 20.

A. Generic Versus Specific Questionnaires

There are two types of HRQL questionnaires, generic and specific (Table 5). Generic health status questionnaires or health profiles are designed to be applicable to patients in all health states. Among the most commonly used and the best-validated in adults are the Sickness Impact Profile (SIP) (33), the Medical Outcomes Survey Short Form 36 (SF-36) (34), the Nottingham Health Profile (35), and the Dartmouth COOP charts (36). In recent years, shorter versions of some of these original instruments have become available. For children, there is the Functional Status II (R) Scale (FSII9R) (37) and a children's version of the Rand SF-36 (38).

The strength of generic instruments is that burden of illness can be compared across different medical conditions. For example, one can compare the burden of illness experienced by patients with rhinitis and asthma (39,40). However, because they are required to be broad in their comprehensiveness to cover all medical conditions, these instruments have very little depth and, as a result, impairments that are important to patients with a specific condition may not be included. Consequently, in many conditions, including asthma, generic instruments may be unresponsive to small but what to the patients are important changes in their HRQL (6,31). Therefore, the use of generic instruments in clinical trials and clinical practice, where one wants to examine the effect of treatment within individuals or groups of patients, is limited.

This lack of depth of focus and lack of responsiveness has led to the development of specific instruments. These instruments may be specific for a group of patients (e.g., the elderly), a particular function (e.g., pain, sexual function), or a disease. Disease-specific questionnaires measure the problems and limitations that patients with a specific disease experience in their day-to-day lives. They are developed by asking the patients themselves about the impairments that are most important to them and therefore these instruments focus on the problems for which patients seek help. Disease-specific questionnaires are consistently

Table 5 Types of HRQL Instruments

Instrument type	Strengths	Weaknesses
Generic health profiles	Comparison across conditions possible	Inadequate focus on areas of specific impairment
	Established reliability and validity	May not be responsive
Utilities	Single number representing quality of life	Cannot examine different aspects of quality of life
	Cost-utility analysis possible	May not be responsive
Disease-specific questionnaires	Focus on problems important to patients	Comparison across different conditions not possible
	More responsive	
	Clinical trials and practice	

more responsive than generic questionnaires to within-patient changes over time that may occur spontaneously or as the result of an intervention. Therefore, they are particularly well suited for monitoring the effect of interventions in both clinical trials and clinical practice. When used in clinical practice, they are much more likely than generic instruments to reveal important patient-specific problems.

B. Utilities

These instruments measure the value or utility that either the patient or society places on various health states. They are very popular with health economists not only because they provide a single number representing HRQL from $0 =$ death to $1 =$ perfect health but also because the majority of instruments meet the assumptions for utility theory and can be used for estimating quality-adjusted life years (QALYs) (41). For measuring the value that patients themselves place on their own health state, the most commonly used instruments are the Standard Gamble (41), the Time Trade-Off (41), and the Feeling Thermometer (41). (The latter is not a true utility but it does provide a HRQL score between 0 and 1.) For measuring the value that society places on various health states, there are the Quality of Well-being Scale (42), the Multiattribute Health Utilities Index (43), and the EuroQol (44). For a long time, these instruments were used only in generic form—i.e., to be applicable in all medical conditions—and in this form they have the same weakness as the generic health profiles in asthma: they are unresponsive to important changes (6,31). Recently, the Standard Gamble and the Feeling Thermometer have been modified for use as disease-specific instruments in children with asthma and appear to have much improved measurement properties (31). Even more recent data have revealed a similar pattern in adults (Juniper et al., manuscript in preparation).

C. Measurement Properties

Face and Content Validity

When selecting an instrument, it is important to ensure that it has both face and content validity; that is to say, the instrument appears to measure what it purports to measure (face validity) (45) and that the items in a questionnaire have been selected using recognized psychometric procedures ensuring that they capture all the areas of function considered important by patients (content validity) (46). Questionnaires, in which items have been selected by clinicians, rarely meet this criterion because some impairments that patients themselves consider important may have been omitted. This is particularly important when considering HRQL questionnaires for children, because even parents often have a very poor perception of the physical and emotional problems their child is experiencing (27–30).

Measurement properties should also be examined to ensure that the instrument is capable of the intended task. Instruments that are to be used in cross-sectional studies (e.g., surveys) need to possess good discriminative properties and those used in longitudinal studies (e.g., clinical trials and clinical practice) must have good evaluative properties (47) (Table 6).

Discriminative Properties

Instruments that are to be used to distinguish between individuals or groups of patients need to possess good discriminative properties. For example, a clinician may wish to examine differences in the HRQL between individuals who do and do not have asthma or, within an asthmatic population, between those who have mild, moderate, or severe impairment. The measurement properties required for good discrimination are reliability (sensitivity to between-subject differences) and cross-sectional construct validity (scores correlating in a predicated way with clinical asthma indices and other measures of HRQL) (47). (Cronbach's alpha is a measure of internal consistency and does not provide evidence of an instrument's discriminative properties. In addition, Fayers and Hand have recently argued very cogently that internal consistency is often an inappropriate measurement property for HRQL questionnaires (48).

Evaluative Properties

Instruments that are to be used to measure longitudinal change within an individual or group of patients must have good evaluative properties. For example, a clinician may wish to examine the effect of an intervention in a clinical trial or follow the progress of a patient in the clinic. The measurement properties required for good evaluation are responsiveness (sensitivity to within-subject change) and

Table 6 Measurement Properties Necessary for Evaluative and Discriminative Instruments

	Discriminative instruments	Evaluative instruments
Signal	Between-patient differences	Within-patient changes related to true within-patient change
Noise	Within-patient differences	Within-patient changes unrelated to true within-patient change
Signal-to-noise ratio (descriptive term)	Reliability	Responsiveness
Construct validity	Cross-sectional	Longitudinal

longitudinal validity (changes in score correlate in a predicted way with changes in clinical indices and other measures of HRQL (47). Questionnaires with good reliability and cross-sectional validity often have poor evaluative properties and fail to detect important changes in asthma quality of life (6,31).

D. Individualized Versus Standardized Questions

Even if one uses a disease-specific quality-of-life questionnaire to focus on the problems most commonly experienced by patients within that condition, no questionnaire is ever going to cover all the problems experienced by all patients from all races, cultures, age groups, etc. Recognizing that one of the aims of HRQL questionnaires is to identify and measure the problems that are most important to patients, some questionnaires include patient-specific or "individualized" questions. At the first visit, a patient will identify the problems that are most important and troublesome, and these same problems will be evaluated at each subsequent visit. Although slightly time-consuming at the first visit, this approach has the advantage of improving content validity; overcoming cultural, age, and gender differences; and improving the appeal to the individual patient who feels that his or her own problems are important to the investigator or clinician and are being taken into consideration.

However, for long-term studies, where individual activities and priorities may change over time and for large clinical trials, where individual patient problems and optimal content validity are less crucial, this feature is less important and standardized activities may be more appropriate (49). Standardized activities are better suited for cross-sectional surveys and studies comparing the burden of illness between patients or groups of patients.

E. How Many Questions Should There Be in a Questionnaire?

The original generic health profiles were very long, often with more than a hundred questions. Although this enhanced breadth and depth of comprehensiveness, they were time-consuming for clinic staff and often wearying for the patient. In the last few years, we have experienced a demand from the pharmaceutical industry, clinicians, and managed-care organizations for ever shorter and simpler questionnaires. Time is money and long questionnaires take time. We have seen the generic Medical Outcomes Survey Short Form 36 (SF-36) collapsed from 36 to 12 items. Under pressure to shorten our own 32-item Asthma Quality of Life Questionnaire (AQLQ), we have developed and validated the 15-item Mini-AQLQ (50). However, there is a price to pay for brevity and simplicity.

The greatest loss is probably in content validity. Even a disease-specific questionnaire is never going to be able to cover all the problems experienced by all patients and, in shortening questionnaires, these individual and often important problems are going to fall by the wayside and become ignored. Is this important?

Maybe not in large clinical trials and long-term practice monitoring, where the sole interest is in obtaining the mean results from a large number of patients. However, we are now beginning to see the inclusion of HRQL assessments in the routine clinical evaluation of individual patients. If HRQL questionnaires are used in this environment to identify individual patient problems and to follow these problems over time to determine the effect of interventions, then the shortened questionnaires are likely to be very inadequate because they will miss important individual problems.

The second loss in shortening questionnaires is to reliability and responsiveness (50). The loss of precision has implications when calculating sample sizes for clinical trials and surveys. In the case of the MiniAQLQ, we have calculated that sample sizes need to be double those required for the AQLQ (50). The cost of having to recruit twice the number of subjects for a study may outweigh the cost of completing a 32-versus 15-item questionnaire.

VI. Interpreting Quality-of-Life Data

Repeated experience with a wide variety of physiological measures allows clinicians to make a meaningful interpretation of results. For instance, the experienced clinician will have little difficulty in interpreting a 0.5 liter increase in FEV_1. In contrast, the meaning of a change in score of 0.5 on a HRQL instrument is less intuitively obvious, not only because there are no units but also because each instrument has its own scoring system. Two approaches have been suggested for interpreting HRQL data: these are "anchor-based" and "distribution-based" (51). The former bases interpretation on clinically meaningful changes in other indices, while the latter depends entirely on statistical distribution. The limitation of using the statistical approach is that even if one calculates the effect size, there is no evidence that this magnitude of change is of any importance to the patient.

Our research group has adopted the anchor-based approach. We have used patient perception of a meaningful change in HRQL as the anchor and defined a minimal important difference (MID) as "the smallest difference in score in the domain of interest which patients perceive as beneficial and would mandate, in the absence of troublesome side-effects and excessive cost, a change in the patient's management" (52). A similar anchor-based approach has been used for the St. George's Respiratory Questionnaire (53).

For many years, statistically aware clinical investigators have cautioned against the sole use of mean data and statistical significance for the interpretation of clinical trial data. One of the reasons for this is that patients may be very heterogeneous in their responses to interventions. Wide heterogeneity (i.e., large standard deviation) may be well hidden if only the standard error of the mean is presented. However, if the MID is known, the problem can easily be addressed by calculating the number needed to treat (NNT) (54). The NNT is the number of patients who need to be treated with the new intervention for one patient to have a clinically important improvement over and above that which he or she would have experienced with the control intervention. Presentation of clinical trial results in this manner is more meaningful and much easier to interpret than standard deviations and confidence intervals for both for clinicians and health policymakers.

Figure 1 shows the results from a Canadian multicenter clinical trial that compared the effect of salmeterol, salbutamol, and placebo on asthma-specific quality of life (5). It was a double-blind, randomized, crossover study with patients taking each trial medication for 4 weeks. At the end of each treatment period, patients completed the AQLQ. It can be seen that for the symptom domain of the AQLQ, the difference between salmeterol and placebo was 0.66 and highly statistically significant. The mean difference between the two treatments was greater than the MID of 0.5 and therefore can be considered of clinical importance. However, the difference between salmeterol and salbutamol in the symptom domain was 0.49—highly statistically significant but on the borderline of being clinically important. In the activity domain, both the difference between

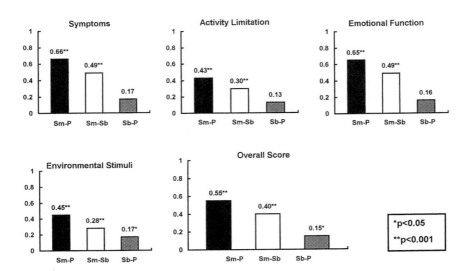

Figure 1 Comparison of the effects of salmetrol (sm), salbutamol (sb), and placebo (P) on asthma-specific quality of life. The vertical bars represent the differences in AQLQ scores between pairs of treatments. (From Juniper et al., 1995.)

salmeterol and placebo (0.43) and the difference between salmeterol and salbutamol (0.33) were highly statistically significant but below the MID. In the past we may have interpreted these data as indicating that the difference between salmeterol and salbutamol for both symptoms and activities was not of clinical importance. However, we would have been basing our interpretation only on the mean data, and this would have been erroneous. Table 7 shows the results of the salmeterol/salbutamol comparison in terms of the proportion of patients benefiting (difference between the two treatments > MID) from the two interventions (55). From these, we have calculated the NNT and shown that even though differences between the two active treatments was less than 0.5, only a relatively small number of patients need to be treated with salmeterol for one to have a clinically important improvement in quality of life over and above that which would have been experienced on salbutamol.

This approach to clinical trial data interpretation is clearly beneficial to clinicians who can tell patients about the probability of benefit from a certain intervention. For instance, for an NNT of 5, the clinician would be able to tell the patient that there would be a 20% chance of benefit from the drug.

VII. Cultural Adaptation of HRQL Questionnaires

The validity of translating HRQL questionnaires for cultures and ethnic groups that are very different from the original development sample has not yet been adequately addressed. The main concern is content validity. Do patients around the world experience different problems because of their asthma? Although we have no formal studies, anecdotal reports are very consistent and suggest that if

Table 7 Number Needed to Treat—Salmeterol Versus Salbutamol

AQLQ domain	Mean difference (p value)	Proportion better on salmeterol	Proportion better on salbutamol	Proportion benefiting from salmeterol	Number needed to treat (NNT)[a]
Symptoms	0.49 (<0.0001)	0.42	0.12	0.30	3.3
Activities	0.30 (<0.0001)	0.32	0.10	0.22	4.5

[a]Number of patients who need to be treated with salmeterol for one to experience a clinically important benefit over and above what he or she would have experienced on salbutamol.
Source: From Ref. 55.

recognized procedures are followed for the translation process, content validity and other measurement properties will be very comparable to the original instrument. For example, during the pretesting of the AQLQ throughout eastern and western Europe, North America, Russia, the Middle East, Australasia, and Japan, patients told us that all their asthma-related problems are well covered by the questions in the AQLQ. In addition, measurement properties (internal consistency, reliability, responsiveness, and construct validity) of high-quality translations are very consistent (6,10,56). Other asthma questionnaire developers have described similar findings (personal communications). This suggests that good-quality cultural adaptations in asthma are acceptable and a new questionnaire for each country is unnecessary.

Adapting quality-of-life questionnaires to other languages and cultures is considerably more complicated than just doing a simple translation (57). This complex procedure is required to ensure that the concept underlying each item is captured accurately in the new language, that the measurement properties of the original instrument are maintained, that there is content validity for the new country, and that the new questionnaire is easily and accurately understood by patients. A recommended procedure for the cultural adaptation of a HRQL questionnaire is as follows: (a) Two independent forward translations by translators whose primary language is the one into which the questionnaire is being translated. These translators should have some training in psychometrics and be familiar with medical terminology. (b) Reconciliation of the two forward translations. (c) Two independent backward translations of the reconciled version by translators whose primary language is that of the original questionnaire. This phase helps to ensure that there are no inaccuracies or ambiguities in the reconciled version. (d) International harmonization. Often it is difficult to find words that exactly reflect the meaning of the original language. For instance, when translating the AQLQ, there is no exact translation of *frustrated* in the Nordic languages. Two words were needed to cover the concept, and these were used in all these languages. (e) Pretesting in patients. The purpose of this phase is to ensure that the patients have no difficulty in understanding the meaning of each question, the instructions, the response options, and their task in completing the questionnaire. In addition, one checks that patients understand the correct conceptual meaning of each question, that all important asthma-related problems are included, and that none of the questions is irrelevant.

Ideally, every translation should undergo a full validation study in every new language to test its measurement properties. However, since these are expensive and time-consuming studies, they are rarely feasible and the organization funding the translation invariably wants the translation yesterday. Fortunately, evidence is now beginning to emerge showing that questionnaires that are translated carefully and following recommended procedures have measurement properties that are very similar to those of the original instrument (6,10,56). This suggests that a full validation study in every language is unnecessary.

Adapting a quality-of-life questionnaire should never be undertaken without the permission of the developer. However, the need should rarely occur because many of the questionnaires used in asthma are available in a very large number of languages and can easily be obtained from the developer.

VIII. Modification of Questionnaires

HRQL questionnaires are scientific instruments in which the items and response options have been selected using carefully standardized and established psychometric methods. Any modifications may seriously affect the measurement properties and validity of the instrument. For this reason most questionnaires are copyrighted and no changes or adaptations should be made without the permission of the developer.

IX. Methods of Questionnaire Administration

HRQL questionnaires are now available for adults in a wide variety of formats, the most common being interviewer-, self-, and telephone-administered paper versions and more recently self-administered computer versions. Each method has its strengths and weaknesses (Table 8), and investigators should choose the one best suited for the task at hand.

Clinicians are often concerned that children are not capable of completing HRQL questionnaires (58). Children certainly need careful teaching to understand their task and interviewers need to be trained in the correct techniques for administering HRQL questionnaires in children. Videos are now available to help inexperienced interviewers. If they are taught properly, children as young as 6 years old are very good at completing questionnaires reliably and providing valid responses (16,24,25). A key problem that we and other investigators have encountered has been with the time specification. The concept of time does not develop until about 7 to 8 years of age and we have found that younger children often require an event marker when asked to recall experiences ''during the last week.''

There is minimal information in the literature about the ability of children to complete self-administered HRQL questionnaires. We addressed this in a recent study in which symptomatic asthmatic children, who had never seen the PAQLQ before, completed the self-administered version on the first day and had it administered by a trained interviewer on the second day. Much to our surprise,

Table 8 Strengths and Weaknesses of Data-Collection Methods

	Interviewer	Self (unassisted)	Telephone	Computer (unassisted)
Missing data	Unlikely	More likely	Unlikely	None
Errors of completion (e.g., two responses, response between two options)	Unlikely	More likely	Unlikely	None
Errors of understanding (items and responses)	Unlikely	More likely	Less likely	More likely
Trained interviewer	Yes	No	Yes	No
Clinic staff time	Quite a lot	Little	Quite a lot	Little
Patient unable to read	Possible	Impossible	Difficult	Impossible
Data transcription errors	Yes	Yes	Yes	No
Availability of summary	Hand calculation	Hand calculation	Hand calculation	Yes
Confidence that responses are the patient's own	Yes	Only if patient completes it when alone	Only if patient's voice is recognized	Only if patient completes it when alone

a number of 7-year-olds completed the self-administered version easily and provided data that was almost identical to those collected on the second day. In contrast, some children, with quite advanced reading skills, made a total mess of the self-administered version. Initial analysis suggested that these were predominantly male and appeared to be unwilling to concentrate on the task at hand.

X. Software

Computerized versions of some questionnaires are now available, often in very simple, patient-friendly, palm-top, touch-screen formats. These are obviously ideal for clinical trial data collection because they eliminate the problems of "missing data" and transcription errors. They will also probably prove very useful in clinical practice because of their ability to provide immediate summary scores and graphical printouts of longitudinal trends.

XI. HRQL in Research

The recognition of the importance of assessing patient well-being, the poor correlation between conventional clinical indices and HRQL, and the advent of HRQL instruments with strong measurement properties has already ensured that many asthma clinical studies include an assessment of HRQL as one of the primary endpoints. Most instruments are short, easily understood, and usually in self-administered format, making completion very little burden either to the investigator or the patient. We have found that patients enjoy completing HRQL questionnaires because they can relate to the questions and know that the things that are important to them are being taken into consideration. In addition, national pharmaceutical regulatory agencies are beginning to ask for evidence of patient benefit for new product submissions.

XII. HRQL in Clinical Practice

The use of HRQL instruments in clinical practice is growing. Disease-specific quality-of-life questionnaires provide a standardized and quantified method for taking a simple patient history. They ask the questions that clinicians have been asking for generations: Does your asthma limit you in your daily activities? Are your symptoms bothering you? Is your asthma giving you problems at work? Are you concerned about having asthma and the need to take medications? Did the new medication help? The advantages of a questionnaire are that the patient can complete it while waiting for the consultation, a quick scan of the responses will save consultation time, and the interviewer does not have to remember all the important questions. In addition, the questionnaire will often reveal problems not spontaneously identified by the patient (particularly children); the clinician can quickly focus on areas of particular bother; and responses at each clinic visit can be compared to determine whether interventions have been beneficial. Changes over time can be recorded more accurately than through patient recall and long-term data bases can be established.

A limitation to the use of quality-of-life questionnaires in clinical practice is that they have been developed to measure the problems that are most important to the majority of patients with asthma. Patients are heterogeneous in their experiences and priorities and no questionnaire is going to cover all the problems experienced by all patients. Therefore, clinicians should never depend solely on HRQL questionnaires to provide them with a complete and comprehensive picture of the patient's concerns and impairments.

The use of HRQL in clinical practice is in its infancy and we now need good clinical studies to evaluate whether its inclusion benefits patient management and is cost-effective. Until such data are available, the beneficial use of these instruments in clinical practice can only be speculative.

XIII. Conclusion

Asthma-specific quality of life correlates poorly with the conventional clinical measures of asthma control in both adults and children. Since one of the aims of treatment must be to ensure that patients themselves benefit, quality of life must be measured directly. Asthma-specific quality-of-life questionnaires are now available for both adults and children and can easily be included in both clinical practice and clinical research.

References

1. Schipper, H., Clinch, J., and Powell, V. (1996). Definitions and conceptual issues. In *Quality of Life and Pharmacoeconomics in Clinical Trials*. Edited by B. Spilker, Philadelphia, Lippincott-Raven, pp. 11–23.
2. Sterk, P.J., Fabbri, L.M., Quanjer, Ph.H., Cockcroft, D.W., O'Byrne, P.M., Anderson, S.D., Juniper, E.F., and Malo J-L. (1993). Airway responsiveness—Standardized lung function testing: official statement of the European Respiratory Society. *Eur. Respir. J.* **6**:54–79.
3. Hargreave, F.E., Pizzichini, M.M.M., and Pizzichini, E. (1997). Assessment of airway inflammation. In *Asthma*. Edited by P.J. Barnes, M.M. Grunstein, A.R, Leff, and A.J. Woolcock. Philadelphia, Lippincott-Raven, pp. 1433–1450.
4. Guyatt, G.H., Naylor, D., Juniper, E.F., Heyland, D., Cook, D., and the Evidence-Based Medicine Working Group (1997). Users' guides to the medical literature: IX. How to use an article about health-related quality of life. *J.A.M.A.* **277**:1232–1237.

5. Juniper, E.F., Johnston, P.R., Borkhoff, C.M., Guyatt, G.H., Boulet, L.P., and Hauki-oja, A. (1995). Quality of life in asthma clinical trials: comparison of salmeterol and salbutamol. *Am. J. Respir. Crit. Care Med.* **151**:66–70.
6. Rutten-van Molken M.P.M.H., Clusters, F., Van Doorslaer, E.K.A., Jansen C.C.M., Heurman, L., Maesen, F.P.V., Smeets, J.J., Bommer, A.M., and Raaijmakers, J.A.M. (1995). Comparison of performance of four instruments in evaluating the effects of salmeterol on asthma quality of life. *Eur. Respir. J.* **8**:888–898.
7. Rowe, B.H., and Oxman, A.D. (1993). Performance of an asthma quality of life questionnaire in an outpatient setting. *Am. Rev. Respir. Dis.*, **148**:675–681.
8. Leidy, N.K., and Coughlin, C. Psychometric performance of the Asthma Quality of Life Questionnaire in a U.S. sample. *Qual. Life Res.* **7**:127–134.
9. Juniper, E.F., Guyatt, G.H., Epstein, R.S., Ferrie, P.J, Jaeschke, R., and Hiller, T.K. (1992) Evaluation of impairment of health-related quality of life in asthma: develop-ment of a questionnaire for use in clinical trials. *Thorax* **47**:76–83.
10. Juniper, E.F., Guyatt, G.H., Ferrie, P.J., and Griffith, L.E. (1993). Measuring quality of life in asthma. *Am. Rev. Respir. Dis.*, **147**:832–838.
11. Marks, G.B., Dunn, S.M., and Woolcock, A.J. (1992). A scale for the measurement of quality of life in adults with asthma. *J. Clin. Epidemiol.*, **45**:461–472.
12. Marks, G.B., Dunn, S.M., and Woolcock, A.J. (1993). An evaluation of an asthma quality of life questionnaire as a measure of change in adults with asthma. *J. Clin. Epidemiol.*, **46**:1103–1111.
13. Hyland, M.E. (1991). The living with asthma questionnaire. *Respir. Med.*, **85**:13–16.
14. Hyland, M.E., Finnis, S., and Irvine, S.H. (1991). A scale for assessing quality of life in adult asthma sufferers. *J. Psychom. Res.*, **35**:99–110.
15. Jones, P.W., Quirk, F.H., Baveystock, C.M., and Littlejohns, P. (1992). A self-com-plete measure of health status for chronic airflow limitation: the St. George's Respi-ratory Questionnaire. *Am. Rev. Respir. Dis.*, **145**:1321–1327.
16. Maille, A.R., Kaptein, A.A., Koning, C.J.M., and Zwinderman, A.H. (1994). Devel-oping a quality of life questionnaire for patients with respiratory illness. *Monaldi Arch. Chest Dis.*, **49**:76–78.
17. Creer, T.L., Wigal, J.K., Kotses, H., McConnaughy, K., and Winder, J.A. (1992). A life activities questionnaire for adult asthma. *J. Asthma*, **29**:393–399.
18. Quirk, F.H., Baveystock, C.M., Wilson, R., and Jones, P.W. (1991). Influence of demographic and disease related factors on the degree of distress associated with symptoms and restrictions on daily living due to asthma in six countries. *Eur. Respir. J.*, **4**:167–171.
19. Malo, J.L., Boulet, L.P., Dewitte, J.D., Cartier, A., L'Archeveque, J., Cote, J., Be-dard, G., Boucher, S., Champagne, F., Tessier, G., Contandriopoulos, A.P., Juniper, E.F., and Guyatt, G.H. (1993). Quality of life of subjects with occupational asthma. *J. Allergy Clin. Immunol.*, **91**:1121–1127.
20. Juniper, E.F. Guyatt, G.H., Feeny, D.H., Ferrie, P.J., Griffith, L.E. and Townsend, M. (1996). Measuring quality of life in children with asthma. *Qual. Life Res.*, **5**:35–46.
21. Townsend, M., Feeny, D.H., Guyatt, G.H., Seip, A.E., and Dolovich, J. (1991). Eval-uation of the burden of illness for pediatric asthmatic patients and their parents. *Ann. Allergy*, **67**:403–408.

22. Creer, T.L., Wigal, J.K., Kotses, H., Hatala, J.C. McConnaughy, K., and Winder, J.A. (1993). A life activities questionnaire for childhood asthma. *J. Asthma*, **30**:467–473.

23. Christie, M.J., French, D., Sowden, A., and West, A. (1993). Development of child-centred disease-specific questionnaires for living with asthma. *Psychosom. Med.*, **55**:541–548.

24. French, D.J., Christie, M.J., and Sowden, A.J. (1994). The reproducibility of the childhood asthma questionnaires: measures of quality of life for children with asthma aged 4–16 years. *Qual. Life Res.*, **3**:215–224.

25. Nocon, A. (1991). Social and emotional impact of childhood asthma. *Arch. Dis. Child.*, **66**:458–460.

26. Usherwood, T.P., Scrimgeour, A., and Barber, J.H. (1990). Questionnaire to measure perceived symptoms and disability in asthma. *Arch. Dis. Child.*, **65**:779–781.

27. Guyatt, G.H., Juniper, E.F., Feeny, D.H., and Griffith, L.E. (1997). Children and adult perceptions of childhood asthma. *Pediatrics*, **99**:165–168.

28. Rosenbaum, P.L., and Saigal, S. (1996). Measuring health-related quality of life in pediatric populations: conceptual issues. In *Quality of life and Pharmacoeconomics in Clinical* Trials. Edited by B. Spilker. Philadelphia, Lippencott Raven, pp. 785–791.

29. Wood, P.R., Hidalgo, H.A., Prihoda, T.J. and Kromer, M.E. (1994). Comparison of Hispanic children's and parents' responses to questions about the child's asthma. *Arch. Pediatr. Adolesc. Med.*, **148**:43.

30. Ronen, G. (1997). Initial steps in the development of a measurement instrument for health-related quality of life in children with epilepsy. MSc. thesis. Hamilton, Ontario, Canada, McMaster University.

31. Juniper, E.F., Guyatt, G.H., Feeny, D.H., Griffith, L.E., and Ferrie, P.J. (1997). Minimum skills required by children to complete health-related quality of life instruments: comparison of instruments for measuring asthma-specific quality of life. *Eur. Respir. J.*, **10**:2285–2294.

32. Juniper, E.F., Howland, W.C., Roberts, N.B., Thompson, A.K., and King, D.R. (1998). Measuring quality of life in children with rhinoconjunctivitis. *J. Allergy Clin. Immunol.*, **101**:163–170.

33. Bergner, M., Bobbitt, R.A., Carter, W.B., and Gilson, B.S. (1981). The sickness impact profile: development and final revision of a health status measure. *Med. Care*, **19**:787–805.

34. Stewart, A.L., Hays, R., and Ware, J.E. (1988). The MOS short-form general health survey: reliability and validity in a patient population. *Med. Care* **26**:724–732.

35. Hunt, S.M., McKenna, S.P., McEwen, J., et al. (1980). A quantitative approach to perceived health status: a validation study. *J. Epidemiol. Commun. Health*, **34**:281–286.

36. Nelson, E., Wasson, J., Kirk, J., Keller, A., Clark, D., Dietrich, A., Stewart, A., and Zubkoff, M. (1987). Assessment of function in routine clinical practice: description of the COOP chart method and preliminary findings. *J. Chronic Dis.*, **40**(suppl 1):S55.

37. Stein, R.E., and Jessop, D.J. (1990). Functional status II(R): a measure of child health status. *Med. Care* **28**:1041–1055.

38. Eisen, M., Ware, J.E., Donald, C.A., and Brook, R.H. (1979). Measuring components of children's health status. *Med. Care*, **17**:902–921.
39. Bousquet, J., Bullinger, M., Fayol, C., Marquis, P., Valentin, B., and Burtin, B. (1994). Assessment of quality of life in patients with perennial rhinitis with the French version of the SF-36 health status questionnaire. *J. Allergy Clin. Immunol.*, **94**:182–188.
40. Bousquet, J., Knani, J., Dhivert, H., Richard, A., Chicoye, A., Ware, J.E., and Michel, F.B. (1994). Quality of life in asthma: 1. Internal consistency and validity of the SF-36 questionnaire. *Am. J. Respir. Crit. Care Med.*, **149**:371–375.
41. Torrance, G.W. (1986). Measurement of health state utilities for economic appraisal. *J. Health Econ.*, **5**:1–30.
42. Kaplan, R.M., Anderson, J.P, Wu, A.W, Matthews, W.C., Kozin, F., and Orenstein, D. (1989). The Quality of Well-being Scale: application in AIDS, cystic fibrosis and arthritis. *Med. Care*, **27**:527–543.
43. Feeny, D., Furlong, W., Barr, R.D., Torrance, G.W., Rosenbaum, P., and Weitzman, S. (1997). A comprehensive multi-attribute system for classifying the health status of survivors of childhood cancer. *J. Clin. Oncol.*, **10**:923–925.
44. The EuroQol Group (1990). A new facility for the measurement of health-related quality of life. *Health Policy*, **16**:199–208.
45. Feinstein, A.R. (1987). The theory and evaluation of sensibility. In *Clinimetrics*. Edited by A.R. Feinstein. Westford, Mass., Murray Printing Co., pp. 141–166.
46. Juniper, E.F., Guyatt, G.H., and Jaeschke, R. How to develop and validate a new health-related quality of life instrument. In *Quality of Life and Pharmacoeconomics in Clinical Trials*. Edited by B. Spilker: Philadelphia, Lippencott Raven, pp. 49–56.
47. Guyatt, G.H., Kirshner, B., and Jaeschke, R. (1992). Measuring health status: what are the necessary measurement properties? *J. Clin. Epidemiol.*, **45**:1341–1345.
48. Fayers, P.M., and Hand, D.J. (1997). Factor analysis, causal indicators and quality of life. *Qual. Life Res.*, **6**:139–150.
49. Juniper, E.F., Buist, A.S., Cox, F.M., Ferrie, P.J., and King, D.R. Validation of a standardized version of the Asthma Quality of Life Questionnaire. *J. Allergy Clin Immunol.* (Conditionally accepted).
50. Juniper, E.F., Guyatt, G.H., Cox, F.M., Ferrie, P.J., and King, D.R. Development and validation of the Mini Asthma Quality of Life Questionnaire. *Am. J. Respir. Crit. Care Med.* (Conditionally accepted).
51. Lydick, E., and Epstein, R.S. (1993). Interpretation of quality of life changes. *Qual. Life Res.*, **2**:221–226.
52. Juniper, E.F., Guyatt, G.H., Willan, A., and Griffith, L.E. (1994). Determining a minimal important change in a disease-specific quality of life questionnaire. *J. Clin. Epidemiol.*, **47**:81–87.
53. Jones, P.W., and Lasserson, D. (1994). Relationship between change in St. George's Respiratory Questionnaire score and patients' perception of treatment efficacy after one year of therapy with nedocromil sodium. *Am. J. Respir. Crit. Care Med.*, **149**: A211.
54. Guyatt, G.H., Juniper, E.F. Walter, S.D., Griffith, L.E., and Goldstein, R.S. (1998). Interpreting treatment effects in randomised trials. *B.M.J.*, **316**:690–693.

55.   Juniper, E.F. (1997). The value of quality of life in asthma. *Eur. Respir. Rev.*, **49**: 333–337.
56.   Sanjuas, C., Alonso, J., Sanchis, J., Casan, P., Broquetas, J.M., Ferrie, P.J, Juniper, E.F., and Anto JM. (1995). The quality of life questionnaire with asthma patients; the Spanish version of the Asthma Quality of Life Questionnaire. *Arch. Bronconeumol.*, **31**:219–226.
57.   Guillemin, F., Bombardier, C., and Beaton, D., (1993). Cross-cultural adaptation of health-related quality of life measures: literature review and proposed guidelines. *J. Clin. Epidemiol.*, **46**:1417–1432.
58.   Bender, B.G. (1996). Measurement of quality of life in pediatric asthma clinical trials. *Ann. Allergy Asthma Immunol.*, **77**:438–447.

6

Current Methods in Measuring Health-Related Quality of Life in Children with Asthma

LYNN M. OLSON and LINDA ASMUSSEN

American Academy of Pediatrics
Elk Grove Village, Illinois

I. Introduction

A widespread consensus is emerging that the outcomes of pediatric care should move beyond traditional, clinical measures of morbidity to include assessments of quality of life.* Such tools make central the social and personal impact of disease and enable children and parents to provide input on how they view their quality of life and capacity to function in typical social roles. For example, can children participate in school activities? Can they play in the same activities as their friends? Do they live a life free of uncomfortable symptoms?

In pediatrics, measuring the quality of life for children with asthma has been of particular interest, both out of concern for the quality of care children with asthma receive and as a indicator of the performance of the health care system for children with special needs. While children are generally free from chronic disease, asthma is an exception (see Chap. 3). While significant ad-

---

*The concept of quality of life is used here somewhat broadly. There is no single, agreed-upon definition of quality-of-life measurement. Other, overlapping concepts frequently used include health-related quality of life, health status, functional outcome, and role performance.

vances have been made in the treatment of asthma, recent studies consistently demonstrate substantial gaps between recommendations and actual practice (1–3).

In this chapter, we outline the special challenges involved in developing valid measures to assess the quality of life for children with asthma. We then describe the currently available instruments. We have identified condition-specific and generic measures for which there is some degree of published information on the performance of the measure. For each we describe the scope and purpose of the instrument intended by the developers, the procedures used to obtain information from children or parents, and the available information on the performance of the instrument, including reliability, validity, and responsiveness.

II. Challenges in Developing Measures for Children

Many of the issues involved in developing instruments for children parallel those for adults (see Chaps. 5 and 7). There is no universally accepted definition of quality of life, thus concepts and methods included in instruments for children vary. Measuring outcomes like quality of life or health status, however defined, is challenging. Currently, the demand for measures outpaces the availability of data documenting the validity, reliability, and responsiveness of instruments for use in research or practice. The development of measures for children lags substantially behind the development of measures for adults; as one recent reviewer concluded, child measures for asthma are in their infancy (4). In particular, there is little experience with the ability of pediatric measures to assess change or with using such measures in clinical practice.

In addition to the standard challenges involved in developing methods to assess quality of life (see Chap. 5), several special issues face those developing instruments for children (5–9). As the field has advanced, many questions have emerged about how best to assess children's outcomes (10). While important questions have been outlined, more experience is needed to provide well-informed answers to several issues.

One challenge in the development of pediatric measures is that the criteria for children's functioning is a ''moving target.'' Because children are developing (see Chap. 2), using adult measures for children or one measure for children of all ages will not suffice. Most questions, for example, about activities and limitations for a 2-year-old would not be appropriate for an 8-year-old or a 16-year-old. Further, for the individual child, behaviors are changing as the child matures. Within and across societies, we might also expect varying definitions of age-appropriate behavior. Researchers developing pediatric instruments usually address these issues by restricting the age range of the measure and developing age-appropriate items.

Second, more so than is true for most adults, children's functioning is interdependent with family functioning. For example, whether a child misses school is dependent on physical morbidity, but it is also a measure of the parents' decision about whether the child is sick enough to stay home from school, whether child care can be arranged, and so on. In turn, the child with a chronic condition often affects the functioning of the family. Some of the emotional, social, and financial strain that would be borne by the patient, if he or she were an adult, is assumed by the parents when the patient is a child (8,11). Thus, the impact of pediatric asthma involves caregiver and family burdens as well as the health status of the patient.

A third issue is the potential variability across subpopulations in health status and the way respondents report on their quality of life. An instrument that has been validated for one group should not be presumed valid for another. In particular, are there differences by nationality, gender, racial or ethnic group, economic status, or educational status? It is highly likely that culture shapes families' perceptions and responses to a child's illness, but the specifics are largely unexplored. There may be differences in the interpretation of terms, readability of the instrument, social relevance of the activity being asked about, or varying health beliefs that could influence the respondents' perceptions and reports of health and illness (12,13). For example, most measures ask about limits on activities in which children might participate. Activities relevant for one group (e.g., swimming, bicycling, team sports) might be of little interest or beyond the economic reach of other children. Surprisingly little attention has been given to subgroup differences in the overall field of health status measurement. Much less is known about variations for children or children with asthma. Subgroup variation is particularly a concern with a condition like asthma. In the United States, for example, it is well known that urban, minority children have especially high rates of asthma (14–16; see Chap. 8); thus it is particularly important to develop methods that assess their health status accurately.

Finally, one of the critical debates in the field is whether measures should be answered by children themselves or whether parents should serve as proxies. On the one hand, it is inherent that individuals themselves are best able to know the impact of disease on their life. On the other hand, children might not yet have developed the cognitive skills to provide valid and reliable responses. For example, children tend to apply ''all-or-none'' thinking (17) and to have limited understanding of negatively worded items (6). The issues, of course, vary across by age. For infants and very young children, we must rely on parent or caregiver report. Adolescents are usually best able to report for themselves. It is in the middle that the questions lie: How do parent and child reports differ and how does each contribute to the goal of the particular study? At what age might we expect children to report reliably for themselves? What are the costs, methods, and time required to collect data from children versus parents?

There are a limited number of health research studies that explore these issues. Pantel and Lewis argue that the data from their study of 65 children (ages not specified) with chronic illness indicate ''both the importance and difficulty of using child report data'' (6). They found high correlations between parent and child report on how disease interferes with the child's daily life (0.77) but poor concordance on other issues, e.g., maturity in coping with the disease (−0.02). In a study of 52 children with asthma, Guyatt and colleagues found important differences between parent and child perceptions of symptom change and quality of life (18). In younger children (7 to 10 years of age) the parents' report of symptom change was more closely related to physiological measures than was the child's report of symptom change; the reverse was true for older children (aged 11 to 17 years). In both younger and older children, the child ratings of symptoms were clearly more closely related to quality of life (as reported by the child) than the parent ratings of symptoms. In a study of 242 children age 8 to 11 with asthma, French and colleagues report a correlation of 0.50 between a scale of children's self-reported severity (e.g., frequency of night waking, wheezing, cough) and the parents' rating of severity. Less closely associated was the child report of ''distress'' (e.g., ''how you feel when short of breath'') and the parents' rating of severity (0.25) (19).

While data from health-related studies are limited, there is a far more extensive body of knowledge on the psychological testing of children. This literature suggests that a variety of factors determine the answers to critical questions: How well do children and adults agree, and whose report is more accurate? These factors include the population studied, the substance and logic of the questions, the methods used to gather data, and, of course, the age of the child (17,20). In general, correlations between children and parents are better for more objective, behavioral items than for more subjective symptoms. Older children are found to be reliable reporters, with the caveat that appropriately tailored methods must be used to obtain information from children. Methods to obtain information from children—e.g., administration by trained interviewers—might often be more expensive than methods that can be used with adults, who usually can self-administer paper-and-pencil instruments.

III. Criteria for Measures Selected

Despite the challenges and special considerations required, advances have been made in the development of measures appropriate to assess quality of life among pediatric patients with asthma and their families. Both condition-specific and generic measures have been developed and are beginning to be used, primarily for research applications. We review six asthma-specific and three generic health-related quality-of-life measures (see Table 1).

To generate a pool of instruments for possible inclusion in this review, we conducted searches using Medline and Embase (both are computerized medical/health-related indexing software). Keywords used in the searches included *asthma, pediatric, children, parents, quality of life, outcome, functional status,* and *health status.* Searches were also conducted using several published review articles related to pediatric asthma and quality-of-life assessment (4,21,22). Each of these methods of identification required that at least some type of published work be available about a given measure. Once assembled, the initial list of measures was revised. An instrument was retained for further review if it met the following criteria: (a) the developers intended to assess outcomes that patients and families value and (b) the instrument measures multidimensional aspects of health. We also sent letters to the authors of the identified instruments to identify key references that might have been missed or to learn about important new developments with the measures.

We excluded from this review of quality-of-life measurement those instruments that examined only a single dimension of health, such as asthma symptoms (23–25). We also excluded several measures developed in the 1970s and 1980s to assess the psychological aspects of asthma. The purpose of these instruments was to identify patients who might benefit from counseling interventions (26–28). Thus, they were more narrowly focused than the instruments being developed and tested today. Although the instruments retained in the review represent work from the United States, Canada, and Europe and cover a broad spectrum of approaches, they share a multidimensional approach to better understanding the lives and experiences of children and families with asthma.

IV. Issues Reviewed

We reviewed and abstracted the identified instruments to provide information that would be relevant to those interested in learning about pediatric asthma outcomes measurement or to those who may consider using one of these measures for research or practice application. The findings are summarized in three major areas: purpose, procedures, performance. One note of caution: The information presented is meant to be an overview and therefore cannot address all details of a particular instrument. Interested readers are encouraged to explore the source documents and primary articles for a more comprehensive report on each measure.

Table 1 Summary of Asthma-Specific and Generic Quality of Life Measures for Children: Condition-Specific and Generic Measures

Condition-specific measures	Questionnaire to measure perceived symptoms and disability in asthma	Childhood Asthma Questionnaire (CAQ)	Children's Health Survey for Asthma (CHSA)
Primary reference(s)	Usherwood et al. (29)	Christie et al. (30); French et al. (19,31)	Sullivan and Olson (32)
Number of Items	17	CAQA, 14; CAQB, 22; CAQC, 22	51
Categories/domains/subscales	Perceived disability Perceived nocturnal symptoms Perceived daytime symptoms	Enjoyment of daily activities Feelings about asthma Frequency of symptoms	Physical health Activity (child) Activity (family) Emotional health (child) Emotional health (family)
Administration methods	Parent (self-administered)	Child (with parent assistance) [CAQA] Child (with adult assistance) [CAQB] Child (self-administered) [CAQC]	Parent (self-administered) Parent (interviewer-administered) Parent (telephone-administered) Adolescent (self-administered, in development)
Age range	5–14	CAQA, 4–7; CAQB, 8–11; CAQC, 12–16	5–12 (parent-completed) 12–16 (adolescent-completed)
Recall period	Previous 3 months	None used	Two versions (2 weeks and 2 months)
Internal consistency	Yes	Yes	Yes
Test-retest	No	Yes	In progress
Content validity	Yes	Yes	Yes
Construct validity	No	Yes	Yes, more in progress
Responsiveness	No	No	In progress
Language availability	English	English	English Spanish (in testing)
Demographics on race/ ethnicity/socioeconomic status	Unspecified	Unspecified	Yes
Asthma severity	Unspecified	Unspecified	All
Completion time	Unspecified	10–15 min	Approximately 20 min

Condition-specific measures	Paediatric Asthma Quality of Life Questionnaire (PAQLQ)	Paediatric Asthma Caregiver's Quality of Life Questionnaire (PACQLQ)	Questionnaire to measure pediatric asthma morbidity
Primary reference(s)	Juniper et al. (33); Guyatt et al. (34)	Juniper et al. (35)	Mitchell et al. (36)
Number of Items	23	13	15
Categories/domains/subscales	Symptoms Activity limitations Emotional function Summary score	Activity limitations Emotional function Summary score	Parent perception of severity Parent emotional response Summary score
Administration methods	Child (interviewer-administered) Child (self-administered)	Parent (self-administered)	Parent (interviewer-administered)
Age range	7–17	7–17	6–11
Recall period	Previous 1 week	Previous 1 week	Previous 1 year
Internal consistency	No	No	No
Test-retest	Yes	Yes	No
Content validity	Yes	Yes	No
Construct validity	Yes	Yes	Yes
Responsiveness	Yes	Yes	No
Language availability	English	English	English
Demographics on race/ethnicity/socioeconomic status	Unspecified	Unspecified	Yes
Asthma severity	All	All	All
Completion time	5–15 min	3–5 min	Unspecified

Table 1 Continued

Generic measures	RAND-7/FSQ-S	Child Health & Illness Profile (CHIP-AE)	Child Health Questionnaire (CHQ)
Primary references(s)	Lewis et al. (37)	Starfield et al. (39,40,41)	Landgraf et al. (42)
Number of Items	RAND-7 = 7; FSQ-S= 14	184	50 (98 and 28-item versions available)
Categories/domains/subscales	Parent global ratings of child's health (RAND-7) Parent global ratings of child's susceptibility to illness (RAND-7) Functional limitation due to illness (FSQ-S)	Discomfort Satisfaction with health Risks Resilience Disorders Achievement	Physical functioning; Role/social-physical; General health perceptions; Bodily pain; Family activities; Role/social-emotional/behavioral; Parental impact—time; Parental impact—emotional; Self-esteem; Mental health; Behavior; Family cohesion
Administration methods	Parent (self-administered)	Child (self-administered)	Parent (self-administered) Parent (interviewer-administered)
Age range	4–16	11–17	5+
Recall period	previous 3 months (RAND-7) previous 2 weeks (FSQ-S)	Previous 4 weeks and 12 months (varies by question)	previous 4 weeks
Internal consistency	Yes	Yes (in nonasthma tests)	Yes
Test-retest	Yes	Yes (in nonasthma tests)	No
Content validity	No	Yes	Yes
Construct validity	Yes	Yes	Yes
Responsiveness	No	No	No
Language availability	English	English	English American-Spanish American sign language Others—in development
Demographics on race/ethnicity/socioeconomic status	Yes	Yes	Yes
Completion time	≤10 min	30 min	Unspecified

A. Purpose: Intended Scope and Application of the Measure

Each measure is introduced with a citation to the primary source article(s) and a listing of the authors and their location. The purpose of the measure, stated in the authors' own prose whenever possible, is provided, as well as a listing of the domains/scales included in the instrument.

B. Procedures: Methods to Collect Data

For each measure we examined the methods used to obtain information from the child or parent. Procedures vary on several dimensions: Is the instrument designed for parent or child completion? Is it administered in person, by telephone or by paper and pencil? How many items and what type of items are on the instrument and how long does it take to complete? For what level of asthma severity is the instrument intended? Is a recall period used for individual items? If yes, what time period is used?

C. Performance: Reliability, Validity, and Responsiveness

In this section, we briefly outline issues related to the development of the measure, such as the qualitative and/or quantitative methods used to develop individual items and scales and establish content validity. Any pilot or beta tests of the measure are described and information on procedures and/or the sample is provided when available. The remainder of the section is devoted to reports of reliability, validity, and responsiveness for each measure. For reliability, was internal consistency tested? Was test-retest reliability examined? Were tests of content or construct validity conducted? Are findings of the measure's ability to appropriately measure change over time (responsiveness) reported?

D. Summary

A short summary is provided at the close of each instrument. Comments on strengths and weaknesses are offered as well as information about the appropriateness of using the measure for various applications.

V. Overview of Instruments

A. Asthma-Specific Measures for Children

1990: Questionnaire to Measure Perceived Symptoms and Disability in Asthma

Purpose

Developed by researchers in Great Britain (29), the purpose of this untitled, condition-specific measure is "to develop a questionnaire to be completed by parents of asthmatic children ages 5–14 years inclusive to provide quantitative measures of the symptoms and disabilities that they perceive in their children.'' Domains addressed are perceived disability, perceived nocturnal symptoms, and perceived daytime symptoms.

Procedure

The questionnaire is designed for parent self-report. Fixed-response choice items are included. A sample item from the measure is: ''Your child has been wheezy during the day?'' A five-point response scale ranging from ''every day'' to ''not at all'' is provided. A recall period of ''the past 3 months'' is used for each question. Average completion time for the 17-item questionnaire is described by the authors as ''a few minutes.'' Whether this measure is appropriate for use with all levels of asthma severity and acute and/or chronic asthma is not specified.

Performance

The questionnaire development process involved both qualitative and quantitative methods of questionnaire design. Testing of statistical properties of the measure involved two studies designated by the researchers as Survey A ($N = 164$) and Survey B ($N = 55$). Participants for Survey A were recruited into a multicenter trial of an inhaled steroid for asthma treatment. Demographic information reported for this study included mean child age (9.8 years) and child gender (males $= 108$, females $= 76$). Survey B participants included any parent of an asthmatic child between 5 and 14 years old seen in one of five participating practices over a 3-week study period. No further characteristics of the samples were provided.

Reliability. Internal consistency of the instrument was assessed using principal component analyses and internal reliability. Coefficient alpha calculated for each of the three scales for both Surveys A and B ranged from a low of 0.71 (daytime symptoms, Survey A) to a high of 0.92 (nocturnal symptoms, Survey B). Test-retest data were not presented.

Validity. Content validity was established through input from general practitioners and cognitive interviews with mothers of asthmatic children. No information on construct validity was reported.

Responsiveness. No information was provided on the questionnaire's ability to measure change over time in a child's asthma condition.

Summary

This measure is quite brief and focuses primarily on disability and symptoms, with less attention to the emotional or social effects of asthma on the child and/or family. Limited statistical information about the instrument is available in the published report, making the measure's usefulness as a research or clinical tool difficult to judge. This instrument does not appear to have been widely used following its development.

1993: Childhood Asthma Questionnaire

Purpose

The Childhood Asthma Questionnaire was developed in the 1990s by Christie, French, and colleagues in the United Kingdom (19,30,31). The CAQ is available in three age versions: Form A (CAQA) for 4- to 7-year-olds, Form B (CAQB) for 8- to 11-year-olds, and Form C (CAQC) for 12- to 16-year-olds. The age breakdowns were primarily chosen to reflect the activities that vary across the transition points in the United Kingdom school system.

The authors indicate the "primary purpose of the questionnaires is to evaluate interventions, that is to be responsive to change over time in individuals." These disease-specific questionnaires were specifically developed for children and are designed to assess multiple dimensions of quality of life: enjoyment of daily activities, feelings about asthma, and frequency of asthma symptoms (specific domains and subscales vary across the three versions).

Procedures

The CAQ is designed for child report, with variation in form across the three age groups. The form for the youngest age group (CAQA) requires parental assistance. The form for the middle age group (CAQB) is designed for child completion with adult assistance (e.g., in testing the questionnaire was read aloud to a classroom). The items on the CAQ are four- and five-point scales, using pictorial "bricks" to represent frequency of activity (e.g., "How often do you go to the swimming pool?") and "smiley" faces to represent feelings about the activity (e.g., "Which picture describes how you feel about going to the swimming pool?"). No recall period is specified in the questions. The authors report most children are able to complete the CAQ in 10 to 15 min; in a classroom setting, the entire procedure, including distribution and instruction, requires about 30 min. No specific severity of asthma was specified, though in testing almost all respondents were mild to moderate asthmatics.

Performance

In developing the CAQ, the researchers used qualitative methods to determine content and factor analysis to derive the specific domains. The three forms of the CAQ have been tested among boys and girls in the United Kingdom. According to the published literature, the CAQB has undergone the most extensive testing. Children were recruited from schools and primary health care centers. Testing was done both at school and by sending home forms. No data on the socioeconomic characteristics of the children were provided.

Reliability. The internal consistency of the subscales among children with asthma ranged from alphas of 0.60 to 0.63 for the CAQA, from 0.44 to 0.82 for the CAQB, and from 0.50 to 0.80 for the CAQC. On test-retest, correlations for the CAQA subscales were 0.59 to 0.63, for the CAQB 0.72 to 0.75, and for the CAQC 0.68 to 0.84.

Validity. Content validity for the measure was established by extensive fieldwork with children in the identification of activities important to children of various age ranges. Construct validity was assessed on the CAQB by comparing subscale scores to parent rating of severity, physician rating of severity, and peak expiratory flow rates; results were mixed and inconclusive.

Responsiveness. No information is available on the performance of the CAQ to measure change in health status.

Summary

The Child Asthma Questionnaires rely on child self-report and are sensitive to developmental differences in children between the ages of 4 and 16 by including three separate, age-specific versions of the instrument. The measures are brief and can be completed in a relatively short time period. Statistical evidence for the measures are mixed—reports of internal consistency and test-retest reliability are moderate and published tests of construct validity are inconclusive. No published information is provided about the CAQ's ability to measure change in health status over time, which may make it a less likely candidate to evaluate interventions.

1995: Children's Health Survey for Asthma (CHSA)

Purpose

The Children's Health Survey for Asthma (CHSA) is being developed by the American Academy of Pediatrics (32) as the first instrument in the Academy's Functional Outcomes Project—a program to develop measures of functional status and well-being in children with chronic health conditions. We, the authors of this chapter, are actively involved in this work. As an instrument for parents of children ages 5 to 12, the CHSA includes the domains of physical health (child), activities (child), emotional health (child), activities (family), and emotional health (family). The instrument is currently in testing form, with several validation tests under way.

Procedure

The CHSA, as originally designed, is a parent self-report instrument. All domain items are based on a five-point response scale—e.g., "How much of the time was your child frustrated by having to limit activities because of asthma?" A recall period of the past 2 months was used in the initial pilot test version of the measure (recall periods of 2, 4, and 8 weeks are being compared). In a pilot test with telephone administration, completion time was less than 20 min. The CHSA, which currently includes 51 items, will be further reduced based on testing under way. The CHSA has been used with all levels of asthma severity.

Performance

Development of the CHSA involved both qualitative and quantitative question-naire design methods. Several pilot tests of the CHSA have been completed in the offices of pediatricians and pediatric asthma specialists across the United States (and in Australia). Administration methods are being tested among rural, urban, and suburban samples of varying ethnic and economic composition. Other pilot projects are currently in progress and the measure is included in several ongoing clinical trials in the United States.

Reliability. Scales from the CHSA have shown to have acceptable to excellent internal consistency as evidenced by Cronbach's alpha. In two early pilot tests (N = 95; N = 100) of the measure, alphas ranged from 0.78 (Pilot Test I—activity scale) to 0.93 [Pilot Test I & II—emotional health (child) scale]. A study of test-retest reliability at 48-hr is near completion. Preliminary (unpublished) data indicate good short-term test-retest reliability with correlation coefficients between baseline and 48-hr administration ranging from a low of 0.64 [emotional health (child) scale] to a high of 0.93 [activity (child) scale].

Validity. Content validity was established through input from an expert work group of general and subspecialty pediatricians, focus groups, and cognitive interviews with parents (primarily mothers) of asthmatic children and a survey asking parents and providers to rate the importance of questions asked on the CHSA. In the published pilot test, significant associations were found between scores on the CHSA and the clinician's rating of child's severity of asthma. Construct validity is also currently being assessed in two longitudinal tests. Data from these studies will allow correlation of CHSA scales with scores from a generic measure of child health (the Child Health Questionnaire), parental assessment of asthma symptoms (Symptom Free Day measure), clinical indicators of asthma severity (spirometry), and other measures of quality of life (The Feeling Thermometer and Global Assessment of Change measure).

Responsiveness. The CHSA's ability to measure change is currently being tested. Longitudinal data collected from children recruited during an emergency department visit will help to determine whether the measure is sensitive enough to detect change when change in the child's health status is expected to occur.

Summary

Studies completed or under way will provide comprehensive tests of the performance of the CHSA with diverse groups of U.S. children. The measure covers a broad scope of domains and includes items relevant to both child and family. Further reduction of the number of items will make the CHSA more practical for use in clinical or research applications. The measure has good reliability and validity in cross-sectional tests under various modes of administration; results of the ongoing longitudinal tests will determine the responsiveness of the instrument. The addition of a Spanish-language version of the parent instrument and an adolescent self-report measure (both in development) will allow more comprehensive applications.

1996: Paediatric Asthma Quality of Life Questionnaire (PAQLQ)

Purpose

The Paediatric Asthma Quality of Life Questionnaire (PAQLQ) was developed by Juniper and other health services researchers at McMaster University, Ontario, Canada,(18,33,34). The PAQLQ is designed to ''gain a full picture of the impact of asthma on the lives of children with the condition.'' The PAQLQ was developed, ''in response to the need for an instrument to measure health related quality of life in children with asthma.'' Domains included in the measure, designed for children and adolescents ages 7 to 17, are symptoms, activity limitation, and emotional function. A total quality-of-life score based on the three domains may also be computed.

Procedure

The PAQLQ, as reported, is an interviewer-administered child-report measure. Several response formats are used across the 23 items. An open-ended question asks the children to identify activities in which they participate and whether they are bothered by asthma when they participate. A set list of activities is then used to determine any other activities in which the child is bothered by asthma. For the identified activities, fixed-response-choice questions assess the impact of asthma; the remainder of the items ask about other activities, emotions, and symptoms. An example of a question from the instrument is: ''How often did you feel frustrated because you couldn't keep up with others?'' (seven-point scale ranging from ''all the time'' to ''none of the time''). A recall period of the past week is used for all items. Average completion time for the measure is reported as 10 to 15 min for the initial visit and 5 to 10 min for subsequent follow-up administrations. The PAQLQ is suitable for all levels of asthma severity.

Performance

Development of the PAQLQ involved both quantitative and qualitative questionnaire design methods. Psychometric properties of the measure were tested in a longitudinal study of 52 children in Ontario, Canada, with asthma (defined in concordance with American Thoracic Society guidelines) and a parent or primary caregiver. Families were recruited through local media, pediatric clinics, and a study on adult asthma. Data were collected at enrollment and 1, 5, and 9 weeks after the enrollment visit. The majority of children required some type of medication for their asthma. Further demographic data regarding the socioeconomic status of the sample are not reported.

Reliability. Internal consistency of the scales was not reported. In test-retest administration, intraclass correlation coefficients were calculated for patients who remained clinically stable over the course of the study, ranging from a low of 0.84 (activities scale) to a high of 0.93 (symptoms scale). Three breakdowns by child age are also provided and yield similar results to the overall group.

Validity. Input from health professionals and surveys and interviews with both parents and children contributed to content validity of the measure. Both cross-sectional and longitudinal construct validity were assessed by correlating PAQLQ scales with clinical indicators of severity (e.g., clinical asthma control, spirometry results, and β-agonist use), generic quality of life (as measured by The Feeling Thermometer) and child-reported global ratings of change. In general, PAQLQ scales correlated in the expected ways with clinical asthma indicators and the other quality-of-life measures.

Responsiveness. Within- and between-subject t tests were used to determine the instrument's ability to detect change over time. Results indicate that, overall, the PAQLQ was sensitive to changes in asthma across a designated 4-week period, but more so for overall quality of life and the symptoms and activities scales than for the emotional scale. The measure also distinguished between the children whose asthma stayed stable over the course of the study versus those whose condition changed.

Summary

The PAQLQ is a brief measure that addresses several domains from the child's perspective. The instrument is now being used quite extensively in pediatric asthma research and recently received approval from the Medical Outcomes Trust, a nonprofit membership organization in the United States to promote scientifically sound outcomes measurement. Tests of reliability and validity indicate acceptable to strong statistical properties. Of particular note is the measure's demonstrated ability to detect change; published data on responsiveness are otherwise lacking in pediatric measures. Published knowledge about the instruments' performance is currently limited to a small sample of Canadian children, thus generalizability is yet unknown. The developers report that studies are under way to examine a self-administered version of the PAQLQ, which will provide useful information on how and at what age children can complete the measure without adult assistance.

1996: Paediatric Asthma Caregiver's Quality of Life Questionnaire (PACQLQ)

Purpose

Like its counterpart for children (the PAQLQ), the Paediatric Asthma Caregiver's Quality of Life Questionnaire (PACQLQ) was developed by Juniper and colleagues at McMaster University (35). The rationale for developing the PACQLQ, as stated by the researchers, is that, "Parents and primary caregivers of children with asthma are limited in normal daily activities and experience anxieties and fears due to the child's illness. We have developed the PACQLQ to measure these impairments." Domains included in the measure, designed for parents of asthmatic children ages 7 to 17, are activity limitation and emotional function. An overall quality-of-life score based on the two domains may also be computed.

Procedure

The PACQLQ is designed for parent self-administration. All questions rely on a seven-point scale. A sample item from the measure is: "How often were you bothered because your child's asthma interfered with family relationships?" (Seven-point scale ranging from "all the time" to "none of the time"). A recall period of the past week is used for all items. The 13-item measure takes an average of 3 to 5 min to complete and is appropriate for use with all levels of asthma severity.

Performance

Development of the PACQLQ involved both quantitative and qualitative questionnaire design methods. Psychometric properties of the measure were tested in a longitudinal study of 52 Canadian parents and/or primary caregivers and their asthmatic child. Data were collected at enrollment and 1, 5, and 9 weeks after the enrollment visit. Further information regarding the socioeconomic status of the sample is not reported.

Reliability. Internal consistency of the scales was not reported. Intraclass correlation coefficients were calculated for test-retest data provided by parents of children whose asthma remained stable over the course of the study. Values for the overall quality of life, emotional function, and activities scales were 0.85, 0.80, and 0.84, respectively.

Validity. Input from health professionals along with surveys and interviews with parents of asthmatic children contributed to content validity of the measure. Both cross-sectional and longitudinal construct validity were assessed by correlating PACQLQ scales with clinical indicators of severity (e.g., clinical asthma control, spirometry results, and β-agonist use), scores from the Impact-on-Family Scale, and parent-reported global ratings of child change. In general, changes in PACQLQ scales correlated in the expected ways with the other parent reports of burden and changes in the child's asthma and weakly with the clinical asthma indicators.

Responsiveness. Within- and between-subject t tests were used to determine the instrument's ability to detect change over time. Results indicate that the PACQLQ was sensitive to changes in asthma across a designated 4-week period. The measure and its scales were also shown to distinguish between the subgroup of children whose asthma stayed stable over the course of the study versus those whose condition changed.

Summary

The parent-completed PACQLQ is similar but not identical to the child-completed PAQLQ, limiting direct item-by-item comparisons between child and caregiver reports. The measure can be completed quickly—a plus for research or practice application. Statistical properties of reliability, validity, and responsiveness are good, though published data are based on a relatively small Canadian sample. The PACQLQ has also been approved by the Medical Outcomes Trust.

1997: Questionnaire to Measure Pediatric Asthma Morbidity

Purpose

Developed by researchers in New Zealand (36), the purpose of this untitled condition-specific measure is "to develop and explore the applicability and validity of other measures of asthma morbidity in children, particularly using parental perception of the morbidity produced by their child's asthma and the parent's emotional response to the child's asthma." Content areas addressed include parental perception of severity and parental emotional response. A composite score can be computed based on four items from the two content areas.

Procedure

The 15-item questionnaire is interviewer-administered to a child's principal caregiver. Fixed-response-choice items are included. A sample item from the measure is "How often did you feel frightened because of your child's asthma?" It has a five-point response scale ranging from "never" to "very often." A recall period of "the last year" is used for most items. An average completion time for the questionnaire is not specified by the authors. The measure is appropriate for use with all levels of asthma severity.

Performance

The development process for individual questionnaire items was not described. Statistical properties of the measure were tested in a study of 381 parents of New Zealand children, ages 6 to 11. Participants were recruited through the offices of general practitioners, schools, and a prior study of community-based asthma prevalence. Demographic information reported for the study included child age and gender (males = 229, females = 152), ethnicity, family structure, and exposure to passive smoke.

   Reliability.   Internal consistency and test-retest data were not presented.

   Validity.   Content validity was not reported. Construct validity was established by correlating individual survey items as well as the composite score with other measures of asthma severity (e.g., emergency room visits, school absences). Of the 15 parental report items, 14 were able to distinguish subjects characterized with high and low morbidity (p < 0.05).

   Responsiveness.   No information was provided on the questionnaire's ability to measure change over time in a child's asthma condition.

Summary

A report of this measure has been published. The measure is brief and appears easy to complete. Evidence on the psychometric properties of the instrument is yet lacking with the exception of construct validity, where the measure seemed able to distinguish low and high morbidity. To date, it appears that the measure has been tested only within New Zealand.

B.   Generic Instruments Tested on Children with Asthma

1989: RAND-7/Functional Status Questionnaire–Specific (FSQ-S)

Purpose

The RAND-7 and FSQ-S are questionnaires to measure generic health status adapted by researchers at the University of California—San Francisco and the University of Washington (37). Both the RAND-7 and FSQ-S are versions of previously developed instruments (Child Health Status Measure from the RAND Health Insurance Experiment and the FSII-R, respectively), modified by the authors to "improve the ease of gathering child health status information." As tested, the instruments are suitable for use with parents of children ages 4 to 16. Scales computed for the RAND-7 are termed RAND 1 (parent's global ratings of children's health) and RAND 2 (parent's global ratings of children's susceptibility to illness). A single scale is created from the FSQ-S—items address functional limitations due to illness.

Procedure

Each measure is self-administered and all items are answered with fixed-response choices. A sample item from the RAND-7 is "How much pain or distress has this child's health caused him or her?" (four-point scale ranging from "a great deal" to "not at all"). The questions "How often did this child seem lively and energetic?" (three-point scale ranging from "rarely or never" to "almost always") and "was this due to asthma?" (three choices: yes, sometimes, no) are representative of items from the FSQ-S. The RAND-7 relies on a recall period of the last 3 months, while the recall period for the FSQ-S is the last 2 weeks. Completion time for the questionnaires is reported as 10 min or less. The measures are appropriate for varying levels of asthma severity.

Performance

Items selected for inclusion were chosen by the authors. The 14 items adopted from the FSII-R were those applicable to the widest age range (0 to 16 years). The measures were tested as part of a larger clinical trial conducted in the San Francisco area. The parents of 100 asthmatic children participated in a cross-sectional study. A subgroup ($N = 47$) of the larger sample took part in a longitudinal study with five data-collection points over the course of 1 year. The racial, economic, educational, and occupational composition of the sample was diverse.

Reliability. Internal consistency was tested and Cronbach's alpha of 0.78, 0.69, and 0.70 was reported for the FSQ-S, RAND 1, and RAND 2, respectively. The authors used repeated measures analysis of variance to assess stability of the scales over time and found only one significant difference, which they attribute to asthma seasonality.

Validity. Tests of content validity were not reported. Construct validity was examined by correlating scores from the FSQ-S and RAND scales with each other as well as with asthma "severity" (computed score based on type, frequency, and amount of medication used) and "illness impact" variables (defined as acute visits, phone calls, attacks, hospital days, parent absence from work, and child absence from school). The FSQ-S and RAND-7 correlated modestly with each other but not with severity. A significant negative correlation was noted between the FSQ-S and acute visits and child school absence. In addition to correlating with these impact variables, the RAND measure was also related to parental absence from work.

Responsiveness. Using stepwise multiple regression analysis, the FSQ-S and RAND-7 measures were not found to be sensitive to change in severity (as measured by medication use) over time. Associations with other outcome measures were not reported. The authors caution, however, that these analyses were based on small sample sizes (only 24 families completed the 12-month follow-up). Associations with other outcome measures were not reported.

Summary

These measures, combined and modified from previously existing generic instruments for use with parents of children with asthma, appear easy to complete. Choices about items for inclusion, however, were based solely on the decision of the authors and did not include parent or child input. Internal consistency was reported as acceptable, but the instrument did not seem to distinguish severity and was not sensitive to change in the asthma condition over time. Although the demographic composition of the sample was quite diverse, the sample was very small, which limits the interpretation of statistical findings.

1995: Child Health and Illness Profile

Purpose

The Child Health and Illness Profile, Adolescent Version (CHIP-AE), was developed by Starfield and colleagues in health policy and management at Johns Hopkins University (38–41). The CHIP-AE was released in 1995 and is intended for youths aged 11 to 18.

This comprehensive health profile is generic, designed for use with all adolescents. The instrument covers the six domains of discomfort, satisfaction with health, risks, resilience, disorders, and achievement; within these domains, 20 subdomains are identified. The developers' purpose is "to document the state of health in adolescent populations, to identify systematic differences in health in subpopulations . . . to assess the impact of health services interventions on health."

Procedure

The CHIP-AE is designed for child completion. The authors acknowledge that some younger adolescents and those with reading impairment may need assistance to complete the measure. Three and five-point response formats are used. Both 4-week and 12-month recall periods are used, varying by type of question. The authors indicate the CHIP can be completed by an adolescent in 30 min. In testing, data gathering was completed in one class period.

Performance

An iterative process of qualitative and quantitative methods was used to develop items and domains in the CHIP-AE. The CHIP-AE has been validated on an ethnically and economically diverse sample of 3003 U.S. adolescents. Data were collected in classrooms in Baltimore, rural Maryland, and rural Arkansas. A separate analysis of 359 children with asthma within the sample of 3003 has also been published.

Reliability. The internal consistency of the subdomains was similar across the geographic samples. Most scales achieved an alpha of at least 0.70. In a 1-week test-retest of the northern Baltimore sample, correlations ranged from 0.49 to 0.87. No data on reliability specific to the asthma subsample have been reported.

Validity. Content validity for the CHIP-AE was established through focus groups with children and parents and reviewed by an interdisciplinary expert group. Several convergent and discriminant tests of validity have been conducted, demonstrating acceptable to excellent correlations with comparable measures. In particular, in a substudy of 74 chronically ill children, the CHIP-AE was found to discriminate adolescents who were well from those with an illness. In the substudy of 379 respondents with asthma, those with active symptoms were found to have significantly lower perceived well-being, higher discomfort, and a greater degree of morbidity than the general sample of children or those who identified themselves as asthmatic but had no active symptoms.

Responsiveness.   No data on responsiveness of the CHIP-AE have been reported.

Summary

The CHIP-AE, designed for self-report by children aged 11 to 17, identifies a broad set of domains and subdomains of child health status, although the length of the questionnaire may be a deterrent to its use in clinical settings and some research projects. The measure has performed strongly in cross-sectional tests with large, demographically diverse samples. Longitudinal data on the responsiveness of the CHIP-AE are not yet reported; however, published reports on cross-sectional data indicate the instrument is able to distinguish well versus ill adolescents and, within an asthma subsample, those with active versus nonactive asthma. A generic measure for younger children is currently being developed at Johns Hopkins by Starfield and colleagues.

1996: Child Health Questionnaire (CHQ)

Purpose

The Child Health Questionnaire (CHQ), a generic measure of child health status, was created by Jeanne Landgraf and collaborators at The Health Institute, New England Medical Center, Boston (42). The project under which the CHQ was developed emphasized "the development and validation of a family of generic, practical yet comprehensive tools for children five years of age and older." The purpose of the new tools was to "provide a broad brushstroke of the functional status and well-being of children along a range of areas." The CHQ is a parent-completed measure applicable to children aged 5 and older. Twelve scales computed from the CHQ include physical functioning, role/social-physical, general health perceptions, bodily pain, family activities, role/social-emotional/behavioral, parental impact-time, parental impact-emotional, self-esteem, mental health, behavior, and family cohesion. Three different versions of the questionnaire (98, 50, and 28 items) are available. The 50-item instrument, known as the CHQ-PF50, has been tested with parents of children with asthma (41). A child-completed version, the CHQ-CF87, is available, but information on its use with asthmatic children has not been reported.

Procedure

The measure can be either self- or interviewer-administered. All items include a four- or five-point scale. "How much pain or distress has this child's health caused him or her?" (four-point scale ranging from "a great deal" to "not at all") is a sample item from the CHQ. The recall period for all questions is the past 4 weeks. Completion time for the CHQ was not reported.

Performance

Both qualitative and quantitative methods of questionnaire design were used in the development of the CHQ. The instrument has been tested widely in groups of well children, and normative data are available. Further, the measure has been used to assess the health status of children with various illnesses and conditions ranging from epilepsy to attention-deficit hyperactivity disorder (ADHD) to asthma. Use of the CHQ with asthmatic children was tested in four separate studies including over 3000 subjects. Primarily the results from these four studies will be reported here. Two of the asthma studies were conducted through health maintenance organizations (HMOs); the other two were randomized clinical trials. Extensive demographic information is available for the larger general samples; in addition, race and education of the responder were reported for the asthma substudies.

Reliability.   Tests from four studies of the measure with asthmatic samples indicate acceptable levels of internal consistency (≥ 0.70), although some exceptions were noted for various scales within certain studies. No data on test-retest reliability are presented.

Validity.   Content validity for the questionnaire, overall, was established through interviews and focus groups with parents and children. Good item discriminant validity is reported for the CHQ items and scales in each of the four asthma substudies. By comparing normative data with substudy scores, the measure has been found to discriminate between healthy children and children ill with asthma and other chronic conditions [epilepsy, juvenile rheumatoid arthritis (JRA) (42)]. Within the four asthma studies, further evidence of construct validity using other measures of functional status or clinical outcome was not specified.

Responsiveness.   The CHQ's ability to detect change over time was not reported.

Summary

The generic CHQ taps a wide variety of health-related domains; it addresses impact of health on both the child and the family and is likely to be widely used in health research. There are extensive cross-sectional data on the instrument collected in the United States, and it has been approved by the Medical Outcomes Trust. The data on national norms are particularly helpful. Asthma-specific studies indicate acceptable internal consistency reliability and suggest construct validity for this population. Data regarding test-retest reliability and responsiveness are not yet available. Different versions of the instrument are available (28, 50, and 98 items), although most information is reported on the 50-item measure. The shorter version (CHQ-PF28), if shown to be statistically sound, may prove the most useful of the three for clinical application. A child-completed measure is available, and translations of the CHQ into several different languages are available or in progress. A parent-completed instrument for very young children (under 5) is in development.

VI. Discussion

We leave the reader with two basic conclusions to our review of the instruments currently available to assess health-related quality of life among children with asthma. First, pediatric outcome measurement has rapidly matured in a relatively short period of time. Although still clearly lagging behind measures for adults, in less than a decade, significant progress has been made to develop, test, and disseminate instruments that address the impact of asthma on the lives of children and their families. Second, there is still an enormous amount of work to be done. Further discussion, debate, and most of all data are needed to meet the challenges in this complex field.

What has been established is a strong interest in developing measures to assess outcomes from the patient's point of view and in understanding the multi-faceted way that child and family well-being may be affected by asthma. Based on the increasing number of organizations allocating resources to the area and the conferences adding outcomes-related topics to their meeting agendas, it is clear that patient-centered outcomes have moved beyond ''buzzword'' status. Also, especially in pediatrics, there is increased understanding of a systems approach; because of the obvious link between child and family, the family unit is considered.

The necessary differences between measures for adults and children have become clear. The special challenges involved in developing pediatric measures have been acknowledged and good research questions are under debate. Multidisciplinary teams are often involved in the development of measures, taking advantage of the expertise of clinicians, statisticians, psychologists, sociologists, and child developmentalists. Most pediatric measures in use today were created with attention to developmental and situational issues and are not simply adult measures modified for children.

Several health care organizations and academic centers now have solid programs under way to develop and use pediatric quality-of-life measures. While some choose to focus exclusively on parent- or child-report measures, others work to develop both. In addition, different administration methods are being tested (e.g., in-person versus interviewer-administered, telephone versus mail). The multiple approaches being tested will provide a comparison of strategies and expand choices for users. While most instruments are still in their infancy, in nearly all cases, tests of existing measures indicate acceptable construct validity and strong reliability.

New developments in this field are very promising, several weaknesses remain. Existing publications on the performance of measures are almost exclusively authored by the same researchers who developed the measures. The field will mature as measures are used and critiqued by those beyond the developers themselves. Another limitation is that most tests of disease-specific instruments for children with asthma have been conducted on small, homogeneous samples, sometimes with no demographic information reported. Further instrument testing needs to include larger, more heterogeneous samples and to be sensitive to cultural differences and variation in health beliefs. It is especially important that measures be tested among the populations most likely to suffer with asthma (see Chap. 8). This caution is especially warranted as language translations become more common for pediatric measures. Relatedly, careful attention should be given to questionnaire reading level, whether the instrument is designed for parents or children. Often reading grade level is simply ignored or at best generated by computer word-processing programs, which are too mechanical to assess a questionnaire's reading level accurately. Educational psychologists or reading specialists can provide a more comprehensive evaluation of an instrument's true reading complexity.

Those shaping future projects should also ensure that instruments are validated for their intended uses. To date, pediatric instruments have primarily been tested with cross-sectional data for research applications. While there is strong interest in using measures to evaluate interventions, few longitudinal data are yet available on the responsiveness of most pediatric instruments. Longitudinal data collection is arduous, costly, and time-consuming, but tests of an instruments' ability to measure change are essential if a measure is to be used for evaluation. There is also growing interest in the use of measures in clinical practice, but again, there are currently few or no data on such applications in pediatric care.

An issue likely to remain under close scrutiny is when and how children can report for themselves. It is likely that both child and parent reports will continue to be applied; useful, though different, information can be obtained from both groups. Child and parent reports each have limits, and much more extensive data are needed to clarify these parameters. Practical issues, such as the type of interviewer and cost to collect data from children, will especially need to be clarified to collect data in large multisite studies or in clinical practice.

Similar questions remain surrounding the comparative advantages and disadvantages of condition-specific versus generic measures. Again, it is likely that valuable data can be obtained from both types of measures, but further evidence would clarify the relative strengths and weaknesses of each for various research questions and applications. Practical procedural questions also remain, such as: What is the preferred recall period? As this review indicates, there is no "gold standard" recall period. Times vary from 1 week to 1 year or may not be specified at all. To complicate the situation, what is appropriate for a parent-report instrument may not be feasible for a child-report measure.

We anticipate that the field for pediatric quality-of-life measurement will expand in several areas. Given the activity in this area, new publications and information will likely become available in the time between our writing and the dissemination of this monograph. To date, measures have primarily been applied to research, however we expect to see more "real world" clinical applications being studied. There are compelling reasons to think clinical use of such instruments might improve the quality of pediatric asthma care. Asking patients/parents about symptoms, functional limitations, and asthma-related family stress in a systematic way is likely to enhance accurate assessment of severity and improve patient-provider communication and education. Such applications should be tested before widespread applications are presumed.

Computerization of outcome instruments will also likely play a role in the future advancement of this field. Some of the measures described above (e.g., the CHIP-AE, the CHQ) are already computerizing their scoring schemes for different types of statistical software programs. Instrument administration by hand-held or laptop computers is becoming increasingly popular as well. If outcome instruments are to be used among individual patients in the office setting, the process will benefit greatly from computer technology. Rather than relying on pencil-and-paper administration, an office staff member might administer a questionnaire via computer with outputs available in "real time" in the office setting.

The time is right for pediatric outcome measurement, especially in the field of asthma, as guidelines and new treatment strategies become an integral part of asthma care and long-term management of the disease. Traditional measures of process and clinical measures of morbidity will continue to be needed, but measures that provide a broader look at outcomes from the child's and family's points of view are earning their place as a tool to improve the quality of care and the quality of life for children with asthma.

References

1. Crain, E.F., Weiss, K.B., and Fagan, M.J. (1995). Pediatric asthma care in U.S. emergency departments: Current practice in the context of the National Institutes of Health guidelines. *Arch. Pediatr. Adolesc. Med.*, **149**:893–901.
2. Alario, A., Bergman, D., Slora, E., et al. (1997). Does office-based management of acute asthma affect outcome? *Amb. Child Health*, **3**:163.
3. Homer, C., Susskind, O., Alpert, H., Schneider, L., Rappaport, L., and Fenton, T. (1997). Impact of a computer based guideline education program on clinical practice for children with asthma. *Pediatric. Res.*, **41**:93A.

4. Bender, B.G. (1996). Measurement of quality of life in pediatric asthma clinical trials. *Ann Allergy Asthma Immunol.*, **77**:438–447.
5. Starfield, B. (1987). Child health status and outcome of care: a commentary on measuring the impact of medical care on children. *J. Chronic Dis.*, **40**:109S–115S.
6. Pantell, R.H., and Lewis, C.C. (1987). Measuring the impact of medical care on children. *J. Chronic Dis.*, **40**:99S–108S.
7. Stein, R.K., and Jessop, D.J. (1990). Functional Status II(R): A measure of child health status. *Med. Care*, **28**:1041–1055.
8. McGlynn, E.A., Halfon, N., and Leibowitz, A. (1995). Assessing the quality of care for children: prospects under health reform. *Arch. Pediatr. Adolesc. Med.*, **149**:359–368.
9. Schuster, M.A., Asch, S.M., McGlynn, E.A., Kerr, E.A., Hardy, A.M., Gifford, D.S. (1997). Development of a quality care measurement system for children and adolescents. *Arch Pediatr. Adolesc. Med.*, **151**:1085–1092.
10. Association for Health Services Research (1998). Improving quality of health care for children: an agenda for research. Washington, D.C.
11. Bauman, L.F. (1994). Discussant section: measures of life quality, role performance, and functional status in asthma research. *Am. J. Respir. Criti. Care Med.*, **149**:S40–S43.
12. McCubbin, H.I., Thompson, E.A., Thompson, A.I., McCubbin, M.A., and Kaston, A.J. (1993) Culture, ethnicity, and the family: critical factors in childhood chronic illnesses and disabilities. *Pediatrics*, **91**:1063–1070.
13. Kinsman, S.B., Sally, M., and Fox, K. (1996). Multicultural issues in pediatric practice. *Pediatr. Rev.*, **17**:349–354.
14. Carr, W., Zeitel, L., and Weiss, K.B. (1992). Variations in asthma hospitalizations and deaths in New York City. *Am. J. Public Health*, **82**:59–65.
15. Taylor, W.R., and Newacheck, P.W. (1992). Impact of childhood asthma on health. *Pediatrics*, **90**:657–662.
16. Targonski, P.V., Persky, V.W., Orris, P., and Addington, W. (1994). Trends in asthma mortality among African Americans and whites in Chicago, 1968 through 1991. *Am. J. Public Health*, **84**:1830–1833.
17. Stone, W.L., and Lemanek, K.L. (1990). Developmental issues in children's self-reports. In: *Through the Eyes of the Child: Obtaining Self-Reports from Children and Adolescents*. Edited by A.M. LaGreca, Boston, Allyn and Bacon; pp. 18–56.
18. Guyatt, G.H., Juniper, E.F., Griffith, L.E., Fenny, D.H., and Ferrie, P.J. (1997). Children and adult perceptions of childhood asthma. *Pediatrics*, **99**:165–168.
19. French, D.J., Christie, M.J., and West, A. (1994). Quality of life in childhood asthma: development of the childhood asthma questionnaires. In *Assessment of Quality of Life in Childhood Asthma*. Edited by M. Christie, and D. French. Chur, Switzerland: Harwood Academic Publishers, pp. 157–180.
20. Flanery, R.C. (1990). Methodological and psychometric considerations in child reports. In *Through the Eyes of the Child: Obtaining Self-reports from Children and Adolescents*. Edited by A.M. LaGreca. Boston, Allyn and Bacon, pp. 57–82.

21. Rothman, M.L., and Revicki, D.A. (1993). Issues in the measurement of health status is asthma research. *Med. Care*, **31**:MS82–MS97.
22. Richards, J.M., and Hemstreet, M.P. (1994). Measures of life quality, role performance and functional status in asthma research. *Am. J. Respir. Crit. Care Med.*, **149**: S31–S39.
23. Fritz, G.K., and Overholser, J.C. (1989). Patterns of response to childhood asthma. *Psychosom Med.*, **51**:347–355.
24. Creer, T.L., Wigal, J.K., Kotses, H., Hatala, J.C., McConnaughy, K., and Winder, J.A. (1993). A life activities questionnaire for childhood asthma. *J. Asthma*, **30**(6): 467–473.
25. Rosier, M.J., Bishop, J., Nolan, T., Robertson, C.F., Carlin, J.B., and Phelan, P.D. (1994). Measurement of functional severity of asthma in children. *Am. J. Crit. Care Med.*, **149**:1434–1441.
26. Achenbach, T.M., and Edelbrock, C. (1983). *Manual for the Child Behavior Checklist and Revised Child Behavior Profile*. Burlington, VT. University of Vermont, Department of Psychiatry.
27. Creer, T.L., Marion, R.J., and Creer, P.P. (1983). Asthma problem behavior checklist: parental perceptions of the behavior of asthmatic children. *J. Asthma*, **20**(2): 97–104.
28. Baron, C., Lamarre, A., Veilleux, P., Ducharme, G., Spier, S., and Lapierre, J.-G. (1986). Psychomaintenance of childhood asthma: a study of 34 children. *J. Asthma*, **23**(2):69–79.
29. Usherwood, T.P., Scrimgeour, A., and Barber, J.H. (1990). Questionnaire to measure perceived symptoms and disability in asthma. *Arch. Dis. Child*, **65**:779–781.
30. Christie, M.J., French, D., Sowden, A., and West, A. (1993). Development of child-centered disease-specific questionnaires for living with asthma. *Psychosom, Med.*, **55**:541–548.
31. French, D.J., Christie, M.J., and Sowden, A.J. (1994). The reproducibility of the Childhood Asthma Questionnaires: measures of quality of life for children with asthma ages 4–16 years. *Qual. Life Res.*, **3**:215–224.
32. Sullivan, S.A., and Olson, L.M. (1995). Developing condition-specific measures of functional status and well-being for children. *Clin. Perform. Qual. Health Care*, **3**: 132–138.
33. Juniper, E.F., Guyatt, G.H., Feeny, D.H., Ferrie, P.J., Griffith, L.E., Townsend, M. (1996). Measuring quality of life in children with asthma. *Qual. Life Res.*, **5**:35–46.
34. Juniper, E.F., Guyatt, G.H., Feeny, D.H., Griffith, L.E., and Ferrie, P.J. (1997). Minimum skills required by children to complete health-related quality of life instruments for asthma: comparison of measurement properties. *Eur. Respir. J.*, **10**:2285–2294.
35. Juniper, E.F., Guyatt, G.H., Feeny, D.H., Ferrie, P.J., Griffith, L.E., and Townsend, M. (1996). Measuring quality of life in the parents of children with asthma. *Qual. Life Res.*, **5**:27–34.
36. Mitchell, E.A., Stewart, A.W., Rea, H.H., McNaughton, S., Taylor, G., Smith, L.T., Asher, M.I, Mulder, J., and Seelye, E.R. (1997). Measuring morbidity from asthma in children. *NZ Med. J.*, **110**:3–6.

37. Lewis, C.C., Pantell, R.H., and Kieckhefer, G.M. (1989). Assessment of children's health status: field test of new approaches. *Med. Care*, **27**:S54–S65.
38. Starfield, B., Bergner, M., Ensminger, M., Riley, A., Ryan, S., Green, B., McGauhey, P., Skinner, A., and Kim, S. (1993). Adolescent health status measurement: development of the child health and illness profile. *Pediatrics*, **91**:430–434.
39. Starfield, B., Riley, A.W., Green, B.F., Ensminger, M.E., Ryan, S.A., Kelleher, K., Kim-Harris, S., Johnston, D., and Vogel, K. (1995). The adolescent child health and illness profile, a population-based measure of health. *Med. Care*, **33**:553–565.
40. Starfield, B., Forrest, C.B., Ryan, S.A., Riley, A.W., Ensminger, M.E., and Green, B.F. (1996). Health status of well vs. ill adolescents. *Arch. Pediatr. Adolesc. Med.*, **150**:1249–1256.
41. Forrest, C.B., Starfield, B., Riley, A.W., and Kang M. (1997). The impact of asthma on the health status of adolescents. *Pediatrics*, **99**:1–7.
42. Landgraf, J.M., Abetz, L., and Ware, J.E. (1996). *The CHQ User's Manual*. Boston, The Health Institute, New England Medical Center.

7

Current Methods for Measuring Health-Related Quality of Life in Adults with Asthma

GUY B. MARKS

Institute of Respiratory Medicine
University of Sydney
Sydney, Australia

I. Introduction

A. Selecting Questionnaires for Measuring Quality of Life

Matching questionnaires to research tasks requires consideration of the nature of the research task and the characteristics of the questionnaire. A hierarchy of evaluations of potential questionnaires should be undertaken. First, does the questionnaire reliably and validly measure health-related quality of life? Second, is the questionnaire suitable for the specific task in hand? Third, what is the meaning of data derived from using the questionnaire?

Does the Questionnaire Reliably and Validly Measure Quality of Life?

There is some consensus among workers in this field that physical, psychological, and social domains must all be sampled to adequately encompass health-related quality of life (1–3). Since quality of life is clearly a patient-focused outcome of health or illness, it is important that the specific content of a questionnaire be derived from patients rather than health professionals. A variety of qualitative research methods have been established to achieve this, including focus groups, which have been extensively used in market research settings (4).

Construction of a questionnaire entails processing the complex, unstructured, and often redundant information gained from this initial content-generating procedure. Producing a consistent measure, which faithfully represents the information gained in the initial process, requires a systematic approach to refining the preliminary set of items. Broadly speaking, there have been two approaches to this task. Both are based on examining the responses to the initial set of items from a sample of representative subjects. Principal components or factor analysis examines the correlation among item responses to identify domains or components of meaning. Items that best measure the variation among respondents in the domain of interest are selected for the questionnaire (5). The alternative approach is to empirically identify the domains of interest and select items that respondents most frequently identify as important for those domains (6). There is evidence to suggest that there may be important differences in the results of these approaches (7).

There is no criterion or gold standard against which the final product can be evaluated. The best guarantee that the questionnaire does validly measure health-related quality of life is the demonstration that it samples the core domains of quality of life and that a valid and systematic process of constructing the questionnaire, such as that described above, has been adopted. The consistency, or reliability, of this measurement can be assessed both internally and externally. Cronbach's alpha is a measure of the consistency with which individual item responses are related to each other and the overall scale (8). Test-retest repeatability measures the extent to which information gathered by the questionnaire is the same in stable subjects on different occasions of measurement.

A questionnaire that validly and reliably measures the core domains of health-related quality of life is worthy of consideration for use in research.

Is the Questionnaire Suitable for the Specific Task at Hand?

Although all valid quality-of-life questionnaires should measure physical, psychological, and social domains, some research tasks require a focus on specific aspects of quality of life that are not measured by all questionnaires. For example, in a clinical trial of drug therapy, it is likely that researchers would regard disease symptoms as an important aspect of quality of life to be measured. In other circumstances it may be more important to focus on emotional or social domains. Researchers can choose among suitable questionnaires to select those that have the appropriate content emphasis.

Several pragmatic issues are relevant to the selection of a questionnaire for a research project. The mode of administration, ease of completion, and cultural appropriateness are important features to consider. Also the dependence of scale scores on non-disease-related patient characteristics (such as age, gender, social class, etc.) may be significant in cross-sectional study designs.

Finally, it is relevant to know that the questionnaire has demonstrated expected characteristics in settings similar to the intended research. In cross-sectional study designs, it is expected that the questionnaire will be able to distinguish between subject groups and bear a predictable relation to other measures. In a longitudinal study design, the ability to detect change when this has occurred and the predictable relation to change in other measures are important (6). These characteristics are commonly referred to as *construct validity*, *sensitivity*, and *responsiveness*. These are not absolute attributes of the questionnaire. They simply describe the relation between questionnaire responses and other variables in a specified setting. The intending questionnaire user must judge whether the observed performances in previous settings mean that the questionnaire will be appropriate for the intended research study.

What Is the Meaning of Information Derived by Using the Questionnaire?

The health-related quality-of-life questionnaires described here do not measure quality of life on an absolute scale. There is no gold standard or criterion against which a given questionnaire score or change in score can be evaluated. Although most questionnaires are scored on an ordinal scale, there is no evidence that the measurements represent a ratio scale. In other words, it is possible to say that one individual (or group) has better or worse quality of life than another or has improved or deteriorated since a previous measurement, but it is not possible to validly say by how much this is.

Nevertheless, information based on the questionnaire's performance in previous settings can be used as a basis for comparison with the current research study. For example, the improvement observed after application of an established therapy might be used as reference for assessing other therapies. Unfortunately, the data required for such references are not commonly available.

B. Scope of the Chapter

This chapter aims to catalogue and describe the key features of patient-focused disease-specific and generic quality-of-life questionnaires that have been designed for or used in adult patients with asthma. The questionnaires included here all encompass the core domains of quality of life: physical, psychological, and social. The purpose of this catalogue is to permit the reader to make an informed decision about the choice of appropriate questionnaires for research purposes.

Questionnaires designed primarily for use in patients with chronic respiratory illness and generic questionnaires that have not been used in patients with asthma are excluded. Questionnaires that do not deal substantially with quality of life, such as asthma knowledge and self-efficacy scales, and those that are not patient-focused, such as clinical severity scores, are not discussed here.

The questionnaires described here are primarily designed for use in research. Although it is feasible to use them in routine clinical practice, it is unlikely that the restricted range of information elicited by a questionnaire will be more useful than that which is gained by an open-ended clinical interview. However, clinicians may find the content of these questionnaires useful in guiding the interview process.

C. Methods

Medline (1987–1997) and Embase (1988–1997) databases were searched using the terms *asthma* and *quality of life* to identify reports of questionnaires falling within the scope of this review. These reports were reviewed to identify published reports of studies that contain relevant information about each of the questionnaires. In addition, for the disease-specific questionnaires, the Science Citation Index was used to find papers citing the original descriptions of the questionnaires.

This search produced six asthma- or respiratory-focused health-related quality of life instruments and two generic instruments. The asthma- or respiratory-focused HRQOL instruments include: The St George's Respiratory Questionnaire (SGRQ), the Living with Asthma Questionnaire (LWAQ), the Asthma Quality of Life Questionnaire (McMaster), the Asthma Quality of Life Questionnaire (Sydney), the Asthma Impact Record (AIR) Index, and the Quality of Life for Respiratory Illness Questionnaire (QOL-RIQ). The generic HRQOL instruments include the Sickness Impact Profile (SIP) and the Medical Outcomes Study Short Form 36 (SF-36).

D. Description of Each Questionnaire

For each questionnaire, the following aspects are described based on information abstracted from published reports:

- Scope and format of the questionnaire
- Development of the questionnaire
- Evidence for construct validity and responsiveness
- Cross-cultural appropriateness and availability in languages other than English
- Summary of applications
- Conclusion regarding strength and weakness of the instrument

II. Descriptions of the Questionnaires

A. St George's Respiratory Questionnaire (SGRQ)

Description of the Questionnaire

Intended Purpose and Scope
The SGRQ was intended for use as a discriminative and evaluative instrument to measure the outcome of care of patients with airways disease. It is designed

for patients with chronic obstructive pulmonary disease (COPD) and patients with asthma (9).

The questionnaire deals with symptoms of airways disease, physical activities causing or limited by breathlessness, impacts of disease on employment, sense of control, panic, stigmatization, need for medication (and consequent side effects), expectations for health, and disturbance of daily life (10). Symptoms of anxiety and depression are not included in this questionnaire.

Format and Method of Administration

This is a 76-item questionnaire divided into three parts. The first part, Symptoms, has ordinal scale responses that generally denote the frequency of specific symptoms of airways disease. Items for the other two parts, Activity and Impact, are constructed in the form of statements with dichotomous (yes or no) response options.

The questionnaire takes about 10 min to complete (11). It can be administered by computer-assisted telephone interview, and the results of this form of administration are reliable when compared with face-to-face interview (12).

Scoring

Each item is associated with empirically derived weights. Scores for the total questionnaire and for the three sections are calculated by adding the weights attached to each item response. The final scores are scaled from zero (no impairment in quality of life) to 100% (maximum possible impairment).

Subscales

As described above, three subscale scores are calculated: Symptoms, Activity, and Impact.

Development of the Questionnaire

The source and method of selecting items for the SGRQ have not been reported. Reports on the development of the questionnaire have focused on the procedure for assigning appropriate weights to each of these items. The degree of distress associated with each of the 76 items comprising the questionnaire was assessed in 140 patients with asthma in six countries (13,14). This degree of distress was mainly independent of age, gender, lung function, duration of asthma, and country. These data were used to calculate empirical weights applied to each item in the SGRQ.

Psychometric Properties of the Questionnaire

Distribution of Scores

In 141 patients with COPD, the SGRQ scores were normally distributed, with mean values for Symptoms, Activity, and Impacts being 62, 55, and 34%, respectively. The overall mean score was 48% (10). Among patients with asthma enrolled in a trial of nedocromil sodium, the mean baseline scores in the treatment group were 55, 39, 34, and 39%, respectively (15).

Reliability: Internal Consistency and Test-Retest Repeatability

The repeatability of the SGRQ was tested in 40 patients with asthma who completed the questionnaire on two occasions, 2 weeks apart. The intraclass correlation coefficient for the total scale score was 0.91, indicating good repeatability (10). Internal consistency has not been reported for the English-language version. However, the Spanish-language version of the SGRQ is highly reliable: Cronbach's alpha 0.94 (16).

Effect of Age, Gender, and Other Subject Characteristics

It has been demonstrated that the degree of distress (and hence weight) associated with individual items in the questionnaire is independent of age and gender (13).

Construct Validity and Responsiveness

Relation to Other Measures: Cross-Sectionally

The cross-sectional relation of the SGRQ was investigated in 141 patients with obstructive airways disease (10). The mean age of these patients was 63 years. Their mean prebronchodilator FEV_1 was 47% predicted and the mean response to inhaled bronchodilator aerosol was 13%. Most of these patients had COPD but some had asthma. In this population, the Symptoms scale was closely related to independently reported symptoms (wheeze, cough, and sputum). The Activity and Impact scales were moderately to strongly correlated with exercise tolerance, degree of dyspnea, and quality of life as measured on the generic Sickness Impact Profile (Table 1). The total score was moderately or strongly correlated with most of the clinical and quality-of-life measures.

Relation to Other Measures: Longitudinally

Changes in SGRQ total scores were correlated with changes in most clinical and other quality of life measures in 133 patients (mainly with COPD) who were assessed on two occasions over a 1-year period (Table 2) (10). However, the strength of correlations was less than observed cross-sectionally in the same population.

Cross-Cultural Appropriateness and Availability in Languages Other Than English

Initial development of the questionnaire included testing of questionnaire items in patients from England, Holland, Finland, Thailand, Italy, and the United States

Table 1 Cross-Sectional Correlation Between SGRQ Scores and Other Clinical and Quality-of-Life Measures in 141 Subjects with Obstructive Airways Disease

	Symptom	Activity	Impact	Total
Cough	0.59[a]	0.17	0.3	0.33
Sputum	0.49	0.0	0.25	0.25
Wheeze	0.57	0.35	0.50	0.50
FEV_1	−0.10	−0.28	−0.26	
FVC	−0.24	−0.32	−0.45	−0.42
Sa_{O_2} at rest	−0.14	−0.2	−0.10	
6-min walk distance (m)	−0.26	−0.59	−0.59	−0.61
MRC dyspnea grade	0.36	0.71	0.66	0.71
Anxiety	0.34	0.44	0.62	0.58
Depression	0.28	0.48	0.62	0.59
SIP, physical	0.35	0.62	0.69	
SIP, psychosocial	0.26	0.53	0.65	
SIP, total	0.33	0.62	0.73	0.71

[a]Correlation coefficient, r, derived from regression analysis. All values >0.2 are significant at the 1% level.
Abbreviations: MRC, Medical Research Council; SIP, Sickness Impact Profile.
Source: From Ref. 10.

(14). Although there were between-country differences in item scores, these differences were small compared with the variation between individuals.

The SGRQ has been translated into Dutch, Danish, Finish, French, Italian, Portuguese, Swedish, and Thai for a multicentered clinical trial (15). Translations were performed using a systematic method involving forward and backward translation.

For another study, the SGRQ was translated into Spanish, once again by the forward and backward translation method (16). It was tested in 318 male patients with COPD and found to be internally consistent (Cronbach's alpha = 0.94). Moderate correlations with a dyspnea scale (R = 0.59 for overall score) and weak to moderate correlations with FEV_1 (ranging from R = −0.29 for symptoms to R = −0.53 for Activity subscale) were observed.

Applications

The SGRQ has been applied in evaluative and descriptive settings in patients with asthma.

The SGRQ was used as an outcome measure in a parallel-group randomized controlled trial of nedocromil sodium in 719 patients with asthma. There was a

Table 2 Longitudinal Correlation
Between SGRQ Scores and Other
Clinical and Quality-of-Life Measures in
133 Subjects with Obstructive Airways
Disease Measured on Two Occasions, 1
Year Apart

	Total
FEV$_1$	-0.22[a]
FVC	-0.26
6-min walk distance (m)	-0.36
MRC dyspnea grade	0.47
Anxiety	0.17
Depression	0.35
SIP, physical	0.14
SIP, psychosocial	0.30
SIP, total	0.32

[a]Correlation coefficient, r. Values > 0.15 are
significant at the 5% level.
Abbreviations: MRC, Medical Research Council; SIP, Sickness Impact Profile.
Source: From Ref. 10.

significant between group difference in improvement from baseline for SGRQ
Impacts subscale (8.1 versus 5.4, p $<$ 0.05) but not for the other scales. Some
clinical outcomes also improved (15).

A randomized controlled trial of a self-management strategy for asthma
demonstrated benefits in several clinical outcomes compared with a traditional
approach to management. Quality of life, which was evaluated using modified
25-item version of the SGRQ (17), improved significantly in the self-management
group compared with the traditional management group.

The SGRQ was used to describe the impact of obstructive airways disease
in older people (18). In subjects aged > 45 years selected at random from the
general community, impaired lung function was associated with worse scores for
the total SGRQ and all three subscales. In the subgroup aged 45 to 64 years,
airway hyperresponsiveness was also associated with worse SGRQ scores.

Conclusion: Summary of Strengths and Weaknesses

The SGRQ comprehensively measures physical and social factors associated with
obstructive airways disease. However, coverage of psychological symptoms is
limited and the authors recommend using a separate questionnaire to measure
these. Although the source of items has not been described, weights for individual

items have been derived by a well-described empirical method based on patient responses.

One of the strengths of the SGRQ is the extent to which cross-cultural and linguistic considerations were included in the design of the questionnaire. Its main limitation, from the standpoint of research in asthma, is its attempt to encompass patients with asthma and those with COPD. Much of the development and testing of the questionnaire has been in populations predominantly composed of subjects with COPD. This poses problems in interpreting the results of the questionnaire in patients with asthma.

B. The Living with Asthma Questionnaire

Description of the Questionnaire

Intended Purpose and Scope

The Living with Asthma Questionnaire (19) is intended for use "by researchers to evaluate the effectiveness of treatment management programs for adult asthma sufferers" (20). The questionnaire does not measure symptoms of asthma but does cover a range of physical, social and psychological domains including social and leisure activities, sports, holidays, sleep, work and other activities, colds, mobility, effects on others, medication use, sex, and dysphoric states and attitudes.

Format and Method of Administration

There are 68 items, each with a three-point response option: "untrue of me," "slightly true of me," and "very true of me." Respondents may also choose "not applicable." There is a mixture of positively and negatively constructed items. It is designed to be self-administered but can be interviewer administered and takes approximately 15 min to complete.

Scoring

Negative items, for which agreement indicates an adverse impact, are scored 1 ("untrue of me") to 3 ("very true of me"). Positive items are scored in the reverse direction. The scale score is calculated by adding the individual item scores and dividing by the number of applicable items (i.e., "not applicable" items are excluded). There is no weighting of items. The final score ranges from 1 to 3: higher scores represent a worse quality of life (19). In some cases it has been scored from 0 to 2 (21).

Subscales

The questionnaire can be analyzed in terms of the 11 domains listed above. However, the authors caution that the small number of items in some domains limits the reliability of these domain scores (22).

Although initial factor analysis of the questionnaire suggested that it consisted of a single dimension (i.e., factor or construct), subsequent analysis has revealed the existence of two dimensions. These have been labeled "problems" or limitations due to illness and "evaluations" of the emotional impact of those limitations (22).

Development of the Questionnaire

Source of the Initial Pool of Items

The items for the initial questionnaire were derived from six focus groups: four conducted in two general practices and two conducted with people recruited by advertising on a university campus. Participants at the focus groups were asked to provide information about their experiences of asthma. The content arising from these groups was formulated into a 103-item questionnaire with four-point response options.

Method of Selecting the Final Item Set

The initial questionnaire passed through three iterative phases of item reduction. Each phase consisted of administration to a sample of people with asthma and principal-components analysis of the responses. Most of the subjects were identified through general practices, but one sample was recruited through an Asthma Society newsletter. On each occasion, highly skewed items, those with low factor loading, and those adversely commented upon by respondents were deleted. At each stage, the principal-components analysis identified a single-factor (component) solution that fitted the data most appropriately.

Psychometric Properties of the Questionnaire

Distribution of Scores

Among patients with moderately severe asthma enrolled in a parallel-group clinical trial, the mean scores at baseline (scored from 0 to 2) were 0.78 (SD 0.36) and 0.77 (SD 0.31), respectively, in the two groups (21).

Reliability: Internal Consistency and Test-Retest Repeatability

The questionnaire was administered on two occasions 2 months apart to 95 volunteers with asthma. The correlation between scores was 0.95, indicating good test-retest reliability.

The two dimensions or constructs that make up the LWAQ, problems (49 items) and evaluations (19 items), are both internally consistent. Coefficient alpha values were 0.94 and 0.90, respectively (22). The 10 domains that contain more than one item are moderately consistent, with coefficient alpha values ranging from 0.57 (medication usage, 6 items) to 0.91 (dysphoric states and attitudes, 23 items).

Effect of Age, Gender, and Other Subject Characteristics

Living with Asthma Scale scores are slightly higher (worse) in women than men (2.00 versus 1.89, p = 0.05) and tend to increase with age (1.71 in 18- to 24-year-olds versus 2.05 in 55- to 64-year-olds, p < 0.001) (20). Similar gender differences were noted among Japanese patients with asthma (23) and similar age effects were noted in Italy (24).

Construct Validity and Responsiveness

Relation to Other Measures: Cross-Sectionally

LWAQ scores are correlated with scores on a generic quality-of-life instrument, the Sickness Impact Profile (r = 0.66), and with concurrently measured peak expiratory flow rate (r = −0.44) (19). They were also observed to be predictive of physician's prescription of steroids to patients with asthma (25).

In patients with moderately severe asthma, LWAQ scores were, at best, weakly correlated with measures of lung function (R = −0.15, p > 0.05, for FEV_1; R = −0.26, p < 0.001, for FVC) but were moderately well correlated with symptom scores (R = 0.42 for daytime symptoms and for nighttime symptoms) (21). In patients with mild asthma, LWAQ scores were not correlated with airway hyperresponsiveness (24).

Relation to Other Measures: Longitudinally

Data from a parallel-group randomized controlled trial of salmeterol (Table 3) have shown that the "problems" construct of the LWAQ is responsive to change (22). Since most items fall within this construct, the overall LWAQ is also responsive to change (p = 0.008 for treatment by time interaction in analysis of variance).

However, in another, similar trial conducted in patients with moderately severe asthma, changes in LWAQ total scores were unrelated to changes in lung function or nocturnal symptom score (21). There was a weak correlation

Table 3   Parallel-Group, Randomized Controlled Trial of Salmeterol—Mean Construct Scores for the Living with Asthma Questionnaire

	Salmeterol (n = 41)		Control (n = 38)		
	Pretreatment	Posttreatment	Pretreatment	Posttreatment	Value[a]
Problems	0.82	0.63	0.76	0.73	0.007
Evaluations	0.66	0.57	0.62	0.58	0.3

[a]P value for treatment by time interaction in two-way analysis of variance.
Source: From Ref. 22.

with change in daytime symptom score (R = −0.24). Also in this study, the LWAQ did not identify a significant difference in treatment effect between the active and control arms of the study in spite of substantial benefits assessed by other means.

Cross-Cultural Appropriateness and Availability in Languages Other Than English

English-language versions of the LWAQ have been used in the United Kingdom and the United States. Translated versions of the questionnaire have been used in Italy (24,26), Japan (23), the Netherlands (21), and France (27).

Applications

The principal applications of the LWAQ have been in clinical trials of asthma therapy including salmeterol (22,27) and fluticasone (28). In one parallel-group randomized trial comparing salmeterol with salbutamol, patients in the salmeterol group improved more than those in the salbutamol group in the sport, sleep, and work domains but not in the other domains (22). In another study comparing salmeterol with slow-release oral terbutaline, subjects in the former group improved significantly more than those in the latter group (27). In a parallel-group clinical trial, subjects with asthma who received fluticasone propionate had significantly greater improvements in LWAQ scores than did those receiving placebo (28).

The LWAQ has been used in the evaluation of community-based management strategies (29–31). In each of these studies, the intervention did not have a substantial impact on any of the outcomes measured, including the LWAQ score.

Conclusion: Summary of Strengths and Weaknesses

The main strength of the LWAQ is the extensive qualitative research undertaken to generate the initial content and the systemic approach taken to construct a consistent and valid measure of asthma-related quality of life. The major focus of the LWAQ is on psychological and social aspects of quality of life.

Limited information on the cross-sectional and longitudinal correlations of the LWAQ with other measures is available. This shows good correlations with other quality-of-life measures but weak to moderate correlations with clinical measures of asthma.

The limited range of response options (three) and the exclusion of asthma symptoms from the questionnaire cause it to be less responsive to the effect of asthma drug treatment than other questionnaires, particularly the AQLQ (McMaster).

C. Asthma Quality of Life Questionnaire (McMaster University)

Description of the Questionnaire

Intended Purpose and Scope

The questionnaire was intended for use as an outcome measure in clinical trials and hence was designed to be capable of measuring change in status (32). It contains items dealing with physical and emotional function, including symptoms. Respondents are asked to refer to their status over the preceding 2 weeks.

Format and Method of Administration

The questionnaire may be interviewer-or self-administered and takes 5 to 15 min to complete. It comprises 32 items, each of which is associated with one of four sets of 7-point Likert-scale response options. Five items in the activities domain are individualized for each respondent. This is achieved, on the first administration of the questionnaire, by asking subjects to select the five most important activities for them which are limited by their asthma. A list of 26 activities is offered as a prompt. The subjects are then asked to rate the degree of limitation they have experienced in undertaking that task. It is intended that subjects completing the questionnaire for the second or subsequent time should see their previous responses at that time.

Scoring

The total scale score is the mean score for all the items. Domain scores are the mean of all items in the domain. No weighting has been used. Items are scored from 1 (totally limited, very great distress, etc.) to 7 (not at all limited, no discomfort or distress, etc.). In other words, lower scores represent worse quality of life.

Subscales

Four domains are identified: symptoms, emotional function, activity limitation, and exposure to environmental stimuli.

Development of the Questionnaire

Source of the Initial Pool of Items

An initial pool of 152 items was drawn from several sources including the Asthma Symptom Checklist (33), two general quality-of-life questionnaires (34,35), interviews with health professionals, and detailed structured interviews with six patients with asthma (32).

Method of Selecting the Final Item Set

Items were selected for inclusion in the final questionnaire on the basis of their importance to patients with asthma. A questionnaire was constructed listing 152 items in six domains: asthma symptoms, emotional problems caused by asthma, troublesome environmental stimuli, problems associated with avoidance of environmental stimuli, activities limited by asthma, and practical problems. The responses of 150 patients with asthma were analyzed to identify which items in each domain were most frequently nominated as troublesome and were most important for those whom they troubled. It was shown that the rank order of importance was not different between age groups, gender, or severity grades for asthma. Respondents nominated a wide range of activities. For this reason the investigators left five items in the activities domain open to allow individual respondents to select activities that were most important to them.

The final wording of the questionnaire was developed by an iterative process of administering the questionnaire to a series of patients with asthma and reviewing its performance after each administration.

Psychometric Properties of the Questionnaire

Distribution of Scores

As with other questionnaires, scores on the AQLQ (McMaster) are skewed toward less impact on quality of life (higher scores). Among patients with moderately severe asthma who were enrolled in one parallel-group clinical trial in the Netherlands, the mean baseline AQLQ (McMaster) scores were 5.55 (SD 1.01) and 5.62 (SD 0.84), respectively, in the two groups (21). In another clinical trial in the United States mean baseline scores were 4.20, 4.18, and 4.11 in three parallel groups, respectively (36). In Australian patients with asthma attending retail pharmacies to purchase bronchodilator inhalers, the mean AQLQ score was 5.22; whereas in a group who had recently been discharged from hospital, the mean score was 4.46 (37).

Reliability: Internal Consistency and Test-Retest Repeatability

Twenty six subjects completed the questionnaire on two or three occasions (total 38 pairs of observations) at four weekly intervals, during which time they were judged to be clinically stable by other criteria. On each follow-up occasion, subjects were shown their previous responses. Under these circumstances, the scores were highly repeatable. The intraclass correlation was 0.92 for overall quality of life and ranged from 0.89 to 0.94 for the subscales (38). Internal consistency has not been reported.

Effect of Age, Gender, and Other Subject Characteristics

The effects of age and gender were examined during the development of the questionnaire. Younger subjects and women had higher scores for the frequency and importance of symptom-related and emotional items in the original 152-item set (32).

Construct Validity and Responsiveness

Relation to Other Measures: Cross-Sectionally

Table 4 shows that, in a clinic-based population of people with asthma, AQLQ (McMaster) scores were moderately correlated with a clinical asthma score but were not correlated with measures of lung function or airway hyperresponsiveness (32). Moderate to strong correlations with generic quality-of-life questionnaires were observed.

There were similar findings in patients with moderately severe asthma enrolled in a clinical trial (21). AQLQ (McMaster) scores at baseline were not correlated with measures of lung function but were strongly correlated with symptom scores (R = -0.59 for daytime symptoms and -0.70 for nighttime symptoms) and other quality-of-life indices (R = -0.73 with Living with Asthma Questionnaire).

For use among patients attending an emergency department for exacerbations of asthma, the AQLQ (McMaster) was modified to refer to the preceding 3 days only. AQLQ scores were strongly correlated with symptoms and a global self-assessment of severity, moderately well correlated with scores on the Sickness Impact Profile, but only weakly correlated with lung function (Table 5) (39).

Relation to Other Measures: Longitudinally

The relation of change in AQLQ (McMaster) scores to other indices was examined in a cohort of 39 subjects assessed on three occasions at four weekly intervals (38). Table 6 shows that changes in scores were strongly correlated with changes

Table 4 Cross-Sectional Relation Between Domains of the AQLQ (McMaster) and Other Measures in a Clinic Setting ($N = 39$)

	Activities	Symptoms	Emotions	Environment
FEV_1 % predicted	0.06[a]	0.11	0.18	0.08
$PC_{20}FEV_1$[b]	0.07	0.00	0.11	0.14
Asthma control[c]	0.31	0.69	0.36	0.45
SIP, physical	0.52	0.38	0.28	0.43
SIP psychosocial	0.37	0.30	0.39	0.40
SF 36, physical[d]	0.81	0.60	0.53	0.69
SF 36, emotional	0.09	0.38	0.49	0.32

[a]Correlation coefficient: values > 0.36 are significant at the 5% level.
[b]Lower values represent more severe airway hyperresponsiveness.
[c]Composite score based on symptoms, lung function, and bronchodilator requirement.
[d]MOS General Health Survey, Short Form 36.
Abbreviations: SIP, Sickness Impact Profile.
Source: From Ref. 38.

Table 5   Cross-Sectional Correlation Between AQLQ (McMaster) and Other Measures in an Emergency Department Setting ($N = 52$)

	Total	Activities	Symptoms	Emotions	Environment
Sickness Impact Profile total score	0.49[a]	0.40	0.47	0.45	0.30
Symptom score	0.74	0.63	0.77	0.57	0.36
Global self-assessment	0.67	0.66	0.60	0.61	0.29
FEV$_1$ % predicted	0.27	0.41	0.18	0.20	0.09

[a]Correlation coefficient: values > 0.31 are significant at 1% level.
Source: From Ref. 39.

in the value of a clinical asthma control index and also with subjects' own global assessment of their change in status. There were weak to moderate correlations with changes in lung function, airway hyperresponsiveness, and quality-of-life measured using generic indices.

These findings were confirmed in a subsequent randomized parallel-group

Table 6   Longitudinal Relation Between Change in AQLQ (McMaster) Domain Scores and Change in Other Measures in a Clinic Setting ($N = 39$)

	Activities	Symptoms	Emotions	Environment
FEV$_1$ % predicted	0.28[a]	0.27	0.43	0.29
PC$_{20}$FEV$_1$[b]	0.26	0.26	0.30	0.30
Asthma control[c]	0.57	0.67	0.63	0.40
SIP, physical	0.24	0.20	0.23	0.17
SIP, psychosocial	0.07	0.19	0.27	0.00
SF 36, physical[d]	0.51	0.46	0.49	0.36
SF 36, emotional	0.34	0.31	0.30	0.37
Global rating of change, activities	0.79	0.76	0.75	0.64
Global rating of change, symptoms	0.78	0.82	0.70	0.66
Global rating of change, emotions	0.43	0.49	0.52	0.38

[a]Correlation coefficient: values > 0.24 are significant at the 5% level.
[b]Lower values represent more severe airway hyperresponsiveness.
[c]Composite score based on symptoms, lung function, and bronchodilator requirement.
[d]MOS General Health Survey, Short Form 36.
Abbreviations: SIP, Sickness Impact Profile.
Source: From Ref. 38.

clinical trial comparing salmeterol with salbutamol (40). Changes in total AQLQ (McMaster) score were correlated with changes in morning peak expiratory flow (R = 0.58), evening peak expiratory flow (R = 0.48), morning symptoms (R = 0.47), nights without sleep disturbances (R = 0.28), daytime symptoms (R = 0.54), FEV_1 (R = 0.38) and rescue salbutamol use (R = 0.43).

In patients with moderately severe asthma enrolled in a clinical trial in the Netherlands, changes in AQLQ (McMaster) were moderately well correlated with changes in lung function (R = 0.32 for change in FEV_1% predicted) and strongly correlated with changes in symptom scores (R = 0.51 for change in daytime symptom score) (21).

There were similar findings among patients with asthma studied in India. Changes in AQLQ (McMaster) scores were strongly correlated with changes in global self-assessment of severity (R = 0.56) and weakly correlated with changes in lung function (R = 0.26) (41).

The AQLQ (McMaster) is responsive to changes in asthma-related quality of life. In the Dutch clinical trial referred to above, the AQLQ was capable of distinguishing an active treatment group (salmeterol, $n = 53$) from a control group (salbutamol, $n = 54$). Furthermore, the effect size (a measure of difference which is independent of the units of measurement) was larger for the total AQLQ score and for the Activities and Symptoms subscales than for other quality-of-life indices (21). The AQLQ (McMaster) was also responsive to change in the Indian clinical trial (41).

Cross-Cultural Appropriateness and Availability in Languages Other Than English

The AQLQ has been translated into Spanish, using the forward and backward translation method (42). French-Canadian and Dutch translations have also been used and evaluated (21,43). The validity and responsiveness of a Tamil translation has been evaluated in India (41). A Japanese translation has also been used (44).

Applications

The AQLQ (McMaster) has mainly been used as an outcome measure in clinical trials. Two studies comparing regular with "as needed" use of albuterol have used the AQLQ (McMaster) as an outcome measure. One was a crossover study in moderate to severe asthma and the other was a parallel group study in patients with mild asthma. Both showed no significant difference in quality of life (45,46) and no differences in clinical measures except that in the crossover study (45) peak flows were higher and need for a rescue bronchodilator was less in the regular-use treatment period.

The effectiveness of salmeterol and regular salbutamol were compared in a randomized crossover trial (40). Significant differences in favor of salmeterol were demonstrated for several clinical indices as well as the AQLQ total and all subscale scores.

A parallel-group randomized controlled trial of a 5-lipoxygenase inhibitor demonstrated significant benefits in terms of reduced exacerbations and improved lung function (36). Mean (SE) improvements from baseline in AQLQ (McMaster) scores at the conclusion of treatment were 0.78 (0.11), 0.60 (0.11), and 0.37 (0.11). The improvement from baseline was greater than placebo for one treatment arm but not the other.

The effect of nedocromil sodium (4 mg qid) in patients with asthma who were not responsive to oral steroids was assessed in a 3-month randomized controlled trial (47). Clinical benefits were accompanied by significant improvements in AQLQ (McMaster) score during treatment. The mean AQLQ score in the active treatment group increased from 4.1 to 4.6 ($P<0.007$).

The AQLQ (McMaster) was used in a clinical trial of a new class of anti-asthma drugs, a platelet-activating factor antagonist. The experimental treatment showed no benefit compared to placebo in any of the clinical or quality-of-life outcomes (48).

The effect of inhaled corticosteroids on patients with occupational asthma, after cessation of exposure to the occupational allergen, was assessed in a randomized crossover design (49). The active treatment period was associated with significant improvements in the total AQLQ (McMaster) score as well as the Symptom and Emotion subscales.

There have been applications of the AQLQ (McMaster) in cross-sectional studies. The impact of an occupational etiology on quality of life in asthma was evaluated in a study in Quebec (43). Compared to patients with non-occupational asthma, those with occupational asthma of similar severity had worse quality of life on all scales of the AQLQ.

One Australian study investigated the relation between quality of life and patients' desire for autonomy in decision making about asthma (37). AQLQ (McMaster) scores were not related to self-management autonomy.

A study in Quebec used the AQLQ (McMaster) to compare patients with asthma with frequent emergency department (ED) attendances with a control group who did not attend the ED (50). There were no differences in quality-of-life scale scores.

Conclusion: Summary of Strengths and Weaknesses

The AQLQ (McMaster) contains items relevant to the central domains of quality of life. There is a major focus on physical symptoms and activity limitations. The method used to select the content for the final questionnaire was an empirical one—based on items subjects thought were most important, most frequently to them. This method, which differs from the psychometric approach, is reflected in the inclusion of some items which other investigators have not found central to quality of life: for example, identification of environmental triggers to symptoms.

The key feature of this questionnaire is that it is designed to detect change. The method of selection of questions for the final questionnaire—the inclusion of five individualized questions, the focus on disease symptoms, the use of 7-point Likert scale responses, and the practice of showing subjects their previous responses—all point toward enhanced responsiveness. This characteristic of the questionnaire has been confirmed in a number of settings. The AQLQ (McMaster) has been used extensively in clinical therapeutic trials. On the whole, results from the AQLQ have been consistent with results for other clinical outcomes in these trials.

As the AQLQ (McMaster) is optimized for longitudinal studies, it is less suitable for cross-sectional or between-subject study designs. The internal consistency of the scale has not been reported, but—since factor loadings were not a criterion for item selection—the scale may be less homogeneous than other scales. Together with the use of individualized items, this means that the scale could be less useful for discriminating between subjects.

Revised Versions of the Questionnaire

Two revised versions of the questionnaire have been developed, with the aim of improving the utility of this questionnaire in certain circumstances.

One revision consists of replacing the five individualized activity items by five standardized items dealing with strenuous activities, moderate activities, social activities, work-related activities, and sleeping (51). The aim of this change was to make the questionnaire more suitable for use in cross-sectional studies. It was expected that it would be less responsive in longitudinal studies. However, in a sample of 40 patients with asthma, scores for the new standardized questionnaire [AQLQ(S)] were highly correlated with scores for the original AQLQ. Furthermore the measurement characteristics of the two questionnaires—including reliability, responsiveness, and cross-sectional and longitudinal relation to other measures—were similar.

An abbreviated questionnaire was developed for use in long-term patient monitoring and large clinical trials. The MiniAQLQ comprises 15 of the 32 items of the standardised AQLQ (52). Comparison of the MiniAQLQ with the original AQLQ reveals strong correlations for the overall score and the symptoms, emotions, and environmental stimuli domains and a moderate correlation for the activity domain. The reliability, responsiveness, and cross-sectional and longitudinal correlations of the MiniAQLQ were found to be generally satisfactory but lower and weaker than those of the original AQLQ.

At the current time, the role and performance of these revised versions of the AQLQ (McMaster) are not clearly defined.

D. Asthma Quality of Life Questionnaire (University of Sydney)

Description of the Questionnaire

Intended Purpose and Scope

This questionnaire was designed for use as an outcome measure in clinical trials of therapeutic interventions for asthma (53,54). It incorporates content from physical, psychological, and social domains, including disease symptoms. The impact of symptoms is measured in terms of how much the respondent has "been troubled" by the symptom. The questionnaire deals with the preceding 1-month period.

Format and Method of Administration

The questionnaire is self-administered but can be interviewer-administered (55). It consists of 20 statements with a common set of 5-point, Likert-scale responses and takes approximately 5 to 10 min to complete.

Scoring

Items are scored 0 ("not at all") to 4 ("very severely"). The total score is calculated by averaging across the items. There is no weighting of individual items. For convenience, the final score is multiplied by 2.5, so that it lies in the range 0 to 10. Higher scores reflect a more adverse impact on quality of life (i.e., best quality of life scores zero).

Subscales

Four subscales have been identified: breathlessness, mood disturbance, social disruption, and concerns for health. Each subscale includes 5 to 7 items from the total 20-item scale. Some items are included in more than one subscale. Subscales are scored by averaging across the relevant items.

Development of the Questionnaire

Source of the Initial Pool of Items

An initial set of items was derived from analysis of the output of a single focus group and discussion with asthma nurse educators. The focus group comprised eight patients who had attended a specialist asthma clinic. Issues raised by this group included physical incapacity, control, emotional states, role fulfilment, social interaction, and general health perceptions. The focus group avoided discussion of physical symptoms. Items for this content area were contributed from the experiences of asthma nurse educators, which were based on patients' descriptions to them.

Method of Selecting the Final Item Set

The initial item pool was formulated into a self-administered questionnaire comprising 69 items with 4- to 6-point Likert-scale responses. The questionnaire was administered to 283 patients with asthma identified from the patient registers of a number of physicians treating people with asthma.

Items with highly skewed distributions or with many missing responses were deleted. The remaining items were subjected to principal-components analysis, which identified the four components that form the subscales of the final questionnaire. Items relating to two other components, "cough" and "control," explained a small proportion of the overall variance and were not correlated with the total (i.e., overall quality of life). Hence these items were excluded from the final questionnaire. Redundant items, those with low item-total correlations for the overall scale, and those that were not correlated with any of the subscales (that is, did not load onto any of the principal components) were excluded. A final set of 20 items was selected to represent the four principal components.

Psychometric Properties of the Questionnaire

Distribution of Scores

The distribution of scores is negatively skewed in most populations of asthmatics that have been studied (53,56). Square-root transformation has been applied to allow parametric analysis (logarithmic transformation is not suitable because of the zero values). Although a floor effect has been observed (i.e., zero values), it has fallen within the lowest quartile in all populations studied.

In subjects identified in a general population survey in Greenwich, United Kingdom, the median score was 2.0 (interquartile range 1.1 to 3.5) (56). In a similar study in Australia, the median score was 1.0 (interquartile range 0.6 to 1.8) (55). In a clinic-based population in Australia, the median score was 2.6 (interquartile range 1.8 to 4.0) (54). In patients with asthma attending allergists in a health maintenance organization, the mean score for subjects with mild asthma was 1.7 (SD 1.2); for moderate to severe asthma, it was 2.2 (SD 1.5).

Reliability: Internal Consistency and Test-Retest Repeatability

Table 7 shows that the total scale and the four subscales were internally consistent, as measured by Cronbach's alpha, in four separate studies: two clinic-based populations and two community-based samples.

Short-term test-retest repeatability was found to be satisfactory in 58 clinic patients with asthma. The intraclass correlation coefficient for the total scale score was 0.80 and for the subscale scores ranged from 0.61 (breathlessness) to the 0.80 (concerns for health).

Effect of Age, Gender, and Other Subject Characteristics

In two Australian community-based samples, the scale scores were not related to age or gender except that females had slightly higher scores on the mood

Table 7 Internal Consistency of AQLQ (Sydney) in Four Settings:
Cronbach's Alpha

	Community sample 1	Community sample 2	Clinic sample 1	Clinic sample 2
Total	0.94	0.89	0.92	0.94
Breathlessness	0.89	0.90	0.89	0.93
Mood	0.89	0.77	0.82	0.90
Social	0.94	0.75	0.88	0.89
Concerns for health	0.87	0.80	0.84	0.85

Source: From Ref. 53.

disturbance subscale (53). In a large community-based sample from the United Kingdom, older subjects and smokers had higher (worse) scores than younger subjects and nonsmokers, respectively (56).

Construct Validity and Responsiveness

Relation to Other Measures: Cross-Sectionally

The cross-sectional relation between scale scores and other measures of quality of life and asthma has been examined in clinic and community-based populations in Australia and in a large community-based population in the United Kingdom.

The total scale score was found to be moderately correlated with other subjective measures of disease severity, such as symptoms, medication use, and global self-assessment of severity (Table 8). On the other hand, correlations with objective measures such as lung function, peak flow variability, and airway hyper-responsiveness were weaker. The scale was moderately correlated ($R = 0.44$) with scores on the Sickness Impact Profile, a generic measure of quality of life in asthma (53). Similar findings were observed in patients attending pulmonary and allergy specialists in California (57). Scores were moderately correlated with a severity index ($R = 0.59$) and weakly correlated with FEV_1 ($R = -0.12$).

The scale discriminates between groups of patients who would be expected to differ in quality of life. In London, subjects with asthma who experienced symptoms three or more times per week were 4.3 times more likely to have scale scores > 3.5 than those with less frequent symptoms (56). Similarly, subjects who were woken from sleep due to asthma symptoms three or more times per week were 2.7 times more likely to have a high scale score than those with less frequent waking.

Table 8 Relation Between Scale Scores for the AQLQ (Sydney) and Measures of Disease Severity in an Australian Population Sample (N = 98)

	Global severity rating[a]	Number of β-agonist inhalers/year	FEV$_1$ (% predicted)	Airway hyper-responsiveness[b]
Total	0.64[c]	0.41	−0.44	0.24
Breathlessness	0.69	0.46	−0.43	0.29
Mood	0.28	0.05	−0.14	0.06
Social	0.38	0.25	−0.48	0.21
Concern	0.45	0.50	−0.46	0.26

[a] Self-assessed rating.
[b] Histamine challenge test, dose-response ratio. Higher values represent more severe airway hyperresponsiveness.
[c] Spearman's correlation coefficient. All values > 0.20 are significant at the 5% level.
Source: From Ref. 53.

Relation to Other Measures: Longitudinally

The relation between change in the scale and change in related measures was examined in 44 patients with asthma who were assessed on two occasions 4 months apart (Table 9) (54). Change in the total scale score was weakly correlated with change in diary card symptom score and change in airway hyperresponsiveness. Change in the social subscale score was more strongly related to the other measures.

The scale was found to be responsive to change in asthma-related quality of life. It was able to distinguish between two groups of subjects judged to be

Table 9 Relation Between Change in AQLQ (Sydney) Score and Change in Other Measures (*N* = 44)

	Total	Breathlessness	Mood	Social	Concerns for health
Symptoms	0.37[a]	0.13	−0.06	0.52	0.37
Peak flow variability	0.12	−0.15	−0.06	0.51	0.02
DRR[b]	0.38	0.21	0.14	0.47	0.32
Sickness Impact Profile	0.18	0.03	0.19	0.20	0.23

[a] Correlation coefficient. Values > 0.33 are significant at the 5% level.
[b] Dose-response ratio, a measure of airway hyperresponsiveness.
Source: From Ref. 54.

improved or stable by independent criteria. The scale was more responsive to change than the Sickness Impact Profile and a diary card symptom record (54).

Cross-Cultural Appropriateness and Availability in Languages Other Than English

The English version of the questionnaire has been used in Australia (55), the United Kingdom (56) and the United States (57–59). Translated versions have been used in Norway, France (60) and Spain (61,62). Investigations with the Spanish and French versions have shown that it has psychometric properties similar to those of the English language version.

Applications

In contrast to the stated purpose of the AQLQ (Sydney), most reports of its use have been in cross-sectional analytic studies.

It was used to describe the relation between disease management and the impact of asthma on quality of life in an Australian provincial center (55) and in an area of London (56). Subjects who perceived that asthma had a major impact on their quality of life were much more likely to have and to use inhaled steroids and peak flow meters and to keep oral steroids in the home. They also showed a stronger tendency to measure their peak flow during an exacerbation compared to those with better quality-of-life scores. This strong relation between perceived quality of life and self-management practices was still apparent after adjustment for disease severity (56).

The AQLQ (Sydney) has been used to investigate the cross-sectional construct validity of a new questionnaire for measuring perceived control of asthma (63). Significant correlations were observed with all four subscales of the AQLQ.

Asthma-specific quality of life, as measured by the AQLQ (Sydney), did not differ between patients with asthma attending an allergist compared with those attending a generalist (59) in spite of the fact that allergists' patients were older and had more severe asthma and more associated diseases. This difference may have been counterbalanced by more intensive treatment prescribed by allergists.

The AQLQ (Sydney) was used as an evaluative measure in an audit of outcomes of patients with asthma attending a specialist clinic in Colorado. This study demonstrated improvements in total and subscale scores over the follow-up period (58). The mean baseline score was 3.5, and this decreased to 2.7 at the follow-up assessment.

Conclusion: Summary of Strengths and Weaknesses

The questionnaire has items dealing with the three major areas that impact on quality of life: physical, psychological, and social functioning. The use of a single focus group could potentially have limited the range of items for the initial item pool. However, the large number of items that were selected means that this was probably not an important limitation. The use of principal components analysis to select items for the final questionnaire ensures that the reduced item set adequately measures and describes the information about impact on quality of life contained in the initial item pool.

This scale is reliable and relatively independent of subject characteristics. Its cross-sectional relation to other measures has been well described. These relations appear to be reproducible in several settings. Although the questionnaire was designed as an evaluative instrument, the longitudinal characteristics of its performance have, so far, only been addressed in a single study. This study showed weak correlations with change in other measures but did demonstrate that the AQLQ (Sydney) is responsive to change.

The AQLQ (Sydney) has been used in a number of different cultural settings to address a wide range of research questions concerning asthma.

E. Asthma Impact Record (AIR) Index

Description of the Questionnaire

Intended Purpose and Scope

This questionnaire was designed to measure quality of life in French-speaking patients with asthma (64). It was intended to be capable of detecting change in quality of life. The scale encompasses physical, psychological, and social aspects of quality of life related to asthma.

Format and Method of Administration

The questionnaire, which is suitable for self-administration, comprises 63 statements: 52 negative and 11 positive items. Subjects are asked to tick each statement that relates to their current health status and can be attributed to asthma. The questionnaire can be completed in approximately 15 min.

Scoring

Negative items are scored 1 if ticked and 0 if not ticked. Positive items are scored in reverse. The total scale and subscale scores are calculated by summing across the relevant items. The maximum possible score is 63. Higher scores correspond to worse quality of life. The authors developed weights for each item. However, their evaluation of the questionnaire showed that these did not add anything to its interpretation. Hence, the authors now recommend an unweighted scoring system.

Subscales

Four mutually exclusive subscales or dimensions can be scored: psychological, physical activity, physical symptoms, and social.

Development of the Questionnaire

Source of the Initial Pool of Items

The initial set of 123 items was constructed as a result of open interviews with 17 patients with asthma. These interviews covered domains of relevance to asthma—including emotions and anxiety; physical limitations; familial, social, and professional limitations; and sleep problems. Items arising from these interviews that were applicable to all respondents were retained for inclusion in the initial questionnaire.

Method of Selecting the Final Item Set

The initial 123-item questionnaire, which was in the same format as the final questionnaire (described above), was administered to 387 patients with asthma. Items selected by <5% of respondents, ambiguous items, and those thought to be not responsive to change were deleted at this stage. The items were then grouped into subscales as described above. The internal consistency of each of these subscales and the total scale were measured, and items whose removal improved internal consistency were deleted.

This reduced 73-item questionnaire was then administered to 32 patients with stable asthma on two occasions, 3 days apart. Items dealing with "acceptance of the disease and its treatment," which were not reproducible, were deleted from the questionnaire.

The final questionnaire comprised 63 items in four subscales.

Psychometric Properties of the Questionnaire

Distribution of Scores

The distribution of scores is skewed toward lower scores. However, the full range of possible scores was observed in a sample of 387 outpatients with asthma. Scores <20% of the maximum were observed in 42% of subjects.

Reliability: Internal Consistency and Test-Retest Repeatability

The questionnaire was found to be internally consistent: Cronbach's alpha was 0.94 for the total scale and ranged from 0.79 to 0.85 for the subscales.

In subjects with stable asthma, tested on two occasions 3 days apart, results were highly repeatable. The intraclass correlation coefficient was 0.97 for the total scale and ranged from 0.91 to 0.93 for the subscales.

Effect of Age, Gender, and Other Subject Characteristics

Women had higher scores (worse quality of life) than men. Scale scores increased with age (Table 10).

Table 10 AIR Index Scores in Patients with
Asthma by Age and Gender (maximum possible
score is 63, $N = 387$)

	Men	Women
18–29 years	12.2	13.9
30–50 years	13.5	18.6
>50 years	18.9	21.9

Source: From Ref. 64.

Construct Validity and Responsiveness

Relation to Other Measures: Cross-Sectionally

Scores on the AIR index were, as expected, strongly correlated with general measures of quality of life: the Sickness Impact Profile and a global self-assessment by visual analogue scale. There were moderate correlations with clinical indices of asthma severity (Table 11). Clinical measures of asthma were more strongly correlated with AIR index scores than Sickness Impact Profile scores.

Relation to Other Measures: Longitudinally

Analysis of the AIR index in a longitudinal setting has not yet been published.

Table 11 Relation Between AIR Index Scores and Other Quality-of-Life and
Asthma-Related Variables ($N = 387$)

	Total scale	Psychological	Physical activity	Physical symptoms	Social
Sickness Impact Profile (total)	0.66[a]	0.54	0.57	0.60	0.60
Peak expiratory flow rate (% predicted)	−0.31	−0.22	−0.33	−0.28	−0.23
Severity of attacks in last month	0.37	0.32	0.33	0.34	0.26
Exertional dyspnea in last month	0.44	0.33	0.44	0.42	0.36
Oral steroid use in last year	0.34	0.29	0.29	0.29	0.28

[a]Correlation coefficients. All are significant at $p < 0.01$.
Source: From Ref. 64.

*Cross-Cultural Appropriateness and Availability in Languages
Other Than English*

The questionnaire was developed among patients in France. Applications in other
settings have not been reported.

Applications

Applications of this questionnaire have not yet been reported.

Conclusion: Summary of Strengths and Weaknesses

The AIR index covers the core domains of quality of life. It has been developed
in a systematic manner to yield a questionnaire which is a reliable and valid
measure of quality of life. Its performance as a measure of change has not yet
been evaluated.

F. Quality of Life for Respiratory Illness Questionnaire (QOL-RIQ)

Description of the Questionnaire

Intended Purpose and Scope

This questionnaire was designed for evaluating outcomes in patients with asthma
and COPD seen in a general practice setting in the Netherlands (65).

Format and Method of Administration

The final version of the questionnaire comprises 55 items with various 7-point
Likert-scale responses. The questionnaire was administered by mail.

Scoring

The method of scoring is not specifically described but appears to be by simple
addition of item scores, with higher scores representing more severe impact on
quality of life.

Subscales

There are seven subscales: breathing problems; physical problems; emotions;
general activities; situations triggering or enhancing breathing problems; daily
and domestic activities; and social activities, relationships, and sexuality.

Development of the Questionnaire

Source of the Initial Pool of Items

Published reports on quality of life in patients with lung disease, existing generic
quality-of-life questionnaires, health professionals involved in the care of patients
with lung disease, and experts in quality-of-life assessment in patients with

chronic lung disease were consulted to identify the initial pool of items for the questionnaire (65). Further items were added after interviews with 11 patients with chronic lung disease. The initial questionnaire comprised 221 items.

Method of Selecting the Final Item Set

The initial questionnaire was administered to 146 patients who were identified through general practitioners. Based on their responses to a symptom and medication history questionnaire, 98 of these subjects probably had asthma, 32 probably had COPD, and the remainder could not be classified. Subjects responded to each item on a 7-point Likert scale.

Items with >30% not applicable responses were deleted. Items with pairwise correlations >0.8 were combined. Factor analysis was used to select for retention those items that loaded most strongly onto predefined content domains (65).

Psychometric Properties of the Questionnaire

Distribution of Scores

This has not been reported.

Reliability: Internal Consistency and Test-Retest Repeatability

The split-half reliability (internal consistency) for the total scale was 0.92 and for the subscales ranged from 0.68 to 0.89 (65).

Effect of Age, Gender, and Other Subject Characteristics

The total questionnaire score was unrelated to age or gender and there was no difference in total scores between those who probably had asthma and those who probably had COPD (65). Some of the subscale scores did differ between patient groups.

Construct Validity and Responsiveness

Relation to Other Measures: Cross-Sectionally

The total score on the QOL-RIQ was moderately correlated with measures of disease severity, including degree of dyspnea ($R = 0.49$), frequency of attacks ($R = 0.45$), subjective severity ($R = 0.49$), number of general practitioner visits ($R = 0.47$), and frequency of absence from work ($R = 0.46$) (65).

Relation to Other Measures: Longitudinally

This has not been reported.

Cross-Cultural Appropriateness and Availability in Languages Other Than English

The questionnaire was developed in Dutch for use in the Netherlands. An English translation has been published (65).

Applications

Applications of this questionnaire have not been reported.

Conclusion: Summary of Strengths and Weaknesses

This new questionnaire is psychometrically sound and yields scores that are correlated with other quality-of-life and clinical outcome measures. However, its attempt to encompass both COPD and asthma in the one questionnaire may limit its utility in settings where one of these entities is the focus of the investigation.

G. Sickness Impact Profile

Description of the Questionnaire

Intended Purpose and Scope

The Sickness Impact Profile is a behavioral measure of health status (34,66,67). It was designed as a measure of self-perceived health status for use in discriminating between groups or evaluating changes in outcomes over time. It was intended to be broadly applicable across a range of types and severities of illness and in a variety of sociocultural settings (34). It measures a wide range of behavioral impacts of illness.

Format and Method of Administration

The final version of the SIP comprises 136 items. Each item is a sentence, written in the first person, present tense, describing a behavior. Respondents are requested to select the items that apply to them on that day and can be attributed to their health status. Behaviors that apply to them but are not attributable to health problems are not to be selected.

The SIP may be interviewer- or self-administered. There is some evidence that self-completion of a mailed out questionnaire may give slightly different responses to personal administration of the questionnaire (34). The questionnaire takes about 20 to 30 min to complete.

Scoring

Each item has an empirically derived weight. The weights of all the selected items are summed to yield a total score out of 100. Higher scores represent more severe dysfunction.

Subscales

There are 12 categories in the final version of the SIP. Three categories (ambulation, mobility, and body care and movement) may be grouped together as a physical dimension. Four categories (social interaction, alertness behavior, emotional behavior, and communication) may be grouped together as a psychosocial dimension. The remaining categories, which do not form part of any dimension, are sleep and rest, eating, work, home management, and recreation and pastimes. Each category and dimension can be scored separately to yield a profile of scores.

Development of the Questionnaire

Source of the Initial Pool of Items

The initial pool of items was collected during 1972 by a survey of 1100 health care professionals, patients, carers, and healthy people. This was supplemented by items drawn from the literature. The initial version of the questionnaire comprised 312 items in 14 categories (34).

The weights used to scale the questionnaire were derived from 25 health care professionals and students who rated the degree of dysfunction associated with each listed behavioral statement.

Method of Selecting the Final Item Set

A series of three field trials were conducted in a variety of patient groups in 1973, 1974, and 1976. In each trial the reliability and discriminative ability of each item was assessed. Items were deleted from successive versions if they did not account for a significant proportion of between subject variance and were not regarded as substantively important (34). At the conclusion of this process, there were 136 items in 12 categories.

Psychometric Properties of the Questionnaire

Distribution of Scores

In a parallel group study of patients with moderately severe asthma, the mean total SIP scores at baseline in the two groups were 6.99 (SD 6.43) and 9.03 (SD 7.56), respectively (21).

Reliability: Internal Consistency and Test-Retest Repeatability

The repeatability of the SIP over a 24-hr period is good for the overall score (0.88 to 0.92) (34). However, there is some variation in the responses to individual items. The total scale and all the category scales are internally consistent [Cronbach's alpha 0.63 to 0.90 for categories and 0.96 overall (66)].

Construct Validity and Responsiveness

Relation to Other Measures: Cross-Sectionally

SIP scores have been shown to be moderately or strongly correlated with other self-assessed measures of health status (67). As expected correlations with clinical indices or physician/health professional assessments are lower. Scores for the psychosocial dimension are moderately correlated with a range of psychological measures, whereas scores on the physical dimension are more strongly related to clinical measures (67).

In patients with asthma, SIP scores were moderately correlated with daytime and nighttime symptom scores (R = 0.39 and 0.38, respectively) but only weakly correlated with lung function (R = -0.17 for FEV_1) (21).

Relation to Other Measures: Longitudinally

This aspect of the SIP was not assessed in its initial evaluation. In a study of patients with lower back pain, correlations of change in SIP scores with change in clinical indices were modest (0.2 to 0.4) (68).

The SIP does not appear to be a good measure of change in patients with asthma. Changes in SIP score were not correlated with changes in lung function or symptom measures (21). In settings where change in health status has been detected by other means, no significant change in SIP score was observed (15,21,54).

Cross-Cultural Appropriateness and Availability in Languages Other Than English

The SIP has been translated into Spanish, Dutch, Swedish, and French. Evidence of the reliability and validity of these translated versions has been published (67,69).

Translations into Dutch, Danish, Finish, French, Italian, Portuguese, Swedish, and Thai have been used in patients with asthma (15,21).

Applications in Patients with Asthma

Most of the applications of the SIP in patients with asthma have been in the development of disease-specific questionnaires, as described in this chapter. In drug trials of nedocromil sodium (15) and salmeterol (21), the SIP did not detect change even when other clinical and quality-of-life measures did change.

Conclusion: Summary of Strengths and Weaknesses

The SIP has a long history of use in a wide variety of disease. However, it is not strictly a quality-of-life questionnaire; instead, it assesses behaviors, many of which are closely related to factors that affect subjects' quality of life.

There is good evidence to suggest that it is not useful for measuring the impact of asthma on quality of life.

H. Medical Outcomes Study: 36-Item Short Form Health Survey (SF-36)

Description of the Questionnaire

Intended Purpose and Scope

The Short Form 36 (SF-36) questionnaire was designed as a comprehensive yet practical and efficient version of a previous longer questionnaire (70). It was intended for use in health policy evaluations, general population surveys, and clinical research and practice (71). It addresses basic human values such as functioning and emotional well-being (70).

Format and Method of Administration

The questionnaire comprises 36 items in the form of questions with various response options ranging from dichotomous (yes or no) to five-level responses. Most questions refer to the preceding 4-week period. It may be self- or interviewer-administered, either face to face or over the telephone (70). It takes approximately 5 to 10 min to complete.

Scoring

The items of the SF-36 are grouped into eight scales and a single transition question (see below). The results are summarized as a profile of eight scale scores. No single overall score is computed. Scale scores are calculated by summing across the items in each scale. Low scores represent more severe levels of dysfunction. The maximum score in each scale corresponds to no abnormality on that scale.

Subscales

Six health concepts common to most health status measures are represented by scales in the SF-36: physical functioning, role limitations due to physical problems, social functioning, general mental health, role limitations due to emotional problems, and general health perceptions. In addition, two other scales were incorporated to widen the applicability of the instrument: bodily pain and vitality. A single item dealing with change in general health now as compared with 1 year ago does not lie within any of the scales.

Two aggregate summary measures, a physical component summary and a mental component summary, may be estimated by principal components factor analysis. These have been shown to contain much of the information arising from the eight individual scales (72).

Development of the Questionnaire

Source of the Initial Pool of Items

The SF-36 was derived from a previous 245-item questionnaire developed for use in the Medical Outcomes Study (MOS) (73). Items for that questionnaire had been collected over a long period of time and were themselves included in a number of other questionnaires (70).

Method of Selecting the Final Item Set

Eight scales from the full-length questionnaire were selected for inclusion in the SF-36. Some of these had been used in previous shorter forms: the SF-18 and SF-20. Items to represent each scale were selected in a manner that reproduced the original longer questionnaire as much as possible (70). The number of items per scale varies from 2 ("bodily pain" and "social functioning") to 10 ("physical functioning").

Psychometric Properties of the Questionnaire

Distribution of Scores

In outpatients with a range of cardiovascular illnesses, diabetes, and/or depression, the full range of scores was utilized in each scale (71). Distributions were skewed, but significant floor and ceiling effects were observed in only a minority of scales (Table 12). Among stable patients with asthma, mean SF-36 scores ranged from 57 (general health perceptions) to 84 (social functioning).

Reliability: Internal Consistency and Test-Retest Repeatability

The internal consistency of the scales has been established in the MOS sample (outpatients with cardiovascular disease, diabetes or depression) and in a sample of patients with asthma (Table 13).

Test-retest repeatability has been assessed over a 2-week interval among patients registered with two general practices in Sheffield, United Kingdom. Sim-

Table 12 Descriptive Statistics and Score Distributions for SF-36 in a Medical Outcomes Study (MOS) Sample ($N = 3445$)

	No. of items	No. of levels	Median score	Percent of scores at floor	Percent of scores at ceiling
Physical functioning	10	21	80	0.8	19.2
Role, physical	4	5	75	24.3	36.7
Bodily pain	2	11	72	0.9	17.8
General health perception	5	21	62	0.2	1.4
Vitality	4	21	55	1.1	0.9
Social functioning	2	9	87.5	0.9	46.3
Role, emotional	3	4	100	18.1	56.1
Mental health	5	26	76	0.1	4.4

Source: From Ref. 71.

Table 13 Internal Consistency (Cronbach's alpha) of SF-36
Scales

	Medical Outcomes Study sample ($N = 3445$)	Asthma sample ($N = 252$)
Physical functioning	0.93	0.98
Role, physical	0.84	0.87
Bodily pain	0.82	0.87
General health perception	0.78	0.83
Vitality	0.87	0.86
Social functioning	0.85	0.42
Role, emotional	0.83	0.76
Mental health	0.90	0.79

Source: From Refs. 71 and 76.

ple correlation coefficients between scores from repeat administrations ranged from 0.60 (''social functioning'') to 0.81 (''physical functioning''). The coefficients of repeatability—that is, the range within which 95% of repeated observations lie—were between 2.7 (''bodily pain'') and 9.8 (''physical functioning'') on a 100-point scale (74,75). Intraclass correlation coefficients for repeated administrations in stable patients have not been reported.

Effect of Age, Gender, and Other Subject Characteristics

Among patients recruited from general practice lists, men had higher (better) scores than women on all scales except general health perceptions (74). Similar findings were observed in patients with asthma: men had better scores on all scales except ''social functioning'' and ''physical role limitations.'' Among these patients, older subjects had worse (lower) scores for all scales except ''social functioning,'' ''mental health,'' and ''vitality'' (76).

Construct Validity and Responsiveness

Relation to Other Measures: Cross-Sectionally

In the Medical Outcomes Study, mean scores on all eight SF-36 scales differed significantly between 576 patients with minor medical conditions and 144 patients with serious medical problems (77). As expected, the differences were greatest for the physical functioning, general health perceptions, role-physical, and vitality scales. The mental health, role-emotional, and social functioning scales performed best in discriminating patients with depression from those with minor medical illness.

Among patients with chronic, stable asthma, the physical functioning SF-

Table 14 Correlation of SF-36 Scores with Clinical
Asthma Severity Index and Lung Function ($N = 252$)

	Aas score[a]	FEV_1
Physical functioning	0.50[b]	0.40
Role physical	0.33	0.28
Bodily pain	0.33	0.32
General health perception	0.45	0.38
Vitality	0.27	0.18
Social functioning	0.35	0.16
Role emotional	0.20	0.16
Mental health	0.19	0.09

[a]Clinical index of asthma severity based on symptoms and requirement for medication over the preceding year. 1 = very
mild, 5 = very severe.
[b]Spearman's correlation coefficient. Values > 0.20 are significant at the 0.005 level.
Source: From Ref. 76.

36 scale was moderately correlated with lung function and a clinical index of
asthma severity based on symptoms and medication usage (76). Most of the other
scales were weakly correlated with these measures of severity of asthma (Table
14). Similar findings were observed among hospitalized elderly patients with
asthma. Compared with controls, patients with asthma had worse scores on the
physical functioning, role-physical, vitality, pain, and general health perception
scales. The physical functioning scale was moderately correlated with FEV_1
(R = 0.37), but the other scales were not correlated with lung function (78).

Relation to Other Measures: Longitudinally

The role of the SF-36 as a tool in longitudinal assessment has not been extensively
reported. Among subjects enrolled in the Medical Outcomes Study who reported
a change in their physical health status at the 1-year follow-up, all SF-36 scales
were significantly different from baseline. The physical functioning, general
health perceptions, and social functioning scales changed the most in these
subjects.

Cross-Cultural Appropriateness and Availability in Languages Other Than English

Normative data for the SF-36 and its translations are available for the United
States, Denmark, Germany, Sweden, the United Kingdom, Australia, France, It-

aly, and the Netherlands (79). The French version has been used in patients with asthma.

The SF-36 has recently been used in patients with asthma, mainly for cross-sectional studies, but it has also been used in clinical trials.

In a study comparing patients with asthma attending an allergist with those attending a generalist (59), the former patients had more severe asthma and were on more treatment than the generalists' patients. They had better scores on Physical Functioning, General Health Perceptions, and Bodily Pain scales of the SF-36.

The SF-36 has been used to examine the construct validity of a new questionnaire for assessing perceived control of asthma (63). Significant correlations were observed with several SF-36 scales.

The SF-36 was used to assess health status in a descriptive study of patients with asthma attending allergy and pulmonary specialists (57). Patients with lower (worse) scores on the General Health Perceptions scale were more likely to also be completely or partially disabled for work, independent of the severity of their asthma.

The effect of asthma on the quality of life of patients aged over 55 who had been hospitalized for asthma has been compared to the effect on age-matched controls who were admitted for other diagnoses (78). Patients with asthma had worse scores than controls on most of the SF-36 scales except mental health, emotional role, and bodily pain (Table 15). For the last of these, bodily pain, the controls were worse than the patients with asthma.

The effectiveness of fluticasone propionate (FP) in two dosage schedules

Table 15 Impact of Asthma on Quality of Life in the Elderly: SF-36 Scores for Patients with Asthma and Patients with Other Diseases

	Asthma	Controls	Difference (asthma, control)	95% CI difference
Physical functioning	33.8	45.8	−12.0	−23.5 to −0.4
Role, physical	36.0	57.9	−22.0	−39.4 to −4.4
Bodily pain	66.1	50.1	16.0	1.6 to 30.2
General health perception	41.2	54.9	−13.7	−25.4 to −2.0
Vitality	36.0	49.4	−13.4	−23.5 to −3.3
Social functioning	49.0	57.3	−8.3	−22.1 to −5.5
Role, emotional	70.1	79.5	−9.4	−26.5 to 7.7
Mental health	72.2	71.3	1.1	−10.6 to 12.3

Source: From Ref. 78.

was assessed in 96 subjects with moderately severe asthma followed for 16 weeks in a parallel-group, randomized, placebo-controlled trial (80,81). SF-36 demonstrated improvement compared with placebo for the Physical Functioning, Role Physical, and General Health scales. Changes in these scale scores were moderately correlated with changes in lung function. Another 12-week study comparing fluticasone propionate with placebo also found significant improvements in these scales and, in addition (for higher doses of fluticasone), found benefits in the Vitality and Mental Health scales (28).

In a parallel-group randomized controlled trial comparing salmeterol ($n = 98$) with oral slow-release terbutaline ($n = 96$) in patients with moderately severe asthma, there were trends in favor of salmeterol in several scales, but the difference was significant only for vitality (27). In contrast, the between-group difference in the disease-specific Living with Asthma Questionnaire was significant.

Conclusion: Summary of Strengths and Weaknesses

The SF-36 includes items relevant to the core domains of quality of life. However, the origin of the specific items that make up the questionnaire is obscured by the complex history of its ancestors. It has been found to be useful in cross-sectional studies of patients with asthma, but its value in longitudinal studies has not been established.

III. Summary and Conclusions

The questionnaires described here all measure health-related quality of life. However, they differ in important respects that are relevant to investigators proposing to use them to address research questions. Two questionnaires, the AIR Index and the QOL-RIQ, are quite new, and only preliminary data are available. It is probably too early to determine their place in the assessment of asthma-related quality of life.

A. Type of Quality of Life Measured

A major source of variation in the way the questionnaires measure quality of life is the source of the initial item content. The Living with Asthma Questionnaire was developed by investigators without clinical expertise in respiratory medicine and all content was derived from patients: initially from focus groups and then by an iterative process based on psychometric principles. The content of AQLQ (Sydney) and the AIR Index was also predominantly patient-based and refined by factor analysis. On the other hand, the AQLQ (McMaster) and the QOL-RIQ derived their initial content from existing questionnaires, literature, and health professionals, with a smaller input from patient interviews. The major patient focus of these questionnaires arose in the second phase: selection of items from the initial pool for the final questionnaire. The SIP also included a large input from health professionals and patient carers in derivation of initial content. The source of content of the SGRQ and the SF-36 is not entirely clear but, at least for the latter, probably includes a significant component of expert and health professional input in its origins.

All the questionnaires described here can be said to validly measure quality of life, as all have undertaken a systematic process to select and refine quality-of-life content items. However, the differences among these processes are reflected in the differences among the questionnaires. For example, the LWAQ has a focus on psychological and social impacts, whereas the AQLQ (McMaster) has a strong focus on physical symptoms and activity limitations. These differences in the conceptualization of health-related quality of life may be important for investigators selecting questionnaires for specific research tasks.

B. Disease-Specific Versus Generic Questionnaires

Another obvious way in which questionnaires differ is in their degree of specificity for asthma. Disease-specific questionnaires were developed to focus attention on key issues relevant to a given disease. This tends to make the questionnaires more sensitive to differences among patients with the disease and more responsive to changes in status. The disadvantage of this specificity is that it may exclude some relevant content areas. For example, treatment side effects and interactions with other diseases may not be detected by a highly specific questionnaire. The other major advantage of generic (that is, not disease-specific) questionnaires is that they allow comparison between subjects with different disease states.

The AQLQ (Sydney), AQLQ (McMaster), LWAQ, and AIR Index are suitable only for use in patients with asthma. They include items that may be relevant only to patients with asthma: for example, the need to avoid triggers for symptoms and the fear of impending attacks. The SGRQ and the QOL-RIQ were developed for use in patients with asthma and COPD. These questionnaires deal with the many common problems associated with these illnesses. The SIP and SF-36 are both generic quality-of-life indices that encompass problems common to all forms of illness.

In selecting a questionnaire for a research task, the investigator must decide the extent to which specificity or generalizability is an important attribute of the instrument. The population in which the study is being conducted and the nature of the research question will influence this decision.

C. Suitability for Between-Subject Designs

In studies where the research question concerns differences between subjects— that is, cross-sectional studies—the reliability and discriminatory capacity of the outcome measurement affects the power of the study. This characteristic of questionnaires is best measured by administering the questionnaire on two occasions to a sample of subjects that is representative of the population of interest and calculating the intraclass correlation coefficient (82). This is the proportion of the total variance of scores attributable to variation between subjects. A high intraclass correlation coefficient indicates that the differences between subjects are much greater than the differences between repeated measurements within subjects. A questionnaire with a high intraclass correlation coefficient (>0.8) will be efficient for measuring differences between subjects.

The intraclass correlation coefficients of the AQLQ (Sydney), AQLQ (McMaster), SGRQ, and AIR index were generally satisfactory. However, the AIR index was tested over a very short interval (3 days) and the AQLQ (McMaster) was tested with subjects shown their previous responses at the second interview, which may have led to an underestimate of the potential for within-subject variation. Furthermore, in the AQLQ (McMaster), which was not designed for comparing results between subjects, five of the items are individually specified. This means that some of the observed variation between subjects arises because the questionnaire itself varies between subjects.

Intraclass correlation coefficients for repeated administrations of the LWAQ and the SF-36 have not been reported, and although there is evidence that they demonstrate short-term test–retest validity, their discriminatory capacity has not been assessed.

The other, pragmatic way to evaluate the potential value of these instruments in discriminating between subjects is to examine their performance in a variety of settings. These data are presented in detail in the sections describing each questionnaire. As expected, all questionnaires have stronger correlations with other quality-of-life indices, symptom scores, and self-assessed severity than with objective measures such as lung function. Unfortunately, it is difficult to use this information to predict whether, in a specified research setting, the questionnaire will be capable of distinguishing subjects in a way that is relevant to the research question.

D. Suitability for Longitudinal Designs

A questionnaire will be suitable for use as an evaluative instrument if it gives meaningful information about subjects' changes in status over time. This implies two characteristics: scores should be repeatable in stable subjects and scores should change, in the expected direction, in subjects whose quality of life has improved or deteriorated.

The problem in making this assessment of responsiveness is the need to identify change, or lack of change, in asthma-related quality of life by some independent criteria. The criteria that are used will necessarily influence the conclusions about responsiveness. For practical purposes, there have been two approaches that are often combined: measures of responses to known effective therapies and classification of change status according to clinical criteria. It is important to recognize that the ability of the questionnaires to respond to changes in quality of life not accompanied by changes in clinical outcomes cannot be assessed by this method.

The AQLQ (McMaster) has been used extensively as an outcome measure in clinical trials of therapeutic drugs. In this setting it has been demonstrated to be responsive to change in a manner consistent with the observed changes in clinical outcomes. Experience with the other questionnaires in this setting is less extensive. The AQLQ (Sydney) has also been demonstrated to be responsive to change in patients who improve by clinical criteria. The LWAQ was able to detect change in one drug trial but is apparently less responsive than the AQLQ (McMaster). The responsiveness of the SGRQ in patients with asthma has not been established, although significant changes were observed in the Impacts subscale in one clinical trial. The SIP does not appear to be responsive to change in status in people with asthma. This characteristic of the SF-36 has not been adequately evaluated.

E. Conclusions

The need for a more holistic, patient-centered approach to assessing outcomes of asthma care led several investigators in the early 1990s, independently, to develop questionnaires for this purpose. Their different perspectives have produced questionnaires that vary in important respects. Each has used a systematic approach to refining the content of the questionnaire, although the nature of that content and extent of patient versus expert or health professional input varies.

Intending questionnaire users must look closely at the content of the questionnaire, and the way it was derived, before deciding whether it measures what they wish to know. Data on the psychometric properties of the questionnaire and its performance in previous applications can then be used to decide whether it is likely to be useful in the proposed setting.

Appendix

Summary Table: Questionnaires Used for Measuring Health-Related Quality of Life in Adults with Asthma

	St George's Respiratory Questionnaire (SGRQ)	Living with Asthma Questionnaire (LWAQ)	Asthma Quality of Life Questionnaire (McMaster)
Primary references	9, 10	19, 20	32
Intended purpose	Discriminative and evaluative outcome measure	As an outcome measure in clinical therapeutic trials	As an outcome measure in clinical therapeutic trials
Disease scope	Airway disease	Asthma	Asthma
Number of items	76	68	32
Categories/domains/subscales	Symptoms Activity Impact	Social and leisure activities, sports, holidays, sleep, work, colds, mobility, effects on others, medication use, sex, dysphoric states, attitudes	Symptoms Emotional function Activity limitation Environmental stimuli
Administration methods	Interview (face-to-face or telephone)	Interviewer- or self-administered	Interviewer- or self-administered
Completion time	10 min	15 min	5 to 15 min
Scoring	Sum empirical derived weights for total and subscale scores Range 0 (no impairment) to 100 (maximum possible impairment)	Items scored 1 to 3 and averaged without weighting Higher scores = worse QoL	Items scored 1 to 7 and averaged without weighting Lower scores = worse QoL
Recall period	1 year (but shorter periods have been used)	Variously specified by investigators	2 weeks

Initial source of content	Not reported	Six focus groups of patients with asthma	Previous questionnaires, interviews with health professionals and six patients
Selection of items for final questionnaire	Not reported	Principal components analysis (three iterations)	Frequency importance product in 150 subjects with asthma
Internal consistency demonstrated in subjects with asthma	Yes (for Spanish language version)	Yes	Not reported
Short-term test-retest reliability in subjects with asthma	Yes	Only simple correlation has been reported	Yes
Cross-sectional relation to clinical asthma measures reported	Yes	Yes	Yes
Application has demonstrated ability to discriminate between groups	Yes (mainly COPD patients)	No	Yes (but limited use in this setting)
Longitudinal relation to clinical asthma measures reported	Yes (mainly COPD patients)	Yes	Yes
Application has demonstrated responsiveness in clinical trial setting	Yes	Yes	Yes (extensive use in this setting)
Languages	English, Dutch, Finnish, Danish, French, Italian, Portuguese, Swedish, Thai, Spanish	Italian, Japanese, Dutch, French	Spanish, French, Dutch, Tamil, Japanese

Summary Table: Continued

	Asthma Quality of Life Questionnaire (Sydney)	Asthma Impact Record (AIR) Index	Quality of Life for Respiratory Illness Questionnaire (QOL-RIQ)
Primary references	53, 54	64	65
Intended purpose	As an outcome measure in clinical trials	To measure and detect change in quality of life in French patients with asthma	Evaluating outcomes in general practice setting
Disease scope	Asthma	Asthma	Asthma and COPD
Number of items	20	63	55
Categories/domains/subscales	Breathlessness; Mood disturbance; Social disruption; Concerns for health	Psychological; Physical activity; Physical symptoms; Social	Breathing problems; physical problems; emotions; general activities; triggers; domestic activities; social activities; relationships and sexuality
Administration methods	Self-administered or questionnaire	Self-administered	Self-administered (by mail)
Completion time	5 to 10 min	15 min	Not reported
Scoring	Items scored 0 to 4 and averaged without weighting; Higher score = worse QoL	Items scored 0 to 1 and summed without weighting; Higher score = worse QoL	Not reported; Higher scores = worse QoL
Recall period	1 month		
Initial source of content	Single focus group; interviews with asthma educators	Open interviews with 17 patients with asthma	Published reports, experts and health professionals

Selection of items for final questionnaire	Principal components analysis	Criteria: to avoid redundancy and optimize internal consistency	Principal components analysis
Internal consistency demonstrated in subjects with asthma	Yes	Yes	Yes
Short-term test-retest reliability in subjects with asthma	Yes	Yes	Not reported
Cross-sectional relation to clinical asthma measures reported	Yes	Yes	Yes
Application has demonstrated ability to discriminate between groups	Yes	Not reported	Not reported
Longitudinal relation to clinical asthma measures reported	Yes	Not reported	Not reported
Application has demonstrated responsiveness in clinical trial setting	Yes (limited use in this setting)	Not reported	Not reported
Languages	English, French, Spanish, Norwegian	French	Dutch, English

Summary Table: Continued

	Sickness Impact Profile (SIP)	Medical Outcomes Study Short Form 36 (SF 36)
Primary references	34	70, 71, 77
Intended purpose	Discriminating between groups and evaluating changes over time	Clinical research and practice, general population surveys, and health policy
Disease scope	Generic health status	Generic health status
Number of items	136	36
Categories/domains/subscales	Ambulation; mobility; body care and movement; social interaction; alertness; emotional behavior; communication; sleep and rest; eating; work; home management; recreation	Physical functioning, role limitations (physical), role limitations (emotional), social functioning, general mental health, general health perceptions, bodily pain, vitality
Administration methods	Interviewer or self-administered	Interviewer- (face-to-face or telephone) or self-administered
Completion time	20 to 30 min	5 to 10 min
Scoring	Empirically derived weights for each checked item are summed	Simple addition for profile of eight scale scores (no single overall score)
	Higher scores = worse QoL	Lower scores = worse QoL
Recall period	1 day	4 weeks

Initial source of content	Survey of health professionals, patients, carers, and healthy people; literature	Previous, larger questionnaire
Selection of items for final questionnaire	Items selected for reliability and discriminative ability	To reproduce results of original questionnaire
Internal consistency demonstrated in subjects with asthma	Yes	Yes
Short-term test-retest reliability in subjects with asthma	Yes (for 24-hr recall)	Not reported
Cross-sectional relation to clinical asthma measures reported	Yes	Yes
Application has demonstrated ability to discriminate between groups	No	Yes
Longitudinal relation to clinical asthma measures reported	Yes	Not reported
Application has demonstrated responsiveness in clinical trial setting	No	Yes
Languages	English, Spanish, Dutch, Swedish, French, Danish, Finnish, Italian, Portuguese, Thai	English, Danish, German, Swedish, French, Italian, Dutch

Abbreviations: QoL, quality of life; COPD, chronic obstructive pulmonary disease.

References

1. Spitzer, W. (1987). State of science 1986: quality of life and functional status as a target variable for research. *J. Chronic Dis.*, **40**:459–463.
2. Ware, J. (1987). Standards for validating health measures: definition and content. *J. Chronic Dis.*, **40**:473–480.
3. Schipper, H., Clinch, J., and Olweny, C. (1996). Quality of life studies: definitions and conceptual issues. In *Quality of Life and Pharmacoeconomics in Clinical Trials.* Edited by B. Spilker. Philadelphia, Lippincott-Raven, pp. 11–23.
4. Basch C. (1987). Focus group interview: an underutilized research technique for improving theory and practice in health education. *Health Ed. Q.*, **14**:411–448.
5. Anastasi, A. (1988). *Psychological Testing.* New York, Macmillan.
6. Kirshner, B., and Guyatt, G. (1985). A methodological framework for assessing health indices. *J. Chronic Dis.*, **38**:27–36.
7. Juniper, E., Guyatt, G., Streiner, D., and King, D. (1997). Clinical impact versus factor analysis for quality of life questionnaires. *J. Clin. Epidemiol.*, **50**:233–238.
8. Cronbach, L. (1951). Coefficient alpha and the internal structure of a test. *Psychometrika*, **16**:297–334.
9. Jones, P., Quirk, F., and Baveystock C. (1991). The St. George's Respiratory Questionnaire. *Respir. Med.*, **85**(suppl b):25–31.
10. Jones, P., Quirk, F., Baveystock, C., and Littlejohns, P. (1992). A self-complete measure of health-status for chronic airflow limitation—the St. George's Respiratory Questionnaire. *Am. Rev. Respir. Dis.*, **145**:1321–1327.
11. Jones, P. (1991). Quality of life measurement for patients with diseases of the airways. *Thorax*, **46**:676–682.
12. Anie, K., Jones, P., Hilton, S., and Anderson, H. (1996). A computer-assisted telephone interview technique for assessment of asthma morbidity and drug use in adult asthma. *J. Clin. Epidemiol.*, **6**:653–656.
13. Quirk, F., Baveystock, C., Wilson, R., and Jones, P. (1991). Influence of demographic and disease related factors on the degree of distress associated with symptoms and restrictions on daily living due to asthma in six countries. *Eur. Respir. J.*, **4**:167–171.
14. Quirk, F., and Jones, P. (1990). Patients perception of distress due to symptoms and effects of asthma on daily living and an investigation of possible influential factors. *Clin. Sci.*, **79**:17–21.
15. Jones, P., and the Nedocromil Sodium Quality of Life Study Group. (1994). Quality of life, symptoms and pulmonary function in asthma: long-term treatment with nedocromil sodium examined in a controlled multicentre trial. *Eur. Respir. J.*, **7**:55–62.
16. Ferrer, M., Alonso, J., Prieto, L., Plaza, V., Monso, E., Marrades, R., Aguar, M., Khalaf, A., and Anto J. (1996). Validity and reliability of the St George's Respiratory Questionnaire after adaptation to a different language and culture: the Spanish example. *Eur. Respir. J.*, **9**:1160–1166.
17. Lahdensuo, A., Haahtela, T., Herrala, J., Kava, T., Kiviranta, K., Kuusisto, P., Perämäki, E., Poussa, T., Saarelainen, S., and Svahn, T. (1996). Randomised comparison of guided self-management and traditional treatment of asthma over one year. *B.M.J.*, **312**:748–752.

18. Renwick, D., and Connolly, M. (1996). Impact of obstructive airways disease on quality of life in older adults. *Thorax*, **51**:520–525.

19. Hyland, M. (1991). The Living with Asthma Questionnaire. *Respir. Med.*, **85**(suppl b): 13–16.

20. Hyland, M., Finnis, S., and Irvine, S. (1991). A scale for assessing quality of life in adult asthma sufferers. *J. Psychosom. Res.*, **35**:99–110.

21. Rutten-van Molken, M., Custers, F., Van Doorslaer, E., Jansen, C., Heurman, L., Maesen, F., Smeets, J., Bommer, A., and Raaijmakers, J. (1995). Comparison of the performance of four instruments in evaluating the effects of salmeterol on asthma quality of life. *Eur. Respir. J.*, **8**:888–898.

22. Hyland, M., Kenyon, C., and Jacobs, P. (1994). Sensitivity of quality of life domains and constructs to longitudinal change in a clinical trial comparing salmeterol with placebo in asthmatics. *Qual. Life Res.*, **3**:121–126.

23. Mashima, I., Tukada, T., Katagiri, A., Yoshimine, H., Muramatsu, Y., Arakawa, M., and Tsukada, K. (1995). Quality of life in asthmatic patients. *Jpn. Psychosom. Med.*, **35**:601–606.

24. Cocco, G., D'Agostino, F., Piotti, L., Schiano, M., Zanon, P., Melillo, G. (1993). Evaluation of quality of life in asthma. *Eur. Respir. Rev.*, **3**:369–372.

25. Hyland, M., Kenyon, C., Taylor, M., and Morice, A. (1993). Steroid prescribing for asthmatics: relationship with Asthma Symptom Checklist and Living with Asthma Questionnaire. *Br. J. Clin. Pyschol.*, **32**:505–511.

26. Irvine, S., Wright, D., Recchia, G., and De Carli, G. (1994). Measuring quality of life across cultures: some cautions and prescriptions. *Drug Info. J.*, **28**:55–62.

27. Didier, A., and Oriola, R. (1997). A two-month comparison of salmeterol/beclomethasone and slow-release terbutaline/budesonide in moderate asthma management. *Clin. Drug Invest.*, **14**:1–11.

28. Mahajan, P., Okamoto, L., Schaberg, A., Kellerman, D., and Schoenwetter, W. (1997). Impact of fluticasone propionate powder on health-related quality of life in patients with moderate asthma. *J. Asthma*, **34**:227–234.

29. Jones, K., Mullee, M., Middleton, M., Chapman, E., Holgate, S., and the British Thoracic Society Research Committee. (1995). Peak flow based asthma self-management: a randomised controlled study in general practice. *Thorax*, **50**:851–857.

30. Drummond, N., Abdalla, M., Beattie, J., Buckingham, J., Lindsay, T., Osman, L., Ross, S., Roy-Chaudhury, A., Russell, I., Turner, M., Friend, J., Legge, J., and Douglas, J., for the Grampian Study of Integrated Care (GRASSIC). (1994). Effectiveness of routine self monitoring of peak flow in patients with asthma. *B.M.J.*, **308**:564–567.

31. Drummond, N., Abdalla, M., Buckingham, J., Beattie, J., Lindsay, T., Osman, L., Ross, S., Roy-Chaudhury, A., Russell, I., Turner, M., Douglas, J., Legge, J., and Friend, J., for the Grampian Study of Integrated Care (GRASSIC). (1994). Integrated care for asthma: a clinical, social, and economic evaluation. *B.M.J.*, **308**:559–564.

32. Juniper, E., Guyatt, G., Epstein, R., Ferrie, P., Jaeschke, R., and Hiller, T. (1992). Evaluation of impairment of health related quality of life in asthma: development of a questionnaire for use in clinical trials. *Thorax*, **47**:76–83.

33. Kinsman, R., Luparello, T., O'Banion, K., and Spector, S. (1973). Multidimensional analysis of the subjective symptomatology of asthma. *Psychosom. Med.*, **35**:250–267.

34. Bergner, M., Bobbitt, R., Carter, W., and Gilson, B. (1981). The sickness impact profile: development and final revision of a health status measure. *Med. Care*, **19**: 787–805.
35. Stewart, A., Hays, R., and Ware, J. (1988). The MOS short term general health survey. *Med. Care*, **24**:724–732.
36. Israel, E., Cohn, J., Dubé, L., and Drazen, J., for the Zileuton Clinical Trial Group. (1996). Effect of treatment with Zileuton, a 5-lipoxygenase inhibitor, in patients with asthma: a randomized controlled trial. *J.A.M.A.*, **275**:931–936.
37. Gibson, P., Talbot, P., Toneguzzi, R., and the Population Medicine Group 91C. (1995). Self-management, autonomy, and quality of life in asthma. *Chest*, **107**:1003–1008.
38. Juniper, E., Guyatt, G., Ferrie, P., and Griffith, L. (1993). Measuring quality of life in asthma. *Am. Rev. Respir. Dis.*, **147**:832–838.
39. Rowe, B., and Oxman, A. (1993). Performance of an asthma quality of life questionnaire in an outpatient setting. *Am. Rev. Respir. Dis.*, **148**:675–681.
40. Juniper, E., Johnston, P., Borkoff, C., Guyatt, G., Boulet, L., and Haukioja, A. (1995). Quality of life in asthma clinical trials—comparison of salmeterol and salbutamol. *Am. J. Respir. Crit. Care Med.*, **151**:66–70.
41. Thomas, K., Ruby, J., Peter, J., and Cherian, A. (1995). Comparison of disease-specific and a generic quality of life measure in patients with bronchial asthma. *Natl. Med. J. India*, **8**:258–260.
42. Sanjunas, C., Alonso, J., Sanchis, J., Casan, P., Broquetas, J., Ferrie, P., Juniper, E., and Anto, J. (1995). Cuestinario de calidad de vida en pacientes con asma: la version espanola del Asthma Quality of Life Questionnaire. *Arch. Bronconeumol.*, **31**:219–226.
43. Malo, J.-L., Boulet, L.-P., Dewitte, J.-D., Cartier, A., L'Archevêque, J., Côté, J., Bédard, G., Boucher, S., Champagne, F., Tessier, G., Contandriopoulos, A.-P., Juniper, E., and Guyatt, G. (1993). Quality of life in subjects with occupational asthma. *J. Allergy Clin. Immunol.*, **91**:1121–1127.
44. Katada, H., Suguro, T., and Kikuchi, H. (1996). Quality of life of patients with bronchial asthma under the inhaled corticosteroid therapy. *Jpn. J. Chest Dis.*, **55**:652–657.
45. Apter, A., Reisine, S., Willard, A., Clive, J., Wells, M., Metersky, M., McNally, D., and ZuWallack, R. (1996). The effect of inhaled albuterol in moderate to severe asthma. *J. Allergy Clin. Immunol.*, **98**:295–301.
46. Drazen, J., Israel, E., Boushey, H., Chinchilli, V., Fahy, J., Fish, J., Lazarus, S., Lemanske, R., Martin, R., Peters, S., Sorkness, C., and Szefler, S., for the National Heart LaBIsACRN. (1996). Comparison of regularly scheduled with as -needed use of albuterol in mild asthma. *N. Engl. J. Med.*, **335**:841–847.
47. Marin, J., Carrizo, S., Garcia, R., and Ejea, M. (1996). Effects of nedocromil sodium in steroid-resistant asthma: a randomised controlled trial. *J. Allergy Clin. Immunol.*, **97**:602–610.
48. Kuitert, L., Angus, R., Barnes, N., Barnes, P., Bone, M., Chung, K., Fairfax, A., Higenbotham, T., O'Connor, B., Piotrowska, B., Rozniecki, J., Uden, S., Walters, E., and Willard, C. (1995). Effect of a novel potent platelet-activating factor antagonist, modipafant, in clinical asthma. *Am. J. Respir. Crit. Care. Med.*, **151**:1331–1335.

49. Malo, J.-L., Cartier, A., Côté, J., Leblanc, C., Paquette, L., Ghezzo, H., and Boulet, L.-P. (1996). Influence of inhaled steroids on recovery from occupational asthma after cessation of exposure: an 18 month double-blind crossover study. *Am. J. Respir. Crit. Care Med.*, **153**:953–960.

50. Boulet, L.-P., Bélanger, M., and Lajoie, P. (1996). Characteristics of subjects with a high frequency of emergency visits for asthma. *Am. J. Emerg. Med.*, **14**:623–628.

51. Juniper, E., Buist, A., Cox, F., Ferrie, P., and King, D. (1998). Validation of a standardised version of the Asthma Quality of Life Questionnaire. *J. Allergy Clin. Immunol.*, **101**:S177.

52. Juniper, E., Guyatt, G., Cox, F., Ferrie, P., and King, D. (1998). Development and validation of the Mini Asthma Quality of Life Questionnaire. *Am. J. Respir. Crit. Care Med.*, **157**:A750.

53. Marks, G., Dunn, S., and Woolcock, A. (1992). A scale for the measurement of quality of life in adults with asthma. *J. Clin. Epidemiol.*, **45**:461–472.

54. Marks, G., Dunn, S., and Woolcock, A. (1993). An evaluation of an asthma quality of life questionnaire as a measure of change in adults with asthma. *J. Clin. Epidemiol.*, **46**:1103–1111.

55. Marks, G., Mellis, C., Peat, J., Woolcock, A., and Leeder, S. (1994). A profile of asthma and its management in a New South Wales provincial centre. *Med. J. Aust.*, **160**:260–268.

56. Marks, G., Burney, P., Premaratne, U., Simpson, J., and Webb, J. (1997). Asthma in Greenwich: impact of the disease and current management practices. *Eur. Respir. J.*, **10**:1224–1229.

57. Blanc, P., Cisternas, M., Smith, S., and Yelin, E. (1996). Asthma, employment status, and disability among adults treated by pulmonary and allergy specialists. *Chest*, **109**:688–696.

58. Storms, B., Olden, L., Nathan, R., and Bodman, S. (1995). Effect of allergy specialist care on the quality of life of patients with asthma. *Ann. Allergy Asthma Immunol.*, **75**:491–494.

59. Vollmer, W., O'Hollaren, M., Ettinger, K., Stibolt, T., Wilkins, J., Buist, A., Linton, K., and Osborne M. (1997). Specialty differences in the management of asthma: a cross-sectional assessment of allergists' patients and generalists' patients in a large HMO. *Arch. Intern. Med.*, **157**:1201–1208.

60. Lurie, A., Guillemin, F., Djaballah, K., Marks, G., Woolcock, A., and Dusser, D. (1997). Quality of life in ambulatory care patients with asthma: validity and reliability of the French version of the University of Sydney Asthma Quality of Life Questionnaire (abstr.) *Am. J. Respir. Crit. Care Med.*, **155**:A721.

61. Perpina, M., Belloch, A., Pascual, L., De Diego, A., and Compte, L. (1995). Calidad de vida en el asma: validacion del cuestionario AQL para su utilizacion en poblacion espanola. *Arch. Bronconeumol.*, **31**:211–218.

62. Colás, C., Lezaun, A., Fraj, J., Dominguez, M., Duce, F., and Larrad L. (1997). Calidad de vida y ECP sérica en pacientes asmáticos. *Rev. Esp. Alergol. Immunol. Clin.*, **12**:58–60.

63. Katz, P., Yelin, E., Smith, S., and Blanc, P. (1997). Perceived control of asthma: development and validation of a questionnaire. *Am. J. Respir. Crit. Care Med.*, **155**:577–582.

64. Letrait, M., Lurie, A., Bean, K., Mesbah, M., Venot, A., Strauch, G., Grandordy, B., and Chwalow, J. (1996). The Asthma Impact Record (AIR) index: a rating scale to evaluate quality of life of asthmatic patients in France. *Eur. Respir. J.*, **9**:1167–1173.
65. Maillé, A., Koning, C., Zwinderman, A., Willems, L., Dijkman, J., and Kaptein A. (1997). The development of the "Quality-of-Life for Respiratory Illness Questionnaire (QOL-RIQ)": a disease-specific quality-of-life questionnaire for patients with mild to moderate chronic non-specific lung disease. *Respir. Med.*, **91**:297–309.
66. Damiano, A. The Sickness Impact Profile. In *Quality of Life and Pharmacoeconomics in Clinical Trials*. Edited by B. Spilker: Philadelphia, Lippincott-Raven, pp. 347–354.
67. de Bruin, AF., de Witte, L.P., Stevens, F., and Diederiks, J.P.M. (1992). Sickness Impact Profile: the state of the art of a generic functional status measure. *Soc. Sci. Med.*, **35**:1003–1014.
68. Deyo, R., and Centor, R. (1986). Assessing the responsiveness of functional scales to clinical change: an anthology to diagnostic test performance. *J. Chronic Dis.*, **39**:897–906.
69. Chwalow, A., Lurie, A., Bean, K., Parent du Chatelet, I., Venot, A., Dusser, D., Douot, Y., and Strauch, G. (1992). A French version of the Sickness Impact Profile (SIP): stages in the cross cultural validation of a generic quality of life scale. *Fundam. Clin. Pharmacol.*, **6**:319–326.
70. Ware, J.J., and Sherbourne, C. (1992). The MOS 36-item short-form health survey (SF-36): I. Conceptual framework and item selection.*Med. Care*, **30**:473–483.
71. McHorney, C., Ware, J.J., Lu, J., and Sherbourne, C. (1994). The MOS 36-item short-form health survey (SF-36): III. Tests of data quality, scaling assumptions, and reliability across diverse patient groups. *Med. Care*, **32**:40–66.
72. Ware, J.J., Kosinski, M., Bayliss, M., McHorney, C., Rogers W., and Raczek A. (1995). Comparison of methods for scoring and statistical analysis of SF-36 health profile and summary measures: summary of results from the Medical Outcomes Study. *Med. Care*, **33**:AS264–AS279.
73. Tarlov, A., Ware, J.J., Greenfield, S., Nelson, E., Perrin, E., and Zubkoff, M. (1989). The Medical Outcomes Study: an application of methods for monitoring the results of medical care. *J.A.M.A.*, **262**:925–930.
74. Brazier, J., Harper, R., Jones, N., O'Cathain, A., Thomas, K., Usherwood, T., and Westlake, L. (1992). Validating the SF-36 health survey questionnaire: new outcome measure for primary care. *B.M.J.*, **305**:160–164.
75. Brazier, J., Harper, R., Jones, N., Thomas, K., and Westlake L. (1992). Validating the SF-36. Author's reply (letter). *B.M.J.*, **305**:646.
76. Bousquet, J., Knani, J., Dhivert, H., Richard, A., Chicoye, A., Ware, J., and Michel, F.-B. (1994). Quality of life in asthma: I. Internal consistency and validity of the SF-36 questionnaire. *Am. J. Respir. Crit. Care. Med.*, **149**:371–375.
77. McHorney, C., Ware, J., and Raczek, A. (1993). The MOS 36-item short-form health survey (SF-36): II. Psychometric and clinical tests of validity in measuring physical and mental constructs. *Med. Care*, **31**:247–263.
78. Dyer, C., and Sinclair, A. (1997). A hospital-based case control study of quality of life in older asthmatics. *Eur. Respir. J.*, **10**:337–341.

79. Ware, J.J. (1996). The SF-36 Health Survey. In *Quality of Life and Pharmacoeconomics in Clinical Trials*. Edited by B. Spilker: Philadelphia, Lippincott-Raven, pp. 337–345.

80. Okamoto, L., Noonan, M., DeBoisblanc, B., and Kellerman, D. (1996). Fluticasone propionate improves quality of life in patients with asthma requiring oral corticosteroids. *Ann. Allergy Asthma Immunol.*, **76**:455–461.

81. Noonan, M., Chervinsky, P., Busse, W., Weisberg, S., Pinnas, J., DeBoisblanc, B., Boltansky, H., Pearlman, D., Repsher, L., and Kellerman, D. (1995). Fluticasone propionate reduces oral prednisone use while it improves asthma control and quality of life. *Am. J. Respir. Crit. Care. Med.*, **152**:1467–1473.

82. Snedecor, G., Cochrane W. (1989). *Statistical Methods*, Ames, IA., Iowa State University Press, pp. 242–245.

8

Psychosocial Factors in Chronic Asthma

CYNTHIA S. RAND and ARLENE MANNS BUTZ

Johns Hopkins University School of Medicine
Baltimore, Maryland

I. Introduction

Both the scientific understanding of the pathophysiology of asthma and the quality of available asthma therapies have dramatically improved over the past twenty years. These advances, however, have not yielded comparably significant reductions in asthma morbidity. Instead, epidemiological data document that concordant with the development of improved therapies, there has been a concomitant rise in asthma morbidity in the United States and worldwide (1–4).

Researchers have examined the possibility that this increased risk is attributable to the pharmacological toxicity of some asthma therapies (5–7). In addition, a significant focus has also been directed to the underutilization of preventive asthma management strategies by both health care providers and patients (8–10). This medical framework (Fig. 1), however, still fails to adequately explain why asthma morbidity remains high in this country, despite the wide availability of effective and safe asthma therapies and intensive public efforts to educate health care providers and patients. This traditional explanatory framework may fail to explain the continuing high levels of asthma morbidity, in part because asthma, like all chronic diseases, is best understood within the context of the social, familial, behavioral, and psychological environment in which it occurs

Figure 1   The impact of asthma: a medical framework.

(Fig. 2). Individual differences in the impact of asthma on quality of life can only partially be attributed to the underlying pathophysiological differences in disease severity and variable treatment options. For each patient, the experience of asthma is a complex interaction of multiple factors, including disease severity, medical treatment, and psychological reactions (11). This experience is uniquely filtered through the personality and behavior patterns of each person with asthma, resulting in the personal ''costs'' of asthma. The disease exacerbations and the burden of day-to-day asthma management can, in turn, create stressors that impact on both individuals and families. This chapter reviews research that has examined the social and psychological factors associated with pediatric and adult asthma morbidity.

Asthma has a long history of being considered a psychogenic disease (12). The episodic nature of asthma exacerbations, the absence of biochemical markers to clearly document physical pathology, and the overt urgency and stress associated with acute attacks has led clinicians and researchers to look to psychiatric, familial, and social characteristics as important contributors to asthma etiology and morbidity. Comorbid genetic risk may also predispose some individuals to both asthma and psychiatric symptoms, such as anxiety and depression (13). Other researchers have interpreted the same observed associations between psychiatric, family, and behavioral variables and asthma morbidity and concluded

Figure 2 The impact of asthma: a psychosocial framework.

that chronic asthma is a psychosocial stressor that can negatively impact on emotions, behavior, mental health, and family dynamics. Causal inferences about the associations between asthma morbidity and psychological and family characteristics are necessarily limited by the cross-sectional design of most studies. Understanding the nature of the relationships between psychosocial variables and asthma is further complicated because of the inherent limitations in the self-report instruments often used to measure and quantify psychosocial and behavioral variables as well as asthma morbidity variables, such as symptom frequency and medication use. Respective of these caveats, research that has examined psychosocial factors as contributors to asthma morbidity or as consequences of asthma morbidity is presented as originally conceptualized by the investigators. Finally, we consider how these psychosocial factors influence asthma morbidity within the broader framework of the social environment (Fig. 3). Specifically, the moderating effect of socioeconomic status on the physical, behavioral, psychological, and social/familial factors that determine asthma's social impact is discussed.

II. Social/Familial Factors and Asthma

Asthma is an unpredictable disease that can interfere with the daily lives of both patients and their families (see Chaps. 2 and 3). Acute asthma episodes can be frightening and disruptive, and the daily care required to prevent asthma attacks may create an additional burden of time and responsibility. Parents of children with asthma may be stressed by their fears for the child's well-being as well as the tangible impact of days of lost work, financial demands, disrupted sleep, and

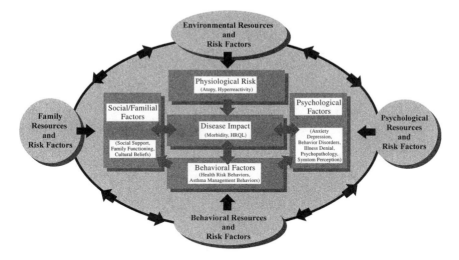

Figure 3   The impact of socioeconomic status on asthma: a social-environmental framework.

altered family plans. Coping with the demands and uncertainties of a chronic illness may be facilitated by social and family resources that support the individual with asthma and their family members. Chaotic families with poor communication, marital discord, or other significant stressors—such as mental illness, financial problems, or substance abuse—may be ill equipped to manage the care of a child with a chronic illness. In turn, the impact of the disease itself may contribute to the stress level within the household. For these reasons, research has examined the role of social and family variables as contributing factors in the severity and impact of asthma.

A.   Social Support

Managing chronic diseases such as asthma often requires individuals with asthma to rely on family and friends for both emotional and material support and assistance. This social support can act as a mediator of the disease's negative impact. However, cooperative management of asthma will be complicated for individuals lacking supportive family and friends or for persons with asthma living in dysfunctional or chaotic households.

Social support is generally considered the emotional, instrumental, and informational help available to an individual within his or her home and community environment (14). It is hypothesized that social support can act as a direct influence on health and overall quality of life as well as acting as a ''buffer'' that helps to minimize the negative impact of chronic illness on well-being. While social support has received more attention in research examining the effects of other chronic diseases—such as arthritis, diabetes, and cardiovascular disease—some investigators have examined the role of social support in moderating the impact of asthma.

Bazargan and Hamm-Baugh (15) report that low social support was associated with depression in a large group of elderly black patients with chronic illness ($n = 1022$), including respiratory diseases such as asthma and chronic obstructive pulmonary disease (COPD); arthritis; kidney disease; diabetes; gastrointestinal problems; dental, hearing, and vision problems; and cardiac disease. Depression was greatest in individuals who described having less support from friends, less instrumental or material support (running errands, assistance with household chores, providing transportation), more stressful life events, lower self-perceptions, and more financial difficulties. However, patients with kidney, vision, and/ or circulation problems had higher rates of depression than elderly black patients with respiratory disease.

Fisher et al. (16) have reported that African-American mothers who were socially isolated were more likely to seek emergency asthma care for their children, independent of asthma severity. Butz et al. (17) found that urban African-American mothers of children with more severe asthma were more likely to report lower levels of social support. In this same project, mothers with lower social support were more apt to seek emergency care for their children's asthma than mothers with higher social support. This may reflect that caregivers with less instrumental (i.e., practical) and affective support have greater difficulty managing their children's day-to-day asthma, resulting in asthma flares, or that caregivers without support may feel less capable of managing an after-hours acute asthma attack without the aid of emergency care. The 24-hr availability of professional care and advice at an emergency department for a wheezing child may be most readily utilized by the mother with the fewest alternative sources of support.

Fathers may play an important moderating role in the impact of asthma on maternal well-being. In a study of 228 low-income Hispanic and African-American mothers, Wasilewski et al. (18) tested the hypothesis that paternal involvement in asthma care and the presence of adults living in the household would be associated with reduced impact of asthma on mothers' daily activities. While the presence of other adults in the household did not influence the level of asthma-related disruption, paternal participation in asthma management was inversely related to the level of disruption, regardless of whether the father lived in the home.

B. Family Functioning

The asthma morbidity and mortality literature has been slow to recognize the association between family dysfunction and poor asthma outcome. Family functioning and coping have been suggested as important factors that can have a significant impact on the psychological adjustment of children diagnosed with a chronic illness, including asthma (19).

Family dysfunction has been reported as a consequence of having a child with asthma (20) as well as contributing to poor asthma outcomes in children (21). Caring for children with asthma may result in family stress and strain on available resources (20). The additional demands of caring for a child with asthma can include tangible burdens, such as the costs and time associated with asthma medical care and environmental control measures, as well as the emotional burden of fear and concerns about the child's well-being. Asthma can impact on the whole family in multiple ways, including altering family plans and increasing sibling jealousy. Families with existing stressors—such as marital discord, substance abuse, or other health problems—may be the least equipped to cope with the requirements associated with preventive asthma care.

Neglect and/or abuse will influence both the medical and psychological morbidity of a child with asthma. Some families are unable to assume the responsibility of their child's complex medical requirements. Chaotic families (defined as families with lack of order and regularity in family life, lack of age-appropriate expectations, and disintegration of executive structure in the family) have been identified among children with asthma admitted to a tertiary care hospital for moderate to severe asthma. In a study by Boxer et al. (21) family chaos was associated with failures in past medical care for asthma. While the incidence of abuse and neglect suspected or identified in this child sample was similar to the estimated incidence in the normal U.S. population (10%), 42% of these children admitted for asthma were transferred to the inpatient psychiatric unit of the hospital prior to discharge. Boxer et al. (21) argue that dysfunctional families have difficulty coping with chronic illness due to the demands of the particular disease. For chaotic and dysfunctional families, having a child with asthma may impose demands that burden them beyond their capacity to cope, resulting in poor asthma control for the child.

Poor asthma outcomes resulting from family dysfunction were reviewed in 201 asthma deaths. Again, parental failure to administer proper asthma medications, a proxy of family dysfunction, was listed as one factor contributing to fatal asthma in children (22).

Strunk et al. (23) have described the family, personal, and medical characteristics that characterized pediatric survivors of severe asthma attacks as well as nonsurvivors. Fatal asthma was not only associated with indices of severe disease such as a history of hypoxic seizures or respiratory failure but was also related to evidence of a poor family support system, psychological problems in the child, noncompliance, and other family management problems. Strunk concluded that asthma deaths in children are due to the interaction of severe disease with psychosocial problems of both the child and the family.

Family communication between parents and children has been shown to be related to adherence with asthma therapy. Christiaanse et al. (24) interviewed 38 children and adolescents recruited from an allergy clinic who were prescribed theophylline on a regular basis. These investigators found that compliance in this sample was only fair (56% compliant) and that gender and socioeconomic status were unrelated to compliance levels. Regression analysis indicated that family cohesiveness and the child's psychological adjustment were both positively related to adherent theophylline levels. The best predictor of compliance was the interaction between family cohesion (versus conflict) and the number of child behavior problems, with the worst adherence found in families with high conflict and high levels of child behavior difficulties.

C. Cultural Factors

Individual and family behavior is shaped by shared values, beliefs, and traditions that are derived from cultural norms. These behaviors and beliefs are nurtured and transferred across generations through modeling, tradition, and family problem-solving efforts (25). Health-related beliefs and behaviors are strongly rooted in these cultural norms and may be discordant with the traditional biomedical model of the health care provider. Pachter (26) has described clinical encounters as ''an interaction between two cultures—the 'culture' of medicine and the 'culture' of patients.'' Differences between the lay person's explanatory model for the causes and treatments of asthma and that of the physician can result in miscommunication, poor adherence with therapy, and inappropriate health care utilization. These differences may result in patients using home remedies as an adjunct to prescribed regimens, or an outright rejection of prescribed therapies, and these practices will not usually be revealed in the standard medical office visit. Culture and experience may create distrust of the prophylactic pharmacological model of asthma management and lead to noncompliance (27). For many parents, daily use of medication is troubling, particularly when a child is not symptomatic. In one study, urban African-American mothers of children with asthma commonly expressed concern that daily medication use would lead to ''addiction'' to the medicine or that the medicine would ''not work as well when really needed'' if used too often (28). Episodic treatment of asthma exacerbations may be considered appropriate and sufficient asthma care in a child with frequent periods of remission. For a mother who considers her child with asthma essentially healthy, daily use of medications may seem excessive and unnecessary. In some communities, home remedies or over-the-counter drugs (teas, coffee, cough medicines, decongestants, etc.) for asthma may be prevalent and viewed as ''safer'' than conventional prescribed asthma medications (28).

III. Psychological Factors and Asthma

Asthma remains a complex illness. There is now considerable evidence that psychological factors play an important role in asthma; however, there is little agreement on the extent to which these factors occur. Depression has been associated with increased asthma morbidity and mortality. Anxiety, specifically panic-fear, is associated with increased health care utilization for asthma. In a study of inpatients with severe asthma, psychosocial problems were reported in 13% of patient medical records, but this figure increased to 33% on further interview (29). Understanding the nature of the psychiatric and social factors in severe and poorly controlled asthma is critical for optimal asthma management.

A. Anxiety: Adult Asthma and Anxiety

One type of anxiety disorder, panic disorder, has been suggested to occur at higher rates in patients with asthma than the general public and is the most frequently reported anxiety disorder in association with medical illness (30). Although the research in this area is still controversial regarding the detrimental effects of panic disorder on the course of asthma, evidence suggests that panic is associated with increased health care utilization. Patients with panic disorder report seven times as many physician visits and lose twice as many workdays as members of the general public (31). Patients with an increased panic-fear tendency have been found to take more as-needed medication and to be high consumers of medical care (32).

Panic-fear is one of the most commonly studied negative emotions associated with asthma (33,34). Two types of panic-fear have been defined: panic-fear in response to the symptoms of asthma, termed *illness-specific panic-fear* and a more *generalized panic-fear* reflecting a stable personality trait (35). Illness-specific panic-fear reflects levels of attention specifically focused on breathing difficulties ranging from symptom disregard (low panic-fear) to symptom vigilance or focused concern of breathing problems (high panic-fear) (36). Generalized panic-fear may predispose a patient to react to his or her breathing problems in a particular way. For instance, high panic-fear personalities tend to neutralize the symptom vigilance of high illness-specific panic-fear, leading to poor medical outcomes (37). High panic-fear personality levels, in contrast to low panic-fear personality levels, are associated with high rates of rehospitalization following chronic intensive asthma therapy (38) as well as longer and more frequent hospitalizations (39), and increased utilization of health care services such as those provided by emergency departments.

The physiology of acute asthma may encourage increased anxiety. Alternations of respiration are very anxiety-provoking (13). One study examined 23 cases of hyperventilation or hyperventilation syndrome presented to an emergency department for organic and psychogenic causes and referred to a chest clinic for full lung-function testing. In this study, almost one-third (30%) of the patients had asthma (40). The authors suggest that "the persistently low P_{CO_2} in these asthmatic patients suggests that asthma made a significant contribution to the initiating hyperventilation attack, probably by long-term lowering the resting Pa_{CO_2} closer to the threshold for symptom production'' (40).

Pattern of β_2-agonist use were studied in relation to anxiety in adult patients with asthma (41). Mawhinny et al. (42) reported that adult patients who used their rescue inhalers (β_2-agonist as needed) in an arbitrary manner scored higher on a standardized trait anxiety measure. The investigators suggested that this higher trait anxiety might lead such patients to turn to their rescue medication when they felt anxious, even when they were not experiencing true airway obstruction. Alternatively, anxiety may interfere with a patient's ability to accurately distinguish chest tightness due to stress and tension from airway obstruction secondary to asthma.

Bosley et al. (43) identified a high incidence of anxiety disorders in a group of 102 patients with asthma requiring inhaled steroids and β_2-agonist treatment for their asthma. They suggest that some degree of anxiety may allow a patient to respond appropriately to respiratory symptoms, motivate them to take medication on a regular basis, and comply with environmental control measures. Alternatively, too much or overwhelming anxiety may make patients too fearful to act.

B. Anxiety: Pediatric Asthma and Anxiety

Mrazek (44) argues that although the cooccurrence of asthma and psychiatric disturbance should be expected at rates equal to the general childhood prevalence of psychiatric conditions (12%), children with severe chronic illness have a higher incidence of anxiety disorders and other psychological problems. Several pediatric studies have investigated the relationship between anxiety and asthma morbidity.

In a cross-sectional study of children attending a tertiary setting, children with asthma had a substantially higher rate of anxiety disorders than a comparison group of healthy children, according to Bussing et al. (45). The prevalence of anxiety disorders during the preceding year in the asthma group was significantly higher than that in the control group (43.2% versus 19.4%, $p = 0.04$). A high rate of separation anxiety was also detected in the children with asthma. This may be explained by the heightened fears and worries of the parent of a child with asthma, including frequent emergency department visits, possible hospitalizations, and the potential loss of the child, which may increase the separation anxiety in the child to meet the mother's needs (45).

''Panic feelings'' were reported by almost two-thirds (64.5%) of the children with asthma during an acute attack, suggesting that anxiety of some form appears to be present in most children at some time during an acute asthma attack (46). Child state anxiety, or transient anxiety, was associated with children reporting ''being upset'' at the beginning of an acute asthma attack and having more than one asthma attack during the preceding year (46). Child trait anxiety, the stable personality trait, was associated with reports of feeling "panic" at the beginning of an asthma attack.

Asthma medications do not appear to contribute to increased rates of anxiety in children with asthma, according to Bussing et al. (47). Theophylline has been linked to both improvement and worsening of cognition and mood. Theophylline has not demonstrated any noticeable neuropsychological side effects in children (48). No evidence of steroid-induced psychiatric disturbance was found at levels typically used to treat children with asthma (49).

Psychosocial functioning, including anxiety, was examined in 100 children 1 to 15 years of age who were referred to a Swiss pediatric asthma clinic (50). Each child received psychosocial assessments regarding family functioning (Family Adaptation and Cohesion Scales, or FACES) and the Child Behavior Checklist (CBLC) in addition to pulmonary function, bronchial reactivity, and immunological tests. Children were classified into five etiological groups based on clinical symptoms: infection-induced ($N = 13$), seasonal ($N = 23$), perennial ($N = 38$) (symptoms independent of infections and allergen exposure), emotional ($N = 1$), and atypical asthma ($N = 25$). Children with emotional etiology were excluded. Children classified with infection-induced asthma were reported by their parents to be more anxious than those in the other four groups. In the seasonal group, there was a high level of immunological abnormality, but very few psychological alterations were detected. Children with atypical asthma were more likely to have psychiatric symptoms as measured by the CBCL. The authors conclude that psychosocial findings are heterogeneous in children with asthma and should be interpreted as being related to their somatic symptoms (50).

C. Depression: Adult Asthma and Depression

Conflicting information exists about the relationship between depression and asthma. While a number of studies have reported that depression is associated with increased asthma mortality and morbidity and that depression appears to be closely related to impaired pulmonary function (51–54), others indicate that depression plays little role in the severity or illness course of asthma (55,56).

In a study of 715 adults, Janson et al. (57) found a significant correlation between self-reported symptoms of wheezing, waking with breathlessness, attacks of breathlessness, and higher levels of depression. However, there was no significant association between depression and either doctor-diagnosed asthma or objective asthma-related variables, such as peak flow. Dyer and Sinclair (58) examined overall quality of life in 40 older hospitalized patients with asthma as compared with that of age-and sex-matched controls without asthma and reported that depressive symptoms were not significantly different between the two groups but were common in both. Furthermore, there were no significant increases in social isolation or emotional problems reported by these hospitalized patients with asthma as compared with a control group without asthma.

The relationship between depressed mood and physiological variables in asthma has been investigated with mixed findings. Allen et al. (59) evaluated the relationship between the level of maximal voluntary activation of the diaphragm and psychological distress in 21 volunteers. For participants with asthma, depressed mood increased the risk of impaired maximal voluntary activation of the diaphragm by 3.5 times. This observation was not noted in the control, nonasthmatic subjects, suggesting an interaction between depression and diaphragmatic function. Rubin (60) has hypothesized that depression and severe asthma are synergistic and exacerbate each other. Although the exact mechanisms involved are not clearly defined, Rubin suggests that depression is associated with cholinergic dominance. Belloch et al. (55), however, using the Minnesota Multiphasic Personality Inventory—Depression (MMPI-D), found that depression was not related to impaired pulmonary function in 51 adult patients with asthma. None of the patients qualified for the clinical diagnosis of depression. However, the results suggest that there is a complex relationship between psychological traits, demographic factors, and clinical symptoms (55).

Disruption of lifestyle appears to be one factor that may be associated with depression in some patients with asthma. In a study of 95 adults with asthma, Janson-Bjerklie et al. (61) found that four variables explained 37% of the variance in depression in this sample; specifically, the number of anticipatory self-care strategies, the appraisal of perceived stress and life change during the previous 6 months, the presence of nocturnal asthma symptoms, and the amount of distress experienced during an asthma episode. Dyspnea predicted only 6% of the variance in depression (61). These findings suggest that the degree to which life is disrupted by asthma and other stressors (such as sleeplessness) is the critical determinant of depressive symptoms in adults with asthma.

Severe asthma may not only lead to depression but depression itself may contribute to poor asthma management via poor self-management behaviors and adherence with therapy. Increased depression has been reported to be a risk factor for poor adherence and increased morbidity and mortality for a wide range of chronic diseases. Bosley et al. (43) evaluated the relationship between electronically monitored asthma compliance and psychological state, including depression. The authors found that the nonadherent patients had significantly higher mean scores for depression [4.7 (SD 3.3)] than the adherent group [3.2 (SD 2.5)].

D. Depression: Pediatric Asthma and Depression

As with adult studies, the association between asthma and depression in children is inconclusive. Functional impairment, such as some limitation in activity, may be partly responsible for any emotional problems detected in children with asthma (62). Data from the 1988 U.S. National Health Interview Survey of 17,110 households revealed that 30% of children with asthma had some limitation in activity, compared with only 5% of children without asthma (63). This alteration of daily activities may be due to the unpredictability of asthma, leading to overprotectiveness by parents and resulting in excessive and burdensome restrictions on the child's daily activities (62).

The association between severity of disease and increased depressive symptoms remains unclear (64). In children with cancer, more depressive symptoms were reported when their general health status was poor; however this relationship was not found among children with asthma (65). Perrin et al. (66) found a curvilinear effect between asthma severity and psychological dysfunction, with the greatest psychological dysfunction occurring among children with both severe and mild asthma.

Suris et al. (67) examined emotional distress and suicidal ideation (by self-administered questionnaire) among adolescents with and without chronic illness (asthma, diabetes, seizures, and cancer). No differences in the prevalence of emotional distress or suicidal ideation were found among the four groups of illness, suggesting that it was not the disease per se; rather, noncategorical factors such as disease severity or uncertainly of disease were associated with increased emotional distress.

Wamboldt et al. (13) examined adolescents with severe asthma and found that they did not have higher rates of affective disorders (including depression) as compared with the general population. However, family members of the adolescent *did* have higher rates of affective, antisocial, and substance abuse disorders than a comparison sample of people who were not ill and also compared with relatives of either the not ill or depressed comparison sample. Wamboldt et al. submit that the linkage may be (a) genetic, in that severe asthma and affective disorders may have a genetic link, or (b) environmental—i.e., having family members with depression or anxiety disorders may provide an environmental stressor to the child that leads to more severe asthma.

E. Behavior Disorders

Many investigators have studied the relationship between asthma or its treatment and school and behavioral problems. The rate of behavior problems in school-age children with asthma has been reported to be twice that found in the general population, based on scoring above the 98th percentile on the Child Behavior Checklist (CBCL) (68). One underlying reason for this increase in behavior problems may be the fact that psychological vulnerability in children is primarily expressed as more behavior problems and less adaptability to social challenges (69).

Using data from the 1988 U.S. National Health Interview on Child Health database, several investigators examined the association between chronic health conditions and behavior problems (47). Children with asthma and medical comorbid conditions (infectious diseases, allergic conditions, and chronic headaches) had a higher mean Behavior Problem Index (BPI) score than did children without chronic conditions. Total BPI scores were significantly different between the asthma and comorbid group, the group without chronic conditions, and the group with asthma alone. Using logistic regression to control for confounding variables, children with severe asthma alone had nearly three times the odds (odds ratio = 2.96; CI = 1.22 to 7.17) and children with asthma plus comorbid conditions nearly twice the odds (odds ratio = 1.86; CI: 1.20 to 2.90) compared with children without chronic conditions in reporting a severe behavior problem. The investigators conclude that severe asthma and asthma with medical comorbidity represent significant risk factors for emotional and/or behavioral problems.

Butz et al. (17) in a study of 392 inner-city children, found that children with high levels of asthma symptoms were more than twice as likely to experience a behavior problem than children classified with a low level of asthma symptoms (p = 0.002). Use of theophylline medication was not correlated with behavior problems. Variables significantly associated with the presence of a behavior problem in the final logistic regression were low level of social support and reporting a high to moderate level of asthma symptoms. The proportion of children with behavior problems in this sample was comparable with the rate (34%) found in an inner-city pediatric clinic population, including children with and without asthma from single-parent families.

An association between pediatric asthma and attention deficit hyperactivity disorder (ADHD) has been suggested, but the research is inconclusive. Biederman et al. (70) showed that the overall rate of asthma did not differ significantly between a group of 140 children with ADHD and 120 normal comparison children. The risk for asthma was significantly elevated only among relatives of children with ADHD who also had asthma. Despite these negative findings, the investigators warn that asthma per se and/or asthma treatments may aggravate ADHD symptoms in some children with asthma, resulting in comorbidity.

Child behavior via parental report was assessed in a large population-based study of 2534 children, including children with asthma. Children with asthma were reported to sleep less well than normal or to be hyperactive (p < 0.001) (71). In further analysis, asthma medication intake during the preceding 12 months was found to be significantly associated with the occurrence of sleep disturbances, which, in turn, may be confounded by the severity of the asthma. Use of theophylline and B_2 agonist drugs was a risk for sleep disturbance. The investigators conclude that psychosocial differences of children with asthma are less remarkable than expected and suggest that children with asthma are influenced more by secondary factors, such as medical treatment than by any primary effect of the illness.

F. Symptom Perception

The critical premise of asthma management is the patient's or parent's ability to accurately identify symptoms and lung function compromise. Perceptions and interpretations of physiological sensations, such as airway obstruction, vary from one individual to another. Symptom perception is likely not static; rather it changes across developmental stages and through experience with asthma exacerbations (72). Accurate perceptions and reports of asthma symptoms are critical to optimal asthma management. Poor perception of airway obstruction may be a contributing factor in dangerous delays in seeking medical treatment for asthma or to medication nonadherence. Inadequate symptom perception has been suggested as one potential cause of fatal and near-fatal asthma (73). In one study of adults with asthma, approximately 15% of the patients failed to recognize bronchoconstriction despite significant airway obstruction, indicating that they were unaware of their level of respiratory distress (74).

Longitudinal research with large samples is required to determine whether changes in symptom perception are associated with morbidity and mortality. Few studies have linked poor symptom perception or denial of asthma symptoms and risk for mortality. Strunk and colleagues (23) demonstrated that global disregard of asthma symptoms was one of the variables that differentiated children who died with asthma compared with children who did not die (matched for age, gender, and severity). This was supported by Zach and Karner (75), who found that ''poor perception of pulmonary function compromise differentiated children who died from asthma from those who did not.'' Fritz et al. (72) corroborated this by reporting that accurate symptom perception was associated with lower functional morbidity (number of schooldays missed, emergency department visits, and nights awakened by asthma symptoms) after controlling for asthma severity.

Respiratory responses to hypoxia and hypercapnia were studied in patients with near-fatal attacks of asthma ($N = 11$) and compared with those of patients who had no near-fatal attacks ($N = 11$) and normal subjects without asthma ($N = 16$) (73). This study was an attempt to examine symptom perception in patients with severe asthma. Using the Borg scale, a linear scale of numbers (0 to 10) ranking the magnitude of difficulty in breathing, the perception of breathing was measured during increasing difficult inspiratory resistances. After breathing for 1 min at each level of resistance, subjects rated the difficulty in breathing or dyspnea. Additionally, chemosensitivity to hypoxia and hypercapnia were measured in terms of slope of ventilation and airway occlusion pressure as a function of the percentage of arterial oxygen saturation and end-tidal carbon dioxide tension. Blunted chemosensitivity to hypoxia and hypercapnia in patients with asthma can result in severe respiratory failure. Results of this study revealed that mean Borg score was significantly lower in the patients with near-fatal asthma than in normal subjects but not significantly lower than the mean score for patients without near-fatal attacks. However, most of the patients with near-fatal asthma had a decreased chemosensitivity to hypoxia as well as blunted perception of dyspnea during resistive loading or higher lung resistance. The authors conclude that relying on patients perception of their asthma symptoms may result in undertreatment of the asthma and ultimately fatal attacks of asthma. Further-more, the use of peak flow monitoring is clearly indicated in patients who are identified at risk for a fatal attack of asthma due to the potential blunting percep-tion of respiratory impairment found in these subjects.

In contrast to this blunted perception found by Kikuchi et al. (73), Boulet et al. (76) found that mean perception scores for airway obstruction were higher in patients with asthma than control subjects during methacholine inhalation tests to induce a 20–50% decrease in FEV_1 and breathlessness. Anxiety and broncho-dilator needs during the induced bronchoconstriction were low and did not corre-late with breathlessness in both the patients with asthma and control subjects. The investigators hypothesize that patients are familiar with change in lung func-tion and that the level of perception of induced breathlessness does not predict whether a patient is at risk for a severe attack. These results were corroborated by Nouwen et al. (77), who also report that patients with asthma perceived symp-toms of bronchial closing and discomfort more accurately than normal controls during a first methacholine-induced bronchoconstriction, but less accurate during a second induction of bronchoconstriction in which the controls became more accurate in symptom perception. This suggests that either the patients with asthma became habituated to their symptoms or to the experimental situation, the latter being proposed by the authors. This study further supports the use of objective lung function—i.e., training patients to measure peak flow levels on a consistent basis—rather than trying to fine-tune symptom perception as a tool for asthma management.

Differences in symptom perception have been attributed to anxiety. In a sample of 78 asthmatic subjects, ''anxious perceivers of histamine induced air-ways obstruction had higher scores for both perceived breathlessness and level of anxiety at a 20% fall in FEV_1'' (78). Anxious perceivers were also more likely to be accurate in their perception of induced bronchoconstriction than nonanxious perceivers. The association between anxious and accurate perceiving of airways obstruction may be interpreted in different ways, which are not mutually exclu-sive. It is conceivable that subjects became more anxious because they accurately perceived progressing degrees of airways obstruction (78). The lack of a signifi-cant difference in anxiety at baseline between anxious and nonanxious perceivers supports this hypothesis. In contrast, Fritz et al. (72) found that anxiety was not related to the accuracy of symptom perception in children with asthma. Overall, Fritz et al. (72) propose that anxiety may not have a linear relationship with symptom perception in children, only that high levels of anxiety interfere with accurate symptom perception. Alternatively, anxiety may influence asthma symp-toms by appropriate asthma management rather than how the asthma symptoms are perceived (72).

Fritz et al. (72) propose that perceptual accuracy in pediatric asthma may be affected by physiological (disease severity), psychological (defensive style), cognitive (intelligence), and parent-child factors (parent modeling). Understanding the factors associated with perceptual accuracy of symptoms would allow for development of intervention programs that maximize the child's ability to self-manage his or her asthma.

G. Psychiatric Diagnosis and Illness Denial

Psychiatric diagnosis and illness denial have been identified as risk factors for asthma morbidity and fatal asthma. Several authors hypothesize that high levels of denial may militate against successful management of potentially life-threatening asthma. Campbell et al. (79) evaluated the association between denial, psychiatric illness, and self-reported asthma morbidity (as measured by questionnaire and semistructured interview) among a sample of patients who had experienced life-threatening asthma episodes. Using the General Health Questionnaire (GHQ), 43% of these patients had scores consistent with psychiatric morbidity. This psychiatric morbidity was correlated with levels of asthma morbidity (number of asthma attacks, interference with daily activities, days lost from work, number of doctor visits in the month prior to the near-fatal attack), with those reporting more symptoms having higher GHQ scores. Although all of these subjects had recently (usually within 12 weeks) experienced a life-threatening asthma attack and been hospitalized for asthma, the mean scores on the Illness Behavior Questionnaire was 3.6 (out of 5), suggesting significant denial of the severity of their illness. Regardless of whether the observed illness denial and psychiatric morbidity are the consequences of living with severe asthma, contributory factors to poor adherence and treatment delays, or both, it is evident that psychiatric comorbidity will complicate asthma management. The investigators suggest that clinicians screen for these factors when evaluating a high-risk patient and make appropriate psychiatric referrals when necessary.

Martin et al. (80) evaluated 30 cases of near-fatal asthma in children over a 3 year period. Through patient/family/provider interviews, questionnaires, and review of medical records, the investigators identified possible contributing factors in the occurrence of near-fatal asthma. Although 83% of patients were classified as having severe asthma and 70% had a hospitalization for asthma in the previous 12 months, 80% of the patients or their families had high illness denial scores. In 73% of these cases, psychosocial factors—such as gross psychiatric illness, substance abuse, intellectual impairment, or social isolation—were considered to be a contributing factor in the near-fatal attack. Overall, Martin et al. concluded that 83% of the episodes were preventable and that significant denial, psychosocial pathology, and delays on seeking treatment contributed to the life-threatening nature of these attacks.

Wareham et al. (81) report that psychosocial factors can contribute to asthma mortality via the patient's capacity to manage his or her asthma appropriately. Of the 28 fatal cases of asthma studied, they found that 17 (71%) demonstrated evidence of contributing psychosocial risk factors, including social isolation, abuse as a child, neurotic illness, marital or legal problems, and alcohol abuse. The research of Mascia et al. (82) confirms this association. Factors associated with fatal outcomes of asthma included severe psychopathology, psychotic signs, low IQ, anxiety, and depression.

Beausoleil et al. (83) found that children and teenage β_2-agonist inhaler overusers (being treated in-hospital for severe asthma), were more likely to have lower IQs and show tendencies toward shrewdness, dominance, and lack of discipline on the Children's Personality Questionnaire (CPQ). The authors concluded that personality-related, intellectual, and cultural characteristics of patients with asthma should be considered when teaching patients regarding the safe and effective use of β_2-agonist inhalers.

H. Patient Beliefs

The way in which individuals with asthma construe their illness and their ability to control the disease has been found to been an important factor in asthma management behaviors. For example, the perceived social stigma of having a chronic illness may encourage illness denial in some individuals (84). For others the unpredictable, episodic nature of asthma can create uncertainty about the severity of the disease and the need for preventive care. Patients may hesitate to seek urgent care because of an unwillingness to give up control of the management to others or because of concerns about the stigma associated with illness and hospitals. Other patients with asthma may fail to manage asthma effectively because they perceive that that there is little that they can do to control asthma outcome (85).

Adams et al. (84) evaluated the asthma-related beliefs and medication compliance of a sample of asthmatic patients in Wales who had been prescribed prophylactic medications. Using qualitative interviewing strategies, they identified three common self-perspectives among this group: deniers/distancers, acceptors, and pragmatics. These perspectives were associated with very different patient beliefs about the nature of asthma and use of preventive medication. Deniers/distancers represented half of the sample ($n = 15$) and either claimed that they did not have asthma (despite a doctor diagnosis and prescribed medications) or reported that they had ''slight'' or ''not proper'' asthma. These patients stated that asthma had no effect on their lives, and they rarely took their reliever medications. On further interviewing, however, these patients frequently revealed that they used their reliever surreptitiously and that they had developed complex avoidance behaviors to avoid physical symptoms (e.g., not running, staying indoors in certain seasons). None of these patients were using their prophylactic asthma medications. All of these individuals refused to accept the stigmatizing (in their view) label of "asthmatic" and instead relabeled their breathing problems as an acute, situation-specific problem or as a "bad chest." Patients identified as acceptors, on the other hand, acknowledged the chronic nature of asthma and had assimilated the social identity of "asthmatic." These patients sought to achieve normality not through denial but rather through the use of asthma management behaviors that allowed asthma control. In contrast to the deniers, who perceived preventive medications as a source of stigma, acceptors saw these medications as an aid to normalization. Pragmatics ($n = 6$) were less neatly categorized, although in general they were closer to the acceptors. These individuals were less positive and zealous about embracing an asthma diagnosis than the Acceptors; however, they were attempting to reconcile their lives and self-image with the social identity of "asthmatic." While they used their prophylactic medications, they might not have been using them in the approved manner. These individuals' level of self-disclosure and self-presentation shifted according to the relevant audience. This analysis of patient beliefs suggests that asthmatics' self-perception of their disease may influence asthma management behaviors.

Another way in which patient beliefs may influence asthma management is the degree to which asthmatics perceive that their behaviors can control asthma exacerbations. Three constructs from social learning theory—self-efficacy, learned helplessness, and locus of control—have been suggested as relevant psychological factors in the perceived control of asthma. *Self-efficacy* refers to an individuals' confidence that he or she can perform a task or behavior in the future; *learned helplessness* is a consequence of perceived lack of control, resulting in an individual "giving up"; finally, *locus of control* is a construct suggesting that individuals vary in the degree to which they believe that events are within their control ("internal") versus outside their control ("external"). In developing the Perceived Control of Asthma Questionnaire (PCAQ) evaluating these factors, Katz et al. (85) found that decreased perceived control was significantly associated with increased risk of hospitalization (after controlling for asthma severity and demographics), frequent activity restrictions, and asthma-related cessation of employment. The authors suggest that asthma interventions that target factors related to perceived control might improve asthma outcomes.

IV. Behavioral Factors and Asthma

Asthma is a chronic disease that is powerfully mediated by patient behaviors. Inadequate or inappropriate health-related behaviors can contribute to poor asthma control and excess asthma morbidity (86). For example, delays in seeking treatment or overreliance on urgent care can lead to dangerous escalations in asthma risk (79,87). Poor adherence with asthma therapy can result in unnecessary and potentially risky disease exacerbations (88). Other health-risk behaviors, such as substance abuse, can contribute to asthma morbidity and mortality by interfering with asthma self-management behaviors, directly exacerbating symptoms, or masking symptoms, thus leading to treatment delays.

While risky health behaviors and poor self-management of asthma result in increased asthma morbidity, positive asthma self-management behaviors are associated with better disease control and reduced health care utilization. Asthma self-management interventions have been developed to promote positive health-related behaviors in asthma, such as adherence with prescribed therapy, correct metered-dose inhaler (MDI) technique, allergen avoidance, preventive primary care, use of an asthma action plan, self-monitoring of symptoms, and peak flow monitoring. These interventions are generally based on both education and behavioral models and may be delivered one on one or in structured group programs. Overall, asthma self-management interventions have been associated with positive changes in asthma management behaviors and improved asthma outcomes in both children and adults.

A. Inappropriate Asthma Management

Because much of the mortality from asthma appears to be associated with avoidable inadequacies in the professional and personal management of asthma, Campbell et al. (79) undertook a descriptive case-series study designed to identify problems in asthma management associated with a near-fatal asthma attack. They interviewed 121 consecutive patients over the age of 15 years who presented to emergency departments in South Australia for treatment of asthma that resulted in respiratory arrest, an altered state of consciousness, and/or a Pa_{CO_2} greater than 50 mmHg on blood gas analysis. While over one-third of the patients reported persistent asthma attacks several times a week for the month prior to the event, fewer than half of these patients (45.8%) reported using an inhaled corticosteroid with their β_2-agonist. One-third of patients refilled their prescriptions without further medical consultation, and one-quarter of patients obtained their β_2-agonist medication "over the counter," without prescription. Over one-quarter (24.5%) of these patients were regular cigarette smokers (similar to the rate in the general population) despite the risks posed by their smoking. Overall, Campbell et al. concluded that these high-risk patients appeared to underutilize opportunities for medical advice, despite their evident symptoms.

Effective asthma management by patients and doctors is believed to prevent emergency department (ED) visits and hospitalizations. Lieu et al. (89) conducted a case-control study of children with asthma who were members of a regional health maintenance organization. Cases were children who had been hospitalized or seen in the ED and matched controls were children with asthma without urgent health care utilization during the study time frame. They reported that the relative odds of a hospitalization (after controlling for demographic variables and asthma severity) were lower for families with a written asthma action plan (odds ratio (OR): 0.54; 95% CI: 0.30, 0.99) and those who washed bedding in hot water at least twice a month (OR: 0.45; 95% CI: 0.21, 0.94). Similarly, ED visits were lower for children with a written asthma action plan (OR: 0.45; CI: 0.27; 0.76) and starting medications at the start of a cold (OR: 0.40; 95% CI: 0.19, 0.86). Attending an asthma education class and using a peak flow meter were not associated with reduced risk. The authors concluded that health practices of families that promote early intervention at home for asthma episodes were associated with reduced risk of hospitalization and ED use.

It is commonly assumed by health care professionals that poor asthma self-management results from inadequate asthma knowledge. To test this assumption, Kolbe et al. (29) evaluated the relationship between asthma knowledge and actual self-management behaviors in 137 patients admitted to the hospital with slow-onset (96% of subjects) severe asthma. They found marked discrepancies between knowledge and action for seeking medical help and calling an ambulance. An increased gap between knowledge and behavior was associated with anxiety, pessimism, being non-European, concerns about medical costs, and the only household income being a Social Security benefit. Understanding that the discrepancy between knowledge and behavior is associated with psychological and socioeconomic factors may be of critical importance in designing more effective asthma treatment strategies (90).

B. Substance Abuse

Substance abuse may be an important risk for increased asthma morbidity and mortality. Abuse of alcohol and drugs has the potential to increase the risk of fatal episodes for the patient with asthma in several ways. Substance abusers may be negligent about preventive asthma care. Patients under the life-disrupting influence of drugs may not perceive the symptoms of worsening asthma; they may be at increased risk because of the potential drug interactions between asthma medications and recreational drugs and/or because they fail to adhere with therapy or engage in appropriate asthma management.

Ernst et al. (91) have evaluated the relationship between asthma severity, psychosocial variables—including substance abuse, and use of albuterol in a case-control study of fatal asthma. They reported that an increased risk of fatal and near-fatal asthma was associated with substance abuse as well as amount of albuterol used, depression, conflict, a history of psychiatric illness, and non-compliance.

The high rates of both asthma morbidity and substance abuse found in inner-city communities (where poverty, poor access to health care, social isolation, joblessness, family dysfunction are common) may be associated. Levenson et al. (92) investigated the circumstances associated with fatal asthma in a sample of 102 cases of fatal asthma in adults younger than 45 years that occurred over a 2½ year period in Cook County, Chicago, an area notable for its unusually high asthma mortality rate. Medical examiner, autopsy, and toxicology reports were reviewed in this study, and, when possible, surviving kin were interviewed about the deceased's history of symptoms, medication use, asthma management, and substance abuse. Based on all available information, asthma deaths were reclassified as either clearly death from asthma, death from an indeterminate cause, or death coincidental to asthma. The investigators found that there was a 32% incidence of excessive alcohol use and/or illicit drug use among the patients who died from asthma. Of these substance abusers who died from asthma, 45% ($N = 13$) had evidence of cocaine use on toxicology screening. This rate was comparable to that observed in a comparison group of homicide deaths, where 47% of the deceased substance abusers tested positive for cocaine or its metabolite.

The most common form of substance abuse is cigarette smoking. Maternal smoking during pregnancy and infancy has been associated with increased risk of children developing asthma (93,94). Acute exposure to smoke can trigger asthma attacks and chronic exposure to smoke in the home environment can lead to increased respiratory infections, worsening symptoms, and decreased pulmonary function (93,95–98).

C. Poor Adherence with Therapy

Inadequate adherence with asthma therapy is associated with increased asthma morbidity and mortality. Milgrom et al. (88) found, in a study of pediatric asthma patients, that asthma exacerbations (as measured by number of prednisone bursts) were more common in those patients who were found by electronic monitoring to be the least adherent with inhaled anti-inflammatory therapy. Several studies have reported that patients presenting to the emergency department for acute asthma episodes were likely to have subtherapeutic levels of their prescribed theophylline (99,100). The risk of fatal and near fatal asthma episodes has also frequently been associated with poor patient compliance with therapy.

Studies that have examined patient adherence with preventive asthma therapies have reported that rates of nonadherence are often over 50% (101). Using electronic monitoring techniques, Spector et al. (102) reported that patients were adherent for a mean of 47% of the days in a 12-week study. Mawhinney et al. (103) electronically monitored adult patients' compliance over a 3- to 4-week period and found that they used their medication as prescribed on average for 37% of the days. In another study using electronic monitoring, Yeung et al. (104) found that when patients were unaware of the adherence monitoring, 6 out of 11 took from 30–51% of the prescribed doses; however, when patients were aware of monitoring, 60% of the patients were 100% adherent, 20% were partially adherent (taking just 70% of the prescribed dose), and 20% were nonadherent. In studies of children's adherence with anti-inflammatory therapy, both Coutts et al. (105) and Gibson et al. (106) have found similar rates of noncompliance.

Inappropriate adherence with asthma therapy may involve other behaviors beside underuse of preventive medications. Some researchers have speculated that overreliance on inhaled bronchodilators may contribute to patient delays in seeking medical care for acute asthma or that overuse of β_2-agonists may pose direct health risks to the asthmatic patient (91,107,108). As with inhaled anti-inflammatory therapy, patients may not be accurate reporters of their level of adherence with this treatment. For example, when Yeung et al. examined adherence with β_2-agonist therapy using electronic monitors they found that, in contrast to anti-inflammatory therapies, patients tended to underreport β_2-agonist use (104). Other investigators have reported that patients frequently fail to adhere to other asthma management behaviors such as environmental control and peak flow monitoring (109).

D.   Asthma Self-Management Interventions

Because of the significant relationship between behavior and asthma morbidity, both clinicians and researchers have examined the value of patient and family education programs designed to improve asthma management skills. Just as risky health behaviors such as nonadherence can increase asthma morbidity, effective asthma self-management behaviors may result in increased asthma control and decreased impact of asthma on daily life. While all asthma self-management interventions include asthma education, numerous studies have suggested that education alone is not sufficient to change complex behaviors (29). Effective intervention programs use behavioral and cognitive strategies such as self-monitoring, relaxation, and reinforcement to establish asthma management skills (110,111). Specific techniques and strategies may be taught and modeled, such as MDI technique, peak flow monitoring, and environmental control. Encouraging objective self-monitoring by careful attention to symptoms and peak flow variability may also increase symptom perception skills. Group or peer-led programs may offer social support and positive role models for patients with asthma and their families. Supportive, informative interventions may also help moderate negative psychological variables, such as anxiety and depression.

Studies of asthma self-management interventions developed by Bailey et al. (112,113), Evans et al. (114), Creer et al. (115–117), Wilson et al. (118,119), and others (120–124) have demonstrated that asthma knowledge and health outcomes can be improved by participation in an asthma self-management program. For example, Bailey et al. compared an individual self-management program for adult asthmatic with a control group and found that functional status was improved among the intervention participants (112,113). One possible mechanism for the reduced asthma morbidity might be the improved medication adherence demonstrated among the intervention participants. These subjects had significantly better adherence (self-reported) than usual-care participants (62 versus 92% fully compliant). For these same participants, staff rating indicated that 78% of the intervention group as compared with 51% of the usual-care group had "excellent" adherence. In addition, inhaler-use skills were significantly improved by participation in this behavioral intervention program, with 95% of intervention participants demonstrating eight out of ten inhaler use skills compared with 48% of usual-care participants (112). Wilson et al. (125) evaluated a clinic-based asthma self-management program targeted at elementary-age children. They found that intervention children had decreased asthma morbidity as compared with control children and improved asthma management behaviors, including MDI skills. Control patients who received only written instruction in MDI use showed no such improvement in technique. Most significantly, increases in MDI skills, as measured by the checklist, were directly correlated with decreases in patients' self-reports of how much their asthma symptoms bothered them. Studies by other investigators of asthma self-management interventions set in schools, outpatient clinics, and hospitals have shown promising results in increasing asthma management behaviors and reducing asthma morbidity (120–124).

V. Understanding Asthma Management Within a Social–Environmental Framework

The dynamic interaction between disease morbidity and psychosocial variables for asthmatics and their families necessarily takes place within the context of the larger community. And within this community environment, effective asthma management will require external as well internal resources. Socioeconomic status (SES), in particular, has been shown to be a powerful predictor of asthma prevalence, hospitalizations, and death. As with many other diseases, such as cancer and heart disease, poverty and minority race are associated with increased risk of asthma morbidity and mortality (126–130). However, the mechanisms by which lower SES and minority status increase risk are not well understood. Some investigators have speculated that the explanatory variable is decreased access to care; others have pointed to lower educational level, lack of personal control and lifestyle variables. Incorporating this broad perspective, we suggest that the most useful framework for understanding how SES contributes to the impact of asthma will be one that considers both the medical management and the contribution of psychosocial variables within the context of the physical, economic, and social environment. As shown in Figure 3, we propose that the physical, behavioral, psychological, and social/familial factors that determine disease impact will be profoundly moderated by the social environment.

A. The Impact of Socioeconomic Status on Physiological Risk for Asthma

Researchers have speculated that the physical environment associated with poverty and inner-city housing may be causally related to the increased asthma prevalence and morbidity found in inner-city minority communities. Poor housing may increase exposure to allergens and irritants that cause or exacerbate asthma. Allergens, cigarette smoke, and inadequate ventilation as well as inferior heating sources, water damage, and lack of air conditioning have all been cited as possible risk factors. Call and associates (131) reported on a study in 144 poor children attending an inner-city emergency department. Of the children with asthma in the sample, 69% had IgE antibody to mite, cockroach, or cat, as compared with 27% of controls. In a large clinical trial of asthma among inner-city children who were both sensitized and exposed to cockroach allergens, experienced 3.3 times as many hospitalizations and 1.8 times more unscheduled visits as well as having significantly more days and nights of wheezing (132). Toyias et al. (133) have reported on a cross-sectional study of adolescents with asthma and found that the relationship between asthma morbidity and cockroach sensitization was strongest in those families with the lowest income. Household and maternal smoking are also known risk factors for asthma prevalence and morbidity, and several investigators have reported high rates of smoking exposure among low-income families (93,95–98).

B. The Impact of Socioeconomic Status on Social/Familial Factors in Asthma Management

The high unemployment, single-parent households, and culture of poverty associated with low SES can all take their toll on the strength and resiliency of the family. Both internal and external family resources will be moderated by income and education level. When families lack the social and structural support network provided by financial resources, two parents to share household and child responsibilities, or friends that can offer tangible support, managing asthma can create a significant additional burden. Young, single mothers may be ill equipped to cope with a child's chronic illness. Fox et al. (134) evaluated parenting behaviors in a sample of 1056 urban mothers and found less positive parenting practices among mothers who were single, had lower incomes, and had lower education levels. Families in low-SES communities must manage all daily activities, including asthma management, against a backdrop of crime, substance abuse, and unemployment. In a study of the influence of family resources and demand on family well-being, Fink (135) found that lower SES was significantly related to decreased family resources and lower family well-being. Other family and social factors that have been shown to be associated with SES include patient beliefs, social support, and communication skills (18,24,25).

C. The Impact of Socioeconomic Status on Psychological Factors in Asthma Management

Higher rates of some mental disorders are associated with lower SES. The stress and hopelessness that can accompany poverty and racism may create an environment that exacerbates the risk of a range of psychopathology, including depression, behavior disorders, anxiety disorders, and schizophrenia. Decreased personal resources resulting from existing mental disorders may limit an individual's ability to improve his or her economic or educational level. As presented above, increased asthma morbidity has been associated with higher levels of depression, anxiety, behavior disorders, and psychopathology. In the U.S. National Institute of Mental Health (NIMH) Epidemiological Catchment Area survey of 18,571 people, the risk of having any mental disorder in the past month was 2.5 times higher for the lowest-SES group than for the highest-SES group (136). Similarly, Kessler et al. (137), reporting on the National Comorbidity Survey, found that lifetime and 12-month prevalence of most mental disorder was significantly increased with lower SES. Studies in primary care patients have found that the risk for depression and anxiety was higher among the unemployed, those with lower education, and those with lower income (138,139). Gazmararian et al. (140), using national survey data, found that black women had a twofold risk of depression (OR = 2.2, CI, 1. to 2.8); however, when poverty status was included in the model, race effects were evident only for nonpoor women. In children the risk of anxiety disorders, depression, and behavior disorders has been found to be associated with SES (141–144).

If mental disorders are more prevalent in lower-SES environments, the increased rate of psychopathology may contribute to poor asthma management and/or increased impact of asthma on the individual or the family. While the causal relationship is unclear, what is evident is that asthmatics in the lowest socioeconomic strata are at risk for both increased psychological morbidity and increased asthma morbidity.

D. The Impact of Socioeconomic Status on Behavioral Factors in Asthma Management

Research has found lower socioeconomic status to be a predictor of a range of behavioral factors in asthma, including the specific patient management behaviors such as use of asthma medications (145) and home remedies (146) and some health risk behaviors, such as substance abuse (147–150). However, it has been the health care utilization behaviors that have been most strongly linked to both SES and race (151–153). The emergency department (ED) is often used by low-income and minority families as a primary source of health care. Mak et al. (154) found that twice as many black than white children were found to use the ED as a primary source of health care. Lozano et al. (151) reported that African-American children using Medicaid were nearly twice as likely to make ED visits or be hospitalized for asthma than white children and that this higher use could not be fully explained by poverty or inadequate health care services. Hanania et al. (153) found that patients who depended on the ED and crisis management of asthma were more likely to have lower incomes, to live alone, and to be less knowledgeable about asthma. Prevention of exacerbations associated with any chronic disease requires continued medical monitoring; however, many low-income families fail to receive adequate ongoing primary health care for chronic illnesses. Wood et al. (155) surveyed 2182 families and found that being uninsured, poor, or nonwhite were independent predictors of children under age 17 having less access to preventive or general medical care. These children less often had a regular care source, more frequently used EDs, and more frequently had financial barriers to care. Even if they had health insurance, low-income and nonwhite children still had less access to care than children from affluent families. Both poor and nonwhite children, regardless of health status (good or bad), had more barriers to care. Weissman et al. (87) interviewed 12,068 patients admitted to five Massachusetts hospitals to determine reasons for delaying care. They found that one in five patients who were black, poor, uninsured, or did not have a regular primary care physician reported delays in obtaining care before hospitalization; these patients often thought that their problems were not serious or would go away. Even after economic barriers are removed, inequities in utilization appear to persist among socioeconomic classes. However, Weissman et al. note that increasing patient knowledge and reduction of financial barriers may reduce the occurrence of these delays.

VI. Summary and Conclusions

Research has clearly demonstrated that social, psychological, and behavioral factors can significantly influence asthma morbidity and patients' quality of life. Asthma, like any other chronic illness, can occur in individuals with a range of personal and familial resources and barriers. When a patient must cope with asthma in the face of significant psychosocial challenge—such as low social support, family dysfunction, or an affective disorder—the impact of asthma may increase. In families struggling with complex personal, social, or economic problems, preventive asthma management behaviors, such as medication compliance, may be low on the hierarchy of that family's priorities. The increased asthma morbidity associated with these psychosocial variables may not be the result only of decreased asthma management behaviors but also of decreased resilience or ability to cope with the symptoms of asthma. The efficacy of asthma self-management interventions in reducing the impact of asthma may result not only from increases in asthma knowledge but from programs that increase psychosocial resources by providing support, enhancing coping skills, and reducing anxiety.

Effective clinical management, therefore, must recognize and address the contributions of psychosocial factors to the management of asthma. Just as the assessment of asthma severity is a fundamental component of developing an asthma treatment plan, so also should psychosocial resources and barriers be evaluated and integrated into the management plan. Clinical history taking for the asthmatic should screen for significant personal or family social or psychological problems, including depression, anxiety, and substance abuse. For many patients with asthma, the education, social support, and structured cognitive-behavioral strategies found in a well-developed asthma self-management intervention are sufficient to decrease fears and enhance asthma coping skills. When families or individuals continue to demonstrate poor asthma control and high asthma impact after asthma self-management education or where they refuse such programs, formal evaluation by mental health experts should be considered to determine the contributing role of psychosocial variables to asthma.

The social environment in which each patient lives in can buffer or exacerbate the impact of asthma. Poverty and low educational levels have been found to be associated with increased risk for virtually every form of psychosocial challenge, including depression, behavioral problems, family dysfunction, and substance abuse. The fact that asthma morbidity is highest in the lowest-SES communities may result partly from the impact of the social environment on the individual's and family's psychosocial resources, access to health care, and physical environment. As Lang and Polansky have noted, the urban poverty and racial differences that are related to an increased risk of asthma death are also associated with "crime, illicit drug use, family dysfunction, hopelessness, and despair" (156). Long-term solutions to the rising rates of asthma morbidity in these communities will therefore require significant social environmental changes as well as effective medical and behavioral interventions.

References

1. Anonymous (1995) Asthma—United States, 1982–1992. *M.M.W.R.*, **43**:952–955.
2. Kolbe, J., Garrett, J., Vamos, M., and Rea, H.H. (1994). Influences on trends in asthma morbidity and mortality: the New Zealand experience. *Chest*, **106**:211S–215S.

3. Strachan, D.P., Anderson, H.R., Limb E.S., O'Neill A., and Wells, N. (1994). A national survey of asthma prevalence, severity, and treatment in Great Britain. *Arch. Dis. Child.*, **70**:174–178.
4. Beasley, R., Pearce, N., and Crane, J. (1997). International trends in asthma mortality. *Ciba Found. Symp.*, **206**:140–150.
5. Lanes, S.F., Birmann, B., Raiford, D., and Walker, A.M. (1997). International trends in sales of inhaled fenoterol, all inhaled beta-agonists, and asthma mortality, 1970–1992. *J. Clin. Epidemiol.*, **50**:321–328.
6. Newhouse, M.T., Chapman, K.R., McCallum, A.L., Abboud, R.T., Bowie, D.M., Hodder, R.V., et al. (1996). Cardiovascular safety of high doses of inhaled fenoterol and albuterol in acute severe asthma. *Chest*, **110**:595–603.
7. Sears, M.R., (1995). Changing patterns in asthma morbidity and mortality. *J. Invest. Allergol. Clin. Immunol.*, **5**:66–72.
8. Boulet, L.P., Belanger, M., and Lajoie, P. (1996). Characteristics of subjects with a high frequency of emergency visits for asthma. *Am. J. Emerg. Med.*, **14**:623–628.
9. Bousquet, J., Knani, J., Henry, C., Liard, R., Richard, A., Michel, F.B., et al. (1996). Undertreatment in a nonselected population of adult patients with asthma. *J. Allergy Clin. Immunol.*, **98**:514–521.
10. Sly, R.M. (1994). Changing asthma mortality and sales of inhaled bronchodilators and anti-asthmatic drugs (review). *Ann. Allergy*, **73**:439–443.
11. Hyland, M.E., Ley, A., Fisher, D.W., and Woodward, V. (1995). Measurement of psychological distress in asthma and asthma management programmes. *Br. J. Clin. Psychol.*, **34**:601–611.
12. Wamboldt, M.Z., and Wamboldt, F.S. (1996). Psychosocial aspects of severe asthma in children. In *Severe Asthma: Pathogenesis and Clinical Management: Lung Biology in Health and Disease*, 86th ed. Edited by S.J., Szefler and D.Y.M. Leung. New York, Marcel Dekker, pp. 465–496.
13. Wamboldt, M.Z., Weintraub, P., Krafchick, D., and Wamboldt, F.S., (1996). Psychiatric family history in adolescents with severe asthma. *J. Am. Acad. Child. Adolesc. Psychiatry* **35**:1042–1049.
14. Williams, H.A., (1993). A comparison of social support and social networks of black parents and white parents with chronically ill children. *Soc. Sci. Med.*, **12**:1509–1520.
15. Bazargan, M., and Hamm-Baugh, V.P. (1995). The relationship between chronic illness and depression in a community of urban black elderly persons. *J. Gerontol. B. Psychol. Sci. Soc.*, **50**:S119–S127.
16. Fisher, E.B., Sylvia, S.C., Sussman, L.J., Arfken, C.L., Sykes, R.K., and Strunk, R.C. (1993). Social isolation of caretakers of African American children with asthma is associated with poor asthma management. *Am. Rev. Respir. Dis.*, **147**:A982
17. Butz, A.M., Malveaux, F.J., Eggleston, P., Thompson, L., Huss, K., Kolodner, K., et al. (1995). Social factors associated with behavioral problems in children with asthma. *Clin. Pediatr.*, **34**:581–590.
18. Wasilewski, Y., Clark, N., Evans, D., Feldman, C.H., Kaplan, D., Rips, J., et al. (1988). The effect of paternal social support on maternal disruption caused by childhood asthma. *J. Commun. Health*, **13**(1):33–42.

19. Hamlett, K.W., Pellegrini, D.S., and Katz, K.S. (1992). Childhood chronic illness as a family stressor. *J. Pediatr. Psychol.*, **17(1)**:33–47.
20. Gustafsson, P.A., Bjorksten, B., and Kjellman, N.I.M. (1994). Family dysfunction in asthma: a prospective study of illness development. *J. Pediatr.*, **125**:493–498.
21. Boxer, G.H. (1988). Neglect contributing to tertiary hospitalization in childhood asthma. *Child Abuse Neglect*, **12**:491–501.
22. Richards, W., and Patrick J.P. (1965). Death from asthma in children. *Am. J. Dis. Child.*, **110**:4–23.
23. Strunk, R.C., Mrazek D.A., Fuhrmann, G.S., and LaBreque, J.F. (1985). Physiologic and psychological characteristics associated with deaths due to asthma in childhood. *J.A.M.A.*, **254**:1193.
24. Christiaanse, M.E., Lavigne, J.V., and Lerner, C.V. (1989). Psychosocial aspects of compliance in children and adolescents with asthma. *J. Dev. Behav. Pediatr.*, **10**:75–80.
25. McCubbin H.I., Thompson, E.A., Thompson, A.I., McCubbin, M.A., and Kaston, A.J. (1993). Culture, ethnicity, and the family: critical factors in childhood chronic illnesses and disabilities. *Pediatrics*, **91**:1063–1070.
26. Pachter, L.M., (1994). Culture and clinical care: folk illness beliefs and behaviors and their implications for health care delivery. *J.A.M.A.*, **271**:690–694.
27. Pachter, L.M., and Weller, S.C. (1993). Acculturation and compliance with medical therapy. *J. Dev. Behav. Pediatr.*, **14**:163–168.
28. Rand, C.S., Butz, A.M., Huss, K., Eggleston, P., Thompson, L., and Malveaux, F. (1994). Adherence with therapy and access to care: the relationship to excess asthma morbidity among African-American children. *Pediatr. Asthma Allergy Immunol.*, **8(3)**:179–184.
29. Kolbe, J., Vamos, M., Fergusson, W., Elkind, G., and Garrett, J. (1996). Differential influences on asthma self-management knowledge and self-management behavior in acute severe asthma. *Chest*, **110**:1463–1468.
30. Cassem, E.H. (1990). Depression and anxiety secondary to medical illness. *Psychatr. Clin. North Am.*, **13**:597–612.
31. Siegel, L., Jones, W.C., and Wilson, J.O. (1990). Economic and life consequences experienced by a group of individuals with panic disorder. *J. Anxiety Dis.*, **4**:210–211.
32. Dahlem, N.W., Kinsman, R.A., and Horton, D.J. (1977). Panic-fear in asthma: requests for as-needed medications in relation to pulmonary function measurements. *J. Allergy Clin. Immunol.*, **60**:295–300.
33. Kinsman, R.A., Dahlem, N.W., Spector, S., and Staudenmayer, H. (1976). Observations on subjective symptomatology, coping behavior and medical decisions in asthma. *J. Clin. Psychol.*, **32**:285–291.
34. Jones, N.F., Kinsman, R.A., Schum, R., and Resnikoff, P. (1976). Personality profiles in asthma. *J. Clin. Psychol.*, **32**:285–291.
35. Dirks, J.F., Kinsman, R.A., Jones, N.F., and Fross, K.H. (1978). New developments in panic-fear research in asthma: validity and stability of the MMPI panic-fear scale. *Br. J. Med. Psychol.*, **51**:119–126.
36. Kinsman, R.A., Lauparello, T., O'Banion, K., and Spector, S. (1973). Multidimensional analysis of the subjective symptomatology of asthma. *Psychosom. Med.*, **3**:250–267.

37. Dirks, J.F., Kinsman, R.A., Staudenmayer, H., and Kleiger, J.H. (1979). Panic-fear in asthma: symptomatology as an index of signal anxiety and personality as an index of ego resources. *J. Nerv. Men. Dis.*, **167**:615–619.

38. Dirks J.F., Fross, K.H., and Paley, A. (1978). Panic-Fear in asthma state-trait relationship and rehospitalization. *J. Chronic Dis.*, **31**:605–609.

39. Dirks, J.F., Jones, N.F., and Kinsman, K.A. (1977). A personality dimension related to intractability in asthma. *Psychosom. Med.*, **39**:120–126.

40. Saisch, S.G., Wessely, S., and Gardner, W.N. (1996). Patients with acute hyperventilation presenting to an inner-city emergency department. *Chest*, **110**:952–957.

41. Sones, P.K., Jones, S.L., and Katz, J. (1987). Improving compliance for asthmatic patients visiting the emergency department using a health belief model intervention. *J. Asthma*, **24**:199–206.

42. Mawhinney, H., Spector, S.L., Heitjan, D., Kinsman, R.A., Dirks, J.F., and Pines, I. (1993). As-needed medication use in asthma usage patterns and patient characteristics. *J. Asthma*, **30(1)**:61–71.

43. Bosley, C.M., Fosbury, J.A., and Cochrane, G.M. (1995). The psychological factors associated with poor compliance with treatment in asthma. *Eur. Respir. J.*, **8**:899–904.

44. Mrazek, D.A. (1992). Psychiatric complications of pediatric asthma. *Ann. Allergy*, **69**:285–290.

45. Bussing, R., Burket, R.C., and Kelleher, E.T. (1996). Prevalence of anxiety disorders in a clinic-based sample of pediatric asthma patients. *Psychosomatics*, **37**:108–115.

46. Butz, A.M., and Alexander, C. (1993). Anxiety in children with asthma. *J. Asthma*, **30**:199–209.

47. Bussing, R., Halfon, N., Benjamin, B., and Wells, K.B. (1995). Prevalence of behavior problems in U.S. children with asthma. *Arch. Pediatr. Adolesc.*, **149**:565–572.

48. Rappaport, L., Coffman, H., and Guare, R. (1989). Effects of theophylline on behavior and learning in children with asthma. *Am. J. Dis. Child.*, **143**:368–372.

49. Bender, B.G., Lerner, J.A., and Kollasli, E. (1988). Mood and memory changes in asthmatic children receiving corticosteroids. *J. Am. Acad. Child. Adolesc. Psychiatry* **27**:720–725.

50. Weder, M., Speck, S., Spalinger, J., Aebischer, C.C., and Kraemer, R. (1993). Psychosomatic symptoms in asthmatic children and adolescents. *Agents Actions Suppl.*, **40**:27–37.

51. Fritz, G.K., Rubinstein, S., and Lewiston, N.J. (1987). Psychological factors in fatal childhood asthma. *Am. J. Orthopsychiatry*, **57**:253–257.

52. Strunk, R.C. (1989). Identification of the fatality-prone subject with asthma. *J. Allergy Clin. Immunol.*, **83**:477–485.

53. Staudenmayer, H., Kinsman, R., Dirks, J., Spector, S., and Wangaard, C. (1979). Medical outcome in asthmatic patients: Effects of airways hyperreactivity and symptom-focused anxiety. *Psychosom. Med.*, **41**:109–117.

54. Boulet, L.P., Deschesnes, R.N., Turcotte, H., and Gignac, F. (1991). Near-fatal asthma: clinical and physiologic features, perception of bronchoconstriction and psychologic profile. *J. Allergy Clin. Immunol.*, **88**:838–846.

55. Belloch, A., Perpina, M., Paredes, T., Gimenez, A., Compte, L., and Banos, R. (1994). Personality dimensions: a multifaceted association. *J. Asthma*, **31**:161–170.

56. Spittle, B.J., and Sears, M.R. (1984). Bronchial asthma: lack of relationship between allergic factors, illness severity and psychosocial variables in adult patients attending an asthma clinic. *Psychosom. Med.*, **14**:847–852.

57. Janson, C., Bjornsson, E., Hetta, J., and Boman, G. (1994). Anxiety and depression in relation to respiratory symptoms and asthma. *Am. J. Respir. Crit. Care Med.*, **149**:930–934.

58. Dyer, C.A.E., and Sinclair, A.J. (1997). A hospital-based case-control study of quality of life in older asthmatics. *Eur. Respir. J.*, **10**:337–341.

59. Allen, G.M., Hickie, I., Gandevia, S.C., and McKenzie, D.K. (1994). Impaired voluntary drive to breathe: a possible link between depression and unexplained ventilatory failure in asthmatic patients. *Thorax*, **49**:881–884.

60. Rubin, N.J. (1993). Severe asthma and depression. *Arch. Fam. Med.*, **2**:433–440.

61. Janson-Bjerklie, S., Ferketicii, S., and Benner, P. (1993). Predicting the outcomes of living with asthma. *Res. Nurse Health*, **16**:241–250.

62. Padur, J.S., Rapoff, M.A., Houston, B.K., Barnard, M., Danovsky, M., Olson, N.Y., et al. (1995). Psychosocial adjustment and the role of functional status for children with asthma. *J. Asthma*, **32**:345–353.

63. Taylor, W.R., and Newacheck, P.W. (1992). Impact of childhood asthma on health. *Pediatrics*, **90**:657–662.

64. Bennett, D.S. (1994). Depression among children with chronic medical problems: a meta-analysis. *J. Pediatr. Psychol.*, **19**:149–169.

65. Gizynski, M., and Shapiro, V.B. (1990). Depression and childhood illness. *Child Adolesc. Soc. Work*, **7**:179–197.

66. Perrin, J.M., MacLean, W.E., and Perrin, E.C. (1989). Parental perceptions of health status and psychological adjustment of children with asthma. *Pediatrics*, **83**:26–30.

67. Suris, J.C., Parera, N., and Puig, C. (1996). Chronic illness and emotional distress in adolescence. *J. Adolesc. Health Care*, **19**:153–156.

68. MacLean, V.V.E., Perrin, J.M., Gortmaker, S., and Pierre, C.B. (1992). Psychological adjustment of children with asthma: effects of illness severity and recent stressful life events. *J. Pediatr. Psychol.*, **17**:159–171.

69. Orr, D.P., Weller, S.C., Satterwhite, B., and Pless, I.B. (1984). Psychosocial implications of chronic illness in adolescence. *J. Pediatr.*, **104**:152–157.

70. Biederman, J., Milberger, S., Faraone, S.V., Guite, J., and Warbuton, R. (1994). Associations between childhood asthma and ADHD: issues of psychiatric co-morbidity and familiarity. *J. Am. Acad. Child. Adolesc. Psychiatry*, **33**:842–848.

71. Wjst, M., Roell, G., Dold, S., Wulff, A., Reitmeir, P., Fritzsch, C., et al. (1996). Psychosocial characteristics of asthma. *J. Clin. Epidemiol.*, **49**:461–466.

72. Fritz, G.K., McQuaid, E.L., Spirito, A., and Klein, R.B. (1996). Symptom perception in pediatric asthma: relationship to functional morbidity and psychological factors. *J. Am. Acad. Child. Adolesc. Psychiatry*, **35**:1033–1041.

73. Kikuchi, Y., Okabe, S., Tamura, G., Hida, W., Homma, M., Shirato, K., et al. (1994). Chemosensitivity and perception of dyspnea in patients with a history of near-fatal asthma. *N. Engl. J. Med.*, **330**:1329–1334.

74. Rubinfeld, A.R., and Pain, M.C.F. (1976). Perception of asthma. *Lancet*, **1**:882–884.
75. Zach, M.S., and Karner, U. (1989). Sudden death in asthma. *Arch. Dis. Child.*, **64**: 1446–1451.
76. Boulet, L.P., Cournoyer, I., Deschesnes, F., Leblanc, P., and Nouwen, A. (1994). Perception of airflow obstruction and associated breathlessness in normal and asthmatic subjects: correlation with anxiety and bronchodilator needs. *Thorax*, **49**:965–970.
77. Nouwen, A., Freeston, M.H., Cournoyer, I., Deschesnes, F., and Boulet, L.P. (1994). Perceived symptoms and discomfort during induced bronchospasm: the role of temporal adaptation and anxiety. *Behav. Res. Ther.*, **32**:623–628.
78. Spinhoven, P., van Peski-Oosterbann, A.S., Van der Does, W.A.J., Willems, L.N.A., and Sterk, P.J. (1997). Association of anxiety with perception of histamine induced bronchoconstriction in patients with asthma. *Thorax*, **52**:149–152.
79. Campbell, D.A., Yellowlees, P.M., McLennan, G., Coates J.R., Frith, P.A., Gluyas, P.A., et al. (1995). Psychiatric and medical features of near fatal asthma. *Thorax*, **50**:254–259.
80. Martin, A.J., Campbell, D.A., Gluyas, P.A., Coates, J.R., Ruffin, R.E., Roder, D.M., et al. (1995). Characteristics of near-fatal asthma in childhood. *Pediatr. Pulmonol.*, **20**:1–8.
81. Wareham, N.J., Harrison, B.D.W., Jenkins, P.F., Nicholls, J., and Stableforth, D.E. (1993). A distant confidential inquiry into deaths due to asthma. *Thorax*, **48**:1117–1120.
82. Mascia, A., Frank, S., Berkman, A., Stern, L., Lamp, L., Davies, M., et al. (1989). Mortality versus improvement in severe chronic asthma: physiologic and psychologic factors. *Ann. Allergy*, **62**:311–317.
83. Beausoleil, J.L., Weldon, D.P., and McGeady, S.J. (1997). b 2-Agonist metered dose inhaler overuse: psychological and demographic profiles. *Pediatrics*, **99(1)**: 40–43.
84. Adams, S., Pill, R., and Jones, A. (1997). Medication, chronic illness and identity: the perspective of people with asthma. *Soc. Sci. Med.*, **45(2)**:189–201.
85. Katz, P.P., Yelin, E.H., Smith, S., and Blanc, P.D. (1997). Perceived control of asthma: development and validation of a questionnaire. *Am. J. Respir. Crit. Care Med.*, **155**:577–582.
86. Detry, J.M., Block, P., De, B.G., Degaute, J.P., and Six, R. (1994). Patient compliance and therapeutic coverage: amlodipine versus nifedipine (slow-release) in the treatment of angina pectoris: Belgian Collaborative Group. *J. Int. Med. Res.*, **22**: 278–286.
87. Weissman, J.S., Stern, R., Fielding, S.I., and Epstein, A.M. (1991). Delayed access to health care: risk factors, reasons, and consequences. *Ann. Intern. Med.*, **114**:325–331.
88. Milgrom, H., Bender, B., Ackerson, L., Bowry, P., Smith, B., and Rand, C. (1996). Noncompliance and treatment failure in children with asthma. *J. Allergy Clin. Immunol.*, **98**:1051–1057.
89. Lieu, T.A, Quesenberry, C.P., Capra, A.M., Sorel, M.E., Martin, K.E., and Mendoza, G.R. (1997). Outpatient management practices associated with reduced risk

of pediatric asthma hospitalization and emergency department visits. *Pediatrics*, **100**:334–341.
90. Garrett, J.E., and Kolbe, J. (1996). Near-fatal asthma in South Australia: descriptive features and medication use. *Aust. N.Z. J. Med.*, **26**:487–489.
91. Ernst, P., Habbick, B., Suissa, S., Hemmelgarn, B., Cockcroft, D., Buist, A.S., et al. (1993). Is the association between inhaled beta-agonist use and life-threatening asthma because of confounding by severity? *Am. Rev. Respir. Dis.*, **148**:75–79.
92. Levenson, T., Greenberger, P.A., Donoghue, E.R., and Lifschultz, B.D. (1996). Asthma deaths confounded by substance abuse. *Chest*, **110**:604–610.
93. U.S. Environmental Protection Agency. (1992). *Respiratory Health Effects of Passive Smoking: Lung Cancer and Other Disorders*. EPA/600/6-90/006F. Washington, D.C., Office of Health and Environmental Assessment.
94. Dekker, C., Dales, R., Bartlett, S., Brunekreef, B., and Zwanenburg, H. (1991). Childhood asthma and the indoor environment. *Chest*, **100**:922–926.
95. Weitzman, M., Gortmaker, S., Walker, D.K., and Sobol, A. (1990). Maternal smoking and childhood asthma. *Pediatrics*, **85**:505–511.
96. Harlap, S., and Davies, A.M. (1974). Infant admissions to hospital and maternal smoking. *Lancet*, **1**:529–532.
97. Chilmonczyk, B.A., Salmun, L.M., Megathlin, K.N., Neveux, L.M., Palomaki, G.E., and Knight, G.J. (1993). Association between exposure to environmental tobacco smoke and exacerbations of asthma in children. *N. Engl. J. Med.*, **328**:1665–1669.
98. Stoddard, J.J., and Miller, T. (1995). Impact of parental smoking on the prevalence of wheezing respiratory illness in children. *Am. J. Epidemiol.*, **141(2)**:96–102.
99. Wood, P.R., Casey, R., Kolski, G.B., and McCormick, M.C. (1985). Compliance with oral theophylline therapy in asthmatic children. *Ann. Allergy*, **54**:400–404.
100. Weinstein, A.G., and Caskey, W. (1985). Theophylline compliance in asthmatic children. *Ann. Allergy*, **54**:19.
101. Rand, C.S., and Wise, R.A. (1996). Adherence with asthma therapy in the management of asthma. In *Severe Asthma: Pathogenesis and Clinical Management: Lung Biology in Health and Disease*, 8th ed. Edited by S.J. Szefler. New York, Marcel Dekker, pp. 435–464.
102. Spector, S.L., Kinsman, R., Mawhinney, H., Siegel, S.C., Rachelefsky, G.S., Katz, R.M., et al. (1986). Compliance of patients with asthma with an experimental aerosolized medication: implications for controlled clinical trials. *J. Allergy Clin. Immunol.*, **77**:65–70.
103. Mawhinney, H., Spector, S.L., Kinsman, R.A., Siegel, S.C., Rachelefsky, G.S., Katz, R.M., et al. (1991). Compliance in clinical trials of two nonbronchodilator, antiasthma medications. *Ann. Allergy*, **66**:294–299.
104. Yeung, M., O'Connor, S.A., Parry, D.T., and Cochrane, G.M. (1994). Compliance with prescribed drug therapy in asthma. *Respir. Med.*, **88**:31–35.
105. Coutts, J.A.P., Gibson, N.A., and Paton, J.Y. (1992). Measuring compliance with inhaled medication in asthma. *Arch. Dis. Child.* **67**:332–333.
106. Gibson, N.A., Ferguson, A.E., Aitchison, T.C., and Paton, J.Y. (1995). Compliance with inhaled asthma medication in preschool children. *Thorax*, **50**:1274–1279.

107. Campbell, D.A., Luke, C.G., McLennan, G., Coates, J.R., Frith, P.A., Gluyas, P.A., et al. (1996). Near-fatal asthma in South Australia: descriptive features and medication use. *Aust. N.Z.J. Med.*, **26**:356–362.

108. Sears, J.R., Taylor, S.R., Print, C.G., et al. (1990). Regular inhaled beta-agonist treatment in bronchial asthma. *Lancet*, **336**:1391–1396.

109. Verschelden, P., Cartier, A., L'Archevéque, J., Trudeau, C., and Malo, J.-L. (1996). Compliance with and accuracy of daily self-assessment of peak expiratory flows (PEF) in asthmatic subjects over a three month period. *Eur. Respir. J.*, **9**:880–885.

110. Mahr, T.A., and Evans, R. (1993). Allergist influence on asthma care. *Ann. Allergy*, **71**:115–120.

111. Clark, N.M., Feldman, C.H., Evans, D., Duzey, O., Levison, M.J., Wasilewski, Y., et al. (1986). Managing better: children, parents, and asthma. *Patient Ed. Counsel.*, **8**:27–38.

112. Bailey, W.C., Richards, J.M., Brooks, C.M., Soong, S., Windsor, R.A., and Manzella, B.A. (1990). A randomized trial to improve self-management practices of adults with asthma. *Arch. Intern. Med.*, **150**:1664–1668.

113. Bailey, W.C., Richards, J.M., Manzella, B.A., Windsor, R.A., Brooks, C.M., and Soong, S. (1987). Promoting self-management in adults with asthma: overview of the UAB program. *Health Ed. Q.* **14**:345–355.

114. Evans, D., and Mellins, R. (1991). Educational programs for children with asthma. *Pediatrician*, **18**:317–323.

115. Jones, S.L., Jones, P.K., and Katz, J. (1991). Compliance in acute and chronic patients receiving a health belief model intervention in the emergency department. *Soc. Sci. Med.*, **32**:1183–1189.

116. Dubbert, P.M., King, A., Rapp, S.R., Brief, D., Martin, J.E., and Lake, M. (1985). Riboflavin as a tracer of medication compliance. *J. Behav. Med.*, **8**:287–299.

117. Epstein, L.H., Beck, S., Figueroa, J., Farkas, G., Kazdin, A.E., Daneman, D., et al. (1981). The effects of targeting improvements in urine glucose on metabolic control in children with insulin dependent diabetes. *J. Appl. Behav. Anal.*, **14**:365–375.

118. Wilson-Pessano, S.R., Scamagas, P., Arsham, G.M., Chardon, L., Coss, S., German, D.F., et al. (1987). An evaluation of approaches to asthma self-management education for adults: the AIR/Kaiser-Permanente study. *Health Ed. Q.*, **14**:333–343.

119. Ruffin, R.E., Latimer, K.M., and Schembri D.A. (1991). Longitudinal study of near fatal asthma. *Chest*, **99(1)**:77–83.

120. Berg, J., Dunbar-Jacob, J., and Sereika, S.M. (1997). An evaluation of a self-management program for adults with asthma. *Clin. Nurs. Res.*, **6**:225–238.

121. Forero, H., Bauman, A., Young, L., Booth, M., and Nutbeam, D. (1996). Asthma, health behaviors, social adjustment, and psychosomatic symptoms in adolescence. *J. Asthma*, **33**:157–164.

122. Kotses, H., Stout, C., McConnaughy, K., Winder, J.A., and Creer, T.L. (1996). Evaluation of individualized asthma self-management programs. *J. Asthma*, **33**:113–118.

123. Allen, R.M., Jones, M.P., and Oldenburg, B. (1995). Randomised trial of an asthma self-management programme for adults. *Thorax*, **50**:731–738.

124. Ignacio-Garcia, J.M., and Gonzalez-Santos, P. (1995). Asthma self-management education program by home monitoring of peak expiratory flow. *Am. J. Respir. Crit. Care Med.*, **151**:353–359.

125. Wilson, S., Scamagas, P., German, D., Hughes, G., Lulla, S., Coss, S., et al. (1993). A controlled trial of two forms of self-management education for adults with asthma. *Am. J. Med.*, **94(6)**:56–63.

126. Lynch, J., Kaplan, G.A., Salonen, R., Cohen, R.D., and Salonen, J.T. (1995). Socioeconomic status and carotid atherosclerosis. *Circulation*, **92**:1786–1792.

127. Svetkey, L.P., George, L.K., Burchett, B.M., Morgan, P.A., and Blazer, D.G. (1993). Black/white differences in hypertension in the elderly: an epidemiologic analysis in central North Carolina. *Am. J. Epidemiol.*, **137**:64–73.

128. Gliksman, M.D., Kawachi, I., Hunter, D., Colditz, G.A., Manson, J.E., Stampfer, M.J., et al. (1995). Childhood socioeconomic status and risk of cardiovascular disease in middle aged U.S. women: a prospective study. *J. Epidemiol. Commun. Health*, **49**:10–15.

129. Heck, K.E., Wagener, D.K., Schatzkin, A., Devesa, S.S., and Breen, N. (1997). Socioeconomic status and breast cancer mortality, 1989 through 1993: an analysis of education data from death certificates. *Am. J. Public Health*, **87**:1218–1222.

130. Gorey, K.M., Holofrom, E.J., Fehringer, G., Laukkanen, E., Moskowitz, A., Webster, D.J., et al. (1997). An international comparison of cancer survival: Toronto, Ontario, and Detroit, Michigan, metropolitan areas (see comments). *Am. J. Public Health*, **87**:1156–1163.

131. Call, R.S., Smith, T.F., Morris, E., Chapman, M.D., and Platts-Mills, T.A. (1992). Risk factors for asthma in inner city children. *J. Pediatr.*, **121**:862–866.

132. Rosenstreich, D.L., Eggleston, P., Kattan, M., Baker, D., Slavin, R.G., Gergen, P, et al. (1997). The role of cockroach allergy and exposure to cockroach allergen in causing morbidity among inner-city children with asthma (see comments). *N. Engl. J. Med.*, **336**:1356–1363.

133. Togias, A., Horowitz, E., Joyner, D., Guydon, L., Malveaux, F. (1997). Evaluating the factors that relate to asthma severity in adolescents. *Int. Arch. Allergy Immunol.*, **113**:87–95.

134. Fox, R.A., Platz, D.L., Bentley, K.S. (1995). Maternal factors related to parenting practices, developmental expectations, and perceptions of child behavior problems. *J. Genet. Psychol.*, **156**:431–441.

135. Fink, S.V. (1995). The influence of family resources and family demands on the strains and well-being of caregiving families. *Nurs. Res.*, **44**:139–146.

136. Regier, D.A., Farmer, M.E., Rae, D.S., Myers, J.K., Kramer, M., Robins, L.N., et al. (1993). One-month prevalence of mental disorders in the United States and sociodemographic characteristics: the Epidemiologic Catchment Area study. *Acta Psychiatr. Scand.*, **88**:35–47.

137. Kessler, R.C., McGonagle, K.A., Zhao, S., Nelson, C.B., Hughes, M., Eshleman, S., et al. (1994). Lifetime and 12-month prevalence of DSM-III-R psychiatric disorders in the United States: results from the National Comorbidity Survey. *Arch. Gen. Psychiatry*, **51**:8–19.

138. Parkerson, G.R., Broadhead, W.E., and Tse, C.K. (1996). Anxiety and depressive

symptom identification using the Duke Health Profile. *J. Clin. Epidemiol.*, **49**:85–93.

139. Zung, W.W., Broadhead, W.E., and Roth, M.E. (1993). Prevalence of depressive symptoms in primary care. *J. Fam. Pract.*, **37**:337–344.

140. Gazmararian, J.A., James, S.A., and Lepkowski, J.M. (1995). Depression in black and white women: the role of marriage and socioeconomic status. *Ann. Epidemiol.*, **5**:455–463.

141. Beidel, D.C., and Turner, S.M. (1997). At risk for anxiety: I. Psychopathology in the offspring of anxious parents. *J. Am. Acad. Child. Adolesc. Psychiatry*, **36**:918–924.

142. Chaffin, M., Kelleher, K., and Hollenberg, J. (1996). Onset of physical abuse and neglect: psychiatric, substance abuse, and social risk factors from prospective community data. *Child Abuse Negl.*, **20**:191–203.

143. Straus, M.A., and Kantor, G.K. (1994). Corporal punishment of adolescents by parents: a risk factor in the epidemiology of depression, suicide, alcohol abuse, child abuse, and wife beating. *Adolescence*, **29**:543–561.

144. Fitzgerald, H.E., Sullivan, L.A., Ham, H.P., Zucker, R.A. Bruckel, S., Schneider, A.M., et al. (1993). Predictors of behavior problems in three-year-old sons of alcoholics: early evidence for the onset of risk. *Child Dev.*, **64**:110–123.

145. Haire-Joshu, D., Fisher, E.B., Munro J., and Wedner, H.J. (1993). A comparison of patient attitudes toward asthma self-management among acute and preventive care settings. *J. Asthma*, **30**:359–371.

146. Butz, A.M., Malveaux, F.J., Eggleston, P., Thompson, L., Schneider, S., Weeks, K., et al. (1994). Use of community health workers with inner-city children who have asthma. *Clin. Pediatr.* **33**:135–141.

147. Wyshak, G., and Modest, G.A. (1996). Violence, mental health, and substance abuse in patients who are seen in primary care settings. *Arch. Fam. Med.*, **5**:441–447.

148. Lillie-Blanton, M., Parsons, P.E., Gayle, H., and Dievler, A. (1996). Racial differences in health: not just black and white, but shades of gray. *Annu. Rev. Public Health*, **17**:411–448.

149. Moss, H.B., Mezzich, A., Yao, J.K., Gavaler, J., and Martin, C.S. (1995). Aggressivity among sons of substance-abusing fathers: association with psychiatric disorder in the father and son, paternal personality, pubertal development, and socioeconomic status. *Am. J. Drug Alcohol Abuse*, **21**:195–208.

150. King, G., Barry, L., and Carter, D.L. (1993). Smoking prevalence among perinatal women: the role of socioeconomic status, race, and ethnicity. *Conn. Med.*, **57**:721–728.

151. Lozano, P., Connell, F.A., and Koepsell, T.D. (1995). Use of health services by African-American children with asthma on medicaid. *J.A.M.A.*, **274**:469–473.

152. Gregg, I. (1992). Can measurement of peak expiratory flow enhance compliance in chronic asthma? *Eur. Respir. J.*, **5**(1):136–138.

153. Hanania, N.A., David-Wang, A., Kesten, S., and Chapman, K.R. (1997). Factors associated with emergency department dependence of patients with asthma (abstr). *Chest*, **111**:290–295.

154. Mak, H., Johnston, P., Abbey H., and Talamo, R.C. (1982). Prevalence of asthma

and health service utilization of asthmatic children in an inner city. *J. Allergy Clin. Immunol.*, **70**:367–372.

155. Wood, D.L., Hayward, R.A., Corey, C.R., Freeman, H.E., and Shapiro, M.F. (1990). Access to medical care for children and adolescents in the United States. *Pediatrics*, **86**:666–673.

156. Lang, D.M., and Polansky, M. (1994). Patterns of asthma mortality in Philadelphia from 1969 to 1991. *N. Engl. J. Med.*, **331**:1542–1546.

9

The Impact of Sociodemographic Factors on Asthma

LAUREN A. SMITH

Boston Medical Center
Boston University School of Medicine
Boston, Massachusetts

JONATHAN A. FINKELSTEIN

Harvard Medical School and
  Harvard Pilgrim Health Care
Boston, Massachusetts

I. Introduction

The burden of living with asthma is shared by children and adults across the globe. While reported prevalence varies among regions and countries, asthma is one of the chronic illnesses with the greatest impact on the lives of individuals and populations. The weight of evidence suggests that in almost every region the prevalence of asthma is increasing (1,2). Clinicians, public health officials, and researchers have described the apparent disproportionate burden experienced by those with lower incomes, poorer housing, and who are members of minority groups. Since asthma is an illness that results from a genetic predisposition modified heavily by environmental exposures, it is critical to consider how individuals' life circumstances affect both their risk of developing asthma and the resultant morbidity they experience. The published literature describes complex associations between sociodemographic factors and asthma prevalence, severity, treatment, and morbidity. Our goal is to review and organize the literature into a framework that facilitates an understanding of the available data.

In addition to the impact of the disease itself, asthma provides an excellent model for developing a general understanding of sociodemographic disparities in health. Asthma is a common chronic condition whose underlying pathophysiology is increasingly understood and for which effective treatment strategies exist. Through a series of interrelated expert panels, an international consensus has emerged on the "best practices" for ameliorating the impacts of asthma through pharmacotherapy, environmental control, and building effective partnerships between patients and health care providers (3,4). Although the effective treatment of asthma entails significant costs, it does not require major investments in infrastructure [i.e., magnetic resonance imaging (MRI) machines, intensive care units, etc.]. Three attributes of asthma—its frequency of occurrence, a working biological understanding, and consensus on evidence-based effective treatment—make it a model condition through which to understand how social factors impact health in populations. By exploring the disparities in asthma prevalence, treatment patterns, and outcomes, we can improve our understanding of the interaction of social and biological factors in the production of ill health generally. The acknowledgment of the importance of social factors in influencing the development, distribution, and severity of disease allows for the development of effective intervention strategies across medical, social, and political spheres. Finally, the insights regarding socioeconomic influences on asthma relate not only to issues of clinical practice but also to questions of social justice as they relate to the health of individuals.

We begin by reviewing the definitions of *socioeconomic status* and related terms, particularly as they pertain to asthma. These terms have been used in the literature to represent several related constructs, and many variables or proxies have served to measure them. After discussing evidence for the impact of these factors on environmental risks, biological risks, access to care, quality of care, and treatment impact, we suggest a theoretical model that defines pathways through which social factors may mediate their influence. The goal of this model is to provide a framework to help organize evidence from a broad, complex, and sometimes conflicting literature. We conclude with a discussion of the limitations of the current literature in these areas and implications for further research and intervention directed at reducing the burden of asthma.

We have attempted to integrate the research findings regarding social factors and asthma from the international literature. Though the bulk of the English-language literature relates directly to asthma in the United States, studies from other countries give us perspective on potentially universal pathways for social impact on asthma and unique expressions related to a single nation's particular social framework. We have limited our review to the English-language literature, realizing that this may have excluded important work published only in other languages.

A. Overall Trends in Asthma Prevalence

There are substantial international data to suggest an increase in both the prevalence and severity of asthma over the past several decades, especially in children. Here we summarize what is discussed in more depth in preceding chapters in this monograph. First, the increases in prevalence and severity do not seem to be due solely to increased labeling of respiratory symptoms as asthma. Woolcock and Peat reviewed the international literature and concluded that the increase in prevalence in children cannot be ascribed solely to changing diagnostic thresholds (2). Second, there are significant disparities in the impact of asthma on particular subsets of the population: poor individuals and members of minority groups have higher rates of asthma prevalence (5–10), hospitalization (11–14), and mortality (8,13–18). These differences exist in the United States, as well as in other countries, such as New Zealand, where Maoris and Pacific Islanders have hospitalization and mortality rates that are twice those of white children (19). Because these differences are both large in magnitude and have been seen across a range of populations and study designs, they have spurred worldwide interest in understanding how social and economic factors may influence asthma burden.

II. Defining Social and Economic Factors in the Context of Asthma

The term *socioeconomic status* (SES) was formed to denote a composite measure of occupation, education, and income to represent an individual's social station and power within their society (20). In the epidemiological literature, *SES* is used to refer to social factors such as income, education, place of residence, and occupation, which mediate the daily life experiences of individuals and populations. Researchers have attempted to describe social class using single measures, composite scales such as the Hollingshead Index of Social Position or the Duncan Socioeconomic Index, or multivariate combinations of measures (20,21). Although composite scales have been extensively used in both the sociological and epidemiological literature, they have important limitations. For example, the Hollingshead Index was based on occupation and education in a 1958 study sample in New Haven, Connecticut (20), while the Duncan Index was based on 1950 survey data on occupational prestige and concerned only men. Despite subsequent revisions, it is not clear that current societal experiences are adequately captured by these measures.

In most modern societies, demographic, economic, and sociocultural attributes (e.g., race and ethnicity, place of residence) are intertwined in complex ways that affect an individual's life experience. The somewhat broader term *sociodemographic* is sometimes used to include age, race, ethnicity, and other factors not included in classic definitions of *SES*. It is difficult to study the independent impact of any one of these variables without very large samples and accurate measurement of each variable. Many investigators choose one or two variables to serve as proxies for the broader impact of SES, or as control variables for analysis of non-SES associations. The choice of social variables is more often based on the availability of data rather than the ability of those variables to fully describe an individual's or population's life experience. In the case of asthma, this has given us a literature that evaluates differences by race, income, education, occupation or insurance status as general proxies for what is an unmeasured set of social and economic variables that together have an impact on health. We also note the varied uses of racial and ethnic categories in the health services research literature. For consistency, we have used designations of race (e.g., white) since much of the data is reported this way except when a study uses specific ethnic categories (e.g., African American).

As we examine this literature, it is useful to consider the conceptualization of the impact of social factors on health proposed by Link and Phelan (22). Most asthma literature assumes that social and economic conditions expose individuals to specific factors (increased dust mites, cockroach antigen, inadequate access to care), which increase the likelihood or severity of disease. We assume that an intervention that eliminated such a direct cause (e.g., removal of cockroach antigen) would reduce asthma burden. Link and Phelan encourage us instead to think in terms of "fundamental social causes" of disease, which "involve resources like knowledge, money, power, prestige, and social connections that strongly influence people's ability to avoid risks and to minimize the consequences of disease once it occurs" (22). They suggest that interventions addressing single intermediate mechanisms may not eliminate the effects of social and economic factors on health. Disparities will remain, exerting their effects through unidentified and therefore unaddressed pathways. Krieger and others have also challenged current conceptions of race, gender and economic status in epidemiologic research (21). Fresh thinking about demographic, economic, and cultural impacts on health may guide us toward a better understanding of how these factors affect the worldwide burden of asthma. For the purpose of understanding the epidemiological and health services literature, we will use the term *SES* as it appears in the literature on asthma. We will also use the broader terms *sociodemographic risk factors* and *social risks* as the set of demographic, social, and economic attributes that confer advantage or disadvantage on members of a society. These factors interact with other biological and environmental variables, which may be particular to individuals, groups, or regions, to increase asthma risk. It will not surprise us, then, that the international literature points us toward different conclusions regarding the roles of specific sociodemographic risk factors among the various regions and populations studied.

III. Epidemiological Evidence for the Impact of Social and Economic Factors on Asthma

A. Disparities in Asthma Burden

In the majority of communities studied worldwide, hospitalization and mortality rates show substantial social and economic variation. Compelling research from the United States indicates that children from lower-SES and minority groups bear a disproportionate burden of asthma, especially in urban environments. Data from other countries suggests that these relationships are not universal but rather vary with the particular social structures at work in each country or community.

In the United States, there are substantial data illustrating racial and economic disparities in asthma prevalence. For example, black children have been reported to be 25 to 100% more likely to have asthma than white children (6,7,9,10,23). Lower-income children also have a higher prevalence of asthma (5,7,9,10,12,23). In one of the few studies in which minorities other than blacks are classified separately, Hispanic children in the Bronx had cumulative prevalence rates twice those of their white peers (5). In this report, income differences in prevalence were present only in Hispanic but not black children. Notably, other studies have shown that the poor versus nonpoor differential is greater for white children, though their rates of asthma are lower overall (7). And it is among white children that the prevalence of asthma has risen most steeply in recent years (10).

The trends for asthma hospitalizations are similar (7,8,11,12,14,24). Carr et al. found that among children and young adults in New York, black and Hispanic children have hospital discharge rates that are five times higher than those of white children (14). Although hospitalization for all children has been increasing, the rate for young black children increased almost twice as much as that for white children (12). When looked at by income, hospitalization rates for low-income children were higher than those for nonpoor children (7). Similarly, minority and low-income status were related to more severe limitation in activity, including more school absences and more days spent in bed (7,23). Taylor and Newacheck report that functional status for black children with asthma was lower, even after adjusting for income. Finally, the disparities in mortality rates for members of minorities are striking. Data from national U.S. surveys as well as from studies performed in New York, Chicago, and Philadelphia all indicate that the mortality rate for minorities is three to five times higher than that for the white population (8,13–18).

Evidence from non-U.S. studies also suggests a negative impact of sociodemographic factors on asthma burden. Connolly et al. performed a cross-sectional study of adult asthma clinic patients in Edinburgh and found that poor asthma control was related to lower social class (25). Similarly, Nejjari et al. found a twofold increase in prevalence of asthma among older French blue-collar and farm workers as compared to white-collar workers (26).

In interpreting this literature, it is difficult to sort out the conflicting evidence on the magnitude of the impact of race on disparities in asthma prevalence, treatment, and outcomes. Although racial minorities experience a higher burden of asthma, in many cases it is unclear whether the disparities act through factors other than race, such as lack of income or access to effective care. Some researchers have found that racial disparities remain after controlling for income and other sociodemographic factors (5,14,27). For example, Carr et al. found that although both race and income differences contributed to the racial variation in mortality in New York, race remained a factor even when they controlled for income (14). Other researchers have found that controlling for income or other variables eliminates the contribution of race to multivariate models (9,11).

There is also contradictory evidence from other countries on the direction of the effect of sociodemographic factors on asthma. Several researchers in Great Britain have found an increased risk of asthma among high-SES individuals. Based on a cohort from the late 1960s, Kaplan et al. found increased rates of asthma in regions with larger homes and more professional parents (28). They also found that asthma attacks were more frequent in children whose parents were employed in nonmanual, professional jobs. Likewise, Lewis et al. evaluated an English birth cohort from 1970 at ages 5 and 16 years and concluded that the persistence of wheezing at age 16 was related to higher social status (29). However, the same study reported that an increased risk of wheezing by age 5 years was related to low social status based on housing, income, parental education, and parental occupation. To explain these differences, the investigators hypothesized that wheezing at younger ages is related to injury to small airways and viral illnesses that may be more susceptible to social influences, whereas wheezing at older ages is an expression of allergic predisposition. Similarly, two studies from different countries in Africa, Zimbabwe, and Ethiopia found that asthma prevalence was greater in areas with greater economic advantage (30,31). Here, the authors hypothesize that asthma risk is related to new exposures brought about by westernization.

The contradictory evidence cited above raises the question of whether the findings reported for specific sociodemographic factors are directly related to a given factor or are due to poverty more generally. In the end, determining the precise contribution of each factor may not be possible or even necessary in order to intervene effectively in disadvantaged populations.

B. Biological Risks

Identified biological risk factors for asthma include genetic predisposition, early lung injury from respiratory illnesses, and a history of prematurity or low birth weight. Few dispute that a genetic predisposition contributes to the risk of asthma. Studies in the international literature have consistently shown that a positive family history of asthma is a predictor of the development of asthma (32–34). The immunogenetics of asthma are rapidly being elucidated (35) and may finally define the roles of allergic sensitization and early infection, especially in the presence of specific genetic markers.

Increasing data support the association between a prior history of lower respiratory illness, such as that caused by respiratory syncytial virus, and the subsequent development of asthma. Prospective and retrospective cohort studies from the United States (36–39), Finland (40), and Sweden (41) have shown that children with a history of lower respiratory illnesses, particularly bronchiolitis, are three to four times more likely to develop asthma than controls. This increased risk was evident both in hospitalized and nonhospitalized children. The Finnish investigators (40) found that 29% of exposed children had decreased midexpiratory flow, indicating bronchial obstruction, compared to 10% of controls; 62% demonstrated bronchial hyperreactivity, compared to 19% of controls. There are also consistent data suggesting an association between low birth weight or prematurity and asthma. Researchers from Israel, Scotland, and the United States report that children and young adults with a history of low birth weight are 30–100% more likely to have asthma (42–44).

Although sociodemographic factors do not directly affect an individual's genetic predisposition to asthma, they do affect both the risk of respiratory infections and the risk of prematurity and low birth weight (36,45–47), which interact with genetic susceptibility. For example, McConnochie et al. found that in New York, the infant hospitalization rates for lower respiratory illness showed significant geographic variation related to such factors (45). In one county, the hospitalization rate for the inner city was three times that for a nearby suburb. In addition, specific sociodemographic factors, such as the unemployment rate and the proportion of mothers with a high school education, correlated with the hospitalization rates for lower respiratory illness. This evidence supports the assertion that one of the mechanisms through which sociodemographic factors exert an impact on asthma prevalence and severity is through differential exposure to predisposing biological risks.

The role of bacterial and viral infection at an early age in the development of asthma through activation of subsets of T lymphocytes is an important new area of research (48). The role of nutritional factors in early childhood is even less well understood. Ongoing research about these and other biological factors may help us to further understand the mechanisms through which sociodemographic risks affect asthma prevalence and morbidity. However, even the deepest knowledge of the biology of asthma genetics and pathogenesis may never produce a solution to the disparities in asthma morbidity and mortality affected by SES.

C. Environmental Exposures

Over the past several decades, there has been a significant international effort to delineate the relationship between environmental exposures and both the development of asthma and the severity of respiratory symptoms. Investigators have focused on outdoor air pollution and indoor exposures, such as dust mites, cockroaches, pets, and tobacco smoke.

Outdoor Air Pollution

Studies from Liverpool, England, and Nairobi, Kenya, suggested a correlation between outdoor air pollution and asthma (49,50). Brabin et al. performed a cross-sectional study of coal dust exposure in Liverpool schoolchildren and found that there were increased respiratory symptoms—such as cough, wheezing, and dyspnea—in the exposed areas. They also found a higher rate of school absences for respiratory symptoms among children in these locations. Similarly, Mohamed et al. correlated the level of outdoor air pollution with the prevalence of asthma in Kenyan schoolchildren (50).

Somewhat contradictory findings were reported in a retrospective study of Philadelphia air quality between 1965 and 1990. Asthma prevalence and mortality initially decreased during the first decade but then increased significantly during the last half of the study period, despite continuing declines in five major air pollutants (15). The fact that asthma mortality increased in Philadelphia during a time when outdoor pollution decreased suggests that other risk factors have been more potent influences on asthma prevalence and severity, at least in U.S. cities.

Indoor Allergens

There are abundant U.S. and international data describing the relationship between exposure to allergens, including dust mites, cockroaches, pets and molds, and the development and severity of asthma. Reports from the United States, England, Sweden, Kenya, and Australia suggest that children and adults exposed to higher levels of these allergens are more likely to become sensitized to them (50–54). Such early sensitization is hypothesized to cause bronchial hyperresponsiveness, which ultimately contributes to airway obstruction (55,56). For example, Sporik et al. in the United States (51) and Lindfors et al. in Sweden (52) reported that the combination of high levels of exposure and sensitization to dust mites and pets led to significantly increased risk of developing asthma symptoms among young children. Similarly, Gelber et al. performed a case-control study of adults presenting to emergency departments and found that individuals both exposed and sensitized to cockroach allergen were six times more likely to have asthma (54).

Finally, there is evidence demonstrating the correlation of exposure to indoor allergens with the degree of symptoms. In a prospective Canadian study, Chan-Yeung et al. related allergen level to daily symptom score among sensitized children (57). Similarly, Peat et al. found that, among Australian children, the risk of wheezing doubled for every doubling of allergen level (53). The evidence from the National Cooperative Inner-City Asthma Study, a prospective study conducted in eight major urban areas in the United States is even more striking. Children who were exposed and sensitized to cockroach allergen had three times more hospitalizations, almost twice as many unscheduled medical visits, and more school absences than children who were not exposed and sensitized (58).

Since sensitization to indoor allergens is related to asthma, it is critical to determine how sociodemographic factors may affect the exposures that result in sensitization. A recent cross-sectional study of asthmatic children in Baltimore by Sarpong et al. explored the relationship between SES, race, and cockroach sensitization (59). The researchers defined SES based on type of residence as well as the educational level and occupation of the head of household. Fully 70% of the low-SES group was sensitized as compared with only 23% and none of the middle- and upper-SES groups, respectively. Both cockroach exposure and sensitization were 16 times more likely in African-American than in white children. The data also suggested that this racial disparity may be present even within the same SES group.

In a study of over 300 children with chronic asthma in San Diego, Willies-Jacobo evaluated the effect of SES on the incidence of dust mite allergy (60) using coverage under Medicaid versus private insurance as a proxy for SES. Children insured under Medicaid were more likely to be sensitized to dust mites. However, children with private insurance were more likely to be sensitized to pets, trees, and molds. The case-control study of Gelber et al. in Wilmington, Delaware, found that uninsured and black adults were more likely to be sensitized to at least one indoor allergen (cat, dust mite, or cockroach) (54), with urban houses five times more likely to contain cockroach allergen than suburban homes. Two other studies demonstrate the impact of allergen exposure among urban subjects. The National Cooperative Inner-City Asthma Study found significant asthma morbidity among predominantly black and Hispanic children who lived in poor neighborhoods, where 30% of the population was below the federal poverty level and two-thirds came from families with annual incomes under $15,000 (58). In a study of black inner-city children presenting to Atlanta emergency departments (61), the diagnosis of asthma was nine times more likely among children who were exposed and sensitized than among the control group. Thus, it is likely that one of the mechanisms through which sociodemographic factors affect asthma is by differential housing quality available to asthma-prone individuals. Evidence from the Dominican Republic (62) suggests that this phenomenon is not limited to the United States; high rates of cockroach antigen have also been recently reported in European low-income housing (63).

Tobacco Smoke

Unlike the case of dust mites and cockroaches, most asthmatics are not thought to develop a specific allergic sensitization to cigarette smoke. Rather, cigarette smoke is a bronchial irritant that may potentiate the effect of other exposures or triggers that lead to hypersensitivity, bronchial hyperreactivity, and airway obstruction (55,56). The worldwide literature—including studies from the United States, Australia, South Africa, and Canada—has clearly demonstrated an increased prevalence of asthma among children whose parents smoke (32–34,64–67). Children who are exposed to cigarette smoke are 1.5 to 3 times more likely to be diagnosed with asthma than unexposed children. In addition, Murray and Morrison showed that asthma symptoms were more severe among Canadian children who were exposed to maternal smoking (67,68).

As with indoor allergens, the crucial question is how social and economic factors affect exposure to tobacco smoke. In the United States, 1994 data confirm the inverse relationship of smoking to level of education (69). Adults with incomes below the poverty line had smoking rates 44% higher than those of individuals who were better off. This suggests that smoking-related asthma would be more common among those with lower education and income. These results may not apply to other countries, where the overall rate of smoking and the relationships between sociodemographic factors and smoking may be quite different.

Within the literature from the United States, there is contradictory evidence on the interaction of sociodemographic factors, smoking, and asthma. Several studies show that the impact of maternal smoking on children is greater among those in lower sociodemographic groups. In particular, studies by Martinez et al. and Erlich et al. found an effect of smoking only among children of less educated mothers, using maternal education as a proxy for SES. Martinez et al., in a longitudinal study of white children in Tucson, Arizona, found that heavy maternal smoking was related to the development asthma only in children whose mothers had less than 12 years of education (64). Children of less educated mothers who smoked heavily were 2½ times more likely to develop asthma by age 12 and had lower measures of lung function than children of mothers who were nonsmokers or smoked less than 10 cigarettes per day. For those mothers who had completed high school, there was no difference in the rate of asthma among the children of smoking and nonsmoking mothers. Similar results were reported by Erlich et al. in their case-control study of South African schoolchildren (33). They found that current maternal smoking was related to asthma only for those children whose mothers had less than 8 years of education; these children were 76% more likely to have asthma.

Weitzman et al. also found smoking more likely among less educated and lower-income mothers but reported different associations between maternal education and asthma (65). Using U.S. National Health Interview Survey data, they showed that the children of heavy smokers (greater than half a pack of cigarettes per day) are twice as likely to be diagnosed with asthma, more than twice as likely to develop asthma within the first year of life, and four times more likely to take asthma medications. However, unlike Martinez et al. (64) and Erlich et al. (33), they found that the impact of smoking was independent of sociodemographic factors such as maternal education, family income, the presence of both biological parents, family size, and the size of the residence. It is unclear why this evidence suggests a different role for modification of the effects of smoking by social factors. Finally, a longitudinal study of pulmonary function and incidence of lower respiratory illness (70) showed that infants of mothers who smoked were 47% more likely to develop lower respiratory illness, suggesting that the effects of sociodemographic factors and smoking are intertwined with other biological risks.

D. Access to Care

The term *access to care* includes several elements affecting the ability to obtain or make use of health care services. An obvious economic barrier is the lack of health insurance. However, even insured individuals may have economic barriers to care, such as unaffordable out-of-pocket expenses, inability to take off time from work, or other reasons that may vary across societies and cultures. In addition to economic barriers, there may be organizational, sociocultural, or individual barriers to the use of health services. For example, access may be limited by transportation restrictions, limited hours, long waiting times for appointments, or language difficulties.

We also include assumptions about the quality of care in our definition of access. Access to effective care (i.e., care of sufficient quality to maximize health) is the only access that matters. For asthma, this includes access to providers with appropriate knowledge and skills, to effective medications and technologies (e.g., home nebulizers), and to education (e.g., regarding trigger avoidance). Though primary care providers treat the vast majority of asthma patients, access to specialty care is an important element of high-quality care for some patients. Access, therefore, is not only about the number of physician visits per year but is also inextricably connected to the quality of care provided when contact is made.

There is convincing evidence that sociodemographic factors have a significant impact on patterns of health care utilization. Low-income and minority patients with asthma are more likely to use emergency departments rather than primary care providers for their asthma care (6,7,71). In their review of U.S. National Health Interview Survey data, Halfon and Newacheck demonstrated that poor children were five times more likely than nonpoor children to use an emergency department for acute asthma care (7). In a cross-sectional study of Baltimore schoolchildren, Mak et al. found that 50% of the children obtained their asthma care in emergency departments and that black children were twice as likely to use an emergency department as a primary care physician (6). Mak et al. showed that patients who used emergency departments for acute asthma care had higher rates of hospitalization and school absence (6). In addition, minority and low income patients were more likely to use hospital-based clinics and neighborhood health centers than private physicians (7).

Studies have also indicated that lower SES is related to decreased numbers of physician visits (7,71,72). Stoddard et al. (73) demonstrated the negative impact of being uninsured on access to care for children with asthma and other conditions. In another study, the income differential persisted even after adjustment for degree of illness, with low-income children 40% less likely to see a physician even if they were sick (7). Others have shown racial or ethnic rather than income differences. In a study of Medicaid patients with asthma in Seattle, Lozano et al. (71) found that compared with white children, African-American children had fewer office visits, more emergency department visits, and higher rates of hospitalization. This difference in patterns of asthma care is particularly striking given the absence of variation in the number of well-child visits, though the results were not adjusted by income.

There is also evidence suggesting that race and other sociodemographic factors affect the technical quality of care received. Current consensus recommendations for asthma treatment include anti-inflammatory agents for all cases of persistent asthma. These controller medicines should be supplemented sparingly with β-agonists for symptomatic relief (74). Though the latest U.S. guidelines were published in the spring of 1997 (3), this paradigm for asthma treatment has been promulgated since the late 1980s. Differential prescribing or utilization of such efficacious treatments is a reasonable index of the technical quality of care delivered. Mitchell found that Maoris and Pacific Islanders were less likely than white New Zealanders to have received medication prior to an asthma hospitalization (19). In addition, Polynesian patients were also less likely to be discharged on anti-inflammatory medications, despite similar severity of asthma symptoms at the time of admission. Several other studies suggest that race or other sociodemographic factors may affect the quality of asthma care. Finkelstein et al. showed, in a study of hospitalized patients, that minority children were 4 to 5 times less likely to have received anti-inflammatory medications before hospital admission and were 5 to 15 times less likely to receive a nebulizer for home use at discharge (75). Bosco et al. studied medication use among Medicaid patients and found that black patients received fewer prescriptions for steroids (76). In addition, the use of outmoded fixed-combination oral therapy persisted longer among black patients than among white patients despite its replacement by newer treatments. Both of these studies indicate that even when minority patients had the same type of insurance as white asthmatics, they received different care.

In addition to pharmacotherapy, other interventions including patient education and control of environmental triggers are critical aspects of asthma care. These indicators of quality are much more difficult to measure using automated sources or chart review, so there is less evidence for disparities in these aspects of care. Denson-Lino et al. found that patients with public insurance were two times less likely to have obtained recommended mattress and pillow covers (77). These families cited lack of funds as the primary reason for not complying with this aspect of the treatment regimen.

The data do not directly show how differential access affects treatment. However, there are several plausible mechanisms. First, episodic care in a setting that does not promote follow-up care with the same individual or small group of providers may adversely affect treatment. Providers may have inadequate information about prior episodes and treatment regimens. They may also have limited information about family and social factors that are likely to exacerbate patients' symptoms and/or impede their ability to utilize treatments. Providers in such settings may appropriately focus on managing the acute episode rather than instituting a longer-term management plan that would include patient and family education, environmental control, and the prescription of long-term control medications. Second, episodic care could adversely affect treatment through patient behavior. Patients may be less likely to adhere to treatment plans prescribed by unfamiliar care providers. Obtaining care in such settings may reinforce a patient's belief that asthma care should focus on treating acute exacerbations rather than managing the disease on a daily basis to prevent symptoms.

Studies on differential prescribing according to race, income, or social class have not exposed the mechanisms through which these differences occur. For example, do patients from less advantaged backgrounds have access to providers who use less effective therapies for all of their patients? Or are the same providers making different treatment decisions for patients in their practices according to sociodemographic variables? Even the latter explanation does not imply an intention to provide substandard care. Rather, we must understand what assumptions about patients' ability to obtain medicines or adhere to complex regimens may consciously or unconsciously drive provider behavior.

IV. A Model for Understanding the Impact of Social Risk on Asthma Burden: Definitions and Proposed Relationships

A theoretical framework used to analyze this body of data should meet several criteria. It should include the major components that empirical research suggests are linked to the condition and include pathways and relationships suggested by currently understood biological mechanisms. The model should assist in organizing the data, explaining conflicting results, and suggesting possible directions for future research and intervention. Finally, we believe that the model should be useful in explaining pathways of increased disease burden both in individuals and populations.

The model we present (Figure 1), which focuses specifically on the impact of social and economic factors on a single disease, fits into more general conceptualizations of health. The World Health Organization (WHO) (78) and the Institute of Medicine (79) have developed definitions of health as a state of well-being that goes beyond the absence of disease. Evans and Stoddart (79) have proposed a general model in which disease, and its impact on an individual, is only one determinant of well-being. Building on this broad view of health, our model has the more narrow goal of explicating the influences of sociodemographic factors on a specific condition. How disease affects an individual's ''health'' will depend on other characteristics of the individual and his or her community, such as the ecological issues described by Halfon and Newacheck in this volume (see Chap. 3) (80). Likewise, we have consciously omitted from our model the psychological and behavioral attributes of individuals and families that affect the course of a chronic disease. Among these are patients' adherence to medications and other treatment plans, issues of family function and support, and others included in the social-environmental framework outlined in this monograph by Rand and Butz (see Chap. 9) (81).

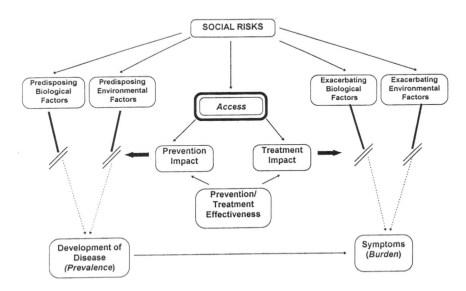

Figure 1 A model of the impact of social risks on the prevalence and severity of asthma.

A. Model Outcomes: Disease Development and Disease Burden

We have addressed separately the pathways through which sociodemographic factors may lead to the *development of asthma* and the pathways through which these factors may affect the severity of asthma among individuals who already have the condition—e.g., *asthma symptoms*. In Figure 1, the box labeled *development of disease*, an outcome for an individual, is also marked *prevalence*, since the same factors that predispose an individual to develop the illness will, aggregated over a population, increase prevalence. We use the term *asthma burden* to include respiratory symptoms as well as functional impact on work, school, or other activities. Examined from the population perspective, asthma burden is the aggregate impact on functional status of a society measured in health or economic terms.

B. Biological Factors

Biological factors appear on both the disease development and disease burden sides of the model. On the development side they are "predisposing" factors, which include individual genetic endowment, but also the other predisposing anatomic and physiological factors such as atopy, size of airways, and level of airway hyperresponsiveness. As discussed earlier, social factors cannot affect genetic risk; however, there is ample evidence for the impact of social factors on other biological risks, such as prematurity, low birth weight, and tobacco exposure in utero or during early infancy. We also include in this category lung injury from early infections, such as lower respiratory illnesses.

On the disease burden side of the model are many of the same biological factors, which can act as "exacerbating factors" by modulating severity or triggering attacks. Again we include individuals' genetic makeup and attributes of immune function, which express themselves in a given degree of airway responsiveness, as well as infectious exposures.

C. Environmental Factors

In this category we include aeroallergens and lung irritants, such as dust mites, cockroaches, and environmental tobacco smoke. The evidence reviewed earlier justifies the placement of these factors as intermediate mechanisms between sociodemographic risk factors and asthma prevalence and burden.

D. Access, Effectiveness, and Impact

In the center of the model is the potential for medical, environmental, or behavioral intervention to prevent the development of disease or ameliorate its burden among those who have already been affected. In both individuals and populations, it represents the ability of treatment or prevention to uncouple the increased risks posed by exposure to social, biological, and environmental factors from their effects.

Treatment/Prevention Effectiveness

We use the term *treatment effectiveness* to refer to the capacity of interventions to affect outcomes in the real-life circumstances in which they will be applied. Wise has framed this in terms of an intervention's capability to "modulate the impact of elevated risk on outcome" (82). Implicit in this notion is the impact of expected, less than perfect rates of adherence to prescribed treatments.

Prevention effectiveness is included in the model as a goal rather than a current reality in asthma. Unfortunately, there is little evidence to date for effective primary prevention strategies. We include prevention in the model because the development of such strategies should be a fundamental goal of work in asthma and will require a deep understanding of the social and economic factors that predispose to this condition.

Access

As discussed above, *access* refers to the ability to obtain appropriate health care services of high quality and not simply the availability of contact with the health care system.

Treatment/Prevention Impact

In our model, the combination of effective treatments and the access of individuals to those interventions produces "treatment impact." Even a treatment that is 100% effective has minimal impact if access to it is inadequate. Similarly, prevention impact is the result of access and prevention effectiveness. When effective prevention strategies are developed for asthma, access to those programs for individuals and populations at risk will be critical to their success.

The model illustrates how the components we have discussed, biological factors, environmental factors, and access are the pathways through which sociodemographic risk factors affect asthma prevalence and burden. The arrows are not meant to imply unique causal relationships. For example, as we have discussed, not all biological factors are affected by social and economic factors. However, by demonstrating those potential pathways supported by the literature, the model may suggest effective approaches to interrupting these pathways.

V. Methodological Issues and Limitations of the Literature

Studies to date have contributed greatly to our understanding of the role of social factors in the development of asthma and the severity of its expression, but important gaps remain. First, the epidemiological literature is limited by inconsistent use of the terms *social class, social status,* and *socioeconomic status*. This reflects both a lack of a consistent underlying model of social and economic factors as well as a tendency to use measures that are convenient to obtain but do not necessarily capture the complexity of the social situation of an individual or group. The use of single variables—such as race, insurance status, or income—as proxies for social conditions has, in many cases, clouded the issue. Sources of data on these variables range from individual self-report to ecological sources (e.g., using the average income for a census tract). Even a variable such as self-reported income may not really capture differences in wealth, which includes savings as well as other assets (82). Disadvantaged minorities are more likely to live in neighborhoods of concentrated poverty than are poor white individuals with similar incomes (21). This could expose them to different neighborhood risk factors that will not be measured by income, education or occupation. Krieger et al. suggest that epidemiological research on race and social class should include individual, household, and neighborhood measures to construct a "contextual analysis . . . to avoid the 'individualistic fallacy,' that is the assumption that individual-level data are sufficient to explain social phenomena, including population patterns of health and disease" (21). Applying this construct across diverse societies will be a new challenge for health services researchers.

Second, in virtually all societies, social and economic variables are highly interrelated. Because of this, studies of social factors are susceptible to confounding: "a mixing of effects between the exposure, the disease, and a third factor that is associated with the exposure and independently affects the risk of developing the disease" (83). Even the best attempts at multivariate modeling have limited ability to tease apart the complex relationships of race, ethnicity, wealth, education, and less tangible attributes of social status that may impinge on health and access to health care. For example, if income is found to be a univariate predictor but then is eliminated when other control variables are entered into a statistical model, the frequent conclusion is that income has no independent effect. However, the elimination of income as a predictor may merely signify inadequate power to unravel confounding relationships. Alternatively, income may act *through* another factor (collinearity) and can therefore never be statistically separated. In all cases, investigators should report that they were unable to determine the independent impact of income in the context of other variables, which is quite different from reporting that none exists. These relationships are especially important when explanations of racial disparities are sought. When such differences in asthma burden persist despite controlling for variables such as income or insurance status, it is important to consider unmeasured factors, such as neighborhood-specific exposures, that differ between racial or ethnic groups. Focusing on potential confounding and collinear relationships encourages investigators to look for more complex and perhaps more realistic explanations for observed associations.

Third, the international literature includes studies from diverse cultures and regions. In studying the biological pathways underlying asthma, one might expect to find common mechanisms across all humans. However, it is not surprising that in one region the role played by social factors, or the predictive power of a particular variable, differs markedly from that found somewhere else. The literature as a whole clearly tells us that social disadvantage—through living conditions, access to care, and other as yet undefined pathways—puts children and adults at increased risk for asthma. However, understanding the details of how a particular risk factor exerts an effect requires a deep understanding of a particular region and its people. Likewise, in designing interventions to uncouple these social risks from their effects on asthma, we should take lessons from each other but know that ultimately solutions must be tailored to particular communities.

Fourth, we tend to focus attention on the impact of a sociodemographic factor based on the strength of its association (often expressed as a p value) or the magnitude of its effect (e.g., relative risk or odds ratio) with the development or severity of asthma. A more important issue, from a public health perspective, is the fraction of overall asthma burden accounted for by that factor. Asthma researchers rarely report the attributable risk or attributable risk percent, which are measures of the absolute effect of the exposure or risk on the outcome in question (83). In other words, what proportion of asthma morbidity is due to dust-mite exposure in the inner city and how much would asthma symptoms be reduced if dust-mite exposure were eliminated. Wise (82) reminds us that it may be ineffective to concentrate on risk factors with the highest relative risks but which account for a small degree of morbidity overall.

Finally, the experience of racial minorities or persons living in poverty is unlikely to be fully captured by currently used demographic and social measurement techniques. Even if we could measure dozens of variables, epidemiological techniques would not be able to capture the full experience of a family living in poor housing, in a dangerous neighborhood, with inadequate access to medical services. For some individuals, reducing the risk of asthma may actually be less important to meeting the goal of overall health than working to meet other basic needs.

VI. Implications for Research and Intervention

Though much remains to be clarified about the role of social and economic factors in asthma, we believe that the literature highlights three important areas. First, there are differences in exposure to predisposing factors that are strongly influenced by sociodemographic factors. The rates of low-birth-weight children and exposure to cigarette smoke in infancy are two examples. Second, there are clear differences in exposure to exacerbating factors, most prominently demonstrated by the increasing data on the role of indoor allergens. Finally, there are important disparities in the access to and quality of care received that have a significant impact on asthma burden. The model introduced suggests pathways through which sociodemographic factors may be linked to asthma prevalence and severity, pointing out areas for subsequent work that might be fruitful in reducing the disparities in asthma burden by race, income, and social class.

We believe that epidemiologists and health services researchers need to continue to track differences in the prevalence and burden of asthma on a population basis, with many of the tools and data sources (e.g., U.S. National Health Interview Survey data) that have been used to date. As in the case of tracking infant mortality rates over many years, this is the only way to measure whether progress is being made. This approach, however, must be expanded to many parts of the world where such data have not been reported, so that we are not making the mistake of extrapolating experience from a few developed countries to nations where very different mechanisms may be at work.

Also a more integrative approach is needed to examine how the various risk factors and pathways interact to produce increased risk for individuals and populations. Instead of focusing on the association of small sets of risk factors in particular settings, it is time to make judgments regarding the proportion of asthma burden for which each accounts. Discussions of the attributable risk of individual factors, in the context of an overall model of the development and severity of asthma, may help guide interventions to reduce asthma morbidity.

It is also important to investigate the *mechanisms* for the differences in the quality of care provided to persons of differing race or social class. Several studies have documented such differences, but none have gone the next step to address how these occur. Are health care personnel overtly or unintentionally racist or "classist" in the care they provide? Do they make fair or unfair judgements about the likelihood of compliance with particular treatment regimens? Or, are there systems issues in health care settings that make providing the highest-quality care to low-income and minority individuals a goal that is difficult to reach? The elucidation of these mechanisms will require integrating classical epidemiological and health services research with more qualitative and anthropological investigations. These must address how individual practitioners operate within systems of care as well as how patients are seen by such systems. It will also be critical to integrate the issues raised in the chapter by Rand et al. in this volume to understand how family circumstances and individual behavior patterns affect patient adherence to regimens for asthma treatment (see Chap. 8). By using this multidisciplinary approach, we will begin to develop an integrated understanding of how access to care, continuity with providers, cultural sensitivity to patients, models for patient education, and factors that influence the adherence to treatment of individuals all contribute to the differences in asthma outcomes measured to date.

Finally, we believe that the most significant gains to be made in the next generation of work in asthma will be in the area of prevention. We included prevention and access to preventive services in our model despite the fact that there has been little progress in these areas to date. As prevention strategies emerge, it will be critical to remain clearly focused on the populations at highest risk. Examination of the history of infant mortality rates in the United States yields an important lesson. Though the overall rates have decreased markedly, the interventions that have served to lower rates overall have done little to reduce disparities between subpopulations (47). As we continue to work toward the reduction of asthma burden across the world, we will need to develop and test interventions that not only target asthma in general but also specifically seek to reduce the additional risk born by disadvantaged populations.

Acknowledgments

The authors would like to thank Paul Wise, Charles Homer, Thomas Inui, Howard Bauchner, and Scott Weiss for their careful reading and helpful suggestions.

References

1. Jackson, R., Sears, M.R., Beaglehole, R., and Rea, H.H. (1988). International trends in asthma mortality: 1970 to 1985. *Chest*, **94**:914–919.
2. Woolcock, A.J., and Peat, J.K. (1997). Evidence for the increase in asthma woldwide. In *The Rising Trends in Asthma* (Ciba Foundation Symposium 206). Edited by D. Chadwick and G. Cadrew. Chichester: Wiley, pp. 111–121.
3. National Asthma Education and Prevention Program. (1997). *Guidelines for the Diagnosis and Management of Asthma*. Bethesda, Md., National Institute of Health.
4. Global Initiative for Asthma. Global strategy for asthma management and prevention. NHLBI/WHO workshop report March 1993. Bethesda, Md., National Institute of Health, pp. 70–117.
5. Crain, E.F., Weiss, K.B., Bijur, P.E., Hersh, M., Westbrook, L., and Stein, R.E.K. (1994). An estimate of the prevalence of asthma and wheezing among inner-city children. *Pediatrics* **94**:356–362.
6. Mak, H., Johnston, P., Abbey, H., and Talamo, R.C., (1982). Prevalence of asthma and health service utilization of asthmatic children in an inner city. *J. Allergy Clin. Immunol.*, **70**:367–372.
7. Halfon, N., and Newacheck, P.W. (1993). Childhood asthma and poverty: differential impacts and utilization of health services. *Pediatrics*, **91**:56–61.
8. Anonymous. (1995). Asthma–United States, 1982–1992. *M.M.W.R.*, **43**:51–52.

9. Weitzman, M., Gortmaker, S., and Sobol, A. (1990). Racial, social, and environmental risks for childhood asthma. *Am. J. Dis. Child.*, **144**:1189–1194.
10. Weitzman, M., Gortmaker, S.L., Sobol, A.M., and Perrin, J.M. (1992). Recent trends in the prevalence and severity of childhood asthma. *JAMA*, **268**:2673–2677.
11. Wissow, L.S., Gittelsohn, A.M., Szklo, M., Starfield, B., and Mussman, M. (1988). Poverty, race, and hospitalization for childhood asthma. *Am. J. Public Health*, **78**: 777–782.
12. Gergen, P.J., and Weiss, K.B. (1990). Changing patterns of asthma hospitalization among children: 1979 to 1987. *JAMA*, **264**:1688–1692.
13. Weiss, K.B., Gergen, P.J., and Crain, E.F. (1992). Inner-city asthma: the epide ol ogy of an emerging U.S. public health concern. *Chest*, **101**:362S–367S.
14. Carr, W., Zeitel, L., and Weiss, K.B. (1992). Variations in asthma hospitaliz   ons and deaths in New York City. *Am. J. Public Health*, **82**:59–65.
15. Lang, D.M., and Polansky, M. (1994). Patterns of asthma mortality in Philadelphia from 1969 to 1991. *N. Engl. J. Med.*, **331**:1542–1546.
16. Weiss, K.B., and Wagener, D.K. (1990). Changing patterns of asthma mortality: identifying target populations at high risk. *JAMA*, **264**:1683–1687.
17. Marder, D., Targonski, P.V., Orris, P., Persky, V.W., and Addington, W. (1992). Effect of racial and socioeconomic factors on asthma mortality in Chicago. *Chest*, **101**:426S–429S.
18. Targonski, P.V., Persky V.W., Orris, P., and Addington, W. (1994). Trends in asthma mortality among African Americans and whites in Chicago, 1968 through 1991. *Am. J. Public Health*, **84**:1830–1833.
19. Mitchell, E.A. (1991). Racial inequalities in childhood asthma. *Soc. Sci. Med.*, **32**: 831–836.
20. Liberatos, P., Link, B.G., and Kelsey, J.L. (1988). The measurement of social class in epidemiology. *Epidemiology*, **10**:87–121.
21. Krieger, N., Rowley, D.L., and Herman A.A. (1993). Racism, sexism, and social class: implications for studies of health, disease, and well-being. *Am. J. Prevent. Med.*, **9**:82–122.
22. Link, B.G., and Phelan, J.C. (1996). Understanding sociodemographic differences in health—the role of fundamental social causes. *Am. J. Public Health*, **86**:471– 475.
23. Taylor, W.R., and Newacheck, P.W. (1992). Impact of childhood asthma on health. *Pediatrics*, **90**:657–662.
24. Weiss, K.B., Gergen P.J., and Hodgson, T.A. (1992). An economic evaluation of asthma in the United States. *N. Engl. J. Med.*, **326**:862–866.
25. Connolly, C.K., Chan, N.S., and Prescott, R.J. (1989). The influence of social factors on the control of asthma. *Postgrad. Med. J.*, **65**:282–285.
26. Nejjari, C., Tessier, J.F., Barberger-Gateau, P., Letenneur, L., Dartigues, J.F., and Salamon R. (1995). Asthma history and sociodemographic characteristics in elderly French people. *J. Epidemiol, Commun. Health*, **49**:324–325.
27. Cunninghan, J., Dockery, D.W., and Speizer, F.E. (1996). Race, asthma and persistent wheeze in Philadelphia schoolchildren. *Am. J. Public Health*, **86**:1406–1409.
28. Kaplan, B.A., and Mascie-Taylor, C.G.N. (1987). Asthma and wheezy bronchitis in a British national sample. *J. Asthma*, **24**:289–296.

29. Lewis, S., Richards, D., Bynner, J., Butler, N., and Britton, J. (1995). Prospective study of risk factors for early and persistent wheezing in childhood. *Eur. Respir. J.*, **8**:349–356.
30. Keeley, D.J., Neill, P., and Gallivan, S. (1991). Comparison of the prevalence of reversible airways obstruction in rural and urban Zimbabwean children. *Thorax*, **45**: 549–553.
31. Yemaneberhan, H., Bekele, Z., Venn, A., Lewis, S., Parry, E., and Britton, J. (1997). Prevalence of wheeze and asthma and relation to atopy in urban and rural Ethiopia. *Lancet*, **350**:85–90.
32. Young, S., Le, Souef, P.N., Geelhoed, G.C., Stick, S.M., Turner, K.J., and Landau, L.I. (1991). The influence of a family history of asthma and parental smoking on airway responsiveness in early infancy. *N. Engl. J. Med.*, **324**:1168–1173.
33. Ehrlich, R.I., du Toit, D., Jordaan, E., Zwarenstein, M., Potter, J., Volmink, J.A., et al. (1996). Risk factors for childhood asthma and wheezing: importance of maternal household smoking. *Am. J. Respir. Crit. Care Med.*, **154**:681–688.
34. Infante-Rivard, C. (1993). Childhood asthma and indoor environmental risks. *Am. J. Epidemiol.*, **137**:834–844.
35. Holgate, S.T. (1997). Asthma genetics: waiting to exhale. *Nature Genet.*, **15**:227–229.
36. Brown, R.W., and Weiss, S.T. (1991). The influence of lower respiratory illness on childhood asthma: defining risk and susceptibility. *Semin. Respir. Infect.*, **6**:225–234.
37. Sherman, C.B., Tosteson, T.D., Tager, I.B., Speizer, F.E., and Weiss, S.T. (1990). Early childhood predictors of asthma. *Am. J. Epidemiol.*, **132**:83–95.
38. McConnochie, K.M., and Roghmann, K.J. (1984). Bronchiolitis as a possible cause of wheezing in childhood: new evidence. *Pediatrics*, **74**:1–10.
39. McConnochie, K.M., Mark, J.D., McBride, J.T., Hall, W.J., Brooks, J.G., Klein, S.J., et al. (1985). Normal pulmonary function measurements and airway reactivity in childhood after mild bronchiolitis. *J. Pediatr.*, **107**:54–58.
40. Korppi, M., Kuikka, L., Reijonen, T., Remes, K., Juntunen-Backman, K., and Launiala, K. (1994). Bronchial asthma and hyperactivity after early childhood bronchiolitis or pneumonia. *Arch. Pediatr. Adolesc. Med.*, **148**:1079–1084.
41. Sigurs, N., Bjarnason, R., Sigurbergsson, F., Kjellman, B., and Bjorksten, B. (1995). Asthma and immunoglobulin E antibodies after respiratory syncytial virus bronchiolitis: a prospective cohort study with matched controls. *Pediatrics*, **95**:500–505.
42. Seidman, D.S., Laor, A., Gale R., Stevenson D.K., and Danon Y.L. (1991). Is low birth weight a risk factor for asthma during adolescence? *Arch. Dis. Child.*, **66**:584–587.
43. McLeod, A., Ross, P., Mitchell, S., Tay, D., Hunter, L., Hall, A., et al. (1996). Respiratory health in a total low birthweight cohort and their classroom controls. *Arch. Dis. Child.*, **74**:188–194.
44. Schwartz, J., Gold, D., Dockery, D.W., Weiss, S.T., and Speizer, F.E. (1990). Predictors of asthma and persistent wheeze in a national sample of children in the United States. *Am. Rev. Respir. Dis.*, **142**:555–562.
45. McConnochie, K.M., Roghmann, K.J., and Liptak, G.S. (1995). Hospitalization for

lower respiratory tract illness in infants: variation in rates among counties in New York State and areas within Monroe County. *J. Pediatr.*, **126**:220–229.

46. Berkowitz, G.S. (1981). An epidemiologic study of preterm delivery. *Am. J. Epidemiol.*, **113**:81–92.

47. Wise, P.H., and Pursley, D.M. (1997). Infant mortality as a social mirror. *N. Engl. J. Med.*, **326**:1558–1560.

48. Shirakawa, T., Enomoto, T., Shimazu, S., and Hopkin, J.M. (1997). The inverse association between tuberculin responses and atopic disorder. *Science*, **275**:77–79.

49. Brabin, B., Smith, M., Milligan, P., Benjamin, C., Dunne, E., and Pearson, M. (1994). Respiratory morbidity in Merseyside school children exposed to coal dust and air pollution. *Arch. Dis. Child.*, **70**:305–312.

50. Mohamed, N., Ng'ang'a, L., Odhiambo, J., Nyamwaya, J., and Menzies, R. (1995). Home environment and asthma in Kenyan schoolchildren: a case-control study. *Thorax*, **50**:74–78.

51. Sporik, R., Holgate, S.T., Platts-Mills T.A.E., and Cogswell, J.J. (1990). Exposure to house-dust mite allergen (Der p I) and the development of asthma in childhood. *N. Engl. J. Med.*, **323**:502–507.

52. Lindfors, A., Wickman, M., Hedlin, G., Pershagen, G., Rietz, H., and Nordvall, S.L. (1995). Indoor environmental risk factors in young asthmatics: a case-control study. *Arch. Dis. Child.*, **73**:408–412.

53. Peat, J.K., Tovey, E., Toelle, B.G., Haby, M.M., Gray, E.J., Mahmic A., et al. (1996). House dust mite allergens. *Am. J. Respir. Crit. Care Med.*, **153**:141–146.

54. Gelber, L.E., Seltzer, L.H., Bouzoukis, J.K., Pollart, S.M., Chapman, M.D., and Platts-Mills T.A.E. (1993). Sensitization and exposure to indoor allergens as risk factors for asthma among patients presenting to hospital. *Am. Rev. Respir. Dis.*, **147**: 573–578.

55. Platts-Mills T.A.E. (1994). How environment affects patients with allergic disease: indoor allergens and asthma. *Ann. Allergy*, **72**:381–384.

56. Platts-Mills, T.A.E., Sporik, R., Wheatley, L.M., and Heymann, P.W. (1995). Is there a dose-response relationship between exposure to indoor allergens and symptoms of asthma. *J. Allergy Clin. Immunol.*, **96**:435–440

57. Chan-Yeung, M., Manfreda, J., Dimich-Ward, H., Lam, J., Ferguson, A., Warren, P., et al. (1995). Mite and cat allergen levels in homes and severity of asthma. *Am. J. Respir. Crit. Care. Med.*, **152**:1805–1811.

58. Rosenstreich, D.L., Eggleston, P.A., Kattan M., Baker D., Slavin, R.G., Gergen P., et al. (1997). The role of cockroach allergy and exposure to cockroach allergen in causing morbidity among inner-city children with asthma. *N. Engl. J. Med.*, **336**: 1356–1363.

59. Sarpong, S.B., Hamilton, R.G., Eggleston, P.A., and Adkinson, N.F. (1996). Socioeconomic status and race as risk factors for cockroach allergen exposure and sensitization in children with asthma. *J. Allergy Clin. Immunol.*, **97**:1393–1401.

60. Willies-Jacobo, L.J., Denson-Lino, J.M., Rosas, A., O'Connor R.D., and Wilson, N.W. (1993). Socioeconomic status and allergy in children with asthma. *J. Allergy Clin. Immunol.*, **92**:630–632.

61. Call, R.S., Smith, T.F., Morris, E., Chapman, M.D., and Platts-Mills T.A.E. (1992). Risk factors for asthma in inner city children. *J. Pediatr.*, **121**:862–866.

62. Barnes, K.C., and Brenner, R.J. (1996). Quality of housing and allergy to cockroaches in the Dominican Republic. *Int. Arch. Allergy Immunol.*, **109**:68–72.
63. de Blay, F., Sanchez, J., Hedelin, G., Perez-Infante, A., Verot, A., Chapman, M., et al. (1997). Dust and airborne exposure to allergens derived from cockroach (*Blattella germanica*) in low-cost public housing in Strasbourg. *J. Allergy Clin. Immunol.*, **99**: 107–112.
64. Martinez, F.D., Cline, M., and Burrows, B. (1992). Increased incidence of asthma in children of smoking mothers. *Pediatrics*, **89**:21–26.
65. Weitzman, M., Gortmaker, S., Walker, D.K., and Sobol, A. (1990). Maternal smoking and childhood asthma. *Pediatrics*, **85**:505–511.
66. Stoddard, J.J., and Miller, T. (1995). Impact of parental smoking on the prevalence of wheezing respiratory illness in children. *Am. J. Epidemiol.*, **141**:96–102.
67. Murray, A.B., and Morrison, B.J. (1989). Passive smoking by asthmatics: greater effect on boys than on girls and on older than younger children. *Pediatrics*, **84**:451–459.
68. Murray, A.B., and Morrison, B.J. (1992). Effect of passive smoking on asthmatic children who have and who have not had atopic dermatitis. *Chest*, **101**:16–18.
69. Anonymous. (1996). Cigarette smoking among adults—United States, 1994. *M.M.W.R.*, **45**:588–590.
70. Tager, I.B., Hanrahan, J.P., Tosteson, T.D., Castile, R.G., Brown, R.W., Weiss, S.T., et al. (1993). Lung function, pre- and post-natal smoke exposure, and wheezing in the first year of life. *Am. Rev. Respir. Dis.*, **147**:811–817.
71. Lozano, P., Connell, F.A., and Koepsell, T.D. (1995). Use of health services by African-American children with asthma on Medicaid. *JAMA*, **274**:469–473.
72. ʼcheck, P.W., and Starfield B. (1988). Morbidity and use of ambulatory care s among poor and nonpoor children. *Am. J. Public Health*, **78**:927–933.
73. Stoddard, J.J., St. Peter, R.F., and Newacheck, P.W. (1994). Health insurance status and ambulatory care for children. *N. Engl. J. Med.*, **330**:1421–1425.
74. National Asthma Education Program. (1991). *Guidelines for the Diagnosis and Management of Asthma*, 1991. Bethesda, Md., U.S. Department of Health and Human Services.
75. Finkelstein, J.A., Brown, R.W., Schneider, L.C., Weiss, S.T., Quintana, J.M., Goldmann, D.A., et al. (1995). Quality of care for preschool children with asthma: the role of social factors and practice setting. *Pediatrics*, **95**:389–394.
76. Bosco, L.A., Gerstman, B.B., and Tomita, D.K. (1993). Variations in the use of medication for the treatment of childhood asthma in the Michigan Medicaid population, 1980–1986. *Chest*, **104**:1727–1733.
77. Denson-Lino, J.M., Willies-Jacobo, L.J., Rosas, A., O'Connor, R.D., and Wilson, N.W. (1993). Effect of economic status on the use of house dust mite avoidance measures in asthmatic children. *Ann. Allergy*, **71**:130–132.
78. WHO. (1994). *Constitution of the World Health Organization: Basic Documents*, 40th ed. Geneva: WHO.
79. Institute of Medicine (1997). Understanding health and its determinants. In *Improving Health in the Community: A Role for Performance Monitoring*, First ed. Edited by J.S. Durch, L.A. Bailey, and M.A. Stoto. Washington, D.C.: National Academy Press, pp. 40–58.

80. Halfon, N., and Newacheck, P.W. (1999). Characterizing the social impact of asthma in childhood. In *Social and Economic Impacts of Asthma*. Edited by K.B. Weiss, A.S. Buist, and S.D. Sullivan. New York, Marcel Dekker.

81. Rand, C.S., and Butz, A.M. (1998). Psychosocial factors in chronic asthma. In *Social and Economic Impacts of Asthma*. Edited by K.B. Weiss, A.S. Buist, and S.D. Sullivan. New York, Marcel Decker.

82. Wise, P.H. (1993). Confronting racial disparities in infant mortality: reconciling science and politics. In *Racial Differences in Preterm Delivery: Developing a New Research Paradigm*. Am. J. of Prev. Med., suppl. to vol. 9(6), November/December 1993. Edited by D. Rowley and H. Tosteston. New York, Oxford University Press, pp. 7–16.

83. Hennekens C.H., and Buring, J.E. (1987). *Epidemiology in Medicine*. Boston, Little, Brown.

Part Two

ECONOMIC IMPACT OF ASTHMA

10

Introduction to Part Two
The Economic Impact of Asthma

SEAN D. SULLIVAN

University of Washington
Seattle, Washington

KEVIN B. WEISS

Rush Medical College
Chicago, Illinois

The field of health economics has recently become comfortably distinct from mainstream economics. Much has happened recently in this field as it is applied to medical technology assessment and health care decision making. Historically, health economists focused on problems of scarcity, market failure, demand, medical labor supply, and pricing. With a growing focus on limited medical resources, health economics has contributed much to the debate about how to allocate these scarce funds in the most cost-effective manner. A fundamental axiom of health economics is that the production of health care should be increased only if the incremental benefits of doing so exceed the incremental costs or if the incremental benefits are judged to be of sufficient value to warrant the allocation of costs from other uses. This basic socioeconomic tenet has found its way into population-based medical care decision making (1). Thus, the need for evaluating the relationship between benefits and costs of medical treatments.

Asthma and its many treatments have not escaped economic scrutiny. As little as 10 years ago, there were but a handful of papers describing the cost of respiratory disorders or the cost impact of medical treatments. Today, there is a rapidly developing literature on the societal impact of asthma, allergy, respiratory chronic obstructive pulmonary disease (COPD), cystic fibrosis, and other respiratory disorders. These data inform policy, assist in the setting of resource priorities, and help medical and financial decision makers to allocate funds for prevention and treatment. The second section of this monograph describes the health care and economic impact asthma and its treatments have on individuals, families, and society at large. The papers presented in this section could not have been written even 5 years ago because the research methods were not fully developed and the data were few. The five essays that make up this section distill and discuss the important advances in health economic methods and their applications in asthma outcomes research.

The first three chapters in this section describe the basic health economics methods used to evaluate disease burden and assess the efficiency of resource allocation by health plans or health authorities to certain management strategies. The first chapter, by Jönsson, illustrates the complex nature of estimating the societal economic consequences of asthma. The goal of estimating economic burden is to derive a figure that best describes the total monetary impact of disease on individuals, health care organizations, and society. Jönsson shows that estimates of asthma costs vary across and within each country, in part because of the inconsistency of the method for evaluating disease burden. He provides a framework for evaluating the cost-of-illness literature and points to the utility of these data for resource allocation.

The next chapter, by Ramsey and Sullivan, reviews approaches to assessing the cost-effectiveness of asthma treatments, including pharmaceuticals, devices, education, disease management programs, and referral to specialty providers. The authors develop, from a clinical perspective, the theory and application of cost-effectiveness assessment in the present health care context. An additional and important contribution made to the monograph by this chapter is the exhaustive literature assessment of the cost-effectiveness of asthma management strategies. One important lesson from this chapter is the need to standardize cost-effectiveness evaluation methods using an accepted reference case (1). In spite of the recent attempt by the U.S. National Asthma Education and Prevention Program (NAEPP) panel on cost-effectiveness assessment, there remains a great deal of room for improvement in standardization (2).

The next two chapters describe the challenge of applying economic evaluation research in the context of medical and health policy decision making to construct a vision of the future. The chapter by Elixhauser and coworkers describes the cost and outcomes implications of prevention. The authors attempt to lay out a unified approach to the study of prevention as applied to asthma, and they do so with very few empirical data on the subject.

The last chapter in this section, by Rutten-van Mölken, describes recent developments in the valuation of the denominator in the cost-effectiveness model. Specifically, the paper describes the elicitation approaches for deriving health-state-preference assessments in asthma health outcomes research. These methods allow the concept of quality of life to be incorporated into the cost-effectiveness analysis directly. These techniques are relatively new, with very little development taking place in asthma. This is changing with the recent independent works of Juniper and Rutten-van Mölken in assessing the validity and reliability of the time trade-off, category rating scale, and standard gamble elicitation approaches in asthma. While it is still early in the development of this research method, we hope to learn much from this work on incorporating quality of life into cost-effectiveness studies.

Today, health plans make adoption decisions about new asthma treatments in the absence of sufficient evidence on population-level costs and outcomes. These decisions result in the assignment of significant medical care resources to new technologies. Inevitably, the scarcity of these resources in the United States will dictate the inclusion of economic evaluation in most population-level decisions. There is evidence that many health plans are currently requiring economic justification—that the incremental benefits are worth the incremental costs—prior to approval of new technology. Kitch et al. describes the development of an economic model of asthma and its treatments. The goal of this model is to make explicit the economic and clinical consequences to a health plan of introducing new asthma technologies. Modeling has become an important part of evaluating the potential impact of new or existing therapies on the cost and health consequences of asthma in situations where data are scarce.

The more skilled health professionals are at recognizing and participating in the process of economic assessment, the better off patients will be. As David Eddy has stated so well: ''Our [clinicians'] current approach to analyzing evidence, estimating the consequences of our actions, and determining the desirability of those outcomes is primitive. We are trying to solve in our heads problems that far exceed the capacity of the unaided human mind. There are tools, already in use in many other disciplines, to help us'' (3).

The authors of this section hope to contribute to increasing the understanding of the tools of health economics as applied to asthma.

References

1. Gold, M.E., Siegel, J.E., Russell, L.B., Weinstein, M.C., eds. (1996). *Cost-Effectiveness in Health and Medicine.* New York, Oxford University Press, pp. 214–246.
2. Sullivan, S., Elixhauser, A., Buist, A.S., Luce, B.R., Eisenberg, J., Weiss, K.B. (1990). National Asthma Education and Prevention Program Working Group Report on the Cost Effectiveness of Asthma Care. *Am J Respir Crit Care Med* **154**:S84–S95.
3. Eddy, D.M. (1990). The challenge. *JAMA* **263**:287–290.

11

Measuring the Economic Burden in Asthma

BENGT JÖNSSON

Centre for Health Economics
Stockholm School of Economics
Stockholm, Sweden

I. Introduction

This chapter reviews the usefulness and problems in estimating the total economic burden of asthma. It is recognized that estimates of the burden of a disease will not provide any direct information for decisions about the allocation of resources for prevention and treatment. However, estimates of the burden of a disease can still be of interest for health policymaking through the provision of relevant information about the magnitude and the changes in the burden of the disease. We will return to this at the end of the chapter.

The methodology for cost-of-illness studies has been much debated. In the following section, the different methodological approaches are presented. Differences in methodology are one reason for problems in comparing the results from different studies. But an even bigger problem is the great variability and uncertainty in the data used for estimating the burden of asthma. The review of results from different asthma studies focuses on identifying both differences in methodology and differences in the data used for the estimates. A couple of methodological points have surfaced more often than others. One of them is the measurement of indirect costs and another is the valuation of unpaid inputs—for example, time input from family members and relatives. These issues are addressed in a separate section.

The chapter concludes with a review of the usefulness of future studies of the burden of asthma and how they may be directed to be most useful for understanding the economic consequences of this disease and the opportunities available to reduce the burden in a cost-effective way.

II. The Cost-of-Illness Method

The idea of estimating the economic burden of illness and disease can be traced over 300 years back to the writing of Sir William Petty. The modern contributions started with the development of the human capital theory in the late 1950s and early 1960s. Weisbrod (1) identified the economic benefits from a better health status in the population as savings in health care expenditures and increased productive capacity. The concept *direct costs* has been used to categorize all costs of prevention, detection, treatment, rehabilitation, and long-term care due to an illness. Loss of production due to the disease has been called *indirect costs*, and a distinction is made between loss of production due to morbidity and premature mortality. For a review of the methodology, see Hodgson and Meiners (2). It is also generally recognized that there are costs that do not fall into these two categories; they are often labeled as intangible costs, since it is difficult to find a monetary valuation of these costs. They are in most cases omitted in the practical application of the cost-of-illness methodology.

The prefix *economic* before "burden of asthma" can be interpreted as the general method used for costing—the valuation of the resources used or lost. Economics is about allocation of scarce resources between competing ends. Resources thus have an opportunity cost. Labor used for health care can be used in other sectors of the economy, and time off work due to illness represents an output foregone. The general rule for costing is that resources should be valued according to their market prices. Market prices give, under very strict assumptions, information about the opportunity cost of different resources. For example, in the labor market, additional workers are hired until the value of the marginal product equals the wage (price) paid.

There are many instances when market prices are either distorted or missing for important resources used or lost due to illness, and most of the controversy around the cost-of-illness methodology relates to these situations. We will later in more detail look at the estimation of indirect costs and the valuation of unpaid inputs. However, the cost-of-illness methodology is not only about valuation but also about the identification and measurement of the resources related to a particular illness.

An illness can be described in terms of incidence and prevalence. To translate incidence and prevalence estimates into resources used or lost is a difficult task. In an incidence study, all future resources used and lost due to the illness should be included. Since these can arise far in the future, it may be difficult or impossible to identify them. There is also the need to discount all costs to present value. A prevalence estimate is simpler, since it relates costs to a defined point in time. However, costs are a "flow concept," which means that in practice we have to estimate costs for a defined period, most often a year, in prevalence-based cost-of-illness studies. For short-term illness, a prevalence-based estimate provides no problem; also chronic illnesses can be handled by identifying everybody with the disease during a given year. But for mortality, it is not very practical to talk about prevalence. In practice therefore, costs due to premature death from a given illness are included in prevalence-based cost-of-illness studies based on the mortality during a given year. Future losses of production are discounted to that year. Very often, loss of production due to early retirement is handled in the same way (3).

Another problem has to do with the definition of the illness or disease. Most cost-of-illness studies define resource use from the use of diagnosis. To avoid double counting, the *main* diagnosis is often used to identify resource use. This method is called the "top-down" method, since the total costs for health care are divided on the basis of the different diseases. The major advantage of this method is that it avoids double counting. It is also possible to use wider definitions of a disease than the main diagnosis or the main cause of sickness, disability, or death. For example in studies of the cost of diabetes, the contribution of diabetes to other diagnoses is often included (4). This may be very relevant, but it poses a problem of aggregation, since if this is done for all diseases, the grand total may be greater than the total health care expenditure. The widest concept is to include, for example, all health care costs for patients with a defined disease. This may be relevant from a managed care perspective.

III. Cost of Asthma Studies

Twelve studies, which all have presented a comprehensive breakdown of the cost components of asthma, are reviewed. They cover a wide range of countries and health care systems. Two studies were carried out in Australia (5,6), the United Kingdom (7,8), Sweden (9,10), and the United States (11,12), and one each in Denmark (13), Canada (14), France (15), and Germany (16). For a study on the cost of asthma in a developing country, see Transkei (17) for South Africa. For an earlier review of cost of asthma studies, see Ref. 18.

Most studies use a variety of data sources. Some studies use a pure top-down approach, like the two Swedish studies, while others use a bottom-up approach, like the Danish study and the study by Smith et al. for the United States.

The latter study uses a single data source, the 1987 National Medical Expenditure Survey. Since this study is based on a representative sample of the population, the result in terms of total cost is not significantly different from that obtained by Weiss et al., whose study used different data sources. However, the relation between direct and indirect costs is very different in the two studies. The problems with using a small unrepresentative sample for the calculations of national costs is shown by the Danish study. The estimated cost for Denmark is nearly four times higher than that for Sweden, despite the fact that the population size is half that of Sweden.

The definitions and levels of detail on costs vary between the studies; for example, only five studies considered the indirect costs due to premature mortality. Table 1 summarizes the relative contributions of direct and indirect costs associated with asthma for each study. A high level of variability is apparent among the studies, which may be the result of differences in health care systems among the countries, different data sources, methodological variations, or genuine differences in cost. In particular, the Teeling-Smith (8) study shows very low direct costs associated with asthma. This may be due to the fact that this early study was carried out when drug costs were low. This component has risen over time and today constitutes a major part of direct costs. This point is illustrated by the two Swedish studies, which were undertaken about 15 years apart, but with a rather similar methodology and based on the same data sources. The share of direct costs has increased over time, and the share of total direct costs represented by drugs has increased. Taking the available data together, it is apparent that direct and indirect costs account for approximately equal shares of the total costs.

If we look at three of the studies presenting cost of mortality (Table 2), we can see that costs due to premature death account for 32% of indirect costs in the United States, 25% in Germany, and 12% in Sweden. It is obviously difficult to make any specific arguments about the distribution of indirect costs due to morbidity in short- and long-term (disability) illness. No such distinction is provided for the United States, and the figures for Sweden and Germany are very different.

Several attempts have been made to compare the absolute level of the cost of asthma in different countries—for example, by relating them to the size of the population or the number of patients with asthma (19). Differences in price levels and methodology as well as uncertainties about the prevalence of the disease make interpretations difficult. The relation between costs of mortality and the total cost may say something about the management of asthma in the three countries, but further analysis is needed to draw such conclusions with some certainty.

The pattern of resource consumption will be very different in individual patients, depending on the severity of the condition and age. Unfortunately, accurate data on this issue are lacking. However, in Canada it has been shown that

Table 1 Summary of Cost-of-Illness Studies for Different Countries (in millions)[a]

	NAC, Australia (5) 1989 AUS $	Mellis (New South Wales), Australia (6) 1989 AUS $	Action Asthma, UK (7) £	Teeling-Smith, UK (8) 1987 £	Tompson, Sweden (9) 1975 SEK	Jacobson and Lindgren, Sweden (10) 1991 SEK	Weiss et al., USA (11) 1990 US $	Smith et al., USA (12) 1994 US $	Sørensen et al., Denmark (13) 1995 DKR	BCG, Canada (14) C $	BCG, France (15) FFR	Nowac et al., Germany (16) 1992 DM
Direct costs	324 (55%)	142 (75%)	344 (50%)	100 (11%)	218 (26%)	1114 (43%)	3638 (59%)	5147 (88%)	3145 (33%)	393 (67%)	4000 (58%)	2520 (56%)
Hospital care	58		83	53	152	306	2045	2800	1075	104	1900	684
Physician services	98		33	18	22	472	493	1530	125	78	1200	768
Drugs/devices	121		228	29	45	336	1100	817	1490	144	900	1068
Other direct costs	47[b]	19							455	67[e]		
Indirect costs	262 (45%)	48 (25%)	342 (50%)	787 (89%)	618 (74%)	1456 (57%)	2568 (41%)	673 (12%)	455 (67%)	196 (33%)	2900[d] (42%)	1976 (44%)
Absence from work	111			223	618	1279	849	222	6377	149		1456
Reduced effectiveness at work	88							218				
Caregiver's time	40						900	213				
Premature death				564		177	819		78			520
Other indirect costs	23[c]							21		47[g]		
Total	**586**	**190[f]**	**686**	**887**	**836**	**2570**	**6206**	**5820**	**9600**	**591**	**6900**	**4496**

[a]Year relates to the year of costing. Data on resource utilization can be from earlier years.
[b]Comorbidity and ambulance costs.
[c]Home care and nursing home treatment.
[d]Lost work time for travel.
[e]Includes invalidity (1450).
[f]Translates to about AUS $400 million for the whole population of Australia.
[g]Not specified.

Table 2 Cost of Asthma in Three Countries (in millions)

	Weis et al. (11), United States, US$	Jacobson (10), Sweden, SEK	Nowac et al. (16), Germany, DM
Indirect costs	**2568 (41%)**	**1456 (57%)**	**1976 (44%)**
Mortality	819 (32%)	177 (12%)	520 (26%)
Disability	—	864 (59%)	616 (31%)
Short-term illness	1749 (68%)	415 (29%)	840 (43%)
Direct costs	**3638 (59%)**	**1114 (43%)**	**2520 (56%)**
Inpatient care	1706 (47%)	306 (27%)	684 (27%)
Outpatient care	832 (23%)	472 (42%)	768 (30%)
Drugs	1100 (30%)	336 (30%)	1068 (42%)
Total cost	**6206 (100%)**	**2570 (100%)**	**4496 (100%)**

Sources: Refs. 10, 11 and 16. For the German study, cash payments for sickness and rehabilitation have been excluded from direct costs, since they are transfer payments and not direct costs.

10% of asthmatic patients account for over 50% of the costs (14). Emergency care, despite its relatively high use in children, remains a small component of the total cost of childhood asthma (less than 7% of the total) (20).

A. Direct Costs

Direct costs will be determined by disease severity, compliance with medication, the overall prevalence of the disease, and the cost of health care; for example, health care costs are higher in the United States than in the UK or Sweden. The relative importance of the components that make up direct costs varies widely among the studies (Table 1). Generally, physician costs make up the smallest component, with the cost of hospitalization being somewhat larger and approximately equal to the cost of drugs, which constitutes the largest component of the direct costs of treating mild to moderate asthma.

Physician Costs

This cost item includes visits to offices and clinics, hospital outpatient departments, and emergency departments. Three of the studies differentiated physician costs into general and specialist practitioners (5,6,14) and one into inpatient and outpatient care (11). Physician costs average 22%, of which 75% relates to general practitioner (GP) consultations and 25% to specialist consultations. Therefore, GP care accounts for the highest proportion of the physician costs. These figures are in agreement with resource data from two additional studies in the United Kingdom (21,22). If we assume that GP care represents part of the cost of controlling asthma, then asthma treated by specialist physicians may represent part of the cost of uncontrolled asthma. Therefore improvements in asthma management by GPs, which require greater patient supervision and assessment of control if it is to be successful, may reduce emergency department use and thus save money in the long term.

Drug Costs

Drug costs make up approximately one-third of the total direct costs of asthma and represent the major cost for mild to moderate asthmatic patients. The share for drugs is higher in, for example, France, Sweden, and the United Kingdom than in the United States, which reflect differences in the relative prices for hospital and physician care. Drugs account for only about 8% of all health care expenses in the United States, while the average in Europe is in the range of 15%. Most drugs and devices can reasonably be considered to be part of the cost of controlling asthma provided that patients are compliant with their medications. Compliance with asthma therapy is poor. A recent study by Bosely et al. (23) has shown that only 15% of patients took drugs as directed for more than 80% of the study period.

Hospital Costs

Cost for hospital care differs widely between studies (Table 1). The figure reported by Thompson (9) is high because it includes hospital outpatient care and ambulatory emergency visits, which accounted for about half of all physician visits in Sweden, while the high figure quoted by Teeling-Smith (8) may relate to the very low estimate for drug costs. In the study by Jacobson and Lindgren (10), the visits to hospital outpatient departments are included in costs of ambulatory care (physician visits). The high percentage reported by Weiss et al. (11) and Smith et al, (12) is probably the result of the relatively high unit cost of inpatient treatment in the United States. Although the cost of hospital care in some estimates includes some ambulatory care, it represents in most studies the single biggest part of direct costs despite the reduction in inpatient care for asthma over time. To understand the opportunities to further decrease the number of hospitalizations by preventive actions, it is necessary to understand the reasons for hospitalization and to define the population being hospitalized.

Hospital costs are incurred mainly by patients with moderate to severe asthma, and hospitalization usually occurs when the management of asthma has failed to prevent an acute severe attack.

Seven of the twelve studies separated hospital costs into their constituent components. Outpatient treatment is an area of hospital care that is predominantly aimed at controlling asthma, while inpatient care, a much larger cost, is primarily concerned with treating acute exacerbations of asthma due to a failure of disease control. Inpatient costs represent the most important component of hospital costs

(70–85%), while emergency department treatment was consistently around 14–18% of the total hospital costs. Children consumed a high proportion of the resources devoted to emergency treatment (45.1%) but a low proportion of the inpatient costs (23.6%). Outpatient treatment, the least expensive constituent of hospital care, consistently accounted for the smallest portion of hospital costs (9–14%).

Other Direct Costs

Other direct costs attributed to asthma include comorbidity (the additional costs incurred in treating asthmatic patients for other diseases), the cost of home care, expenditure on "alternative medicine," nursing home costs, and the costs of ambulance callouts. The study by Mellis et al. included cost of waiting time in the direct costs, while the study by National Asthma Campaign (NAC) for Australia included costs of co-morbidity and ambulance costs. In the Danish study, cost of housekeeping and transports are included in the direct costs. Some studies, like that of Smith et al., include the caregivers' time costs in the indirect costs. Other studies, like the two from Sweden, do not include these costs, since they are not reported in the sources used for the estimations.

B. Indirect Costs

Indirect costs occur only when asthma has become sufficiently intrusive to interfere with a patient's lifestyle; they are therefore mainly associated with uncontrolled asthma.

Indirect costs encompass those costs associated with the loss of productive work by the patient, premature retirement, and premature death. Time spent by others caring for sick relatives is sometimes included in indirect and sometimes in direct costs, representing costs of informal care. Indirect costs are sometimes reported in terms of physical resources—for example, the number of working days lost or the number of premature deaths—without attempting to value these units.

If we look at three studies presenting cost of mortality (Table 2), we can see that cost due to premature death account for 32% of indirect costs in the United States, 25% in Germany, and 12% in Sweden. A distinction is sometimes made between short- and long-term costs, or between early retirement and absence from work when estimating indirect morbidity costs. The Swedish study shows higher costs for long-term absence (disability), while the opposite is true for Germany. No such distinction is provided for the United States. The study from Denmark also makes this distinction, and it is cost for early retirement that explains the very high indirect costs in that study.

Some studies report loss of production from patients with asthma who work but have less than full productivity. Smith et al. report for the United States a "restricted activity loss" that is of the same magnitude as the loss from days off work. A day with restricted activity is valued at 50% of a full workday.

Several studies include housekeeping loss. The magnitude of the estimates vary greatly. Smith et al. reported loss of production from housekeeping at $21 million in 1994, while Weiss et al. reported a cost of $503 million in 1990 prices. These two studies also reported schooldays lost, at a cost of $195 million and $900 million respectively. It should be noted that these estimates do not include an estimate of the value from the loss of education for children, but the time off work for family members to take care of them. These "indirect costs," measured as lost productivity, might alternatively be labeled "costs of informal care." One alternative would be to value this as the opportunity cost of professional care.

It is obvious that there is a need for better guidelines for which types of resource use to include in indirect costs, how these should be quantified, and how they should be valued.

Indirect costs will vary depending on the age of the patient and on the severity of the disease. Weiss et al. (11) and Lenney et al. (20) reported that children accounted for a high percentage of indirect costs (39.4%), reflecting the importance of time spent by others to care for children and the high prevalence of childhood asthma.

C. Intangible Costs

Asthma can significantly impair the quality of a patient's life. A number of instruments have been developed for the formal assessment and measurement of quality of life from the patient's viewpoint rather than from that of the clinician (see Chaps. 5–7). Those used in asthma include both generic health quality-of-life instruments like the Nottingham Health Profile (24) and SF-36 (25) and disease-specific instruments like St. George's Respiratory Questionnaire (26) and the McMaster Questionnaire (27). Using these, it has been demonstrated that patients with asthma have an impaired quality of life and that this can be improved by prophylactic treatment (28). However, in no cost-of-illness study has quality of life been incorporated in a systematic way.

IV. Measurement of Indirect Costs

Indirect cost of illness consists of the loss of production from the persons afflicted with a defined disease. There are good arguments to restrict the concept of indirect cost to persons afflicted with disease and not extend this concept to loss of production from persons who care for those with the disease. In the latter case, it is better to define the costs as nonmedical direct costs. The term *nonmedical* separates them from the resources used for professional medical care—i.e., health care costs. Nonmedical costs may include the costs of specific living arrangements, home help in the person's house, or services (time inputs) from relatives. For many diseases, these inputs are considerable—for example, different types of dementia [see Rice et al. (29)]. The nonmedical costs can be divided into costs of "formal care"(for example, social services) and informal care (services provided by friends and relatives). There is a high degree of substitutability between different types of formal care and between formal and informal care. It is important that all relevant costs be accounted for regardless of how the resources used are classified or paid for (reimbursed). It is therefore better to classify all resources used for treatment and caring for the patient as direct costs and to reserve the concept indirect costs for the loss of production that the illness causes for the patient. This is also consistent with the original definition of the concept [see Weisbrod (1)].

The quantification of indirect costs is rather straightforward; it is the time lost from productive work. This time lost can be identified from statistics of work absenteeism, early retirement pensions, and premature death. This can be measured in days, months, or years. The usual problems with multiple and competing diagnoses is present, but in principle what should be measured is well defined: the amount of working time lost due to the disease from a particular patient or group of patients. The fact that premature death results in the loss of a consumer as well as a producer does not change this. However, it is important to separate loss of production from morbidity and mortality, because the interpretation and relevance of the two concepts for different decision makers may differ. The production loss or gain from changes in mortality cannot be given any meaningful interpretation in an economic evaluation [see Johannesson (30)]. However, the net consumption—consumption minus production—in added years of life should be included in cost-effectiveness studies (31).

One type of loss of production that is not covered by this measurement technique is the loss of productivity at work due to an illness. This concept has been applied to estimates of cost of illness due to depression [see Greenberg et al. (32)] and had a significant impact on the magnitude of the indirect costs for this disease. This concept may also be of importance in asthma, although no estimates have been provided. The measurement problems are considerable, since it is difficult to observe the reduction in productivity for an external observer, and the validity of estimates by the persons themselves may be difficult to assess. However, if tried in practice, the best way would be to measure the reduction in productivity as a percent of full work capacity. That can then be translated into hours or days and added to time off from work. The same valuation can then be applied.

Identification and quantification of time lost from work is difficult, but the great controversy has been around the valuation of the time lost. In principle, the valuation criteria are clear: the economic burden should be valued as the opportunity cost of the time lost. But what is the opportunity cost?

As with direct costs, the natural starting point should be the market price for labor. Average earnings, including nonwage labor costs, are generally used to measure the cost of the time lost from production. This is consistent with neoclassical economic theory, which predicts that the value of production and earnings is equal for the marginal worker. This gives a norm that in a consistent way can be applied to all calculations as an acceptable approximation despite the obvious fact that different forms of market imperfections can invalidate the equality between wages and the value of the marginal product.

The most important market imperfection is unemployment. If there is unemployment, a sick person may be replaced by someone who would otherwise be unemployed. In this case there is no loss of production. Although this may happen, it will not necessarily invalidate the use of the average earnings as a measure of opportunity cost. First, the unemployment may be of a searching, frictional, or structural character, and in this case it may be unlikely to find someone out of work with the same skills who can take the job. There may be periods with very high unemployment, where this probability is much higher, but also periods where there are more jobs available than persons to fill them. In the latter case, the average earnings may represent an underestimate of the opportunity cost of time lost from work.

One may argue that the opportunity cost of time lost from work varies over the business cycle and that a correction for this should be made—for example, a 10% reduction in periods of very high unemployment and a 10% increase in periods of excess demand for labor. But this will not add very much to the estimates. Estimates of the economic burden have, in most cases, a long-term perspective, which makes it more relevant to use the average instead of adjusting to the current economic conditions.

It has been argued [see Koopmanschap et al. (33)] that indirect costs should be measured according to the friction cost method rather than the traditional human capital approach. According to the friction cost method, indirect costs for long-term absence, from disability as well as mortality, mainly occur during the time it takes to replace a worker—i.e., the friction period. For short-term absence, Koopmanschap et al. argue that the traditional method overestimates the production lost due to diminishing returns to labor, internal labor reserves within firms, and the fact that sick employees can sometimes make up for lost work when they return to work after a period of absence. Using the friction method to measure indirect costs means that the opportunity cost of labor is set close to zero after the friction period.

The friction method has been criticized by Johannesson and Karlsson (34). They note that for short-term absence, the differences between the different estimation methods are rather small. The argument that sick employees make up for lost work when they return to work ignores the opportunity cost of the extra effort and time involved. Internal labor reserves can be interpreted as an adjustment to the level of absence due to sickness, and is thus a direct replacement cost for the company. The argument of diminishing returns can be relevant if the supply of labor is significantly increased. However, for marginal changes in the supply of different types of labor, the argument of equality of gross income and the marginal value of the products produced will still hold.

For long-term absence—for example, due to early retirement—the friction method assumes that all vacancies are filled by previously unemployed persons. This does not seem very likely, since some vacancies will be filled with workers who are already employed. That will create a new vacancy and thus a new friction period if the method is applied consistently. It is impossible to follow these chains in practice. But the major problem with the method is the assumption that there are persons available to fill all vacancies at zero cost. If this is the case, it is questionable if we can use wages to estimate the direct costs of health care. The costs of health care are dominated by labor costs. If there is no cost when a doctor is sick, why is there any cost when he is at work? If the price of labor is close to zero, this has to be taken into account for both direct and indirect costs. However, it is not a realistic assumption and not consistent with general economic principles.

The discussion about the friction method reminds us that markets are not perfect and that market prices, including wages for different types of labor, may deviate from opportunity cost. It is also relevant to try to correct for these imperfections in specific situations where reliable corrections can be made. But it is not an argument to change the basic principles for valuation. There is great value in using consistent approaches based on theory, even if it is obvious that the theory is not a perfect description of reality.

The Value of Lost School Days

Asthma also occurs at young ages. For schoolchildren, the disease may result in days lost from school. In human capital theory, schooling is seen as an investment in human capital. In principle, the cost of lost schooldays should be measured as a reduction in the earnings resulting from how the disease affects the return on education.

Kreuger (35) estimates that in the United States, each year of schooling raises wages by about 8%. This estimate can be used as a first approximation by calculating the resulting effect on the discounted lifetime income. But the return on education is difficult to estimate in the first place, and it is even more difficult to assess the value of marginal changes in the time spent on education.

In practice, it is possible to estimate only the consequences of major costs for schooling. For example, if entrance to the labor market is postponed by 1 year, the present value of the year lost from work can be used as measure of the value of lost schooldays. However, for young children, entrance into the labor force lies far ahead, which means that, with discounting, the effect will have a small value.

We should also remember that the human capital theory is only one approach to the economics of education. Other hypotheses, assuming that schooling is a signaling effect or screening instrument, put further question marks behind the valuation of lost school time (36). With this approach, schooling has no direct effect on productivity but helps to select individuals with high productivity. Time lost from school may not have any cost if the cost of producing the signal is not increased.

Two studies from Australia (5) and the United States (11) include the number of schooldays lost in the cost-of-illness estimate but make no attempt to place an economic value on these days.

Childhood asthma may also affect the time lost from work for the parents. The issues related to the measurement of this are addressed in the next section.

V. The Cost of Unpaid Inputs

A large amount of production takes place within the household. Although there is no direct remuneration for this production, no market price, this does not mean that it has no value or cost. When a person is afflicted by an illness, the household production may also be affected. This should be added to the indirect costs.

A great part of unpaid production takes place within the household. Parents provide care for their children and children care for elderly parents. This informal care is part of the direct costs. The valuation problem is the same regardless of whether a direct or indirect cost is involved.

How do we estimate the opportunity cost of unpaid production? One method, the replacement method, has been used in several U.S. cost-of-illness studies. The relevant services provided are identified, the time spent for them is measured, and the market prices for the different types of labor providing these services are used for costing.

Another method is to estimate the value of unpaid household production in accordance with the alternative market occupation that the person working at home might pursue. Since it is difficult to determine what the alternative in each individual case might be, the average market wage paid for an ordinary occupation is most often used.

The first method is to be preferred when the alternative to household production is services in the formal market. For example, if someone caring for a relative cannot provide the service, a direct substitution of the service, hour for hour, is needed. In practice, this may be an unrealistic situation. The substitute service may give more or less care, with resulting changes in costs as well as quality of care. There has been a significant shift from informal care to formal care over time in most countries, and differences between countries as well as within countries (urban versus rural areas) may be significant.

The second method may be preferred in situations where the person providing the service can actually substitute time between providing services within the household and on the market. However, in many instances, the opportunity cost of time may be leisure time rather than time for paid work. In such situations, one may use the wage rate reduced by the marginal tax rate as the value of opportunity cost of time.

It is difficult to provide very explicit rules for assessing the "shadow price" of unpaid services. The purpose of the estimation should be stated as clearly as possible, and the method of identification, quantification, and valuation should be related to the purpose. For example, if a significant amount of time is spent on transportation for treatments, a calculation of the time used may be the most important. This estimate may provide ideas and incentives for an efficient use of this resource, regardless of the specific method used for the valuation of time.

VI. Concluding Remarks

The policy relevance of burden-of-disease studies has been much debated (37–41). One opinion has been that such studies are of no policy relevance at all, since they are not full economic evaluations, comparing costs and benefits of different alternatives for prevention or treatment. Although it is correct that cost-of-illness studies do not give direct evidence on the efficiency of allocation of resources, it is not correct to say that they have no relevance at all. The first studies that were undertaken in the modern area—for example, by Weisbrod (1)—had the explicit aim of guiding decisions about investments in research and development and in prevention. Since there is a great problem in defining explicit alternatives and assessing consequences for many research and development projects as well as preventive actions, an overall assessment of the "potential benefits" may be of value for decisions regarding resource allocation at a more general level. This will not rule out more precise cost-benefit studies for defined projects.

Normative interpretations of cost-of-illness studies must be made with great care. The lack of explicit alternatives does not make the estimations void of policy relevance. For example, it is not useful to criticize descriptive epidemiology for not involving controlled clinical trials.

Asthma is considered to be a mild illness that should be managed by ambulatory care. However, 43% of the cost of asthma is related to the use of emergency departments, hospitalization, and death. This strongly indicates that there is scope for significant cost reduction by improving disease control.

The pattern of costs incurred will vary among asthmatic patients depending on the severity of the disease and the degree of control achieved. Clinicians and health economists perceive "control" differently. The indication of successful control from the clinical viewpoint is the fact that the physician does not see the patient in the clinic, whereas health economists perceive control as the quality of life attained by the patient.

At the present time, more money is spent on rescue therapy than on prophylactic therapy, indicating that further improvement in therapy can be made. International management guidelines recommend an increase in expenditure on prophylactic therapy, which should reduce reliance on rescue therapy, and, by improving the control of asthma, may potentially decrease hospital costs, with consequent savings in total health care costs.

Cost-of-illness studies can be of value to evaluate the long-term consequences of changes in therapy. Studies have, for example, shown that increased use of inhaled steroids has reduced the cost of inpatient care (42). Cost-of-illness studies can be useful to evaluate what is happening in the whole health care system over time, and thus to make sure that the potential benefits based on evidence from clinical experiments can be transformed into clinical practice. Repeated studies with the same methodology in one country generally have more value than international comparisons.

Cost-of-illness studies will not provide all the necessary information for more rational decision making about allocation of resources to and within asthma. But they provide the first step to disease management and cost-effectiveness studies and provide a check for the long-term development if repeated at regular intervals. Cost-of-illness studies are descriptive studies, which means that it is very important that they are undertaken, with a strictly defined methodology for valuation of the consequences. But it is also important that the definition of the disease and its consequences be made as carefully as possible. The great differences observed between different studies seem to reflect these latter differences more than differences in the valuation methods applied.

Cost-of-illness studies can be seen as "health accounts," complementary to the national accounts that describe the total economic activity in a population (42). Undertaken with a well-defined methodology and based on data of good quality, they can make an important contribution to our understanding of the development of diseases and our attempts to control them.

References

1. Weisbrod, B. (1961). *Economics of Public Health*. Philadelphia, University of Pennsylvania Press.
2. Hodgson, T.A., and Meiners, M.R. (1982). Cost-of-illness methodology: a guide to current practicies and procedures. *Milbank Mem. Fund Q. Health Soc.*, **60**:429–491.
3. Lindgren, B. (1981). Cost-of-Illness in Sweden 1964–75. Dissertation, Lund economic Studies 24. Lund, Sweden, Lund University.

4. Jönsson, B. (1997). Health economic aspects of diabetes. *Endocrinol. Metab.*, **4** (**Suppl B**):135–137.
5. National Asthma Campaign (1992). *Report on the Cost of Asthma in Australia.*
6. Mellis, C.M., Peat, J.K., Bauman, A.E., and Woolcock, A.J. (1991). The cost of asthma in New South Wales. *Med. J. Aust.*, **155**:522–528.
7. Action Asthma. (1990). *The Occurrence and Cost of Asthma.* Worthing, U.K., Cambridge Medical Publications.
8. Teeling-Smith, G. (1990). *Asthma.* London, Office of Health Economics.
9. Thompson, S. (1984). On the social cost of asthma. *Eur. J. Respir. Dis.*, **65**:185–191.
10. Jacobson, L., and Lindgren, B. (1995). Astma. *De Samhällsekonomiska Kostnaderna: Studier i Hälsoekonomi 8.* Lund, Sweden, Lund Universitet.
11. Weiss, K.B., Gergen, P.J., and Hodgson, T.A. (1992). An economic evaluation of asthma in the United States. *N. Engl. J. Med.*, **326**:862–866.
12. Smith, D.H. et al. (1997). A national estimate of the economic costs of asthma. *Am. J. Respir. Crit. Care Med.*, **156**:787–793.
13. Sørensen, L., Weng, S., Weng, S.L., Wulf-Andersen, L., Østergaard D., and Bech P.G. (1997). The costs of asthma in Denmark. *Br. J. Med. Econ.*, **11**:103–111.
14. BCG Canada. (1993). *The Costs of Adult Asthma in Canada.* Princeton, N.J., Communications Media for Education.
15. CRESGE France. (1992). *Asthme: Mieux connaitre pour mieux traiter (Asthma: Understand It Better to Treat It Better).* Paris: Glaxo.
16. Nowac, D., Volmer, T., and Wettengel, R. (1996). Asthma bronchiale—eine Krankheitskostenanalyse, *Pneumologie* **50**:364–371.
17. NHLBI/WHO Geneva. (1995) *Exploring the Costs of Asthma: An Illustrative Case Study in Transkei.* NHLBI/WHO Workshop Report, Publication Number 95-3659.
18. Barnes, P.J., Jönsson, B., and Klim, J.B. (1996). The costs of asthma. *Eur. Respir. J.*, **9**:636–642.
19. Weiss, K.B. (1996). The health economics of treating mild asthma. *Eur. Respir. Rev.*, **6(33)**:45–49.
20. Lenney, W., Wells, N.E.J., and O'Neill, B.A. (1994). The burden of pediatric asthma. *Eur. Respir. J.*, **4**:49–62.
21. Action Asthma. (1991). *National Asthma Survey Results.* London: Allen and Hanburys Ltd.
22. Whiteman, I.A., and Gaduzo, S.C. (1993). The Management of mild-to-moderate astmatics in general practice: a retrospective analysis. *Br. J. Med. Econ.*, **6**:25–35.
23. Bosely, C.M., Parry, D.T., and Cochrane, G.M. (1994). Patient compliance with inhaled medication: does combining beta-agonists with corticosteroid improve compliance? *Eur. Respir. J.*, **7**:504–509.
24. Hunt, S.M. et al. (1980). A quantitative approach to perceived health status: a validation study. *J. Epidemiol. Commun. Health*, **34**:281–286.
25. Ware, J.E., and Sherbourne, C.D. (1992). The MOS 36-item short-form health survey (SF-36): I. Conceptual framework and item selection. *Med. Care*, **30**:473.
26. Jones, P.W., Quirk, F.H., Baveystock, C.M. and Littlejohns, P. (1992). A self-complete measure of health status for chronic airflow limitation: The St. Georges Respiratory Questionaire. *Am. Rev. Respir. Dis.*, **145**:1321–1327.

27. Junifer, E.F., Guyatt, G.H., Ferrie, P.J., and Griffith, L.E. (1993). Measuring quality of life in asthma. *Am. Rev. Respir. Dis.*, **147**:832–838.

28. Jones, P.W., and the Nedocronil Sodium Quality of Life Study Group. (1994). Quality of life, symptom and preliminary function in asthma: long term treatment with nedocronil sodium examined in a controlled multicenter trial. *Eur. Respir. J.*, **7**:55–62.

29. Rice, D.P., Fox, P.J., Max, W., et al. (1992). The burden of caring for Alzheimer's disease patients. In Proceedings of the 1991 Public Health Conference on Records and Statistics, Washington, D.C., U.S. Department of Health and Human Services, pp. 119–124.

30. Johannesson, M. (1994). The concept of cost in economic evaluation of health care: a theoretical inquiry. *Int. J. Technol. Assess. Health Care*, **10**:675–682.

31. Meltzer, D. (1997). Accounting for future costs in medical cost-effectiveness analysis. *J. Health Econ.*, **16**:33–64.

32. Greenberg, P.E., Stiglin, L.E., and Finkelstein, S.N. (1993). The economic burden of depression in 1990. *J. Clin. Psychiatry*. **54**:405–418.

33. Koopmanschap, M.A., Rutten, F.F.H., van Ineveld, B.M., and van Rojijen, L. (1995). The friction cost method for measuring indirect cost of disease. *J. Health Econ.*, **14**: 171–189.

34. Johannesson, M., and Karlsson, G. (1997). The friction method: a comment. *J. Health Econ.*, **16**:249–255.

35. Krueger, A.B. (1993). How computers have changed the wage structure: Evidence from micro data, 1984–1989. *Q. J. Econ.*, **108**:33–60.

36. Spence, A.M. (1974). *Marketing Signaling*. Cambridge, Mass., Harvard University Press.

37. Shiell, A., Gerard, K., and Donaldson, C. (1987). Cost-of-illness studies: an aid to decision making? *Health Policy*, **8**:317–323.

38. Hodgson, T.A. (1989). Cost-of-illness studies: no aid to decision making? Comments on the second opinion by Shiell et al. *Health Policy*, **11**:57–60.

39. Lindgren, B. (1990). The cost of ''non-treatment.'' In *Measuring the Benefits of Medicines*. Edited by G. Teeling-Smith. London, Office of Health Economics.

40. Lindgren, B. (1990). The economic impact of illness. In *Cost of Illness and Benefits of Drug Treatment*. Edited by U. Abshagen U and F.E. Münnich. München: W. Zuckschwerdt Verlag. 1990, pp. 12–20.

41. Drummond, M.F. (1992). Cost-of-illness studies: a major headache? *Pharmaco-Economics*, **2**:1–4.

42. Davey, P.J., and Leeder, S.R. (1992). The cost of migraine: more than just a headache? *PharmacoEconomics*, **2**:5–7.

43. Gerdtham, U.-G., Hertzman, P., Jönsson, B., and Boman, G. (1996). Impact of inhaled corticosteroids on asthma hospitalization in Sweden 1978–1991. *Med Care*, **34**:1188–1198.

12

Economic Evaluation of Asthma Treatments

SCOTT D. RAMSEY and **SEAN D. SULLIVAN**

University of Washington
Seattle, Washington

I. Introduction

Public and private health delivery systems are searching for ways to minimize the cost of managing chronic diseases while maintaining high quality care for their member populations. The goals of minimizing cost and ensuring quality are often in conflict, however, particularly in the era of budget constraints, rising demand for health care services, and increased competition. The tension arises because health insurance creates incentives for patients (and often providers) to consume care with little regard for the unit price of that care. Decision makers must select disease management strategies that balance the need for fiscal responsibility with patients' desire to obtain the most technologically advanced and beneficial care that is available. Because the process of allocating scarce resources among competing medical treatments can be emotionally and politically charged, decision makers would prefer to turn to rational and consistent methods of evaluation designed to maximize health for expenditure. Pharmacoeconomic analysis is one tool that has been developed to serve this need.

Asthma is a chronic condition that exemplifies the conflict between economic constraints and the demand for medical care. As highlighted by a recent series of cover stories in popular magazines (1,2), the disease is frightening to

affected children and their parents. There is a great desire among the public to
"cure" or control asthma. Correspondingly, there are a wide variety of therapeutic alternatives from which to choose; pharmaceuticals, specialty care, desensitization regimens, and education programs, to name but a few. These treatment options vary widely in effectiveness and cost. The increasing prevalence of asthma, combined with the recent introduction of several costly new therapies, is generating a rapidly rising "asthma budget" for many health systems. The rising cost of asthma care, however, is at odds, with moves to tighten health care budgets. Thus, there has been intense activity in the areas of "clinical practice guidelines," "disease management," and "critical pathways"; there are also other efforts that are at least in part aimed at reducing expenditure while maintaining quality for asthma care. Because asthma has become such an important topic to the public, decision makers must be mindful of the social as well as clinical aspects of this disease in their efforts to control the costs of asthma care. Since pharmacoeconomics combines a societal perspective with analysis of clinical and economic effectiveness, this methodology holds great promise as an aid to therapeutic decision making for patients with asthma.

The purpose of this chapter is to briefly define the discipline and uses of pharmacoeconomic studies, to review the global literature on the cost-effectiveness of asthma therapies, and to suggest "best practices" for conducting economic evaluations of therapies for asthma.

II. Principles of Cost-Effectiveness Analysis and Pharmacoeconomics

Cost-effectiveness analysis can be defined as a set of research methods to assess and quantify the costs and clinical consequences of medical care treatments in order to estimate the "economic value" of the treatment in relation to alternative treatments (3). Pharmacoeconomic analysis is cost-effectiveness analysis as applied to drug therapies for disease. A cost-effectiveness analysis of competing medical treatments should incorporate evidence on the clinical consequences (efficacy and safety) and the costs and relative cost-effectiveness of treatment alternatives (4).

A. Essential Concepts

The "result" of a cost-effectiveness analysis (CEA) is derived from a simple equation that integrates costs and outcomes:

Incremental cost-effectiveness therapy A =

$$\frac{\text{cost}_A - \text{cost}_B}{\text{effectiveness}_A - \text{effectiveness}_B} \quad (1)$$

Health outcomes

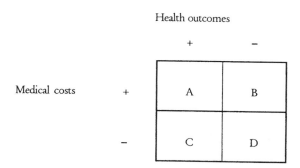

Figure 1 Depiction of possible outcomes of pharmacoeconomic studies.

In CEA two therapies are compared: therapy A (usually the new technology) and therapy B (the established therapy). The incremental cost-effectiveness of A versus B is thus the attributable benefit per incremental level of expenditure for the new technology.

Given this equation, there are only four possible outcomes from a cost-effectiveness analysis, as illustrated in Figure 1 (5). Quadrant B illustrates a treatment that is less efficacious or more harmful and costs more than the current treatment. Quadrant C depicts a dominant technology—one that improves health outcome and achieves cost savings. Outcomes B and C are unambiguous results, indicating that the new therapy should be rejected (B) or accepted (C) technologies by the health care system. Quadrant D represents a less expensive treatment with a reduced health outcome as compared with standard therapy. Quadrant A shows the cost-outcome relationships of most new medical technologies. Here, health benefits improve, but at an additional expense to the health care system. For outcomes in quadrants D and A, clinicians, patients, and payers must decide whether the improvement or loss in health outcome is worth the additional costs or cost saving of providing care with the new technology. Note that in a health care system with a fixed budget over time, additional expenditure on new treatments reduces the amount of resources available to treat other diseases.

III. Methods of Cost-Effectiveness Analysis

Although only four outcomes are possible in a cost-effectiveness analysis, the evaluation task is still far from simple. In particular, the analyst must consider what costs will be included in the numerator and how effectiveness will be measured for the denominator.

A. Cost Measurement

All researchers agree that *direct medical* care costs should be comprehensively evaluated and not limited to the assessment of the cost of asthma therapy alone. For example, if only the costs of medications are assessed in an evaluation of drug therapy for asthma, a number of important economic parameters will be disregarded. These include the direct costs associated with the use of medical resources to treat significant adverse reactions to the drug or the savings that may result from averted hospitalization and emergency department visits due to improved clinical outcome. *Direct nonmedical* care costs can also be important when treating asthma. Examples here include transportation costs to and from the physician and the value of the time the family spends caring for children with asthma. In addition to direct medical and nonmedical care costs, *indirect costs* (also known as *productivity costs*) may also be important. For example, the wage value of a parent's time away from work when his or her child suffers a severe asthma attack should be counted as an economic consequence of the disease and a factor that may benefit from effective therapy. Finally, diseases such as asthma extract an *intangible cost*—the cost of the emotional burden placed on patients and family members. Although seldom valued explicitly in pharmacoeconomic analyses, these costs are sometimes measured in monetary units, particularly when patients and family members are asked what they would be willing to pay to "cure" or remove the disease as a factor in their lives (see "Cost-Benefit Analysis," below.)

B. Outcomes Measurement

One of the most difficult (and controversial) aspects of cost-effectiveness lies in choosing the measure of effectiveness [the denominator in Eq. (1), above]. The term used for the type of pharmacoeconomic analysis varies according to the measure of effectiveness that is included in the denominator. Several approaches have been taken; the most common of these are outlined below. Many different approaches have been applied to pharmacoeconomic evaluations of asthma therapies. These types of pharmacoeconomic studies are reviewed in the following section.

Cost-of-Illness Studies

Cost-of-illness studies seek to estimate the economic burden of a disease on a particular society (see Chap. 11). Cost-of-illness studies are not true cost-effectiveness analyses, since they usually do not compare alternative treatments, and the "denominator" (effectiveness) is usually omitted. Still, they are commonly performed as a way to raise awareness regarding the economic consequences of illnesses, particularly those where the impact on society may be undervalued by health care policymakers and the public. For example, the often cited study by Weiss and colleagues on the economic impact of asthma found that this "mild" chronic illness accounted for $6.2 billion in costs during 1990. Furthermore, more than $1 billion of these costs were "indirect costs," that is, productivity losses due to loss of school days of children with the disease (6).

Cost-Minimization Analysis

Cost-minimization analyses evaluate competing therapies with the goal of finding the least costly treatment option. Implicit in this type of analysis is the assumption that each treatment is equally effective for the condition (thus, the focus on costs only). No cost-minimization studies have been performed for competing asthma therapies, perhaps because therapies have been found to vary substantially in effectiveness.

Cost-Effectiveness Analysis

The most common pharmacoeconomic evaluation technique is cost-effectiveness analysis (CEA). The measure of effectiveness [the denominator in Eq. (1)] in a cost-effectiveness study is an ad hoc measure of benefit that is most suitable to the study. Here, health outcomes of treatments are expressed in "natural" units such as symptom-free days or years of life saved. *Ad hoc* denominators have the advantage of being readily identifiable and unambiguous aspects of a disease that are clearly affected by the treatments in question. An important disadvantage is that important factors beyond that particular measure of effectiveness that may also be affected by the treatment are ignored. For example, focusing on life years gained as the measure of effectiveness ignores improvements in functional status and changes in quality of life, both of which may be affected by the therapies.

Cost-Utility Analysis

Cost-utility analysis is a special form of the cost-effectiveness model in which the health outcomes are expressed in quality-adjusted life years (QALYs) gained. The quality adjustment is derived from preference weights or health utilities (3). The advantages of a cost-utility studies are that they (a) simultaneously capture changes in mortality and morbidity in the measure of effectiveness; (b) are applicable to all disease states and treatments; (c) consider patients' preferences for health outcomes, and (d) conform to normative theory of decision making under uncertainty (7).

Cost-utility studies have a conceptual appeal to researchers and are the most ideal for use in decision making because of the features described above. The U.S. Public Health Service's Panel on Cost Effectiveness and Medicine and the province of Ontario recommend cost-utility analyses of pharmaceuticals to support formulary listing (8,9). However, technical limitations in the measurement of preferences in asthmatics (particularly in children) and a lack of long-term data concerning the impact of asthma interventions on quality of life has limited the use of this approach.

Cost-Benefit Analysis

Cost-benefit analysis is a form of pharmacoeconomic analysis where both costs and benefits are defined in monetary terms and adjusted to net present values. Unlike other forms of cost-effectiveness analysis, which present their results as a ratio of costs over effects, the result of a cost-benefit analysis is simply the *difference* between total costs and total benefits (since both are defined monetarily). As a result, cost-benefit analyses have the advantage of yielding a straightforward result: either the intervention is "cost-effective" (benefits exceed costs), and should be accepted, or it is not. However, there are many technical, social, and ethical difficulties with expressing health outcomes in monetary terms. To obtain dollar estimates of health gains, researchers either measure revealed preferences in actual markets or obtain hypothetical estimations derived from willingness-to-pay studies (10). Revealed preferences, however, are usually confounded because health care purchases are heavily subsidized in most countries. Willingness-to-pay surveys are subject to many interviewer and interviewee biases. As a consequence, cost-benefit analyses are conducted infrequently. No cost-benefit studies have been published for asthma therapies.

IV. Pharmacoeconomic Studies of Asthma Pharmacotherapy

There are a number of pharmacoeconomic analyses of asthma pharmacotherapy. Tables 1 and 2 summarize the important retrospective and prospective pharmacoeconomic evaluations of asthma pharmacotherapy.

V. Inhaled Corticosteroids

There is substantial evidence of the positive clinical effects of combining inhaled corticosteroids with bronchodilator therapy for the management of asthma (11). The therapeutic management guidelines of the U.S. National Asthma Education and Prevention Expert Panel Report (NAEPP), the International Consensus Report (ICR), the Global Initiative for Asthma Report (GINA), and the British Thoracic Society recommend as initial treatment such combination therapy for persons with moderate-to-severe asthma. However, adding inhaled corticosteroid medications to an existing regimen of inhaled or oral bronchodilator therapy contributes significantly to the overall cost of treating asthma in these patients. An

Table 1 Nonrandomized Pharmacoeconomic Studies of Asthma Pharmacotherapy

First author, year, reference no.	Study method used	Sample size	Perspective	Treatments studied	Length of study	Costs measured	Health outcomes measured	Economic outcomes
Adelroth, 1988 (12)	Retrospective; pre/post quasi-experimental design	36 adults	Societal	Budesonide	5 years; 2 years pre, 3 years post	Direct	Reduction in need for oral steroid after introduction of inhaled budesonide	Estimated 55% reduction in direct costs
Ross, 1988 (27)	Retrospective; pre/post quasi-experimental design	53	Health system	Two groups: cromolyn users and nonusers	3.2 to 3.8 years[b]	Direct	None	Estimated 92–96% reduction in use of health services
Gerdtham, 1996 (13)	Retrospective; econometric model	[a]	Societal	All inhaled corticosteroids	11 years	Direct	Reduction in hospital bed days and discharges for asthma	Estimated benefit: cost ratio of between 1.5:1 and 2.8:1
Perera, 1995 (25)	Prospective; pre/post quasi-experimental design	86 children	Societal	Two groups: various doses of beclomethasone and budesonide	4 years	Direct	Reduction in acute severe attacks, hospital admissions, breakthrough wheezing, missed schooldays, and treatment satisfaction	Estimated 83% reduction in total costs of care; $0.04 per unit increase in patient satisfaction with treatment

[a] Unit of analysis is counties and not persons. The study represents a total of 71% of the Swedish population.
[b] Cromolyn users contributed 3.2 years of data and nonusers of cromolyn contributed 3.8 years of data.

Table 2   Randomized Pharmacoeconomic Studies of Asthma Pharmacotherapy

First author, year, reference no.	Study method used	Sample size	Perspective	Treatments studied	Length of study	Costs measured	Health outcomes measured	Economic outcomes
Schulpher, 1993 (26)	Randomized controlled trial	145 adults	Health system	Two groups: salmeterol and placebo	12 weeks	Direct	Episode-free days	No statistically significant difference in clinical effectiveness, thus a cost-outcome was not calculated
Campbell, 1993 (14)	Randomized controlled trial	556 adults	Health system	Two groups: budesonide 400 µg compared to budesonide 800 µg	12 weeks	Direct	Lung function (FEV$_1$) and symptoms	Not cost-effective to increase dose of budesonide from 400 to 800 µg in patients with mild to moderate asthma
Connett, 1993 (17)	Randomized controlled trial	40 children	Societal	Two groups: budesonide compared to placebo	26 weeks	Direct and indirect	Lung function (FEV$_1$), symptoms, symptom-free days	Budesonide is dominant therapy; saved $9.43 for each symptom-free day gained

Reference	Study design	Patients	Perspective	Treatment groups	Duration	Cost type	Outcome measures	Conclusions
Rutten-van Molken, 1993 (18)	Randomized controlled trial	116 children	Societal	Two groups: budesonide and salbutamol, salbutamol alone	3 years[a]	Direct and indirect	Lung function (FEV$_1$), symptom-free days, school absences	Budesonide is cost-effective; $83 per 10% improvement in FEV$_1$, $4.75 per symptom-free day gained
Rutten-van Molken, 1995 (19)	Randomized controlled trial	274 adults	Societal	Three groups: beclomethasone and terbutaline, ipratropium and terbutaline, terbutaline alone	2.5 years	Direct and indirect	Lung function (FEV$_1$, PC$_{20}$), symptom-free days	Beclomethasone is cost-effective; $201 per 10% improvement in FEV$_1$, $5 per symptom-free day gained Ipratropium is not cost-effective
O'Byrne, 1996 (16)	Randomized controlled trial	57 adults	Societal	Three groups: budesonide 400 or 800 μg and bronchodilator compared to bronchodilator alone	16 weeks	Direct	Lung function (PEFR), symptom scores, exacerbations, emergency room visits, and willingness to pay	Budesonide is cost-effective at 400 μg per day but not at 800 μg per day compared to bronchodilator alone
Booth, 1996 (20)	Randomized controlled trial	225 children	Societal	Two groups: sodium cromoglycate 20 mg qid compared to fluticasone 50 μg bid	8 weeks	Direct	Lung function (PEFR) symptom scores, and the probability of successful treatment	Fluticasone is cost-effective compared to sodium cromoglycate CE ratios vary according to outcome measure selected

[a]The study had a planned 3-year follow-up but only 39 patients reached a follow-up period of 22 months.

Key: PEFR, peak expiratory flow rate; CE, cost-effectiveness.

important and as yet not fully explored research question is whether inhaled corticosteroids in combination with bronchodilators are cost-effective compared with
bronchodilator alone for treating persons with mild-to-moderate or moderate-to-
severe asthma.

The first evidence of the beneficial economic effects of inhaled budesonide
was reported in a letter by Adelroth and Thompson (12). The study examined
the relationship between use of high-dose inhaled budesonide (800 μg per day)
and asthma-related inpatient hospital days in 36 oral steroid–dependent patients
with asthma over a 5-year period. The analysis employed a pre-post, quasiexperi-
mental study design where patients served as their own controls. Inpatient admissions, total days, and direct medical care costs fell significantly after starting
budesonide compared with the previous 2 years on oral steroid therapy. Direct
medical care costs per patient declined by over 55% per year for up to 3 years
after the initiation of inhaled budesonide.

Gerdtham and colleagues built on Adelroth and Thompson's initial work
in Sweden by constructing a pooled, time-series economic model to determine
the association between greater use of inhaled corticosteroids and asthma-related
hospital days in 14 counties over an 11-year period, again using a nonexperimen-
tal methodology (13). More than 80% of inhaled corticosteroid use during this
time was with budesonide. Although not a true pharmacoeconomic analysis, the
study did indicate a strong negative association between use of inhaled corticosteroids and hospital-bed days for asthma. An approximate cost-benefit ratio was
developed from the multivariate models suggestive of positive economic benefits
in excess of costs on the order of between 1.5:1.0 and 2.8:1.0, depending on
the analytical model.

Several recent studies have employed experimental research designs to investigate the cost-effectiveness of inhaled corticosteroids. Campbell and colleagues reported on the cost-effectiveness of increasing the daily dose of inhaled
budesonide from 400 to 800μg per day after 6 weeks in persons with mild-to-
moderate asthma (14). Data from a 12-week randomized trial of 556 patients
aged 14 to 84 were used in the analysis. The health outcomes of increasing the
dose of inhaled budesonide in these patients was reported elsewhere and showed
that 800 μg per day of budesonide failed to improve lung function or reduce
symptoms when compared with 400 μg per day (15). The total cost of treatment
(medication only) was estimated to be £3108 (about $4660 U.S.) in the group
taking 400 μg/day (12 weeks) compared with £4662 (about $6993 U.S.) in both
the groups—that taking 400μg/day (6 weeks) and that taking 800 μg/day (6
weeks). The authors concluded that increasing the dose of budesonide from 400
to 800 μg/day was not a cost-effective strategy.

Similar findings were observed by O'Byrne et al. in a randomized trial of
budesonide 400 μg/day, 800 μg/day, and placebo in 57 adult asthmatics with
mild disease (16). Low-dose budesonide demonstrated better asthma morning

and nocturnal symptom control and improved peak expiratory flow rate (PEFR); it was judged to be cost-beneficial compared to placebo. High-dose budesonide did not improve lung function or symptom scores relative to low-dose budesonide.

In a somewhat longer study, Connett and colleagues studied the cost-effectiveness of inhaled budesonide compared with placebo in a 6-month randomized trial of 40 children ages 1 to 3 with persistent asthma (17). The outcome results indicated that budesonide produced a favorable clinical response, increasing symptom-free days when compared with placebo (195 versus 117 days). Direct medical costs (including the cost of budesonide) and indirect costs were tabulated for the numerator of the cost-effectiveness ratio. The results suggested that budesonide is a dominant therapy; that is, compared with placebo, budesonide increases overall effectiveness and reduces overall costs by £6.33 (about $9.45 U.S.) per symptom-free day gained.

Rutten-van Mölken and associates reported on the cost-effectiveness of adding inhaled corticosteroid to as-needed bronchodilator compared with as-needed bronchodilator alone in a 12-month randomized trial of 116 asthmatic children 7 to 16 years of age (18). The investigators evaluated FEV_1 as the primary outcome. Frequency of symptom-free days and number of school absences were included as secondary outcome measures. Patients randomized to inhaled corticosteroid plus as-needed bronchodilator experienced significantly increased lung function (FEV_1) and symptom-free days and reduced days missed from school relative to as-needed bronchodilator alone. Compared to bronchodilator alone, bronchodilator plus inhaled corticosteroid increased FEV_1 by 10% at an additional total cost of about $83 U.S. The additional cost of bronchodilator plus inhaled corticosteroid was about $4.75 U.S. per symptom-free day gained. Thus, inhaled corticosteroid plus bronchodilator was more effective than bronchodilator alone, but at an additional cost. The relative value differed depending on whether one focused on improved lung function (FEV_1) or better symptom control.

In the largest and most comprehensive study to date, Rutten-van Mölken and associates investigated the costs and effects of adding inhaled anti-inflammatory therapy to inhaled β_2-agonist by analyzing data from a randomized trial of 274 adult participants aged 18 to 60 years (19). Patients were selected for inclusion if they met the age criteria and had diagnosed moderately severe obstructive airway disease defined by pulmonary function criteria. Patients were eligible if they had either asthma or chronic obstructive pulmonary disease. Each was randomized to either fixed-dose inhaled terbutaline plus inhaled placebo (BA + PL), inhaled terbutaline plus 800 µg of inhaled beclomethasone per day (BA + CS), or inhaled terbutaline plus inhaled ipatropium bromide 160 µg per day (BA + AC). Patients were followed for up to 2.5 years or until premature withdrawal.

The economic objective of this study was to determine the relative cost per unit of benefit for the three therapeutic arms. The clinical results indicated that addition of the inhaled corticosteroid to fixed-dose terbutaline led to a significant improvement in pulmonary function (FEV_1 and PC_{20}) and symptom-free days, whereas addition of the inhaled ipatropium bromide to fixed-dose terbutaline produced no significant clinical benefits over placebo. The average annual monetary savings associated with the use of inhaled corticosteroid were not offset by the increase in costs from the average annual price of the inhaled product. The incremental cost-effectiveness for inhaled corticosteroid was $201 per 10% improvement in FEV_1 and $5 per symptom-free day gained. The incremental cost-effectiveness of ipatropium bromide was not evaluated because of the lack of clinical benefit relative to placebo.

The cost-effectiveness of fluticasone was studied in a group of 4- to 12-year-old children who required inhaled prophylactic treatment for asthma (20). Over an 8-week study period, 115 patients received sodium cromoglycate 20 mg four times daily and 110 patients received fluticasone propionate 50 μg twice daily. The effectiveness of both treatments was determined by morning and evening PEFR, daily symptom control, safety, proportion of successfully treated patients, and incidence of adverse consequences. The authors concluded that, over an 8-week period, fluticasone was cost-effective when compared to sodium cromoglycate for prophylactic treatment, using treatment success rates as the primary cost-effectiveness outcome measure.

The results from these studies suggest a favorable economic impact of using inhaled corticosteroids. Similarly, other studies have demonstrated that inhaled anti-inflammatory therapy reduces hospitalization rates in persons with chronic asthma (21–25), although they did not include formal pharmacoeconomic evaluation.

VI. Long-Acting β₂-Agonists

Long-acting bronchodilators such as formoterol and salmeterol represent a relatively new approach to prophylactic and symptomatic treatment for asthma. Only one published study has simultaneously evaluated the impact of a long-acting agent on clinical and economic outcomes for patients with asthma (26). In this paper, the authors reported on a retrospective cost-effectiveness analysis of a clinical trial of 145 patients diagnosed with asthma and randomized to receive 12 weeks of maintenance therapy with either long-acting formoterol or short-acting albuterol. The primary clinical outcome measure was cumulative symptom-free days over the 12-week period. The authors concluded that there were no statistically significant differences in symptom-free days between the two treatment groups. Because of these results, no incremental cost-effectiveness ratio was calculated. For illustrative purposes, the authors simulated a range of possible clinical benefits and cost-effectiveness ratios by respecifying the symptom-free composite score to include or not include adverse events.

VII. Inhaled Cromolyn Sodium

Ross and coworkers made use of patient and health services records in one large group practice to estimate the economic consequences of including cromolyn sodium in the treatment regimen of asthma patients (27). A total of 53 patients were retrospectively identified from medical records and categorized into two groups: those who received cromolyn sodium for at least 1 year (n = 27) and those who received no cromolyn sodium as part of the treatment regimen (n = 26). Patients receiving cromolyn sodium provided an average of 3.2 years of health service utilization data, and those in the comparison group provided 3.8 years of data. Medication costs for patients on cromolyn sodium were slightly higher ($27.90 per month) than those for the control group ($25.20 per month). However, emergency department and hospital costs declined significantly for cromolyn sodium patients; after the change in medication, they experienced a 96% reduction in the rate of emergency department visits and a 92% reduction in the rate of hospital admissions. The authors made no direct measurement of outcomes of therapy and did not control for symptom severity or other baseline confounding that might partly explain differences in the results. Thus this study is not a true cost-effectiveness analysis; rather, it is a cost comparison of two retrospective cohorts of asthma patients.

VIII. Other Pharmacotherapy

The remaining economic studies of asthma medications identified in this review were not full cost-effectiveness evaluations. Tierce and colleagues performed a retrospective cost-identification study comparing use of inhaled albuterol to use of inhaled metaproterenol in 1463 Michigan Medicaid patients (28). Asthma-related medications, physician and emergency department visits, and hospital care were assessed and valued using Medicaid prices. The authors concluded that the overall cost of care was significantly lower in the albuterol group as compared with the metaproterenol group. Because this study was not randomized, questions remain about baseline comparability of the two groups.

A modest number of papers exist on the impact of other β_2-agonists on health services utilization (29), methylprednisolone use in the emergency department (30), or aerosolized versus metered-dose inhaler delivery of β_2-agonists (31,32). Three of the studies did not attempt to value the intervention benefits in monetary terms; rather, these studies expressed outcomes in terms such as number of visits (29,30,32). Further, one study was not considered because of a mixed inception sample that included patients without asthma among the evaluable patients (31).

IX. Economic Studies of Asthma Patient Education and Consultation Programs

Several reports document the clinical and economic impact of patient-oriented asthma education programs. Educational interventions have included formal classroom-based medication compliance programs and asthma self-management programs for adults and children and their parents. In general, economic evaluations of these programs have been quite favorable, in particular when the programs have been directed at high-risk patients or those with documented resource-intensive care needs (such as a prior hospitalization) (33–42). In a recent comprehensive (but small) study, Neri and colleagues conducted a prospective randomized trial comparing asthma event rates and costs before and after two education programs: a "complete program" that included classroom-type lessens and a "reduced program" that included educational brochures but no formal instruction (43). There were approximately 33 patients in each arm. The study included cost-benefit and cost-effectiveness analyses. Compared with the year prior to the intervention, asthma-related events (attacks, medical examinations, admissions) fell significantly in the year following the evaluation for both programs. Comparing the years pre- and postintervention, the cost-benefit calculations revealed a cost savings of $1181 for the complete program and $1028 for the reduced program. The value of asthma-related work loss was included in the calculations.

Analyses have also examined the economic impact of referrals of patients with moderate to severe asthma to specialists (44). In retrospective chart reviews, these studies find significant reductions in sick office visits, emergency department visits, hospital days, and costs of care for patients. Most of these analyses, however, suffered from poor design and evaluation methods. Flaws included failing to figure in the cost of the intervention, inadequate specification of the time horizon for treatment, and lack of adjustment for potential confounding in patient selection.

X. "Best Practices" for Economic Evaluation of Therapeutic Agents for Asthma

Pharmacoeconomic evaluation is an evolving science. Still, there are several reasons to establish standard methods of economic evaluation for therapies such as asthma. Drummond and colleagues give the following rationale for establishing standards: (a) to maintain high methodological standards; (b) to facilitate the comparison of the results of economic evaluations for different health care interventions, and; (c) to facilitate interpretation of study findings from health care setting to setting (45–51). The latter issue occurs both within countries with diverse health delivery systems (such as the United States) and for international interpretation of studies.

It is recommended that the criteria listed below be adhered to as a minimum when designing, conducting, and reporting a pharmacoeconomic analysis of new or existing asthma therapies.

One of the most important elements of a pharmacoeconomic evaluation is defining precisely the patient populations and clinical treatment scenarios. This important step is sometimes neglected by health economists but is usually seen as the sine qua non by the clinical audience for the study. Patient inclusion and exclusion criteria, comparison treatments, treatment protocols (including doses and follow-up intervals), and duration of therapy and observation should be well described and justified. Because cost-effectiveness analysis focuses on *comparing* two or more alternative therapies for a given condition, it is particularly important to justify the treatments that will be compared. Ideally, all possible therapies would be identified and compared simultaneously, including the ''no therapy'' option. In practice, resource limitations will force the researcher to focus on a small number of alternatives. As a minimum, a new therapy should be compared with the status quo; that is, the therapy that is most widely used in existing practice.

There are two cautions to this general rule of thumb. The first is that the status quo is often a mixture of therapies that vary according to the clinical situation. For example, asthma can be managed with inhaled β-agonists, inhaled steroids, cromolyn, or a combination of these treatments. One has the option of comparing the new therapy to each individual alternative or to a combination (e.g., inhaled β-agonist and inhaled steroid) that is widely used. In such cases, it is sometimes useful to refer back to the clinical condition and consider narrowing the clinical population that is the focus of the study (e.g., children with asthma to children with mild asthma). Alternatively, selecting a few commonly used combinations may be advisable. The second caution is when the status quo is widely believed to be ineffective. Here, any alternative therapy has a good chance of appearing cost-effective. This situation (which is often not known if the status quo has not been carefully evaluated) is best addressed by including a ''best available'' alternative in the analysis. A good source for finding the best available alternative is a clinical practice guideline that has been created by careful evaluation of clinical evidence. Carefully defining these elements will lend credibility to the study among the practitioners and decision makers who will ultimately decide whether to accept or reject the study's conclusions.

It is also important to define the context of the economic evaluation; that is, whether it was conducted as a part of a clinical trial, a retrospective database analysis, or other type of study design. Controlled clinical trials are usually con-

sidered the ''gold standard'' for investigating the efficacy and safety of pharmacotherapy, yet such trials have both advantages and limitations for pharmacoeconomic evaluation. Controlled clinical trials have high internal validity but may
have limited external validity, particularly in terms of the economic evaluation.
End points that are part of a clinical trial are also sometimes not appropriate for an
economic evaluation. For example, the study by Campbell focused on pulmonary
function, whereas most clinicians, health plans, and patients are interested in
symptoms (14). In contrast, the studies by Connett and colleagues and Rutten-
van Mölken and associates evaluated symptom-free days as the primary outcome
measure (17–19). Even when appropriate end points for an economic analysis
are included, clinical trials are often not statistically powered for evaluation of
these end points.

It is important that economic evaluations consider the effectiveness rather
than the efficacy of alternative therapies. *Effectiveness* refers to the impact of the
intervention or technology under routine clinical conditions when administered
to a more generalized patient population (52). Clinical trials often apply strict
selection criteria, retain highly motivated subjects (and physicians), and involve
close clinical monitoring. Cost-effectiveness analyses that are incorporated into
clinical trials designed to measure efficacy must adjust the outcomes to reflect
what is likely to occur in clinical practice. Such factors as patient noncompliance,
comorbid conditions, and less intensive monitoring should be considered and
outcomes adjusted (usually downward) to reflect these clinical realities.

These issues are highlighted in the studies by Gerdtham and colleagues
and Adelroth and Thompson. The lack of experimental design in the study by
Gerdtham and colleagues and the very small sample size of the Adelroth and
Thompson study restrict the internal validity and conclusions of these two studies.
However, these studies make use of an alternative evaluation strategy wherein
the authors attempt to measure population effectiveness of the inhaled product
in the absence of the constraints of a clinical study design (6). The strength of the
conclusions by Gerdtham and colleagues lies in the longitudinal and generalizable
nature of the data.

A pharmacoeconomic analysis must also have a clearly stated *perspective*.
Because the analysis includes economic as well as clinical information, a variety
of perspectives are possible. In particular, one may take a societal perspective,
a health insurance payer perspective, or a patient perspective when including
economic costs and benefits in the analysis. Obviously, the relative cost-effectiveness will differ depending on which of these perspectives is taken. Most researchers in the field favor the societal perspective because it includes *all* costs and
benefits that occur as a result of treatment, not just those that accrue to single
parties such as insurers or patients. This is particularly important for a disease
such as asthma, since treatments affect family members as well as the patient.

The type of economic analysis (e.g., cost-effectiveness, cost-utility, cost-benefit) should also be clearly defined and justified. As noted above, the patient population and context of the study will often limit the type of economic analysis that can be performed. For example, evaluations of patient preferences for a cost-utility study using the interview technique of the standard gamble would be almost impossible to perform in an asthma study that involved children (although the preferences of the parents may be of some value).

Selection of the type of economic analysis will to a large extent determine the elements that are included as costs and measures of effectiveness for the study. Nevertheless, they should be carefully detailed and justified. As noted above, costs should at least include all direct medical care costs and ideally will include direct nonmedical care costs and indirect costs (production losses). Intangible (psychic) costs are often omitted due to practical difficulties in collecting and valuing them and because it is often unclear whether they should be included as costs or benefits of therapy in cost-effectiveness analyses.

The *time horizon* for the economic analysis must be clearly stated and justified and ideally should reflect the duration of illness for asthma patients. Several of the papers noted above reported clinical and economic results for trials that were 8 to 12 weeks in duration. Asthma is not a disease that lasts 8 to 12 weeks. Such short-term studies can be misleading and are more likely to produce conflicting results if the patterns of disease can vary widely over the long term or if the disease tends to improve or worsen over time in typical patients. Short-term studies are not appropriate for economic evaluations of asthma therapies.

Because asthma is a chronic disease that can last for years or a lifetime, costs and benefits that accrue in the future must be *discounted* to their present value for the analysis. Discounting reflects the notion that individuals prefer to enjoy benefits today rather than the same level of benefits at some future date. Equal discounting of costs and benefits is important for two major reasons. The first is consistency—since the effects are being valued relative to costs, future values of both should be adjusted similarly (53). The second has been popularly referred to as the "Keeler-Cretin paradox," so-named after the authors who first described it. In short, Keeler and Cretin demonstrate that if the effectiveness of a program is discounted at a rate that is less than the discount rate for costs, the cost-effectiveness of that program can always be improved by postponing the start of the program. The result is an illogical scenario where beneficial programs are always delayed indefinitely (54). A "standard" discount rate of 3% per annum for costs and benefits has recently been proposed for economic evaluations of medical therapies (8).

Inevitably, pharmacoeconomic evaluations contain imperfect information and the level and extent of uncertainty within the study necessitates further exploration. Therefore, there is a need for *sensitivity analyses* in every cost-effectiveness study. Sensitivity analysis is the process of varying the level of one or more input parameters (such as the efficacy of a particular asthma medication) to evaluate the impact of varying assumptions on the overall result of the study. Input parameters that greatly affect the outcome when they are varied are examined closely for their robustness and accuracy. In this way, sensitivity analysis gives the reader an appreciation for the validity and reliability of the results.

Finally, the "bottom line" of a pharmacoeconomic analysis should be stated clearly. Therapies should be described as either "cost-effective" or "cost-ineffective" in unequivocal terms whenever possible. Additionally, the discussion should include potential clinical and policy implications of the findings.

XI. Linking Cost-Effectiveness Analysis with the Development of Clinical Practice Guidelines

Ideally, pharmacoeconomic evidence should be weighed along with clinical data when creating clinical practice guidelines for asthma management. Since much of the drive for guidelines has been the growing economic importance of asthma, it makes sense to bring formal economic analysis into the guidelines development process, using methods that are agreed upon by leaders in the field. Economic data can then be linked with clinical data as part of the evidence that justifies the management strategy that is outlined in the guideline.

To date, pharmacoeconomic data have not been explicitly factored into clinical practice guidelines for asthma. This is partly because pharmacoeconomic studies have varied widely in quality and because the outcomes measures vary widely from study to study. Two issues must be addressed before pharmacoeconomic data can be effectively integrated into the clinical practice guideline process. First, the methodological quality of the studies must improve substantially. Second, meaningful and relevant outcome variable(s) must be selected for inclusion in all analyses to facilitate comparison of different interventions. A recent report by the NHLBI Workshop on Asthma Outcome Measures for Research Studies provides a useful review of the many end points available to researchers who study asthma (55). The National Asthma Education and Prevention Program Task Force on the Cost-Effectiveness, Quality, and Financing of Asthma Care has recommended the use of symptom-free days as the standard outcome measure for cost-effectiveness evaluation of asthma treatments, in part because the measure reflects aggregate disease morbidity (56).

XII. Conclusion

Health care decision makers are interested in employing rational approaches to allocating resources among patients with chronic disease. Many embrace pharmacoeconomic evaluations as a set of tools to improve asthma care, given the conflicts generated by constrained health budgets and a rising demand for medical care. However, before pharmacoeconomic data can be integrated into the decision-making process the methodologic standards of these studies must improve and common measures of outcome (such as symptom-free days) must be incorporated into all new evaluations. High standards will ensure that the internal and external validity of these studies is apparent to decision makers and researchers. Common measures of outcome will ensure the comparability of data on the economic value of different treatments, particularly as new therapies are introduced into practice. When methods and outcomes for pharmacoeconomic evaluations of the most commonly used therapies are standardized, this important information can be made part of the process of creating clinical practice guidelines for asthma.

References

1. Cowley, G., and Underwood, A. (1997). Why Ebonie can't breathe. *Newsweek* **129**: 58–67.
2. Health report. (1997). *Time* **149**(20):25.
3. Drummond, M.F., Stoddart, G.L., and Torrance, G.W. (1987). *Methods for the Economic Evaluation of Health Care Programmes.* New York, Oxford University Press.
4. Banta, H.D., and Luce, B.R. (1993). *Health Care Technology and Its Assessment.* New York, Oxford University Press.
5. Ellwood, P. (1988). Outcomes management: a technology of patient experience. *N. Engl. J. Med.*, **318**:1549–1556.
6. Weiss, K.B., Gergen, P.J., and Hodgson, T.A. (1992). An economic evaluation of asthma in the United States. *N. Engl. J. Med.*, **326**:862–866.
7. von Neumann, J., and Morgenstern, O. (1994). *Theory of Games and Economic Behaviour.* Princeton, N.J., Princeton University Press.
8. *Cost-Effectiveness in Health and Medicine.* Edited by M.R. Gold, J.E. Siegal, L.B. Russell, and M.C. Weinstein. New York, Oxford University Press, 1996.
9. Detsky, A. (1993). Guideline for economic analysis of pharmaceutical products: a draft document for Ontario and Canada. *PharmacoEconomics*, **3**:354–361.
10. Johannesson, M., and Weinstein, M.C. (1996). Designing and conducting cost-benefit analyses. In *Quality of Life and Pharmacoeconomics in Clinical Trials*, 2nd ed. Edited by B. Spilker. Philadelphia, Lippincott-Raven.
11. Barnes, P.J., and Pedersen, S. (1993). Efficacy and safety of inhaled corticosteroids in asthma. *Am. Rev. Respir. Dis.*, **148**(4 Pt 2):S1–S26.
12. Adelroth, E., and Thompson, S. (1988). Advantages of high-dose inhaled budesonide. *Lancet*, **1**:476.
13. Gerdtham, U.G., Hertzman, P., Boman, G., and Jonsson, B. (1996). Impact of inhaled corticosteroids on asthma hospitalization in Sweden. *Appl. Econ.*, **28**:1591–1599.
14. Campbell, L.M., Simpson, R.J., and Turbitt, M.L., et al. (1993). A comparison of the cost-effectiveness of budesonide 400 μg/day and 800μg/day in the management of mild-to-moderate asthma in general practice. *Br. J. Med. Econ.*, **6**:67–74.
15. Rees, T.P., Lennox, B., Timney, A.P., et al. (1993). Comparison of increasing the

dose of budesonide to 800 mg/day with a maintained dose of 400 µg/day in mild to moderate asthmatic patients. *Eur. J. Clin. Res.*, **4**:67–77.

16. O'Byrne, P., Cuddy, L., Taylor, D.W., Birch, S., Morris, J., and Syrotuik, J. (1996). Efficacy and cost benefit of inhaled corticosteroids in patients considered to have mild asthma in primary care. *Can. Respir. J.* **3(3)**:169–175.

17. Connett, G.J., Lenney, W., and McConchie, S.M. (1993). The cost-effectiveness of budesonide in severe asthmatics aged one to three years. *Br. J. Med. Econ.*, **6**:127–134.

18. Rutten-van Mölken, M.P., Van Doorslaer, E.K., Jansen, M.C., et al. (1993). Cost-effectiveness of inhaled corticosteroid plus bronchodilator therapy versus bronchodilator monotherapy in children with asthma. *PharmacoEconomics*, **4(4)**:257–270.

19. Rutten-van Mölken, M.P., Van Doorslaer, E.K., Jansen, M.C., Kerstjens, H.A., and Rutten, F.F. (1995). Costs and effects of inhaled corticosteroids and bronchodilators in asthma and chronic obstructive pulmonary disease. *Am. J. Respir. Crit. Care Med.*, **151**:975–982.

20. Booth, P.C., Wells, N.E.J., and Morrison, A.K. (1996). A comparison of the cost effectiveness of alternative prophylactic therapies in childhood asthma. *Pharmaco-Economics*, **10(3)**:262–268.

21. Karalus, N.C., and Harrison, A.C. (1987). Inhaled high-dose beclomethasone in chronic asthma. *N.Z. Med. J.*, **100**:306–308.

22. Wennergren, G., Kristjasson, S., and Strannegard, I. (1996). Decrease in hospitalization for treatment of childhood asthma with increased use of antiinflammatory treatment, despite an increase in prevalence. *J. Allergy Clin. Immunol.*, **97**:742–748.

23. Donahue, J.G., Weiss, S.T., Livingston, J.M., Goetsch, M.A., Greineder, D.K., and Platt, R. (1997). Inhaled steroids and the risk of hospitalization for asthma. *J.A.M.A.*, **277**:887–891.

24. Suissa, S., Dennis, R., Ernst, P., Sheehy, O., and Wood-Dauphinee, S. (1997). Effectiveness of the leukotriene receptor antagonist zafirlukast for mild-to-moderate asthma: a randomized, double-blind, placebo-controlled trial. *Ann. Intern. Med.*, **126(3)**:177–183.

25. Perera, B.J.C. (1995). Efficacy and cost effectiveness of inhaled steroids in asthma in a developing country. *Arch. Dis. Child.*, **72**:312–316.

26. Sculpher, M., and Buxton, M. Episode-free days as endpoints in economic evaluations of asthma therapy. *PharmacoEconomics*, **4(5)**:345–352.

27. Ross, R.N., Morris, M., Sakowitz, S.R., and Berman, B.A. (1988). Cost-effectiveness of including cromolyn sodium in the treatment program for asthma: a retrospective, record-based study. *Clin. Ther.*, **10(2)**:188–203.

28. Tierce, J.C., Meller, W., Berlow, B., and Gerth, W.C. (1989). Assessing the cost of albuterol inhalers in the Michigan and California Medicaid programs: a total cost-of-care approach. *Clin. Ther.*, **11**:53–61.

29. Emerman, C.L., Cydulka, R.K., Effron, D., Lukens, T.W., Gershman, H., and Boehm, S.P. (1991). A randomized, controlled comparison of isoetharine and albuterol in the treatment of acute asthma. *Ann. Emerg. Med.*, **20**:1090–1093.

30. Littenburg, B., and Gluck, E.H. (1986). A controlled trial of methylprednisolone in the emergency treatment of acute asthma. *N. Engl. J. Med.*, **314**:150–152.

31. Jasper, A.C., Mohsenifar, Z., Kahan S., Goldberg H.S., and Koerner, S.K. (1987). Cost-benefit comparison of aerosol bronchodilator delivery methods in hospitalized patients. *Chest*, **91**:614–618.

32. Summer, W., Elston, R., Tharpe, L., Nelson, S., and Haponik, E.F. (1989). Aerosol bronchodilator delivery methods: relative impact on pulmonary function and cost of respiratory care. *Arch. Intern. Med.*, **149**:618–623.

33. Green, L., (1974). Toward cost-benefit evaluations of health education: some concepts, methods and examples. *Health. Ed. Monog.*, **2**:34–64.

34. Boulet, L., Champan, K., Green, L., and FitzGerald, J. (1994). Asthma education. *Chest*, **106(4 suppl.)**:184S–196S.

35. Windsor, R., Bailey, W., Richards, J.J., Manzella, B., Soong, S., and Brooks, M. (1990). Evaluation of the efficacy and cost effectiveness of health education methods to increase medication adherence among adults with asthma. *Am. J. Public Health*, **80**:1519–1521.

36. Muhlhauser, I., Richter, B., Kraut, D., Weske, G., Worth, H., and Berger, M. (1991). Evaluation of a structured treatment and teaching program on asthma. *J. Intern. Med.*, **238(2)**:157–164.

37. Trautner, C., Richter, B., and Berger, M. (1993). Cost-effectiveness of a structured treatment and teaching programme on asthma. *Eur. Respir. J.*, **6**:1485–1491.

38. Bolton, M., Tilley, B., Kuder, J., Reeves, T., and Schultz, I. (1991). The cost and effectiveness of an education program for adults who have asthma. *J. Gen. Intern. Med.*, **6**:401–407.

39. Sondergaard, B., Davidsen, F., Kirkeby, B., et al. (1992). The economics of an intensive education program for asthmatic patients: a prospective controlled trial. *PharmacoEconomics*, **1**:207–212.

40. Fireman, P., Friday, G., Gira, C., Vierthaler, W., and Michaels, L. (1981). Teaching self-management skills to asthmatic children and their parents in an ambulatory care setting. *Pediatrics*, **68**:341–348.

41. Lewis, C., Rachelefsky, G., Lewis, M., De la Soto, A., and Kaplan M. (1984). A randomized trial of ACT (asthma care training) for kids. *Pediatrics*, **74**:478–486.

42. Clark, N., Feldman, C., Evans, D., Levison, M., Wasilewski, Y., Mellins, R. (1986). The impact of health education on frequency and cost of health care use by low income children with asthma. *J. Allergy Clin. Immunol.*, 78(1 pt.1):108–115.

43. Neri, M., Migliori, G.B., Spanevello, A., Berra, D., Nicolini, E., Landoni, C.V., Ballardini, L., Sommaruga, M., and Zanon, P. (1996). Economic analysis of two structured treatment and teaching programs on asthma. *Allergy*, **51**:313–319.

44. Westley, C., Spiecher, R., Starr, L., Simons, P., Sanders, B., Marsh, W., Comer, C., and Harvey, R. (1997). Cost effectiveness of an allergy consultation in the management of asthma. *Allergy Asthma Proc.*, **18(1)**:15–18.

45. Drummond, M., Brandt, A., Luce, B., and Rovira, J. (1993). Standardizing methodologies for economic evaluation in health care: practice, problems, and potential. *Int. J. Technol. Assess. Health Care*, **9**:26–36.

46. Levenson, T., Grammer, L.C., Yarnold, P.R., and Patterson, R. (1997). Cost-effective management of malignant potentially fatal asthma. *Allergy Asthma Proc.*, **18(2)**: 73–78.

47. Windsor, R., Bailey, W., Richards, J., et al. (1990). Evaluation of the efficacy and

cost-effectiveness of health education methods to increase medication adherence among adults with asthma. *Am. J. Public Health*, **80**:1519–1521.

48. Deter, H. (1986). Cost-benefit analysis of psychosomatic therapy in asthma. *Psychosom. Res.*, **30**:173–182.

49. Folgering, H., Rooyakkers, J., and Herwaarden, C. (1994). Education and cost/benefit ratios in pulmonary patients. *Monaldi Arch. Chest Dis.*, **49(2)**:166–168.

50. Sondergaard, B., Davidsen, F., Kirkeby, B., et al. (1992). The economics of an intensive education programme for asthmatic patients. *PharmacoEconomics*, **1**:207–212.

51. Tougaard, L., Krone, T., Sorknaes, A., and Ellegaard, H. (1992). Economic benefits of teaching patients with chronic obstructive pulmonary disease about their illness. *Lancet*, **339**:1517–1520.

52. Drummond, M.F., and Davies, L. (1991). Economic analysis alongside clinical trials: revisiting the methodological issues. *Int. J. Technol. Assess. Health Care*, **7**:561–573.

53. Wienstein, M.C., and Stason, W.B. (1977). Foundations of cost-effectiveness analysis for health and medical practices. *N. Engl. J. Med.*, **296**:716–721.

54. Keeler, E.B., and Cretin, S. (1983). Discounting of life-saving and other nonmonetary effects. *Mgt. Sci.*, **29**:300–306.

55. National Heart, Lung, and Blood Institute. (1994). Asthma outcome measures. *Am. J. Respir. Crit. Care Med.*, **149(2)**:S1–S90.

56. Sullivan, S.D., Elixhauser, A., Buist, A.S., Luce, B.R., Eisenberg, J., and Weiss, K.B. (1996). National Asthma Education and Prevention Program working group report on the cost effectiveness of asthma care. *Am. J. Respir. Crit. Care Med.*, **154(3 pt. 2)**:S84–S95.

13

Cost and Outcome Implications for Prevention

ANNE ELIXHAUSER

Agency for Health Care Policy and
  Research
Rockville, Maryland

**NANCY KLINE LEIDY and
MICHAEL T. HALPERN**

MEDTAP International Inc.
Bethesda, Maryland

I. Introduction

Asthma death rates are increasing steadily and hospitalizations for asthma are on the rise, especially among children (1). The concomitant personal and monetary costs of asthma have received increasing attention and the cost of illness for asthma has been examined in many countries (2,3,4). One unanimous conclusion is that the prevention of asthma and its exacerbations should be a high priority because of the enormous monetary savings that are possible by preventing asthma-related use of health care services and averting loss of productivity due to morbidity and premature mortality (5). One author suggested that the prevalence of asthma in the next generation could be reduced substantially through preventive efforts (6). Although the costs of asthma are well understood, there is a need to assess the relative cost-effectiveness of asthma interventions (2), especially those aimed at the prevention of asthma and its exacerbations.

Asthma is a multifactorial condition related to genetics, the environment, allergens, and socioeconomic status (1). Death rates from asthma in the United States are significantly higher among people living in less affluent countries (7) and hospitalization rates for asthma are higher among people in poverty, particularly among poor children (8). Although the link between poverty and asthma has not been established in all countries, it nonetheless illustrates the capacity for prevention to play a major role in reducing the burden of asthma. Poverty is associated with a host of factors that contribute to increased incidence of asthma and more severe disease. In addition to lack of access to health care services, insufficient continuity of care, and lower likelihood of appropriate treatment with anti-inflammatory drugs, poverty-related causes of asthma-related morbidity and mortality include exposure to allergens and inadequate systems of social and educational support (9).

This chapter examines the health and economic implications of interventions aimed at the prevention of asthma. Compared with the treatment of asthma, considerably less is known about its prevention. Research into this area is a relatively recent phenomenon; thus many of the conclusions about the effectiveness of preventive interventions are speculative. This chapter provides alternative typologies of preventive interventions for asthma, focusing on primary interventions, and reviews evidence for the effectiveness of efforts to prevent asthma. Finally, we provide a conceptual framework for evaluating the costs and outcomes of interventions for the primary prevention of asthma.

II. Prevention of Asthma

A. Typologies of Asthma Prevention

One way of categorizing preventive interventions for asthma entails dividing them by stage of disease (10,11). *Primary prevention* of asthma aims at averting the onset of the condition by avoiding risk factors that would lead to its development. *Secondary prevention* strives to intervene while the condition is not yet symptomatic in order to avoid its progression. *Tertiary prevention* seeks to interrupt the course of active disease to prevent worsening of asthma and development of complications—that is, to prevent morbidity and mortality among patients with known disease. Prevention of asthma exacerbations among patients with known disease would be considered secondary or tertiary depending on the severity of the asthma.

An alternative typology of prevention, which has not been applied to asthma, focuses on how the intervention is delivered and also divides preventive interventions into three categories (12). First, *clinical prevention* relies on the delivery of medical services from health care providers to patients. In the case of asthma, this would include early detection and medical prophylaxis programs to prevent the onset of asthma symptoms among high risk infants and children and the treatment of existing asthma to prevent exacerbations. Second, *behavioral prevention*, or health promotion, focuses on changing individual behavior and lifestyle. Asthma-related behavioral prevention would include encouraging cessation of harmful activities, such as smoking, or promoting healthy behaviors, such as use of insecticides to reduce dust mite or cockroach exposure, or by installing air filters in the home.

Third, *environmental prevention*, or health protection, focuses on changing the environment to a more healthful one. It differs from other types of prevention because it does not require individual behavior change and thus avoids the concomitant problems of individual adherence. Examples of such interventions aimed at asthma would be air pollution prevention strategies to reduce exposure to particulates and ozone or engineering solutions to avoid occupational exposure to hazardous substances through improved ventilation or spillproof containers. Environmental prevention requires some degree of societal or organizational commitment, rather than individual behavior change, and can often be accomplished through governmental regulations. In examining the cost-benefits of such programs for reducing asthma, one finds that the costs are generally borne by society as a whole through increased taxation or by certain sectors of society (such as industry) through imposed costs, while the direct benefits may accrue to a relatively small minority, such as asthma-prone patients. However, the benefits of environmental interventions are likely to have a broader scope, benefiting other at-risk groups as well, such as patients with other respiratory or cardiac ailments.

An ecological model that roughly parallels this intervention-based typology is suggested in this text by Halfon and Newacheck (Chap. 3). This model divides asthma interventions into those aimed at children, at the microsystem surrounding the child (e.g., families and school), at the exosystem (e.g., the community), and at the macrosystem (e.g., air pollution policies).

Bailey et al. (10) provide an another typology of asthma interventions based upon the types of interventions that are available. Because so little is known about the primary prevention of asthma, they group interventions into (a) those related to risk factors and the natural history of the disease and (b) interventions related to therapy of the condition. This chapter focuses on the first group of interventions. Another chapter in this text covers topics related to prevention of respiratory exacerbations in known asthmatics (Ramsey and Sullivan, Chap. 12).

B. Primary Prevention of Asthma

Reducing the Incidence of Asthma: Children

Relatively little is known about interventions to prevent the onset of asthma; however, evidence provided by epidemiological and clinical studies suggests that primary prevention potentially could have an important role in averting the onset of asthma. Environmental exposures have been implicated in the development of asthma. There is clear evidence that passive exposure to tobacco smoke exacerbates asthma symptoms among children with known disease, resulting in additional medication use and increased visits to emergency rooms. However, there is also evidence that passive smoke exposure may be linked to the onset of asthma—that is, passive smoking may actually cause asthma (13). While a longitudinal study of 74,000 women found that smoking does not appear to be a cause of asthma (14), a cross-sectional survey of over 11,000 children found a link between exposure to tobacco smoke and symptoms of wheezing (15). Genetics and exposure to smoking have been implicated in heightened airway responsiveness in infants (16), and there is some suggestion that there may be a link between prenatal exposure to smoking and airway responsiveness. Another study examining the contribution of prenatal factors suggested that maternal age and birth weight are important determinants of asthma as well (8).

Bronchial hyperresponsiveness appears to be one of the most critical risk factors correlated with the subsequent development of asthma, although it is possible to have hyperresponsiveness without asthma and vice versa (17). Murphy (11) suggests that studies are needed to assess the relationship between asymptomatic airway hyperresponsiveness and the risk of developing asthma. Such studies would potentially identify people who are at risk of developing asthma and might enable the development of interventions to intercede early in the course of the disease.

The effects of air pollution on asthma have been examined and a positive association was found between the level of particulates and the symptoms of shortness of breath and wheezing among African-American children with asthma (18). This suggests that air pollution prevention or reducing exposure to outdoor air on days when particulate matter is high may be a feasible approach to reducing the burden of asthma. It has been reported that increases in ozone levels are also associated with declines in lung function (19). Again, the role of air pollution in the onset of asthma has not been explored.

Viral respiratory infection, specifically croup and bronchiolitis, in childhood has been associated with increased airway responsiveness even when controlling for exposure to maternal smoking (20). There has been subsequent evidence linking infections with human rhinovirus, parainfluenza virus, and respiratory syncytial virus early in life to the development of asthma (21, 22). Such research opens the possibility of using antiviral agents or anti-immunological factors as measures to prevent asthma completely; however, additional biomedical research is required to establish this link and to develop specific primary preventive measures.

Studies suggest the possibility of primary prevention of asthma through early childhood interventions among children at risk of developing asthma. Aeroallergens, such as cat allergens, have been implicated in the development of asthma among children (23,24) especially among children with atopy (25). Similar findings have been reported among adults sensitized to cat allergen (26). Cockroach allergen has been implicated in asthma in the National Cooperative Inner-City Asthma Study (27). This study used a multifactorial approach in reducing environmental exposure to cockroach, dust mite, and cat allergens by using plastic bed covers and insecticides. These interventions were found to be effective in reducing asthma symptoms among children; however, their effectiveness in preventing asthma in asymptomatic individuals has not been assessed. Warner (28) identified the need for further prospective studies of reducing aeroallergen exposure among high-risk infants, defined as infants with a family history of atopy. She also suggested that it may be possible to identify high-risk infants through family history and cord blood IgE levels; however, she warned that the specificity of such diagnostic markers is low.

Early observational studies (for example, 29) had indicated that infants who were fed breast milk were much less likely to develop asthma than babies who were bottle-fed, especially among atopic children. In a randomized study, Fabre et al. (30) identified infants with elevated levels of IgE in their umbilical cord serum. These infants were placed on a diet that emphasized breast-feeding and restricted intake of sensitizing foods such beans, wheat, chocolate, eggs, and fish. In addition, measures were taken to reduce exposure to aeroallergens during infancy. The rate of developing asthma was 13.3% in the intervention group compared with 31.7% in a control group. However, the value of breast-feeding as a means of preventing allergy and asthma remains controversial (31), as does the role of nutrition in asthma (32,33).

The role of early exposure to allergens was further investigated in the Isle of Wight Study, where infants at risk of atopy were randomized to treatment and control groups. Patients in the treatment group received soy-based formula or breast milk from their mothers who followed a nonallergenic diet and their families undertook dust mite eradication measures (mattress covers and acaricide treatments of the home). When children were evaluated at 1 year of age, 40% of infants in the control group had evidence of allergy, compared with 18% of infants in the treatment group, and rates of asthma were significantly higher in the control group (34). However, at 2 and 4 years of age, the differences in asthma rates disappeared even though the findings for other allergies persisted (35,36).

There is not complete agreement on the role of the environment in the genesis of asthma. Harris et al. (37) conducted a study among 5864 twin pairs in Norway to examine the relative impacts of genetics and the environment on the development of asthma. They found that 75% of the variability in risk of developing asthma was attributable to genetic influences and that the remaining 25% was explained primarily by nonshared environmental influences. These results led the authors to conclude that shared environment during infancy and childhood is less predictive of development of asthma than genetics and that environmental interventions may have limited impact on reducing asthma risk.

Clearly, there is a critical need for more research into the link between environmental exposure and the onset of asthma and the development of specific interventions to reduce the incidence of asthma. Despite the controversy and need for more information, there was enough evidence for a consensus statement from New Zealand on the preventive management of asthma to conclude that although asthma is largely genetic in origin, environmental factors such as prenatal exposure to maternal smoking during pregnancy, passive smoking during infancy, and exposure to aeroallergens in infancy may have a role in primary prevention (38).

Thus there is a continued need for randomized trials to assess the role of early childhood exposure in the genesis of asthma (33).

We found two studies that examined a pharmacological approach to preventing the development of asthma. Ketotifen is an oral prophylactic medication for the long-term treatment of asthma. Because of its antihistaminic, antianaphylactic and anti-inflammatory effect, ketotifen is an effective treatment for allergies as well. In one study, children without asthma but with non-food-related atopic dermatitis were administered ketotifen for 1 year (39). Approximately 13% of the treated children developed asthma during the course of that year, compared with over 41% of children in the control group. A 3-year study of administering ketotifen to children with elevated serum IgE levels and a family history of asthma reported that 9% of treated children developed asthma, compared with 35% of untreated children (40). Although these results appear to be promising, more work is needed to investigate the effectiveness of pharmacological preventive strategies and to explore practical strategies for identifying high-risk children.

The cost of illness for asthma, including the cost of asthma in children, is described elsewhere in this text (Jönsson, Chap. 11). There have been no economic evaluations of interventions to reduce the onset of asthma among children.

Reducing the Incidence of Occupational Asthma

Occupational asthma is defined as reductions in airflow and airway hyperresponsiveness due to exposure at the workplace. Two major classes of occupational asthma have been defined based on the precipitating causes. Sensitizer-induced asthma is caused by high-molecular-weight (e.g., animals, wood, or plants) or low-molecular-weight (chemicals, dyes, metals) antigens and is an immunologically mediated disease. Irritant-induced asthma is caused by dusts, fumes, and gases and is often referred to as *reactive airway dysfunction syndrome*, or RADS (41). Sensitizer-induced asthma generally has a long latency period following initial exposure, while irritant-induced asthma can result from single or multiple exposures and is often the result of workplace accidents. Approximately 250 substances are known to cause occupational asthma, and up to 20% of all asthma may be attributable to workplace exposure (42).

The hallmark of prevention of occupational asthma is to avoid exposure. Most interventions fall into the environmental prevention category and consist of design modification, appropriate ventilation, and substitution of nonsensitizing substances for those likely to cause asthma. There is also a role for training in safe work practices and in quick response to industrial accidents, monitoring and surveillance, and smoking cessation, since concomitant smoking has been shown to increase sensitivity to workplace exposure (41,43).

The economic outcomes associated with occupational asthma have been examined (44). Workers who developed asthma and who were subsequently removed from the job suffered an average decline in income of 54% because financial compensation did not counterbalance their loss in income, although their respiratory symptoms and lung function improved. Workers who remained on the job and continued to be exposed to the precipitating causes of asthma also suffered some income loss, although to a smaller degree than workers removed from their jobs (35%); however, their lung function continued to deteriorate. The authors speculated that workers chose to remain on the job for financial reasons, despite continued poor health, and suggested that remuneration should aim at retraining and relocation rather than disability compensation. Additional information on occupational asthma is presented by Blanc (Chap. 4).

Summary

In summary, the Guidelines for the Diagnosis and Management of Asthma (45) concluded that there is sufficient evidence implicating occupational exposure in the development of asthma and that the workplace is the only setting where primary prevention has been demonstrated to be effective. Research continues on the role of avoiding early exposure to aeroallergens, tobacco smoke, and food allergens as a means of preventing the development of asthma.

III. Economic Evaluations of Primary Prevention

Rutten-Van Mölken et al. (46) reviewed the health economic literature on asthma care, focusing on the management of known asthma. They suggested that additional study is needed in examining pharmaceutical interventions for asthma treatment as well as diagnostic and monitoring technologies; however, their review did not evaluate primary preventive interventions. An exhaustive literature search was conducted to identify studies assessing the economic impact of primary preventive interventions in asthma and no studies were found. Given the lack of firm evidence on the efficacy and effectiveness of primary prevention in children, it is not surprising that no economic evaluations have been performed.

A. A Framework for Economic Evaluation

The remainder of this chapter outlines a framework for evaluating the health economic implications of primary preventive interventions for asthma. Following the guidelines provided by Gold et al. (47), we develop a research strategy for evaluating an intervention aimed at the primary prevention of asthma among high-risk children, in order to illustrate the principles that should be considered in conducting a health economic assessment.

As more research evidence accumulates on the efficacy of such interventions, a strategy for the primary prevention of asthma among high-risk infants and children could be outlined in detail. However, it is critical that evidence from basic research, consisting of etiological studies and clinical trials, be available to establish the efficacy of the interventions. As efficacy studies are being conducted, economic modeling studies can be undertaken to project the economic impact of the interventions. After efficacy has been demonstrated, effectiveness studies can evaluate the impact of the intervention under conditions of routine use of application, and can include an economic component in the evaluation study (12).

Objective of the Analysis

As described above, the genetic basis of asthma has been established and there is epidemiological evidence of an association between asthma and atopy in both adults and children. Furthermore, there is some evidence that avoiding early exposure to aeroallergens, tobacco smoke, and food allergens may be an effective means of preventing the development of asthma. Given the condition's multifactorial nature, an intervention aimed at primary prevention of asthma among children would ideally be a multifaceted approach that would target interventions based on family history and evidence of atopy, seek to reduce exposure to indoor allergens (such as dust mites and cockroaches) as well as food allergens, and avoid exposure to tobacco smoke. The objective of an economic assessment as outlined here would be to evaluate the cost-effectiveness or cost-benefit of alternative methods of primary prevention of asthma in high-risk children.

Audience for the Study

The primary audience for the study would be health care practitioners who will be most likely responsible for establishing a family history of asthma, identifying patients at risk of developing asthma, prescribing the necessary allergen preventive measures, and recommending smoking cessation for adults in the household. Another audience will be third-party payers, who will bear the costs of preventive medications (if any are prescribed) and smoking cessation medications. The final audience will be groups responsible for enunciating recommendations for prevention of asthma such as the National Asthma Education and Prevention Program and the U.S. Preventive Services Task Force. Individuals will most likely bear the largest burden of preventive interventions such as dust mite eradication and limitation of exposure to other allergens and cigarette smoke.

The choice of the audience for the study influences what parameters are examined. For example, a study that is conducted from the perspective of the health care insurer would be limited to an evaluation of the costs and consequences that are relevant to the third party payer (such as asthma medications and emergency department visits) and may have a relatively short time horizon given the high rates of turnover in some health plans. In general, the societal perspective is preferred, because cost shifting from one sector to another is avoided. For example, the societal perspective will account for out-of-pocket costs borne by families that are not relevant from the perspective of the third-party payer.

Type of Analysis

An elementary approach to evaluating the economic effects of prevention is the Basic Assessment Scheme for Intervention Costs and Consequences, or BASICC (48). This approach evaluates only the costs of the intervention itself and the direct savings in health care resource use attributable to the intervention; it does not include the costs associated with changes in productivity, nor does it include a direct assessment of health outcomes in their natural units (e.g., symptom-free days or cases prevented). Health outcomes are evaluated only insofar as they affect use of health care resources. Such an analysis results in a net cost calculation:

Cost *program* + cost *side effects* − cost *health outcome averted*

While this approach is rudimentary, it is simple and relatively straightforward and may suffice, especially for initial studies and early modeling of the economic consequences of interventions. Furthermore, if the audience for the study is the health care insurer (government or private), then this type of analysis is appropriate because it directly evaluates those factors most relevant to this group.

Alternatively, the study could be framed as a cost-effectiveness analysis (CEA), which would result in incremental cost-effectiveness ratios. The numerator consists of the monetary value of the program or intervention, health care resources, patient and caregiver time costs, and any other costs not related to health care. The denominator consists of the outcomes, which can be cases of asthma prevented, symptom-free days, years of life saved, or quality-adjusted life years (QALYs). The use of QALYs is particularly relevant to asthma interventions because it takes into account both mortality and morbidity. An outcome such as years of life saved measures only the mortality outcomes of a condition and would seriously underestimate the health consequences of asthma, since morbidity and reduced functional capacity during an exacerbation are key features. The use of the outcome measure, cases of asthma prevented, might be appropriate; however, such a study outcome would not allow comparison with interventions for other conditions. Hence, QALYs are the ideal denominator because they facilitate comparisons with other studies, allowing decision makers to make resource allocation decisions across a wide array of conditions and interventions if measures of costs are similar. A cost-effectiveness analysis results in the following calculation:

$$\frac{\text{Total cost}_{program\ 1} - \text{total cost}_{program\ 2}}{\text{health outcome}_{program\ 1} + \text{health outcome}_{program\ 2}}$$

where total cost = cost of the intervention
                   + medical costs
                   + nonmedical costs
                   + productivity lost
                   + future medical costs
Health outcome = nonmonetary valuations of the outcomes of the program

The choice of which specific formulation to use would be based on a number of factors. For example, in the early stages of evaluating an intervention, the net cost approach may be appropriate for initial investigations into the economic consequences of the intervention. The availability of data and the resources available to perform an analysis would be additional determining factors.

Perspective

The purpose of the analysis is to provide information to a wide range of decision makers; thus, in general, the societal perspective should be taken, because it attempts to account for all costs and effects regardless of who experiences them. However, specific subgroups in society may be interested in the costs or benefits that will apply to them specifically. For example, the government may be particularly interested in the impact of an environmental preventive intervention on its budget, through expenditures for the intervention or for health benefit payments. Employers may be interested in interventions that affect worker productivity, worker's compensation claims, or health insurance costs. Individual patients will be interested in out-of-pocket expenditures. One approach is to conduct the study from the societal perspective and from one or more other perspectives of particular interest.

Other factors beyond costs are affected by the choice of perspective. For example, since third-party payers are likely to have a shorter time horizon than society as a whole (see below), the choice of discount rate is likely to be higher for studies conducted from the perspective of the third party payer.

Time Horizon

Time horizon refers to the length of time for which costs and consequences will be assessed. This time period should be defined in order to ensure that all relevant costs of the intervention are accounted for and that all pertinent consequences, both intended and unintended, are included (49). For an asthma prevention intervention, the time horizon will undoubtedly extend beyond the time frame for which data can reasonably be collected. Because of this, it will be necessary to model the lifetime health consequences and medical cost savings of preventing asthma. Information on the costs of treating asthma will be required for this modeling effort. A shorter time horizon can be taken; however, such an approach will disregard costs and effects that occur during a lifetime of dealing with a chronic illness and will tend to underestimate the impact of a preventive intervention.

This study could evaluate the costs of conducting an intervention among a cohort of children for a specified time period, e.g., the length of time required to prevent asthma among a significant proportion of the cohort under study, and then model the lifetime consequences of the program among that cohort. For those children in whom asthma was prevented, the lifetime costs of asthma would be prevented. For those children for whom the intervention failed, the lifetime costs of asthma would be an added cost. A critical factor that such a model will have to account for is that asthma in children or adults is not necessarily a lifetime illness.

Time Preference

In the current example, the costs of the intervention for a particular cohort of children are being incurred in the present and for the next several years, yet many of the consequences of that intervention (preventing a lifetime of asthma) will occur far into the future. Because of the differential timing of costs and consequences, it is necessary to discount future costs and consequences to their net present value, and the same discount rate should be applied to both nonmonetary and monetary components of the equation (50). For any prevention program, discounting future health effects can have a considerable effect on the results of analysis, since the bulk of the program costs are incurred now (at undiscounted dollar values), while the consequences occur far into the future when they are likely to be heavily discounted. This is even more profound for preventive interventions aimed at children when the health effects are even more distant temporally and discounting will reduce them to an even smaller value.

The necessity of discounting costs is not contested, since it is generally accepted that a dollar 1 year from now is worth less than a dollar now. For example, current expenditures for an intervention would not be subjected to any discounting unless they extended beyond a 1 year period. Similarly, any health outcomes expressed in monetary terms (health care resource use and lost productivity due to asthma) are also subjected to discounting if they occur more than 1 year in the future. On the other hand, considerable controversy has surrounded the practice of discounting health effects expressed in natural units because of a reluctance to devalue health outcomes just because they occur in the future. Indeed, guidelines in the United Kingdom, specify a lower discount rate for health outcomes than for costs (51,52). Specifically, there is concern that discounting health outcomes decreases the projected benefit of long-term health initiatives, many of which involved children. However, Lipscomb et al. (50) provide an example of why it is imperative that future health consequences be discounted at the same rate as future costs.

> Assume that an investment of $100 today would result in saving 10 lives (or 1 life per $10 investment). If the $100 were invested at a 10% rate of return, in 1 year it would be worth $110; and with this $110, it would be possible to save 11 lives. ... If the social decision maker is attempting to maximize the health output obtainable from the original $100 and if the value of future lives saved is not discounted, then the cost-effectiveness of the program is improved for every year it is delayed. ... The paradox persists if lives saved are discounted at any rate below 10%, the rate by which costs would be discounted in this example. [p. 221]

The choice of discount rate is another area of controversy. Rates ranging from 3% to 10% have been used; however Lipscomb et al. (50) recommend that 3% be used as the base case discount rate because it is most consistent with a commonly accepted conceptual basis for discounting, the shadow price of capital (based on rates of return for safe long-term investments). For sensitivity analyses, they recommend ranges of 0% (to assess the impact of discounting) to 7% (to reflect the real consumption rate of interest). It is easy to see that the higher the discount rate, the more future costs and consequences will be devalued, an issue especially relevant for preventive programs whose consequences occur far into the future.

The distaste that many express for the practice of discounting health effects can be dealt with through sensitivity analysis (described in more detail below), by differentially discounting health effects and costs. This makes it possible to compare results where both costs and effects are discounted to results that are based on discounted costs and undiscounted effects. Wide variations in results make explicit the trade-offs that will be involved in investing in a particular program and point to the need to consider issues other than efficiency when making decisions about health care interventions. Decisions about investing in such interventions should also take into account the value that we, as a society, place on children's health. Economic evaluations do not consider distributional or equity concerns; these issues must be weighed separately but simultaneously with efficiency in any resource allocation decision.

Target Population

For the current example, the target population is infants and children at high risk of developing asthma. A major determinant of the cost-effectiveness of such a program would be the ability to target a high-risk population. Factors such as elevated IgE levels, evidence of non-food-related atopic dermatitis, and a family history of asthma have shown some promise as screening criteria; however, it is not yet clear that these criteria have sufficient sensitivity or specificity. Without appropriate screening criteria to target a high-risk population, the intervention may be provided to many individuals who would not develop asthma; hence the costs of the intervention would not be offset by the averted costs of asthma prevented in the future.

It is possible to identify a number of subgroups within a population who would have varying levels of responsiveness to an intervention or who would be more or less costly to include in an intervention. For example, infants and children who meet two or more screening criteria might be more likely to develop asthma and could be considered a higher-risk population that would be more likely to benefit from an intervention. Younger children might also benefit more than would older children. Such population subgroups should be defined in the course of early etiologic and efficacy studies. With respect to the costs of delivering a program, it might be less costly to deliver a program to infants and children in a densely populated urban area where outreach is simpler than in rural areas (49).

Defining the Intervention and its Alternatives

In an economic evaluation, an intervention can only be compared with some alternative. That alternative may be doing nothing, or it may be some alternative intervention. All interventions should be described in sufficient detail to allow replication of the program. Screening criteria, age limits for patients, the length of the intervention, personnel involved, number of contacts with children and families, and other relevant characteristics of the intervention should be explicitly defined.

The most relevant comparator in any analysis is the status quo—that is, the most likely intervention for the population under study. Given that no other primary prevention programs exist for asthma, the most relevant comparator would be "no intervention."

A problem facing asthma prevention programs is the multifactorial nature of asthma. It is unlikely that a simple "magic bullet" will become available that will prevent asthma in all children at risk. On the other hand, clinical trials tend to be reductionist, isolating specific interventions in an attempt to identify "what works." Asthma prevention may well require a more global, multifactorial approach, employing a number of factors that interact to achieve success. However, specifying a more global strategy risks the criticism that is not possible to ascertain which feature of the program works for what specific subpopulation; furthermore, such an approach does not provide adequate guidance for those who wish to structure a program with more limited resources.

Scope of the Study

As a part of designing the study, it is necessary to specify its scope or to draw boundaries around the study because an intervention will have immediate as well as more distant effects. These effects can relate to the populations that are examined as well as types of health outcomes (49). A program aimed at preventing asthma among children will have its immediate effects on the children targeted for the intervention. However, other populations will be affected as well; for example, parents are likely to miss less work to care for a sick child. For this analysis, it would seem reasonable to include the impact on parents, since there are immediate economic effects that are associated with caring for sick children.

With respect to the types of health outcomes to be included, it is clear that health effects would be included. However, should non-health effects be considered as well? For example, should the costs of special education needs be included if the child with asthma misses too much school? The key to specifying the scope is to constrain the analysis to those populations and impacts that are likely to have a significant impact on the results of the analysis and to consider the needs of decision makers who will use the study to make resource allocation decisions, keeping in mind that no outcome should be neglected that would unduly impact one group over another.

Consequences

Consequences are the health outcomes associated with an intervention and form the denominator of the cost-effectiveness ratio. There are a number of health outcomes that could be assessed and incorporated into a cost-effectiveness analysis, the most common of which are cases of asthma prevented, symptom-free days, life years saved, and quality-adjusted life years saved.

Because the outcomes of an asthma program are expected to have an impact on morbidity and mortality, ideally we should assess health-related quality of life as well as survival or life-expectancy (47). While other outcomes might include changes in lung function or blood gas oxygenation, these clinically based measures are not amenable to presentation in cost-effectiveness analyses. These outcomes could be reflected indirectly in quality adjustments, thus quality-adjusted life years would be the preferable denominator for our cost-effectiveness ratio.

One of the challenges of measuring quality of life over a lifetime is that asthma is an episodic illness: periods of normal airway functioning are punctuated by exacerbations of the condition during which quality of life is reduced to varying degrees depending on the severity of the episode. A cost-effectiveness analysis that sought to evaluate the lifetime impact of a preventive intervention would have to estimate:

The number of asthma exacerbations over a lifetime

The impact of these exacerbations on quality of life—i.e., what is the divergence from the optimal health state

The length of time patients remain in the less than optimal health state

The reduction in quality of life associated with living with asthma even when the disease is under control

The reduction in quality of life due to side effects of asthma treatment

For use in cost-effectiveness analysis, health-related quality of life is expressed as quality adjusted life years, or QALYs, which are measured in terms of utilities, values that fall between 0.0 (worst possible health state) and 1.0 (best state) (see Chap. 15). We then measure divergences from this perfect state of health (assigning them weights less than 1.0) as well as the length of time the patient spends in that less-than-perfect state. Future QALYs are discounted as described above (47).

One method of obtaining health utility measures is to administer questionnaires to patients, such as the Disability Distress Index, the EuroQol, the Health Utilities Index, and the Quality of Well-Being Scale. All of these measure multiple domains of quality of life, including social functioning, psychological and emotional functioning, physical functioning and impairment, although each of them measures different dimensions with different levels of sensitivity (see Chaps. 5–7). Asthma-specific quality-of-life questionnaires for children have been reported (53).

An alternative is to develop descriptions of various health states, or scenarios, and then to ask patients or other respondents to rate these health states using methods such as the standard gamble and time trade-off techniques (54,55). Such scenarios could be structured so that respondents are asked to consider lifetime effects, including the recurrent and intermittent nature asthma exacerbations, the impact of adhering to a treatment regimen that must be continued despite lack of symptoms, and the short- and long-term side effects of treatments. One of the barriers to accomplishing this is that the long-term consequences of treatments such as inhaled glucocorticoids are not fully understood.

On the other hand, a more elementary analysis can be conducted, particularly as an initial modeling effort, to assess the relative economic impacts of a program. As described earlier, the BASICC approach is limited to an assessment of economic consequences. This approach may be particularly useful if the program results in lower health care costs over patients' lifetimes, and these lifetime cost savings are greater than the total costs of the intervention. Such an assessment could entail calculation of the total cost of the intervention delivered to all targeted individuals as well as the costs of side effects of the program, anticipated or unanticipated. From this sum, we would subtract out the costs that are averted because of cases of asthma prevented. The result of the analysis would be the net costs of the program (48). A study using the BASICC approach would be particularly amenable to using secondary data: effectiveness data could be drawn from early trials of preventive interventions and cost data potentially could be taken from asthma cost of illness studies.

Costs

A major choice facing the analyst is which costs will be included in the health care cost-effectiveness analysis. *Direct medical costs* are always included and reflect the use of medical resources to provide the intervention and to treat asthma. Physician services must be counted and then a dollar value assigned, commonly using national reimbursement rates. Emergency room services must similarly be counted. Outpatient drugs, supplies (such as spacers), and equipment (such as spirometers) are an important part of asthma care and must often be captured through patient self-report when patients' insurance does not cover these items. Also included in this category are the costs associated with the intervention, such as screening and identifying patients, personnel time to educate patients' families about allergen avoidance, costs of special diets, mattress covers, and insecticide treatments for the home.

The resource use associated with acute-care hospitalizations can be captured by measuring total length of stay, length of stay in the intensive care unit, use of a respirator, use of tests and procedures, and use of medications. Alternatively, a global cost of hospitalization can be estimated by using national average payments, such as diagnosis-related group (DRG) payments in the U.S. Another method is to use hospital billing data on inpatient charges, which are often adjusted by cost-to-charge ratios to more closely approximate actual costs (56). Other institutional care, such as nursing home care, will probably not represent an important cost component for asthma care.

Patient-borne direct costs include out-of-pocket medical costs, such as medications not covered by insurance, or nonmedical direct costs, such as costs associated with transportation to and from the doctor's office. In addition, the patient-borne costs of the interventions must be considered.

Indirect costs put into monetary terms the productivity losses associated with asthma-related morbidity and mortality. These can be related to productivity loss for patients or for their caregivers, a category of costs especially salient for childhood asthma.

Sensitivity Analysis

An assessment of preventive interventions will no doubt require a number of assumptions to be made about key parameters in the model. When there is such uncertainty, sensitivity analysis will play a crucial role in testing the impact of changing these parameters on the results of the study. One-way sensitivity analysis, in which one parameter at a time is changed, is the most frequently used method, but it may understate the impact of uncertainty on the results. Multiway sensitivity analyses are appropriate to evaluate the impact of changing several parameters simultaneously; however, this approach complicates the analysis considerably. Precautions should be taken in communicating the results of such analyses so that decision makers can understand the results. Sensitivity analysis will be particularly critical in studies of preventive interventions, particularly when modeling long-term effects and costs.

IV. Conclusion

Compared with the information available on the treatment of asthma exacerbations, relatively little attention has been focused on the primary prevention of asthma. A handful of studies have investigated the possibility of preventing asthma among high-risk children and no economic evaluations of such programs were found during this review. There is a critical need for more research into primary prevention efforts. The Global Initiative for Asthma Workshop report suggested that primary preventive programs be the focus of heightened attention (57). Although there is currently sparse evidence for their effectiveness, the following interventions were identified as the most promising areas for primary prevention:

- Reduce prenatal exposure to cigarette smoke by avoiding smoking during pregnancy
- Improve maternal nutrition during pregnancy
- Limit exposure of infants and children to passive smoking
- Reduce exposure to aeroallergens such as dust mites, cockroach, and cat allergen
- Reduce motor vehicle pollution
- Avoid exposure to occupational sensitizers

Sullivan and Weiss (58) have suggested that economic studies be conducted before major investment into clinical trials of asthma treatments to estimate the potential economic impact of alternative treatments in order to guide research into the most potentially cost-effective strategies. Such advice is even more critical for preventive interventions. A modeling study that postulates the potential economic outcomes associated with asthma interventions could provide the impetus for additional clinical investigation of specific preventive programs and can guide their design and implementation. By evaluating alternative levels of sensitivity and specificity and by positing alternative costs of screening programs, such a study could forecast what would be required for programs to be cost-effective. Such research could provide insight into the level of effectiveness required for interventions and into the expense of those interventions in order to evaluate which programs are most likely to result in cost-effective solutions.

Asthma prevention faces serious challenges. A means of identifying high-risk infants and children or adults is not yet available. Interventions that will prevent the onset of asthma among these high-risk individuals have not been specified, and those that are known require major commitments of individual behavioral change. Many of the primary preventive interventions—such as reducing air pollution, smoking cessation, and prenatal care—will impact not only asthma but other conditions as well, underscoring the need for studies that examine the global impacts of prevention, a consideration that will dramatically increase the difficulty and complexity of conducting such studies. However, as with all prevention, the relationship between an intervention and a prevented outcome is a probabilistic one. The greatest challenge facing the asthma community may be to accumulate the level of evidence required to convince individuals and institutions to change and to develop the means to communicate that evidence effectively.

References

1. Centers for Disease Control and Prevention. (1996). Asthma mortality and hospitalization among children and young adults—United States, 1980–1993. *M.M.W.R.*, **45**:350–353.
2. Weiss, K.B., and Sullivan, S.D. (1996). Understanding the costs of asthma: the next step. *Can. Med. Assoc. J.*, **154(6)**:841–843.
3. Krahn, M.D., Berka, C., Langlois, P., and Detsky, A.S. (1996). Direct and indirect costs of asthma in Canada, 1990. *Can. Med. Assoc. J.* **154**:821–831.
4. Barnes, P.J., Jonsson, B., and Klim, J.B. (1996). The costs of asthma. *Eur. Respir. J.*, **9**:636–642.
5. Sullivan, S., Elixhauser, A., Buist, A.S., Luce, B.R., Eisenberg, J., and Weiss, K.B. (1996). National Asthma Education and Prevention Program working group report on the cost effectiveness of asthma care. *Am J. Respir. Crit. Care Med.*, **154**:S84–S85.
6. Peat, J.K. (1996). Prevention of asthma. *Eur. Respir. J.*, **9**:1545–1555.
7. Lang, D.M., and Polansky, M. (1994). Patterns of asthma mortality in Philadelphia from 1969 to 1991. *N. Engl. J. Med.*, **331**:1542–1546.
8. Schwartz, J., Gold, D., Dockery, D.W., Weiss, S.T., and Speizer, F.E. (1990). Predictors of asthma and persistent wheeze in a national sample of children in the United States: association with social class, perinatal events, and race. *Am. Rev. Respir. Dis.*, **142**:555–562.
9. Buist, A.S., and Vollmer, W.M. (1994). Preventing deaths from asthma. *N. Engl. J. Med.*, **331**:1584–1585.
10. Bailey, W.C., Clark, N.M., Gotsch, A.R., Lemen, R.J., O'Connor, G.T., and Rosenstock, I.M. (1992). Asthma prevention. *Chest*, **102(3 suppl)**:216S–231S.

11. Murphy, S. (1994). Asthma etiology and management: primary to tertiary prevention. *Prev. Med.*, **23**:688–692.

12. Teutsch, S.M. (1992). A framework for assessing the effectiveness of disease and injury prevention. *M.M.W.R.*, **41**:1–12.

13. Environmental Protection Agency. (1992). *Respiratory Health Effects of Passive Smoking: Lung Cancer and Other Disorders.*, EPA/600/6-90/006F.

14. Troisi, R.J., Speizer, F.E., Rosner, B., Trichopoulos, D., and Willett W.C. (1995). Cigarette smoking and incidence of chronic bronchitis and asthma in women. *Chest*, **108**:1557–1561.

15. Cunningham, J., O'Conner, G.T., Dockery, D.W., and Speizer, F.E. (1996). Environmental tobacco smoke, wheezing, and asthma in children in 24 communities. *Am. J. Respir. Crit. Care Med.*, **153**:218–224.

16. Young, S., Le Souf, P.N., Geelhoed, G.C., Stick, S.M., Turner, K.J., and Landau, L.I. (1991). The influence of a family history of asthma and parental smoking on airway responsiveness in early infancy. *N. Engl. J. Med.*, **324**:1168–1173.

17. Macklem, P.T. (1989). Risk factors and prevention strategies for asthma. *Chest*, **96(suppl)**:361S–362S.

18. Ostro, B.D. (1997). Air pollution worsens African American asthmatic children's symptoms. JAMA: Asthma Information Center. Highlights of ALA/ATS meeting. Reuters: Health Information Services (web page); http://www.ama-assn.org/special/ asthma/newsline/conferen/afr520.htm (accessed 23 May, 1997).

19. Dockery, D.W. (1997). Ozone, particulate matter substantially raise asthma morbidity and mortality. JAMA: Asthma Information Center. Highlights of ALA/ATA meeting. Reuters: Health Information Services (web page); http://www.ama-assn.org/special/asthma/newsline/conferen/ozo521.htm (accessed May 23, 1997).

20. Weiss, S.T., Tager, I.B., MoZuz, A., and Speizer, E.F. (1985). The relationship of respiratory infections in early childhood to the occurrence of increased levels of bronchial responsiveness and atopy. *Am. Rev. Respir. Dis.*, **131**:573–578.

21. Ahmad, H. (1997). Exposure to asthma-associated viruses puts neonates at risk. JAMA: Asthma Information Center. Highlights of ALA/ATS meeting. Reuters: Health Information Services (web page); http://www.ama-assn.org/special/asthma/ newsline/conferen/neon519.htm (accessed May 23, 1997).

22. Holtzman, M.J., (1997). Respiratory viruses said to underlie some cases of asthma. JAMA: Asthma Information Center. Reuters: Health Information Services (web page); http://www.ama-assn.org/special/asthma/newsline/reuters/429virus.htm (accessed May 23, 1997).

23. Platts-Mills, T.A., Sporik, R.B., Chapman, M.D., and Heyman, P.W. (1995). The role of indoor allergens in asthma. *Allergy*, **50(suppl 22)**:5–12.

24. Ingram, J.M., Sporik, G., Rose, R., Hosinger, R., Chapman, M.D., and Platt-Mills, T.A. (1995). Quantitative assessment of exposure to dog and cat allergens: relation to sensitization and asthma among children living in Los Alamos, New Mexico. *J. Allergy Clin. Immunol.*, **96**:449–456.

25. Sears, M.R., Burrows, B., and Flannery, G.P. (1991). Relation between airway responsiveness and serum IgE in children with asthma and in apparently normal children. *N. Engl. Med.*, **325**:1067–1071.

26. Litonjua, A.A., Sparrow, D., Weiss, S.T., O'Connor, G.T, Long, A.A., Ohman, J.L.

(1997). Sensitization to cat allergen is associated with asthma in older men and predicts new-onset airway hyperresponsiveness. *Am. J. Respir. Crit. Care Med.*, **156**: 23–27.

27. Rosenstreich, D.L., Eggleston, P., Katten, M., Baker, D., Slavin, R.G., Gergen, P., Mitchell, H., McNiff-Mortimer, K., Lynn, H., Ownby, D., and Malveaux F for the National Cooperative Inner-City Asthma Study. (1997). The role of cockroach allergy and exposure to cockroach allergen in causing morbidity among inner-city children with asthma. *N. Engl. J. Med.*, **336**:1356–1363.

28. Warner J.A. (1991). Prospects for the prevention of asthma. *Allergy Proc.*, **12(1)**: 11–14.

29. Kaufman, H.S., Frick, O.L., (1981). Prevention of asthma. *Clin. Allergy.*, **11**:549–553.

30. Fabre, D., Horta, H., Solís, R.L., Díez, G., Escobar, J.P., Barrios, F., and Jústiz A. (1990). Prevention of allergic diseases and IgE dosification in cord sera. *Allergol. Immunopathol.*, **18(6)**:309–313.

31. Bousquet, J., Michel, F.B. (1991). Overview of the concept of prevention of allergy. *Allergy Proc.*, **12**:239–244.

32. Monteleone, C.A, and Sherman, A.R. (1997). Nutrition and asthma. *Arch. Intern. Med.*, **157**:23–34.

33. von Mutius, E. (1997). Towards prevention. *Lancet*, **350(suppl II)**:14–17.

34. Arshad, S.H., Matthews, S., Gant, C., and Hide D.W. (1992). Effect of allergen avoidance on development of allergic disorders in infancy. *Lancet*, **339**:1493–1497.

35. Hide, D.W., Matthews, S., Matthews, L., Stevens, M., Ridout, S., Twiselton, R., Gant, C., and Arshad S.H. (1994). Effect of allergen avoidance in infancy on allergic manifestations at age two years. *J. Allergy Clin. Immunol.*, **93**:842–846.

36. Hide, D.W., Matthews, S., Tariq, S., and Arshad, S.H., (1996). Allergen avoidance in infancy and allergy at 4 years of age. *Allergy*, **51**:89–93.

37. Harris, J.R., Magnus, P., Samuelsen, J.O., and Tambs, K. (1997). No evidence for effects of family environment on asthma: a retrospective study of Norwegian twins. *Am. J. Respir. Crit. Care Med.*, **156**:43–49.

38. Asher, M.I., Toop, L., and Mitchell, E.A. (1994). Asthma in children: consensus on preventive management in New Zealand. *N.Z. Med. J.*, **107**:108–110.

39. Iikura, Y., Naspitz, C.K., Mikawa, H., Talaricoficho, S., Baba, M., sole, D., and Nishima, S. (1992). Prevention of asthma by ketotifen in infants with atopic dermatitis. *Ann. Allergy*, **68**:233–236.

40. Bustos, G.J., Bustos, D., Bustos, G.J., and Romero, O. (1995). Prevention of asthma with ketotifen in preasthmatic children: a three-year follow-up study. *Clin. Exp. Allergy*, **25**:568–573.

41. Newman, L.S. (1995). Occupational asthma. *Clin. Chest. Med.*, **16**:621–636.

42. Venables, K.M., and Chan-Yeung, M. (1997). Occupational asthma. *Lancet*, **349**: 1465–1969.

43. Venables, K.M. (1994). Prevention of occupational asthma. *Eur. Respir. J.*, **7**:768–778.

44. Gannon, P.F.G., Weir, D.C., Robertson, A.S., and Burge, P.S. (1993). Health, employment, and financial outcomes in workers with occupational asthma. *Br. J. Ind. Med.*, **50**:491–496.

45. National Asthma Education and Prevention Program. (1997). Expert panel report II: guidelines for the diagnosis and management of asthma.

46. Rutten-Van Mölken, M.P.M.H., Van Doorslaer, E.K.A., and Rutten, F.F.H. (1992). Economic appraisal of asthma and COPD care: a literature review 1980–1991. *Soc. Sci. Med.*, **35(2)**:161–175.

47. Gold, M.R., Patrick, D.L., Torrance, G.W., Fryback, D.G., Hadorn, D.C., Kamlet, M.S., Daniels, N., Weinstein, M.C. (1996). Identifying and valuing outcomes. In *Cost-Effectiveness in Health and Medicine*. Edited by M.R., Gold, J.E., Siegel, L.B., Russell, and M.C., Weinstein. New York, Oxford University Press, pp. 82–134.

48. Centers for Disease Control and Prevention. (1995). Assessing the effectiveness of disease and injury prevention programs: costs and consequences. *M.M.W.R.*, **44(No. RR-10)**:1–10.

49. Torrance, G.W., Siegel, J.E., and Luce, B.R. (1996). Framing and designing the cost-effectiveness analysis. In *Cost-Effectiveness in Health and Medicine*. Edited by M.R. Gold, J.E. Siegel, L.B. Russell, and M.C. Weinstein New York, Oxford University Press, pp. 54–81.

50. Lipscomb, J., Weinstein, M.X., and Torrance, G.W. (1996). Time preference. In *Cost-Effectiveness in Health and Medicine*. Edited by M.R. Gold, J.E. Siegel, L.B. Russell, and M.C. Weinstein New York, Oxford University Press, pp. 214–235.

51. Her Majesty's Treasury. (1989). *Discount Rates in the Public Sector*. London, Press Office.

52. Department of Health. (1994). Press Release 94/251. London.

53. Juniper, E.F. (1997). How important is quality of life in pediatric asthma? *Pediatr. Pulmonol. Suppl.*, **15**:17–21.

54. Torrance, G.W., Thomas, W.H., and Sacket, D.L. (1972). A utility maximization model for evaluation of health care programs. *Health Services Res.*, **7**:118–133.

55. Torrance, G.W. (1986). Measurement of health state utilities for economic appraisal. *J. Health Econ*, **5**:1–30.

56. Luce, B.R., Manning, W.G., Siegel, J.E, and Lipscomb, J. (1996). Estimating costs in cost-effectiveness analysis. In *Cost-Effectiveness in Health and Medicine*. Edited by M.R. Gold, J.E. Siegel, L.B. Russell, and M.C. Weinstein. New York, Oxford University Press, pp. 176–213.

57. Global Initiative for Asthma. (1995). Global Strategy for Asthma Management and Prevention. NHLBI/WHO Workshop Report. National Institutes of Health. National Heart, Lung, and Blood Institute, Pub. No. 95-3659.

58. Sullivan, S.D., and Weiss, K.B. (1993). Assessing cost-effectiveness in asthma care: building an economic model to study the impact of alternative intervention strategies. *Allergy*, **48**:146–152.

14

Development of a Pharmacoeconomic Policy Model for Asthma

BARRY KITCH and SCOTT T. WEISS

Channing Laboratory
Harvard Medical School and Brigham and Women's Hospital
Boston, Massachusetts

A. DAVID PALTIEL

Yale School of Medicine and Yale School of Management
New Haven, Connecticut

KAREN M. KUNTZ

Harvard School of Public Health and Brigham and Women's Hospital
Boston, Massachusetts

PETER J. NEUMANN

Harvard School of Public Health
Boston, Massachusetts

I. Introduction

Asthma is a chronic inflammatory disease that affects 14 to 15 million Americans and imposes substantial morbidity, reductions in productivity, and health care costs. Nearly 500,000 emergency department visits a year are attributable to the disease, and it accounts for more restricted activity days than any other chronic illness. Direct and indirect costs of the disease in the United States have been estimated at $3.6 and $2.6 billion, respectively (1).

The good news is that clinicians now have at their disposal an expanding range of potentially effective therapies. Numerous studies have demonstrated the beneficial effect of inhaled corticosteroid therapy in terms of reduced symptoms, improved lung function, and fewer exacerbations (2–4). Additionally, a new class of medications, the antileukotrienes, has given encouraging results in initial clinical trials (5,6). At nearly the same time an increasingly sophisticated literature on nonpharmacological interventions, such as patient education and disease management, has further expanded asthma management options (7–10).

II. Need for Cost-Effectiveness Analysis

Although the asthma community finds itself with a substantial burden of disease, it simultaneously finds itself with an ever-increasing variety of management options. Were resources unlimited, clinicians would merely implement new treatments and programs wherever they yielded an overall health benefit. Given the constraints of limited resources, comparisons among asthma intervention programs in terms of their added health benefit achieved for additional money spent would be valuable to policymakers. The goal of cost-effectiveness analysis (CEA) is to furnish such comparative information (11,12; see Chap. 12).

Broadly stated, the purpose of cost-effectiveness analysis is to provide decision makers at all levels with information to aid them in the efficient allocation of scarce resources across competing alternative uses. Problems such as this, in which some desired outcome is maximized subject to a finite resource limitation, are referred to as "constrained optimization" problems. CEA can assist decision makers in organizing and understanding information regarding complex choices with uncertain outcomes by making explicit the economic costs and health benefits of health-related investments. Moreover, because it can shed light on comparative cost consequences and the benefits forgone when funds are devoted to one activity rather than another, CEA can provide valuable information for resource allocation decisions. Because political, ethical, and legal issues are often relevant to the allocation of resources, CEA should be viewed only as an aid to policymakers.

While the role of cost-effectiveness analysis continues to grow in the health and medical sector, surprisingly few data have been reported comparing the effectiveness and cost impact of alternative interventions for managing asthma. No cost-effectiveness analysis has yet been developed to evaluate the National Asthma Education and Prevention Program's guidelines for the management of asthma and there have been few rigorous considerations of the roles of specialty care, professional education, and quality management procedures or the differing needs of identifiable patient subpopulations (13).

III. Need for a Disease Model

Because no single database contains all of the information needed for a comprehensive cost-effectiveness analysis of asthma care, it is necessary to rely on mathematical models of disease. These models are structured to specify the underlying disease process and impact of intervention and can be used to link data from multiple sources, extrapolate costs and health effects beyond the time horizon of a clinical trial, and investigate how cost-effectiveness ratios might change if the values of key parameters in a model are changed. A typical model describes a disease process as an evolving sequence of transitions among a set of mutually exclusive health states. Once the structure of a disease model is specified, data from a variety of sources are used to fill in the structure in terms of the transition probabilities among health states, costs, and health-related quality of life. Often, long-term prospective observational studies are used to specify the natural history of a disease process, while randomized controlled trials are useful for determining the impact of a particular intervention. The impact of an intervention could be a change in one or more of the transition probabilities (e.g., slowing of the disease process) and/or an increase in quality of life.

Even in situations where costs and quality of life are collected alongside a clinical trial, the use of models is often necessary. Because clinical trials often use an intermediate end point, a model can be used to predict long-term prognosis from an intermediate outcome. HIV trials, for example, frequently use the biological end point of CD4 count as an indicator of effectiveness rather than mortality or years of life saved. As a result, an incremental cost-effectiveness ratio calculated directly from the trial can yield only an incremental cost per decrease in CD4 count averted. A ratio presented in these units would be useful only for comparison to other cost-effectiveness studies that utilize the same units. A modeling effort that specifies the known relationships between CD4 count and AIDS incidence, and AIDS and death, can convert the trial into a more broadly useful measure of effectiveness such as years of life saved or quality-adjusted life years (QALYs) saved—the measure recommended by the Panel on Cost-Effectiveness in Health and Medicine (11,14). Use of these measures may give clinicians and patients a better sense of what the treatment "really" accomplishes and permits comparisons of CEA ratios across diverse medical interventions. The same issue and opportunity for modeling exists in asthma, where physiological parameters such as FEV_1 or methacholine responsiveness are frequent clinical trial end points, while exacerbations requiring emergency department visits or hospitalizations are important drivers of asthma morbidity and costs.

Another example of the value of extending beyond the time horizon chosen within a clinical trial is a CEA based on the Diabetes Control and Complications Trial (DCCT), a multicenter, randomized controlled clinical trial that compared intensive to conventional therapy in patients with insulin-dependent diabetes mellitus (IDDM) (15). While intensive therapy was shown to delay the onset and slow the progression of early complications, the trial did not continue long enough to demonstrate reductions in longer-term complications such as blindness, end-stage renal disease, and lower extremity amputation. A CEA based solely on the trial data would clearly be biased against the intensive therapy because it would exclude the cost and health consequences associated with these late events. The DCCT Research Group, therefore, developed a mathematical model to calculate the lifetime benefits and costs of these two arms. The model employed data from other clinical trials and epidemiological studies, which were used to estimate the risk of progression to late complications. Thus with the aid of modeling, researchers were able to put the up-front costs of intensive therapy in the context of the high costs, morbidity, and mortality associated with the late complications not directly observable in the DCCT. The result was a better understanding of the potential implications of the short-term costs and clinical outcomes observed.

Models are capable of more than filling in, combining, and extending data. Disease models are designed partly to articulate the hidden assumptions and value judgments that underlie decisions. Policy modeling is the systematic and explicit identification of beliefs—a method of holding assumptions up to public scrutiny so that they can be understood, evaluated, and refined by all interested parties (caregivers, patients, insurers, and policymakers). Health policy models can serve as a valuable tool for forecasting future health care resource requirements and projecting costs and consequences of alternative allocations of resources. Models have been successfully employed to guide policy decisions in the areas of coronary heart disease, screening for cancer, AIDS patient care, and dialysis capacity planning (14,16,17). A model can add a dynamic, comprehensive and societal perspective to a wide variety of asthma program evaluations by (a) capturing the systemwide effects of policy decisions; (b) explicitly identifying the relevant trade-offs to both patients and payers; and (c) having the ability to rapidly assimilate new clinical data as randomized, controlled trials are completed.

IV. Methodological Issues

A. Model Specifications

The state-transition model, which tracks hypothetical cohorts of patients throughout the courses of their diseases, is the model type most appropriate for a chronic disease such as asthma (18). It allows the course of each cohort (for example, a cohort enrolled in an asthma disease management program versus a cohort receiving standard care) to be compared in terms of their clinical outcomes and health care costs. Such models are designed to yield incremental cost-effectiveness ratios for comparing health programs or interventions.

State-transition models divide the patient population into mutually exclusive and collectively exhaustive states (or compartments) whose members share particular clinical or intervention-related traits. They employ what is known about the population, the disease, and the effect of interventions, such as asthma education and antileukotriene therapy to govern the flows into and out of each of the compartments. During some time period (for example, 1 month), each cohort of patients faces a set of probabilities of changing states. The model starts with an initial distribution of patients in the various health states and applies the transition probabilities recursively over time, which allows the model user to track how many people are in each state at each point in time.

A state-transition model's usefulness in health economics comes from the model's ability to assign costs and quality-of-life weights to the different states. As patients cycle through the model, they accrue costs and measures of effectiveness (e.g., QALYs, symptom-free days) for each year until death. The average cost and effectiveness measures for each cohort are computed, providing the basis for calculating incremental cost-effectiveness ratios between the policy options. Once the health states and the possible transitions allowable among the health states has been determined, there are a number of ways to formulate the operations of the model.

V. General Framework

A. State Space

An example of a general framework for a state-transition model of asthma is illustrated in Figure 1. The natural history of asthma is classified into three general compartment categories (or ''sectors''): chronic, acute, and death. A newly diagnosed patient is assumed to enter the system via the chronic sector. The onset of an acute exacerbation triggers a transition from the chronic sector to the acute sector. Survivors of acute events either return to the chronic sector or experience yet another exacerbation in the subsequent period; patients who do not survive

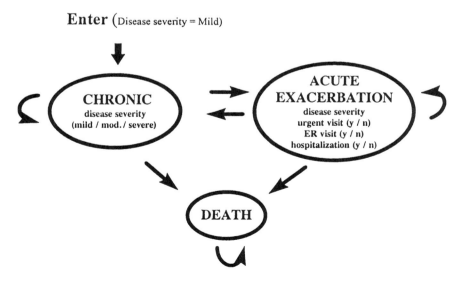

Figure 1 General model framework for asthma.

the acute event enter the death sector. Deaths can also occur from the chronic sector. The death sector is composed of "trapping" states, meaning that no further transitions are possible once a person dies.

Ideally, the various states (or compartments) within any sector would be stratified along a wide variety of dimensions, incorporating a patient's entire sociodemographic and clinical history and noting not only prior illnesses but also such important data as age, risk factors, recent environmental exposures, disease progression, and the time and frequency of any recurrences. Unfortunately, data collection burdens and computational complexities increase with dimensionality; a model that distinguishes among many patient types might "look" more precise, but it would be much harder to establish the statistical credibility and policy relevance of its output. The result is the desire to strike a balance by including only the most essential clinical parameters; for purposes of the present illustration, we consider disease severity, treatment regimen, and acute event category.

Chronic States

There are three chronic states, stratified by level of disease severity: mild, moderate, and severe. (How these severity levels are defined and implemented in our model is discussed in the following section.) The first state, for example, is composed of individuals in the chronic sector who have mild disease.

Acute States

In our model the acute sector is stratified by disease severity (mild, moderate, or severe) and the downstream pathway of events triggered by the acute event. For example, a given acute exacerbation might lead to one or more of the following: a visit to an urgent care facility, an emergency department visit, or a hospitalization. Each of these pathways is distinctive in terms of its likelihood, resource consumption consequences, downstream clinical outcomes, survival rates, quality-of-life implications, and sensitivity to intervention. Figure 2 illustrates the possible pathways triggered by an acute episode.

Death States

The death sector is composed of two absorbing (or trapping) states, representing asthma-related deaths and deaths from other causes.

VI. State Transitions

The natural history of asthma is captured in this framework through the process of transitions (i.e., flows of the population into and out of the various compart-

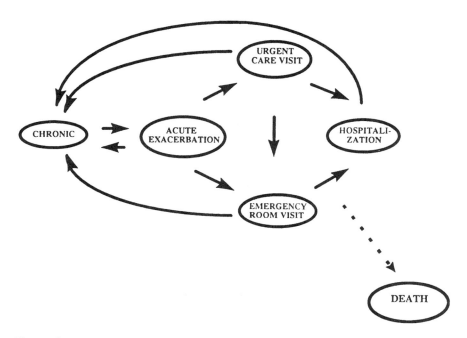

Figure 2 Acute pathways of asthma.

ments). For example, the model will take note, at the start of each time increment (or cycle) of the process of disease progression/remission, the onset of acute exacerbations, survival rates from previous acute events, and any deaths that occur. Some members of the population will remain in the same compartment over several time increments, others will proceed to a more advanced stage of disease, some will experience acute episodes, some will survive acute events, and still others will die.

A. Chronic State Transitions

Figure 3 illustrates the possible flows into and out of a generalized, chronic compartment. The horizontal arrows depict arrivals and departures due to general disease progression. The outgoing downward arrows below the box denote the two other classes of transition out of a chronic state: chronic deaths (both asthma- and non-asthma-related) and onset of acute exacerbations. The incoming downward arrow above the box represents survival of acute events. The arrow re-

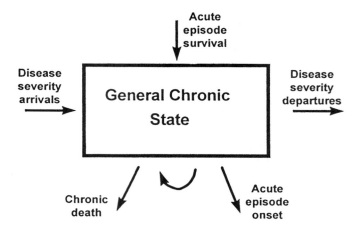

Figure 3 General chronic state of asthma.

turning to the box illustrates the possibility that an individual may simply remain in the same compartment from one time increment to the next.

B. Acute State Transitions

Figure 4 is the general-population flow diagram for the acute sector states. The incoming arrow on the left denotes arrivals from the chronic sector (i.e., the onset of an acute exacerbation). Outgoing arrows represent survival (and a return either to the chronic sector or to some other acute state) and death. Here again, the

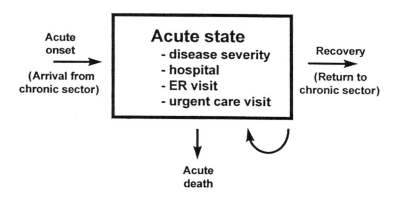

Figure 4 General acute state of asthma.

arrow captures the possibility that an individual may remain in the same compartment from one cycle to the next.

The population flows depicted in Figures 3 and 4 can be represented mathematically by a set of different equations that embody the major variables that influence the natural history of disease and acute events: rates of disease progression, incidence of acute exacerbations, survival probabilities, and both the preventive and therapeutic effects of intervention. These equations will lie at the heart of our final model and will serve as the mechanism by which population levels in each of the model's compartments are tracked over time.

Of course, the model will require credible input data if these calculations are to be performed. Specifically, parameter values will be required in four important areas: (a) the natural history of disease, including acute event incidence, acute event pathway likelihoods, and disease progression rates (all of these stratified by disease severity); (b) efficacy and toxicity of drugs and other interventions; (c) the resource consumption costs of both ongoing care and specific events (e.g., exacerbations, deaths); and (d) the quality-of-life impact of asthma, exacerbations, and alternative intervention options. An overview of how these data will be managed to produce usable output is described in the following section.

VII. Further Methodological Issues

Despite the arguments in favor of a pharmacoeconomic policy model for asthma, none as yet exists. Principal barriers to asthma-related cost-effectiveness research and the development of a model include:

- The absence of a generally agreed upon framework for disease severity
- The existence of multiple disease outcomes with the absence of a single, consensus outcome
- The presence of dramatically different acute and chronic components of disease
- Partly as a result of this complexity, the absence of satisfactory primary data on costs, outcomes, quality of life, and patient preferences

In the following section, we inventory some of the major methodological issues that pertain to the development of an asthma model.

A. Asthma-Related Outcomes

A multitude of outcomes have been tracked in asthma clinical trials. In general, asthma is a chronic disease with acute exacerbations, and a model of outcomes will need to capture both the chronic and acute dimensions of the disease.

Asthma outcome measures can be divided into the broad categories of clinical and physiological. Clinical outcomes include baseline activity restrictions, symptoms (wheeze or shortness of breath, cough, and nocturnal wakings due to asthma), and acute exacerbations; all of these together affect quality of life. Physiological outcomes include principally measures of baseline lung function [FEV_1 and peak expiratory flow rate (PEFR)] and measures of airway reactivity (methacholine or histamine responsiveness and possibly diurnal PEFR variation).

No single, ideal asthma outcome exists—each has its limitations and relevance. A model should therefore be able to report on a number of clinical indicators of disease morbidity and disease-related cost, such as symptom-free days, acute exacerbations, emergency department visits and hospitalizations, and lost work- or schooldays. Below is a description of some of these outcomes and their strengths and weakness for use in disease modeling.

Symptoms

Generally defined as cough, wheeze, shortness of breath, chest tightness, and sputum production, symptoms, along with acute exacerbations, are major determinants of disease morbidity. Symptoms have customarily been reported as number of symptoms or, more recently, as the number of symptom days or symptom-free days in a given time period; they correlate well with risk of acute exacerbation and health care utilization. The major limitation is the absence of a single consensus approach to using symptoms as an asthma outcome. Whether the focus should be intensity, duration, or frequency has not been well studied. As a result, which feature or combination of features correlates best with quality of life or resource utilization is not well known. Other limitations include the subjectiveness of the term and variation across studies in the method of recording symptoms (e.g., some studies may use diaries, others patient recall at periodic visits).

Acute Exacerbations

Acute exacerbations or attacks are defined generally as acute or subacute episodes of progressively worsening asthma symptoms. Many of the direct and indirect costs of asthma are attributable to exacerbations. Thus, both for its relationship to morbidity and to costs, exacerbation is an important outcome. The limitations include the subjectiveness of the term and variation across studies. No rigorous, well-studied definition of acute exacerbation exists; it is often difficult to be specific as to what separates chronic symptoms from exacerbations.

Mortality

Asthma deaths are relatively uncommon, though they appear to have increased markedly in recent years. From 1982 to 1991, the annual number of deaths for persons 35 years of age or younger (where diagnostic accuracy is greatest) increased from 3154 to 5106 (19). Most asthma-related deaths result from acute exacerbations and are thought to be avoidable. Though readily identifiable and specific, especially in younger populations, death attributable to asthma occurs too infrequently to serve as the major disease outcome. Morbidity outcomes are much better indicators of the public health significance of asthma.

Physiological Markers

FEV_1 is linearly related to the severity of airways obstruction. FEV_1 is highly reproducible and baseline FEV_1 gives a reasonable glimpse of severity of disease (20). A principal limitation as an outcome measure is that mild asthmatics tend to have normal values between episodes. As a result, interventions that improve the clinical course of mild disease may not be reflected in a change in FEV_1. PEFR is also a measure of airways obstruction and allows for ambulatory monitoring of degree of obstruction (20). As compared with FEV_1, it is less reproducible and more user-dependent. PEFR lability (diurnal variation) is correlated with respiratory symptoms, baseline spirometry, airway responsiveness, and the use of "rescue" medications. Limitations include the sensitivity of the test to patient effort and considerable measurement "noise." Airway responsiveness (methacholine or histamine) has a sensitivity of 95% for clinical diagnosis of asthma and recent symptoms and has a specificity less than 100% in the general population (20). There are a limited but growing amount of data on the relationship between changes in PC_{20} and clinical outcomes.

Health Care Utilization

Office visits or routine care refer to care delivered on a scheduled or routine basis through a clinic, physician's office, or managed care setting and should be captured in the cost of care of patients in the chronic phase of asthma. Unscheduled physician encounters, or urgent care visits, can be prompted by acute exacerbations as an alternative to emergency department (ED) visits. This category includes non-hospital-based acute care facilities, medical walk-in centers offered within hospitals as an alternative to ED care, unscheduled physician office visits or urgent phone calls which result in self-management steps. Urgent encounters contribute to the cost of acute exacerbation and can influence the rates of ED visits or hospitalizations. An ED visit is also an important outcome for studying the effect of various interventions for asthma exacerbations. Limitations include difficulty in comparing ED rates across populations and time because of alternative settings for acute care delivery (urgent care facilities, urgent office visits).

Hospitalizations for acute exacerbation are also an important contributor to cost. Like asthma deaths, hospitalization rates have increased in recent years

for not entirely understood reasons. Also as for deaths, hospitalizations nevertheless occur too infrequently to serve as the major disease outcome. The advantage
to including hospitalizations is the cost significance of hospitalizations; by some
estimates they account for 47% of the direct costs of asthma (1).

B.   Specification of an Asthma Severity Index

A disease model will be driven by the risk or probability of outcomes of interest
in a given time period. Thus a measure of asthma severity that reflects the risk
of an outcome will be an integral part of the modeling exercise. While no consensus exists as to what the exact criteria ought to be, severity classification schemes
are widely used for asthma both clinically and in research. As indicators of disease severity, clinical markers have the advantage of immediate clinical relevance
and a relative abundance of data in the literature; limitations include the subjectiveness of the markers (there is no consensus among researchers as to what ought
to be measured as an asthma symptom or among patients as to what they ought
to report as symptoms), variation in the way in which the data are collected (daily
diaries versus recall), and imperfect correlation with other measures of clinical
disease. The advantage to using physiological markers as criteria for a severity
index is their objectivity and sensitivity (individuals may be asymptomatic in
the face of persistent obstruction or hyperresponsiveness); limitations include
imperfect correlation with clinical disease, including outcomes such as exacerbations, and paucity of complete physiological data for many clinical trials.

   Given the limitations of both types of disease burden markers, some have
argued for the use of both in severity classification schemes. Both combination
strategies and individual physiological or clinical schemes are discussed below.

No Severity Criteria Specified

One possible strategy would be to use no specific physiological or clinical criteria
to define categories. The distinctions mild, moderate, and severe are frequently
used in the literature, and these same categories would define the severity categories of the model. While the literature employs various strategies to index severity, they would be considered equivalent for the purposes of the model. The
rationale would be that although there are differences in the definitions used in
the literature, the different criteria nonetheless tend to capture the same disease
severity distinctions: a patient whose disease is categorized as mild in one study,
using one set of criteria, is likely to have been placed in the same category by
most other studies where criteria were different. Disadvantages include the potential error of the assumption that different criteria are capturing the same populations. Communicating the model results would also be made more difficult by
not adopting a clear definition for each of the severity categories.

Symptom-Based Classification

In this scheme, severity criteria would be based on symptom frequency, either in terms of the number of symptoms in a given time period, or the number of symptom days in a given time period. A clear advantage compared to the "no specific criteria" scheme is that specific criteria—symptom-based criteria—would be employed. Another advantage is that it uses clinically relevant manifestations of disease. The use of symptoms also corresponds to usual clinical practice; most practitioners judge severity on the basis of symptom frequency. An additional advantage is that many studies record symptom data pre- and postintervention—data for modeling should be readily available. Asthma symptoms are the key factors that affect quality of life in the chronic phases of disease. Disadvantages include the subjectiveness of symptoms, variability in definition of symptom, and imperfect correlation with the risk of exacerbations.

Physiological Classification

An alternative to symptom-based criteria is one which relies entirely upon physiological data (FEV$_1$, PEFR, airway responsiveness). The principle advantage is the greater objectivity of the physiological tests, particularly FEV$_1$. Though methacholine responsiveness data are not recorded in many studies, they are recorded for a substantial number, and FEV$_1$ and PEFR data are recorded in still more. One option would be to use a single physiological test as the basis for the index. For example, all of those with a baseline FEV$_1$ < 60 would be severe, those with an FEV$_1$ 60–80 moderate, and those with an FEV$_1$ > 80 mild. Another option would be to use some combination of both flow (FEV$_1$ or PEFR) and reactivity data. The theoretical underpinnings for such a scheme are that much of the severity of asthma, a disease of reversible airways obstruction, ought to be captured by two tests: one that measures the extent of baseline, or chronic phase, airways obstruction (FEV$_1$ or PEFR), and one that measures the tendency of the airways to obstruct further (methacholine challenge). Though even using both variables to estimate severity will result in inaccurate assessments for some individuals, there is evidence that it might be a reasonably efficient scheme for a population of individuals (e.g., the use of methacholine challenge to predict acute exacerbations in mild asthmatics). Disadvantages to using a single objective test include the inability of any one test to capture all of the variability in burden and risk of disease. Mild asthmatics, for example, may have essentially normal PEFR or FEV$_1$ between episodes. Disadvantages to using airway obstruction and airway responsiveness data include the incompleteness of data from many of the clinical trials that do not include airway responsiveness, the absence of good existing data to model the probability of exacerbation as a function of both parameters, imperfect correlation between tests and clinical disease severity, and the fact that such a strategy is not widely used by clinicians. Following up this last point, there may be good reasons for clinicians not to use such a scheme on a routine basis—clinical measures, which for the treating physician are the ultimate and most important outcomes, are much more readily available.

NAEPP Classification

The National Asthma Education and Prevention Program (NAEPP) (13) developed and endorses an asthma severity classification scheme that uses a combination of physiological and clinical criteria. There are several advantages to the scheme. First, it is comprehensive. It incorporates data on FEV_1, baseline symptoms, and exacerbations. Another principal advantage is that it gives an immediate clinical accessibility and relevance to the scheme. An important disadvantage to the scheme from a research perspective is the categories are not mutually exclusive. Patients can qualify for severity categories in a number of ways, and there may be conflicting data making no one category a perfect fit. A second disadvantage is that differences between patient populations in the tendency to use urgent care or emergency facilities could result in different severity classifications for populations that were, in reality, quite similar from a clinical standpoint. The subjectiveness of the criteria symptoms, and variability in the method of ascertaining symptom frequency, could also result in similar classification variability. An additional disadvantage, particularly as it applies to modeling, is that the NAEPP scheme has not been used in its exact form around the world, or even in much of the clinical research done in the United States.

Other Combinations

Other combination strategies that are simpler than the NAEPP scheme could nonetheless preserve the advantages of basing severity on both clinical and physiological measures. The use of symptoms and objective measures of airways obstruction is attractive in that it is less cumbersome than the NAEPP scheme, incorporates an objective marker of disease severity, and is clinically relevant. Disadvantages include the difficulty in ensuring that categories are mutually exclusive and its complexity compared to a symptom only or physiological test only scheme. This type of scheme would require primary data.

Regardless of the severity classification index used, there is the task of determining what values to assign to each of the chronic severity levels for quality-of-life weight, cost of chronic care, and risk of acute exacerbation. If no specific criteria are used, then the burden of the modeler would be to extract these values from studies that specifically report a severity level. More importantly, these values should be attainable for both populations receiving usual care and for populations receiving the interventions of interest. The use of an explicit criterion (e.g., FEV_1) offers the flexibility of modeling quality of life, cost of chronic care, and risk of acute exacerbation through the variable or variables used for the severity index. Under this paradigm, the task would require the estimation of the relationships between the index variable and the outcome variables (e.g., the mathematical relationship between FEV_1 and risk of acute exacerbation).

C. Costs

There are several important cost components to consider. Direct costs are those that actually consume resources in the delivery of health services. For asthma, these include items such as program costs, inpatient care, outpatient care, physician services (inpatient and outpatient), ED visits, ambulance use, medications, short- and long-term treatment complications, devices, diagnostic services, nursing services, allergy testing and treatment, and hospitalizations. Indirect costs involve losses in productivity due to asthma illness or premature death. These costs include loss of work by patients due to symptoms of asthma or asthma-related health care visits and loss of work by caregivers of school age and adult patients with asthma. Intangible costs capture the value of the pain and anxiety suffered by asthma patients as well as the family members; some of these will be captured in the quality-adjustment process.

In general, costs represent the opportunity cost of resources consumed and not expenditures. For example, services donated should be valued even though they require no expenditures. Also, the use of charges (as opposed to economic costs) can introduce serious geographic and service-specific biases into a cost assessment (21). Cost per unit of service utilization can often be obtained from the literature. Emphasis should be placed on studies that utilize a cost accounting method for estimating costs.

One way to measure economic costs to asthma patients or parents of children with asthma is to use diaries and logs as a means of collecting information about the number of days lost due to asthma-related reasons. Conceptually, time represents a real cost, since time spent seeking or providing care could be productively spent in other endeavors. Valuing time costs has long been controversial. Ideally, we would like to know the value of the time to the consumers themselves. For practical reasons, studies often use proxies such as the average hourly wage of home health care workers. As critics have noted, existing wage rates may undervalue the time of persons whose time is spent in leisure or uncompensated employment such as housewives, the elderly, children, and the unemployed. Thus, it will be important to note the limitations of the estimate and to conduct sensitivity analyses to examine how results vary under different assumptions.

Clearly, the direct cost of medical care of asthma, the cost of asthma-related interventions, and the indirect cost of asthma-related care all contribute to the overall burden of asthma. Because asthma, like many diseases, affects parents, employers, friends, and families as well as the patient, distinguishing relevant from irrelevant costs can be difficult. The best approach may be to perform the analysis numerous times, using a host of different perspectives, with a view (ultimately) to illuminating why reasonable stakeholders might disagree.

D. Other Analytical Considerations

One purpose of an asthma modeling project is the promotion of discussion among decision makers in a variety of settings. For caregivers and patients seeking to prioritize care, the results would highlight the impact of therapy on life expectancy, quality of life, and cost. For purchasers at the institutional, state, and federal levels, it would help project the clinical and cost impact of practice guidelines and financial coverage for medications. Flexibility in the perspective of the analysis (societal, managed care, patient or patient advocacy group) would lead to broader applicability.

VIII. Summary and Conclusions

Cost-effectiveness analysis is a useful analytical tool that can assist efforts to optimize the use of available medical technologies. Disease models permit analysts to (a) calculate the benefits and costs beyond the time horizon of a clinical trial, (b) consider relevant clinical strategies not directly evaluated in a clinical trial, (c) incorporate data from a number of different sources, and (d) evaluate "what if" scenarios for various data parameters and assumptions.

As we have discussed, barriers to asthma related cost-effectiveness research and the development of an asthma model include the absence of a generally agreed upon framework for disease severity, the absence of a single consensus disease outcome, the presence of very different acute and chronic components of disease, and the absence of satisfactory primary data on costs, outcomes, quality of life, and patient preferences.

While there are barriers to formal analysis, the costs of overcoming them are conceivably small compared to those society incurs by leaving them unaddressed. The recent promulgation of practice guidelines by NAEPP, for example, suggests that critical resource allocation decisions are currently being made in the absence of any analysis of costs, outcomes, and implicit trade-offs. Similarly, the fact that a growing number of managed care organizations have designated asthma to be a sentinel health condition means that mechanisms are now being put in place to measure and evaluate the quality of care—once again, in the absence of any formal means of assessing the appropriateness of such mechanisms. Efforts to confront the challenges for the purpose of cost-effectiveness analysis and disease modeling should offer the dividend of a greater awareness of the challenges posed to clinicians, researchers, and decision makers alike by the current body of literature.

Acknowledgments

This work has been funded by a grant from AstraZeneca Pharmaceuticals.

References

1. Weiss, K.B., Gergen, P.J., and Hodgson, T.A. (1992). Asthma in the U.S.: an evaluation of the economic impact of a mild chronic illness. *N. Engl. J. Med.*, **326**:862–866.
2. Haahtela, T., Jarvinen, M., Kava, T., et al. (1991). Comparison of a β_2-agonist, terbutaline, with an inhaled corticosteroid, budesonide, in newly detected asthma. *N. Engl. J. Med.*, **325**:388–392.
3. Van Essen-Zandvliet, E.E., Hughs, M.D., Waalkens, H.J., et al. (1992). Effects of 22 months of treatment with inhaled corticosteroids and/or beta-2 agonists on lung function, airway responsiveness, and symptoms in children with asthma. *Am. Rev. Respir. Dis.*, **146**:547–554.
4. Reed, C.E. (1993). Aerosol glucocorticoid treatment of asthma. *Am. Rev. Respir. Dis.*, **140**:S82–S88.
5. Leff, J.A., Busse, W.W., Pearlman, D., et al. (1998). Montelukast, a leukotriene-receptor antagonist, for the treatment of mild asthma and exercise-induced bronchoconstriction. *N. Engl. J. Med.*, **339**:147–152.
6. Drazen, J.M., Israel, E. (1998). Should antileukotriene therapies be used instead of inhaled corticosteroids in asthma? Yes. *Am. J. Respir. Crit. Care Med.*, **158**:1967–1968.
7. Windsor, R.A., Bailey, W.C., Richards, J.M. Jr., et al. (1990). Evaluation of the efficacy and cost-effectiveness of health education methods to increase medication adherence among adults with asthma. *Am. J. Public Health*, **80**:1519–1521.
8. Mayo, P.H., Richman, J., and Harris, H.W. (1990). Results of a program to reduce admissions of adult asthma. *Ann. Intern. Med.*, **112**:864–871.
9. Bailey, W.C., Richards, J.M. Jr., Brooks, C.M., et al. (1990). A randomized trial to improve self-management practices of adults with asthma. *Arch. Intern. Med.*, **150**:1664–1668.
10. Wilson, S.R., Scamagas, P., German, D.F., et al. (1993). A controlled trial of two forms of self-management education for adults with asthma. *Am. J. Med.*, **94**:564–576.
11. Gold, M.R., Siegal, J.E., Russell, L.B., et al. (1996). Cost-effectiveness in Health and Medicine: Report of the panel on cost-effectiveness in health and medicine. New York, Oxford University Press.
12. Detsky, A.S., Naglie, L.G. (1990). A clinician's guide to cost-effectiveness analysis. *Ann. Intern. Med.*, **113**:147–154.

13. Murphy, S., Sheffer, A.L., Pauwels, R.A. (1997). National Asthma Education and Prevention Program: highlights of the expert panel report II: guidelines for the diagnosis and management of asthma. Bethesda, MD.: National Heart, Lung and Blood Institute. (NIH publication no. 97-4051).

14. Freedberg, K.A., Scharfstein, J.A., Seage, G.R. 3rd, et al. (1998). The cost-effectiveness of preventing AIDS-related opportunistic infections. *J.A.M.A.*, **279**:130–136.

15. Anonymous. (1996). The Diabetes Control and Complications Trial Research Group. Lifetime benefits and costs of intensive therapy as practiced in the diabetes control and complications trial. *J.A.M.A.*, **276**:1409–1415.

16. Tosteson, A.N., Weinstein, M.C., Hunink, M.G., et al. (1997). Cost-effectiveness of populationwide educational approaches to reduce serum cholesterol levels. *Circulation*, **95**:24–30.

17. Salzmann, P., Kerlikowske, K., Phillips, K. (1997). Cost-effectiveness of extending screening mammography guidelines to include women 40 to 49 years of age. *Ann. Intern. Med.*, **127**:955–965.

18. Drummond, M.F., Stoddart, G.L., Torrance, G.W. (1987). Methods for economic evaluation of health care programmes. New York, Oxford University Press.

19. Asthma—United States, 1982–1992. (1995). *MMWR Morb. Mortal. Wkly. Rep.*, **43**: 952–955.

20. Enright, P.L., Lebowitz, M.D., Cockroft, D.W. (1994). Physiologic measures: pulmonary function tests. Asthma outcome. *Am. J. Respir. Crit. Care Med.*, **149**:S9–18.

21. Finkler, S.A. (1982). The distinction between costs and charges. *Ann. Intern. Med.*, **96**:102–109.

15

Health State Preference Estimation in Asthma

MAUREEN P. M. H. RUTTEN-VAN MÖLKEN

Erasmus University
Rotterdam, The Netherlands

I. The Rationale Behind Valuation

Earlier in this monograph several generic quality-of-life instruments, such as the Short Form–36 and the Sickness Impact Profile, are discussed (see Chaps. 5–7). The major similarity between these instruments is that they are primarily descriptive. Generally, they yield a profile of scores for domains such as physical functioning, self-care, emotions, role performance, sleep, symptoms, and discomfort. These profile scores are sometimes aggregated to form a single index.

Generic health profiles and indices are essentially different from instruments designed to elicit values or preferences. Unlike preference scores, profile scores do not reflect the *net effect* of treatment on quality of life. Suppose a new bronchodilator becomes available that improves shortness of breath and wheezing as compared with an already available bronchodilator. The new medication is however, associated with more frequent tremor, arrhythmia, headache, and nausea. To decide whether this new drug is to be preferred to the older drug, its positive and negative effects on quality of life have to be balanced against each other. In other words, a summary measure of the quality-of-life profiles of the two drugs is needed in which the domains are valued with respect to one another. Even when profile scores are aggregated to form a single index, the resulting score is not an assessment of the net effect of treatment because the aggregation is not based on an explicit trade-off between the domains. Simply summing up numerical scores across questions does not recognize the relative importance of individual domains to individuals. For this reason, the currently available health indices like the Short Form–36 or the Sickness Impact Profile are not ideal for use in cost-effectiveness analysis (1).

In daily clinical practice, trade-offs between benefits and side effects are often made in an implicit way. The relative importance of dimensions can also be determined in a more explicit way by using valuation or utility measurement techniques. These techniques measure the values that patients place on their health state or that society places on various health states in terms of a single numerical score on a scale of 0 (death) to 1 (perfect health). Once such a single score for a particular health state is obtained, it can be combined with survival data to form a comprehensive outcome measure such as the quality-adjusted life-year (QALY). The QALY concept was developed by health economists searching for superior ways of assessing the merits of alternative allocations of resources. In an increasingly cost-conscious health care environment, the need for a uniform summary measure of outcome is apparent. The advantage of the QALY concept is that it not only enables the comparison of the cost-effectiveness of different treatments for the same disease but also allows the comparison between interventions for different diseases.

Despite the attractiveness of a uniform outcome measure, the use of utilities and QALYs in asthma was discouraged a few years ago because of the many methodological issues still to be overcome at the time (2). The purpose of this chapter is to review the instruments and methods currently available for valuation and their usefulness in asthma research. The focus is on the empirical application and no attempt is made to cover all methodological issues.

The organization of this chapter follows the three-stage approach required to obtain QALYs. First, actual patients' health states before and after an intervention must be described. These health state descriptions then have to be valued. Finally, these values are combined with survival data to obtain QALYs. Choices that have to be made at each stage of QALY estimation are addressed in the subsequent sections. The end of this chapter reviews the experience with preference measurement in asthma and provides suggestions for future approaches.

II.   Stage I: Describing Health States

In the first stage of QALY estimation, actual patients' health states, as occurring before and after the treatment under evaluation, must be described. This can be done either by using a multiattribute utility instrument (A) or by designing ''holistic'' descriptions (B).

A. Multiattribute Health State Classification

The term *attribute* refers to a domain or dimension of health such as physical functioning, self-care, pain, discomfort, or anxiety. Thus, a multiattribute utility instrument is a multiattribute health state classification system for which multiattribute preference functions have been developed. It provides a direct link between the description and the valuation of health. The four most frequently used instruments are the Quality of Wellbeing Scale (QWB) (3), the Disability/Distress Index (4), the EuroQol instrument (5), and the Health Utility Index (HUI). The latter exists in three different versions: Mark I, II, and III (6). Recently two new instruments, the 15 Dimension (15D) Health Related Quality of Life Questionnaire (7) and the Quality of Life and Health Questionnaire (QLHQ) (8), have been presented. The descriptive systems of these instruments are compared in Table 1. It should be noticed that similarity in scale labels sometimes hides dissimilarities in content or vice versa. In using the QWB or the Disability/Distress Index, patients first have to complete a structured set of quality of life questions. The responses to these questions are then used to classify patients within each attribute. In using the EuroQol, HUI, 15D, or QLHQ, patients directly rate themselves on the attributes of these instruments. The resulting health state descriptions are presented as taxonomies showing the appropriate level of functioning within each attribute. For an example of a health state description based on the QWB, see Table 2. After obtaining the health state descriptions, there are two approaches to the valuation of these descriptions.

Using Multiattribute Preference Functions

The first approach is to link the descriptions directly to a multiattribute preference function. This is a mathematical formula that allows the estimation of preference scores for a large number of health states. The formula is estimated from preference measurements for a small, carefully selected subset of those states (9). The formula is usually estimated using preferences of the general public. Thus, when a multiattribute preference function is used, patients do not have to perform the valuation task themselves. Table 2 gives an example of preference estimation based on the existing QWB weights.

Direct Utility Measurement

The second approach is to elicit preferences directly from the same patients who provided the descriptions.

B. Holistic Health State Descriptions

An alternative to using one of the above-mentioned multiattribute utility instruments is to describe the patients' health states to be valued ''holistically'' and

Table 1 Comparison of the Attributes of Preference Instrument

Disability/ distress index	EuroQol	Quality of wellbeing scale	Quality of life and health questionnaire	15D-Health-related quality of life questionnaire	Health utility index		
					Mark I	Mark II	Mark III
Disability	Mobility	Mobility	Physical suffering	Breathing	Physical functioning	Sensation (vision, hearing, speech)	Vision
Distress	Self-care	Physical activity	Limits on activities	Mental functioning	Role functioning	Mobility	Hearing
	Usual activities	Social activity	Outlook on life	Communicating	Social-emotional functioning	Emotion	Speech
	Pain/discomfort	Symptoms/problems list	Overall quality of life	Seeing	Health problems	Cognition	Ambulation
	Anxiety/depression			Moving		Self-care	Dexterity
				Working		Pain	Emotion
				Perceived health		Fertility	Cognition
				Hearing			Pain
				Eating			
				Elimination			
				Sleeping			
				Distress			
				Pain			
				Social participation			
				Depression			

Table 2 Health State Description and Valuation Based on the QWB Weights

Attribute	Attribute level and symptom	Weight
Mobility	No limitations	−0.000
Physical activity	Had trouble or did not try to lift, stoop, bend over, or use stairs or inclines, health-related	−0.060
Social activity	Limited in major role activity, health-related	−0.061
Symptom/problem	Cough, wheezing, or shortness of breath, with or without fever, chill or aching all over	−0.257
	Total preference weight	1 − 0.060 − 0.061 − 0.257 = 0.622

Source: From Ref. 3.

in great detail using narrative-style scenarios or even multimedia presentations of actual patients. The valuation of these health states can be done either by patients themselves or by the general public. If preferences are elicited from patients currently in those states, then obviously there is no need to describe those states in any detail because the patients already understand the states through experience (9).

In addition to the choice of the health state classification system and the mode of presentation (taxonomic versus holistic scenarios), there are other important issues to be decided in this first phase of QALY estimation. One is whether or not to add information on diagnosis, duration, history, and prognosis to the health state description. There is empirical evidence that information on the duration of health states, preceding and following states, and the presence or absence of a diagnostic label does affect valuation (10,11). In my opinion, adding a disease label provides relevant additional information in that it makes the generic health state classification scheme somewhat more disease-specific. However, careful design of the presentation is needed to prevent unintended positive or negative connotations (e.g., a prognosis of a fatal asthma attack when the label *asthma* is added), which may affect the values given.

III. Stage II: Valuing Health States

A. Values Versus Utilities

Before discussing the different techniques of valuation, it is important to address the distinction that is usually made between utilities and values. Utilities are strengths of preferences under uncertainty and values are strengths of preferences under certainty (12). Since health states that result from medical interventions may occur with a certain probability, the medical decision is thus a problem of choice under uncertainty. Both utilities and values are commonly expressed on a scale ranging from 1 (perfect health or best imaginable health state) through 0 (death or worst imaginable health state). The concept of utilities dates from the 1940s, when the *expected utility theory* of decision making under risk was developed by von Neumann and Morgenstern (13). This theory describes how a decision maker ought to approach a decision problem in a manner consistent with his or her preferences and a particular set of rational axioms (14). Expected utility theory is well accepted as a normative theory, but it is now widely acknowledged that empirical patterns of preference commonly violate the axioms of this theory. In this chapter the term *utility* is reserved for values based on the von Neumann/ Morgenstern expected utility theory. The terms *preference* and *value* are used interchangeably.

B. Preference Elicitation Techniques

It is beyond the scope of this chapter to describe all available techniques. Many descriptions have been given and many methodological issues associated with valuing health states have been addressed. For comprehensive reviews, see Torrance (14) and Froberg and Kane (15–17). The focus of this section is on the most frequently used techniques standard gamble (SG), time trade-off (TTO), and rating scale (RS) and their strengths and weaknesses. All techniques are required to render at least interval scale values—i.e., the differences between 0.7 and 0.8 and between 0.1 and 0.2 should represent equal preference differences. At the end of this section I will also briefly describe the willingness to pay (WTP) approach, because this too has been used in asthma.

Standard Gamble

Published experience with the SG in adult asthma is limited to one clinical trial by Rutten-van Mölken et al. (18), where patients were randomized to receive 6 weeks of treatment with either salmeterol or salbutamol. At baseline and after 6 weeks, patients were offered a choice between the certainty of remaining in the present health state for the rest of their lives by continuing with their current treatment regimen or taking a gamble with a hypothetical new treatment that could either cure their asthma completely (probability p) or cause immediate death (probability $1 - p$). The probability p was varied between 100% and 0%. Patients choose either their current health or the risky treatment at ever-increasing mortality risks until they were indifferent between the current health state and the gamble. At the point of indifference, the utility of the current health state equals $pU_{ph} + (1 - p)U_d$, where U_{ph} is the utility of perfect health, which is 1 by definition, and U_d is the utility of dead, which is 0 by definition. The SG has also been used in children with asthma, who were given the same question as described above (19).

From a normative viewpoint, the SG has been claimed to be the "gold standard" of utility assessment because it obeys the axioms of the von Neumann/Morgenstern expected utility theory. However, the SG has been shown to be subject to bias (20) and framing effects (21), causing internal inconsistencies that undermine this claim.

Time Trade-off

With this technique, two alternatives are presented to a respondent: (a) t years (months, weeks, days) in the current health state under the current treatment regimen and (b) a new treatment that completely cures the disease but reduces the time span to x years (months, weeks, days). The respondent is asked how many years x in perfect health he or she would consider equivalent to t years in the current health state. The utility for the current health state is then calculated as x/t.

The TTO was specifically designed for use in health care by Torrance et al. (22). It is not based on the von Neumann/Morgenstern expected utility theory; therefore an additional assumption is required to treat the TTO values as utilities under uncertainty. It should be assumed that subjects are risk-neutral with respect to life years. This means they should value years now equal to years in the future. However most subjects' utility functions for health years are not linear but concave with respect to time. That is, subjects prefer years in the near future to those further away. No published application of the TTO in asthma was found.

Rating Scale

The RS (feeling thermometer) was used in the quality-of-life study of salmeterol versus salbutamol, mentioned above (18). It was also applied in the study of asthmatic children by Juniper et al. (19). It is a simple method in which subjects are asked to rate their current health or a scale ranging from 0 to 1 (or 0 or 100) anchored by death or the worst imaginable health state (rated 0) and perfect health or the best imaginable health state (rated 1). Subjects are instructed to place health states along the scale such that the intervals between states reflect differences in preferences between them. A variation of this technique, which asks subjects to sort the health states into an equal number of categories, assuming equal intervals between categories, is called *category rating*.

The disadvantage of this technique is that there might be a tendency for subjects to spread the values over the scale and feel a reluctance to rate extreme values (23). Furthermore, because the RS does not involve probabilities, it does not produce von Neumann/Morgenstern utilities.

Other Methods

Other methods of health state valuation, such as the magnitude estimation (24) and the equivalence or person trade-off technique (25), have been used less often. With magnitude estimation, a respondent would be given a standard health state (e.g., the healthiest state) and asked to provide a number or ratio indicating how much better of worse each of the other states (including their own state) were compared with the standard. The main feature of the person trade-off technique is that it asks subjects how many people in health state B are equivalent to a specified number in health state A.

Willingness to Pay

A different approach to assess the strength of individuals' preferences is their willingness to pay for health-improving and/or life-extending interventions (26). When WTP is assessed by direct questioning techniques, it is known as *contingent valuation*. It is used in cost-benefit analyses to express the benefits of health care interventions in monetary terms. Many methodological issues concerning this method are debated (27). Although the WTP is a measure of preference, it cannot be used to calculate QALYs. The WTP approach is rather an *alternative to* the QALY approach (28). Two applications of contingent valuation in asthma are discussed in Sec. V, below. The first is a study by Rowe and Chestnut, described by Kenkel et al., that provides estimates of the value of a reduction in bad asthma days for people with asthma (29). The second is a cost-benefit analysis by O'Byrne, who evaluated the economic consequences of treating very mild asthma with inhaled corticosteroids (30).

C. Measurement Properties

Currently, no consensus exists as to the most appropriate method of eliciting health state preferences. Among considerations such as the perspective of the study and the decision to be taken, selection of a method should also be based on considerations of feasibility, reliability, and validity.

Feasibility

All techniques have been reported to be feasible in adults. The SG and the TTO are cognitively more demanding than the RS. Visual aids are needed to explain these techniques; hence, they are best administered by a trained interviewer. The RS has been reported to be feasible in asthmatic children, but for successful application of the SG, children were found to require considerable reading and comprehension skills (19).

Validity

One approach to assess the criterion validity of the techniques is to study whether people behave in accordance with their elicited preferences. It would be interesting to examine the extent to which the levels of risk people are prepared to take in an SG correspond to the levels of risk in the real medical decision situation. To my knowledge, such studies are not available.

In the absence of a gold standard, construct validity can be assessed by examining the convergence in preference scores elicited using different techniques. Many studies have found the methods to yield different results (for an overview, see Ref. 31). The SG usually renders higher scores than the TTO, and these are, in turn, higher than RS scores. The difference between SG and TTO is most likely explained by risk aversion in the first method. Since the RS does not incorporate attitude toward risk or require a trade-off to be made, its scores tend to be lower than those from the other two methods.

Comparing the correlations between preference measures and generic descriptive health state measures also contributes to the understanding of construct validity. A review of 15 studies containing both health state and preference measures found them to be poorly or moderately related (32). The correlations between preferences and health state measures ranged from 0.14 to 0.49 for the TTO, from 0.17 to 0.46 for the RS, and from 0.01 to 0.30 for the SG. In regression models, health state scores were able to predict 18–43% of preference scores. In adult asthmatics, the RS has demonstrated good cross-sectional construct validity, with correlations ranging between 0.43 and 0.59 (18). The longitudinal validity of the RS was not as good as the cross-sectional validity, and the validity of the SG was poor. Also, in asthmatic children who were able to provide consistent responses, the RS showed good validity (19). The SG worked less well in children. Only in older and more skilled children was its validity found to be acceptable.

The RS generally shows better validity than the SG. This is not surprising, since the RS, like the descriptive health state measures, originates in psychometrics.

Reliability

Test-retest reliability has been scarcely reported in the literature. For the SG a test-retest reliability of 0.80(33) was reported at 1 week and 0.53 at 1 year (34). The test-retest reliability of the TTO was reported to range from 0.63 at 6 weeks (16) to 0.87 at 1 week (35). For the RS, correlations between 0.49 at 1 year (34) and 0.77 at 1 week (33) have been reported. In a study of rheumatic patients, a considerably lower 3-month test-retest reliability was reported, with correlations ranging from 0.24 to 0.33 for the RS and 0.43 to 0.70 for the SG (36). In adult asthmatics, the 6-week test-retest reliability was reported to be 0.65 for the RS and 0.56 for the SG (18). In children with asthma aged between 7 and 17 years, the 4-week reproducibility was found to be 0.56 for the RS and 0.24 for the SG, values which considerably improved in the older and more skilled children (19).

Group mean preferences have been observed to be relatively stable, though individual preferences seem to be relatively unstable. At the individual level, the techniques show many inconsistencies. The relatively poor stability of measurements from individual patients may limit the use of preferences for individual decision making.

In using prepackaged multiattribute systems that directly link health state descriptions with preference scores, investigators should be aware of the techniques which were employed to generate the preference scores. SG and TTO have been used to collect weights for the Health Utility Index. The QWB values and the values of the Disability/Distress Index were based on RS techniques. TTO has been used to collect weights for the EuroQol. Magnitude estimation and paired comparison were used to generate the weights for the 15D and the QLHQ respectively. Since generally only a single estimate of utility is used in cost-utility analysis, this analysis may be very sensitive to the method used to elicit weights, which, in turn, constrains the ability to compare cost-per-QALY ratios for different interventions. Hornberger has shown that the effect of different methods on the final cost-utility ratio may be considerable (37). There is no evidence, however, to suggest that other procedures used to guide resource-allocation decisions are any less susceptible to the effects of different methods of presentation.

D. Levels of Decision Making and Choice of Respondents

In addition to the elicitation technique, another important choice is the source of preferences. This choice is guided by the decision to be taken. Sutherland and Till describe the interaction between levels of decision making and health state information (38). The levels of decision making can be represented on a scale. One end of the scale is formed by the societal or governmental perspective and the other end by the individual patient's perspective. The concept of utilities and QALYs is equally applicable to analyses that guide individual patient decision making and to economic analyses (39). The major difference between the two applications is the source of the utilities (40). In clinical decision making, patient preferences are of importance, as the purpose is to decide upon an optimal treatment policy for an individual patient or groups of patients. Economic evaluations are mostly directed toward planning and reimbursement decisions regarding publicly financed interventions in the context of a limited budged. Thus the relevant values are those derived from a representative sample of ''fully informed'' members of the general public, for it is the general public that collectively pays for health care through taxes and health insurance premiums. The general public sample includes some patients who have experienced the health state, but only in proportion to the prevalence of that health state in the general public (1). It is often argued that it is difficult to obtain informed and unbiased preferences from people who lack the experience of being in a particular health state themselves. The health states remain hypothetical and describing them in excessive detail may lead to cognitive overload.

The choice of respondents would not be an issue if it were to have no influence on preferences. However, literature suggests that people who have a disease value the associated health states more highly than people who do not have the disease (41). Empirical research has also shown that the utility associated with a disabling condition resulting from a life-threatening disease is often higher than the utility of normal functioning. Even though high utilities can be achieved by people who are objectively disabled, I do agree with the Washington Panel (a U.S. group of experts who have written recommendations for cost-effectiveness analyses) that society's goal should be to minimize disability (1). The Washington Panel also argues that using community preferences versus patient preferences does not discriminate against the ill or disabled. This is because if the general public systematically rates ill health lower than those who experience ill health, the gains from intervention will become larger and the costs per QALY will decrease (1). The panel therefore suggests the use of general public preferences and the highlighting of subgroup preferences in the sensitivity analysis. The exception would be when an analysis is designed to evaluate alternative interventions for the same condition; there the use of patient preferences is legitimate.

IV. Stage III: Integrating Preferences and Life Years

To allow comparison of interventions for different patient populations, it should be possible to contrast interventions that primarily improve quality of life with interventions that aim to increase life expectancy or to improve both quality of life and life expectancy. Thus it is required that the quality and the quantity of life be combined into a single summary measure such as the QALY. The quality can be expressed in preference weights and the quantity can be expressed in terms of life expectancy, duration of survival, or interval of observation. The conventional approach to calculate QALYs is to multiply the preference weight for each health state that occurs during a certain observation period by the time in that state and then sum the values. (An example is given in Sec. VI.) The process is simple, which is what makes the QALY approach so appealing.

The QALY approach is controversial for many reasons (42). One of the criticisms is that each health state is assigned a value regardless of the length of time spent in the state or the sequence of health states experienced. A few alternatives have been suggested, such as the Healthy Years Equivalents (HYE) (43,44) and the Saved Young Life Years (SAVEs) (45). The valuation of health paths rather than health states together with the use of a two-step SG technique are the two key features of the HYE's approach. The key feature of the SAVE approach is that changes in health states are valued rather than health states themselves. This is done to avoid the valuation of life per se. Recently the Washington Panel recommended continued use of QALYs, however, these potential alternatives are still in the early stages of development (1). This is therefore not further discussed here.

V. Experience in Asthma

Of the currently available multiattribute health state classification systems, the EuroQol, the Disability/Distress Index, and the Health Utility Index have been used in asthma.

The descriptive scheme of the *EuroQol* was applied in a study by McColl et al. aimed at developing a core set of scales to be used in evaluating the therapeutic effects in asthma and diabetes (46). The EuroQol was not included in the core set because the authors anticipated that, since it has single item dimensions, it would be insufficiently discriminating and responsive. Data to support this were not given in their paper. It can indeed be argued whether the EuroQol or any other multiattribute preference elicitation instrument would be suitable for this purpose, because they are primarily valuation instruments and not descriptive instruments.

The *Disability/Distress Index* was applied as part of a study by Kerridge et al. to asses the feasibility of using QALYs to measure the outcomes of intensive care (47). The study included 248 patients, of whom a small subgroup of 18 patients had asthma. Their health state was retrospectively assessed 3 years after their admission to the intensive care unit (ICU). The results varied considerably between diagnostic groups. The average preference weight for quality of life ranged from 0.70 for patients with pulmonary edema to 0.99 for patients with cardiac arrest. The average for patients with asthma was 0.93. The costs per ICU admission were lowest for asthma, and the gain in life years and QALYs for this group was among the greatest. Average costs per QALY (discounted at 5%) in Australian dollars ranged from $297 for asthma to $2323 for patients with pulmonary edema. Marginal costs per QALY, when treatment on ICU is compared with standard ward treatment, were estimated to range from $256 for asthma to $3177 for vascular surgery. As the authors rightly point out, the accurate measurement of preferences is relatively unimportant in studies assessing ICU, since the gain in QALYs is primarily determined by survival rather than by the change in quality of life. Nevertheless the use of QALYs to evaluate treatment in intensive care was found to be feasible.

The *Health Utility Index* Mark II was applied in a study of 52 children with asthma between 7 and 17 years of age aimed at the determination of the minimum skills required to complete various questionnaires (19). To calculate the utilities, an existing multiplicative multiattribute utility function based on preferences of the general public was used (9). The children had little difficulty completing the instrument. Their average (±SD) preference score at the start of the study was 0.89 (±0.09). The 4-week test-retest reliability in 37 stable patients was 0.93, indicating that the children were able to provide consistent answers. However, since the cross-sectional validity was rather poor, it is impossible to determine whether the children accurately understood the questions. Furthermore, the Health Utility Index was found to be completely unresponsive. It was not able to detect change in patients whose health state changed. However, the reader should remember that this was not an intervention study.

In the above-mentioned experience, patients were not asked to perform the valuation task themselves. The descriptions of their health were mapped to a classification scheme for which preferences were previously determined from a sample of the general public. In contrast, preferences were elicited directly from asthma patients in two studies, one in adults (18) and one in children (19). In both studies, the preferences were used as stand-alone measures of overall net quality of life. They were not used to calculate QALYs.

In the 6-week salmeterol versus salbutamol study by our group, we used an early version of the Health Utility Index to classify the adult patients' health. It had six domains with five levels of dysfunction per domain: (a) physical state and mobility, (b) self-care, (c) emotions, (d) leisure activities, (e) pain and other complaints, and (f) side-effects from treatment. After patients described their own health on these six domains, their preference weights for their own health were elicited using the RS and the SG. Only the RS was found to be sensitive enough to reflect the significantly greater improvement in clinical outcomes and disease-specific quality of life that was found on salmeterol as compared to salbutamol. At baseline the average (±SD) preference weight was 0.68 (±0.15) on the RS and 0.87 (±0.14) on the SG. After 6 weeks, the RS values were improved by 0.07 on salmeterol and 0.04 on salbutamol. The SG was not responsive at all. Most likely this lack of responsiveness can be explained by patients' risk aversion. The more risk-averse a subject, the less he or she is willing to risk death, the higher the utility for the current health state. This causes serious ceiling effects, leaving little room for improvement. Moreover, we varied the chances by steps of 10%, which reinforced the risk aversion. We concluded that the SG as applied in our study was not suitable for use in asthma. The RS however, seemed sufficiently responsive in asthma. Its measurement properties were better than those of the SG, although its longitudinal validity still gave reason to some concern.

Similar conclusions were drawn in the study by Juniper et al., who determined the minimum skills required by children 7 to 17 years of age to complete the RS and SG (19). Mean (±SD) preference weights at baseline were 0.66 (±0.15) for the RS and 0.82 (±0.15) for the SG. Only the youngest patients (younger than 8 years) experienced difficulty completing the RS. In children able to provide reliable answers, the RS showed good validity and responsiveness. However, to provide reliable answers to SG questions, children needed to have at least grade 6 reading skills. Only in these patients, were the measurement properties of the SG acceptable.

There is a fundamental difference between the two studies with regard to the procedures used to obtain patients' preferences. In our study, patients first gave a generic description of their health, after which they valued it. In Juniper's study, patients were first given three scenarios containing disease-specific descriptions of patients with mild, moderate, and severe asthma. After these three scenarios were valued, they were asked to value their own asthma.

The experience with utility measurement in asthma is limited, but there is even less experience with contingent valuation. Kenkel et al., describe a study by Rowe and Chestnut, who asked people with asthma what maximum increase in taxes they would be willing to pay for a program that might reduce their bad asthma days by half (29). The questionnaire was completed by 64 adult asthmatics and 18 parents of children with asthma under 16 years of age; about 80% of the answers could be used in the analyses. The investigators found a mean (±SD) bid of $401 (±$85) (1983 dollars) to reduce bad asthma days by 50%. The experience of a bad day and the number of bad days is different for each subject, and so is the number of bad days avoided by the 50% reduction. The average reduction in bad days was equal to 19. Thus these patients were willing to pay $21 to avoid a bad asthma day.

O'Byrne used the contingent valuation technique to determine whether the use of low doses of inhaled corticosteroids is cost-beneficial in patients with very mild asthma (30). At the end of a 4-month trial (n = 57) in which patients received 400 or 800 μg budesonide a day or placebo, the patients were asked what they were willing to pay per week to continue taking the drug they had received during the trial. Thus, a monetary estimate of the value of the benefits is received. Patients were willing to pay, in Canadian dollars, $368, $320, and $100 to receive 4 months of treatment with budesonide 400 μg/day, 800 μg/day, and placebo respectively. Thus, the additional benefit of 4 months treatment with budesonide over placebo was $268 for the low dose and $220 for the high dose. Because the additional benefits of both the low and the high doses of budesonide exceeded the additional costs of the drug, it was concluded that budesonide is cost-beneficial compared with bronchodilators. The trial did not have enough power to detect differences between the two doses over budesonide.

VI. Suggestions for Future Approaches

In the previous section we examined the experience with preference estimation in asthma. This experience provides little guidance as to the best way to obtain preferences. We still have much to learn about the behavior of the various measurement techniques in asthma, their relation to clinical measures and patient characteristics, and their contribution to individual and societal decision making. The most important reason why researchers are reluctant to perform utility measurement is probably the (presumed) inadequate responsiveness of these measures to clinically relevant changes. Asthma is a fluctuating disease where periods of acute exacerbations, which vary in severity, alternate with periods of relatively normal health. Treatment aims at preventing the acute attacks and improving the symptoms of dyspnea and wheezing. For QALYs to capture the nuances of treatment effects, a fine-tuned preference-elicitation technique is required.

The currently available multiattribute health state classification schemes are probably not sensitive enough to detect clinically relevant changes. None of the existing schemes includes a dyspnea dimension. Many of the schemes include a pain dimension, which is irrelevant in the case of asthma. Comprehensive instruments like the 15D, which has many domains, or the QWB, which includes an exhaustive list of symptoms and problems that may influence function, have the potential to be more responsive to change in asthma than short instruments like the Disability/Distress Index or the EuroQol.

To increase the sensitivity of the multiattribute schemes, a disease-specific module could be added. That module should be linked with the main multiattribute classification scheme for which a multiattribute preference function exists. Instead of adding disease-specific domains, the main multiattribute classification scheme could be made more disease-specific. This disease-specific classification scheme should still capture the entire concept of health and also include the domains where changes are not expected. This approach is less practical because it would require the development of new community-based preference functions. However, when the analysis is not intended to guide overall resource allocation decisions, patient preferences could be used. In this case, using more disease-specific dimensions is legitimate as long as they cover the entire concept of health.

One of the reasons why the results of our study (18) were disappointing is that we asked patients to rate their general level of functioning without explicit recognition of the influence of acute episodes. An alternative approach, proposed by Rothman and Revicki, would have been to obtain separate preferences for health states during asthma attacks of varying severity and health states during periods between attacks (48). To allow for the multiplication of utility during episodes by the duration of the episode, the best time horizon is probably 1 day. This way, it would be possible to develop health state indices that incorporate the frequency and duration of asthmatic episodes. For example, suppose that under the current treatment regimen a patient has one moderate and two severe asthma episodes a year, the moderate episode lasting for 5 days and the severe episodes for 10 days. Furthermore, suppose a new treatment reduces the number and severity of episodes to two moderate episodes each lasting for 5 days. During episodes, the utility equals 0.5 for a severe episode and 0.6 for a moderate episode, whereas the period in between episodes is valued by 0.9. One year of treatment under the current regimen equals $((5 \times 0.6) + (20 \times 0.5) + (340 \times 0.9))/365 = 0.87$ QALYs. One year of new treatment equals $((10 \times 0.6) + (355 \times 0.9))/365 = 0.89$ QALYs. The new treatment gain is 0.02 QALYs.

Another approach would be to ask subjects to value an entire path of health states evolving over time. This path is characterized by alternating periods of symptoms of varying severity and periods with no symptoms. It should be determined whether this approach is feasible and not cognitively too demanding.

An important task for the future might be to establish the minimal clinically important difference in utilities. As for some asthma-specific quality of life questionnaires, we should establish what change in utilities is perceived as at least a small but relevant benefit. This will probably depend on the disease and its prognosis. Knowing the minimal important difference is especially relevant when utilities are used as stand-alone measures of overall net quality of life. As Juniper explained in Chapter 5, knowing the proportion of patients who experienced a small but relevant improvement allows the calculation of the number of patients one would have to treat for a single patient to achieve a relevant improvement in utility. Multiplying the incremental costs of treating a single patient by the "number needed to treat to improve a single patient's utility" would provide an alternative insight into the cost-effectiveness of a treatment (for an example see Ref. 49).

Regarding the choice of the preference elicitation technique, this could be based on considerations of the goal of the study. When the values are used as an overall measure of quality of life without an attempt to make across-disease comparisons, the RS is adequate. However, when the values are used to calculated QALYs in cost-utility analyses, then SG or TTO values are more appropriate. Using the SG and the TTO to obtain patient preferences may prove difficult because these techniques do not reflect the typical choices confronting an asthma patient. As yet, a complete cure for asthma and perfect health is not a realistic option, and immediate death from asthma is relatively rare except in a case of status asthmaticus. Also asthma therapy does not involve an immediate risk of dying or a trade-off between quality and length of life. To avoid using death in an SG, death can be replaced by any other outcome as long as it is worse than the health state being valued. In order to score the utilities on a 0-to-1 scale, this gamble should be chained to a basic reference gamble using perfect health and death as outcomes in which the utility for that worse outcome can be obtained. According to the axioms of expected utility theory, the utility that results from the two-step approach gamble should be equal to the utility that is elicited in a basic reference gamble. Although several studies have shown that differences between the one-step and two-step SG approach do occur, careful design of the SG questions should reduce the number of internally inconsistent responses to a minimum. Furthermore, several alternatives to expected utility theory have been proposed, of which the prospect theory proposed by Tversky and Kahneman in 1992 has the most potential to improve the descriptive validity of the SG (50). However, at this stage, it is too early to predict whether these developments will have any practical implications.

References

1. Gold, M.R., Patrick, D.L., Torrance, G.W., Fryback, D.G., Hadorn, D.C., Kamlet, M.S., Daniels, N., and Weinstein, M.C. (1996). Identifying and valuing outcomes. In *Cost-Effectiveness in Health and Medicine*. Edited by M.R. Gold, J.E. Siegel, L.B. Russell, and M.C. Weinstein. New York, Oxford University Press. pp. 82–134.

2. Richards, J.M., and Hemstreet, M.P. (1994). Measures of life quality role performance and functional status in asthma research. *Am. J. Respir. Crit. Care Med.*, **149 (suppl)**:31–39.

3. Kaplan, R.M., Anderson, J.P., and Ganiats, T.G. (1993). The Quality of Wellbeing Scale: rationale for a single quality of life index. In *Quality of life Assessment: Key Issues in the 1990s*. Edited by S.R. Walker and R.M. Rosser. Dordrecht, Kluwer, pp. 65–94.

4. Kind, P., and Rosser, R.M. (1988). The quantification of health. *Eur. J. Soc. Psychol.*, **18**:63–77.

5. Brooks, R., with the EuroQol Group. (1996). EuroQol: the current state of play. *Health Policy*, **37**:53–72.

6. Feeny, D., Furlong, W., Boyle, M., and Torrance, G.W. (1995). Multi-attribute health state classification systems: Health Utility Index. *PharmacoEconomics*, **7**:490–502.

7. Sintonen, H., Pekurinen, M. (1993). A fifteen dimensional measure of health-related quality of life (15D) and its applications. In *Quality of Life Assessment: Key Issues in the 1990s*. Edited by S.R. Walker and R.M. Rosser. Dordrecht, Kluwer, pp. 185–195.

8. Hadorn, C.S., and Uebersax, J. (1995). Large scale outcome evaluation: how should quality of life be measured? I. Calibration of a brief questionnaire and a search for preference subgroups. *J. Clin. Epidemiol.*, **48**:607–618.

9. Torrance, G.W., Furlong, W., Feeny, D., and Boyle, M. (1995). Multi-attribute preference functions: Health Utility Index. *PharmacoEconomics*, **7**:503–520.

10. Sutherland H.J., Llewellyn-Thomas, H., Boyd, N.F., and Till, J.E. (1982). Attitudes toward quality of survival—the concept of "maximal endurable time." *Med. Decision Making*, **2**:299–309.

11. Gerard, K., Dobson, M., and Hall, J. (1993). Framing and labeling effects in health descriptions: quality adjusted life years for treatment of breast cancer. *J. Clin. Epidemiol.*, **36**:77–84.

12. Keeney, R.L., and Raiffa, H. (1976). *Decisions with Multiple Objectives: Preferences and Value Tradeoffs*. New York, Wiley.

13. Von Neumann, J., and Morgenstern, O. (1947). *Theory of Games and Economic Behavior*. Princeton, N.J., Princeton University Press.

14. Torrance, G.W. (1987). Utility approach to measuring health-related quality of life. *J. Chronic Dis.* **40**:593–600.

15. Froberg, D.G., and Kane, R.L. (1989). Methodology for measuring health-state preferences: I. Measurement strategies. *J. Clin. Epidemiol*, **42**:345–354.

16. Froberg, D.G., and Kane, R.L. (1989). Methodology for measuring health-state preferences: II. Scaling methods. *J. Clin. Epidemiol.*, **42**:459–471.

17. Froberg, D.G., and Kane, R.L. (1989). Methodology for measuring health-state preferences: III. Population and context effects. *J. Clin. Epidemiol.*, **42**:585–592.

18. Rutten-van Mölken, M.P.M.H., Custers, F., Van Doorslaer, E.K.A., Jansen, C.C.M., Heurman, L., Smeets, S.J., and Maesen, F.P.V. (1995). Comparing the performance of four different instruments in evaluating the effects of salmeterol on asthma quality of life. *Eur. Respir. J.*, **8**:888–898.

19. Juniper, E.F., Guyatt, G.H., Feeny, D.H., Griffith, L.E., and Ferrie, P.J. (1997). Minimum skills required by children to complete health related quality of life instruments for asthma: comparison of measurement properties. *Eur. Respir. J.*, **10**:2285–2294.

20. Liewellyn-Thomas, H., Sutherland, H.J., Tibshirani, R., Ciampi, A., Till, J.E., and Boyd, N.F. (1982). The measurement of patients' values in medicine. *Med. Decision Making*, **2**:449–462.

21. Tversky A., and Kahneman, D. (1981). The framing of decisions and the psychology of choice. *Science*, **211**:453–458.

22. Torrance, G.W., Thomas, W.H., and Sackett, D.L. (1972). A utility maximization model for evaluation of health care programs. *Health Serv. Res.*, **7**:118–133.

23. Read, J.L., Quinn, R.J., Berwick, D.M., Fineberg, H.V., and Weinstein, M.C. (1984). Preferences for health outcomes: comparisons of assessment methods. *Med. Decision Making*, **4**:315–329.

24. Kaplan, R.M., Bush, J.W., and Berry, C.C. (1979). Health state index: category ratings versus magnitude estimation for measuring levels of wellbeing. *Med. Care*, **17**:501–525.

25. Nord, E. (1995). The person-trade-off approach to valuing health care programs. *Med. Decision Making*, **15**:201–208.

26. Thompson, M.S. (1986). Willingness to pay and accept risks to cure chronic disease. *Am. J. Public Health*, **76**:392–396.

27. O'Brien, B., and Gafni, A. (1996). When do the "dollars" make sense? Toward a conceptual framework for contingent valuation studies in health care. *Med. Decision Making*, **16**:288–299.

28. Gafni, A. (1997). Alternative to the QALY measure for economic evaluations. *Support Care Cancer*, **5**:105–111.

29. Kenkel, D., Berger, M., and Blomquist, G. (1994). Contingent valuation of health. In *Valuing Health for Policy: An Economic Approach*. Edited by G. Tolley, D. Kenkel, and R. Fabian. Chicago, The University of Chicago Press, pp. 72–104.

30. O'Byrne, P., Cuddy, L., Taylor D.W., Birch, S., Moms, J., and Syrotuik, J. (1996). Efficacy and cost benefit of inhaled corticosteroids in patients considered to have mild asthma in primary care practice. *Can. Respir. J.*, **3**:169–175.

31. Nord, E. (1992). Methods for quality adjustment of life years. *Soc. Sci. Med.*, **34**: 569–560.

32. Revicki, D.A., and Kalpan, RM. (1993). The relationship between psychometric and utility based approaches to the measurement of health-related quality of life. *Qual. Life. Res.*, **2**:477–487.

33. O'Connor, A.M., Boyd, N.E., and Till, J.E. (1985). Methodological problems in assessing preferences for alternative therapies in oncology: the influence of preference elicitation technique, position order and test-retest error on the preferences for alternative cancer drug therapies. Nursing Research: Science for Quality Care; proceedings of the 10th National Nursing Research Conference. Toronto: University of Toronto.

34. Torrance G.W. (1976). Social preferences for health states: an empirical evaluation of three measurement techniques. *Soc. Econ. Plan. Sci.*, **10**:129–136.

35. Nease, R.F. Jr., Kneeland, T., O'Connor, G.T., Summer W., Lumpkins, C., Shaw L., Pryor D., and Sox, H.C. (1995). Variation in patient utilities for outcomes of the management of chronic stable angina: implications for clinical practice guidelines. Ischemic Heart Disease Patient Outcomes Research Team. *J.A.M.A.*, **273**:1186–1190.

36. Rutten-van Mölken, M.P.M.H., Bakker, C.H., Van Doorslaer, E.K.A., and Van der Linden S.J. (1995). Methodological issues of patient utility measurement. *Med. Care*, **33**:922–937.

37. Homberger, J.C., Redelmeier, D.A., and Petersen, J. (1992). Variability among methods to assess patients' wellbeing and consequent effects on a cost-effectiveness analysis. *J. Clin. Epidemiol.*, **45**:505–512.

38. Sutherland, H.J., and Till, J.E. (1993). Quality of life assessments and levels of decision making: differentiating objectives. *Qual. Life Res.*, **2**:297–303.

39. Weinstein, M.C., and Stason, W.B. (1977). Foundations of cost-effectiveness analysis for health and medical practices. *N. Engl. J. Med.*, **296**:716–721.

40. Drummond, MF. (1987). Resource allocation decision in health care: a role for quality of life assessments? *J. Chronic Dis.*, **40**:605–616.

41. Sacket, D.L., and Torrance, G.W. (1978). The utility of different health states as perceived by the general public. *J. Chronic Dis.*, **31**:697–704.

42. Loomes, G., and McKenzie L. (1989). The use of QALYs in health care decision making. *Soc. Sci. Med.*, **28**:299–308.

43. Mehrez, A., and Gafni, A. (1989). Quality-adjusted life years, utility theory, and healthy years equivalents. *Med. Decision Making*, **9**:142–149.

44. Gafni, A., and Birch, S. (1995). Preferences for outcomes in economic evaluation:

an economic approach to addressing economic problems. *Soc. Sci. Med.*, **40**:767–776.

45. Nord, E. (1992). An alternative to QALYs: the saved young life equivalent. *B.M.J.*, **305**:875–877.

46. McColl, E., Steen, I.N., Meadows, KA., Hutchingson, A., Eccles, M.P., Hewison, J. Fowler, P., and Blades, SM. (1995). Developing outcome measures for ambulatory care: an application to asthma and diabetes. *Soc. Sci. Med.*, **41**:1339–1348.

47. Kerridge, R.K., Glasziou, P.P., and Hillman, K.M. (1995). The use of "quality-adjusted life years" (QALYs) to evaluate treatment in intensive care. *Anaesth. Intens. Care*, **23**:322–331.

48. Rothman, ML., and Revicki, D. (1993). Issues in the measurement of health state in asthma research. *Med. Care*, **31(Suppl)**:MS82–MS96.

49. Goldstein, R.S., Gort, E.H., Guyatt, G.H., and Feeny, D. (1997). Economic analysis of respiratory rehabilitation. *Chest*, **112**: 370–379.

50. Tversky, A., and Kahneman, D. (1992). Advances in prospect theory: cumulative representation of uncertainty. *J. Risk. Uncert.*, **5**:297–323.

AUTHOR INDEX

A

Abbey, H., 206, *217*, 221, 223, 229, 230, *238*

Abboud, R.T., 181, *208*

Abdalla, M., 138, *175*

Abdin, A.H., 20, *22*

Abdulrazzaq, T.M., 20, *22*

Abetz, L., 119, *126*

Abramson, M., 57, *71*

Achenbach, T.M., 103, *125*

Ackerson, L., 199, 201, *213*

Adams, S., 197, *212*

Aday, L., 45, *53*

Addington, W., 101, *124*, 221, 223, *239*

Adelroth, E., 278, *287*

Adkinson, N.F., 227, *241*

Aebischer, C.C., 190, *210*

Aguar, M., 132, 133, *174*

Ahmad, H., 294, *309*

Ahn, P., 34, 37, *50*

Aitchison, T.C., 202, *214*

Alario, A., 100, *123*

Alexander, C., 189, *210*

Allen, G.M., 190, *211*

Allen, R.M., 202, 203, *215*

Alonso, J., 90, 91, *98*, 132, 133, 143, *174*, *176*

Alpert, H., 100, *123*

Ameille, J., 68, *74*

Anastasi, A., 128, *174*

Anderson, H., 131, *174*

Anderson, H.R., 13, 19, 20, *21*, *22*, 23, 24, 25, 33, 34, 35, 37, 41, 42, 43, *47*, *49*, *50*, *53*, 59, *72*, 181, *208*

Anderson, J.P., 84, *97*, 333, 335, *347*

Anderson, S.D., 78, *94*

Angus, R., 144, *176*

Anie, K., 131, *174*

Anto, J., 132, 133, 143, *174*, *176*

Anto, J.M., 68, *74*, 90, 91, *98*

Apter, A., 143, *176*

Arakawa, M., 137, *175*

Arfken, C.L., 185, *208*

Aris, R.M., 61, *72*

Armstrong, R., 68, *75*

Arshad, S.H., 295, *310*

SUBJECT INDEX

A

Access to care, 229–231
  definition, 229
  emergency departments, 229
  and technical quality of care, 230–231
Adults and asthma (*see also* Occupational asthma)
  prevalence, 56–57
  work limitations, 57
Africa, asthma prevalence and SES, 224
African Americans
  asthma mortality rates, 223
  asthma prevalence, 223
  and decreased levels of social support, 185
  healthcare utilization, 206, 223, 229–230
Age and asthma prevalence 33–34
Air pollution, 226, 294
Allergens
  cat allergen, 294
  cockroach allergen, 294
  dust mite allergen, 294
  degree of symptoms, 226–227
  sensitization, 226–227
  socioeconomic status, 227

Americans with Disabilities Act, 71
Anxiety and asthma, 188–190
Asthma Impact Record Index, 151–154
Asthma prevalence, 23, 33, 56–57, 220–224
Asthma Quality of Life Questionnaire (McMaster University), 17–18, 64, 86–87, 139–146, 259
Asthma Quality of Life Questionnaire (University of Sydney), 146–151
Asthma severity
  NAEPP (National Asthma Education and Prevention Program) classification, 326
  National Health Interview Survey, U.S., and classification, 36–37
  physiological classification, 325–326
  symptom-based classification, 325
Asthma-specific quality of life instruments, 107–116, 130–156
Attention deficit hyperactivity disorder, 193

379

Wanda Gave it to Sumeet
for Co] Asthma Project
May '2005